Mirror of American Life

A Courses by Newspaper Reader

Edited by
David Manning White
and **John Pendleton**

Courses by Newspaper
is a project of
University Extension,
University of California,
San Diego

Funded by
The National Endowment
for the Humanities

Publisher's Inc.
Del Mar, California

Copyright © 1977 by the Regents of the University of California.
All rights reserved.

Library of Congress Cataloging in Publication Data

Main entry under title:

Popular Culture: Mirror of American Life

   Bibliography: p. 350
   1. U.S.—Popular culture—addresses, essays, lectures.
2. U.S.—Social life and customs—1971-   —addresses,
essays, lectures. I. White, David Manning, 1917-
II. Pendleton, John, 1947-
E169.02.P58   973.92   77-16300
ISBN 0-89163-037-6
ISBN 0-89163-036 8 pbk.

Acknowledgments

SECTION ONE

17: Excerpts from "Popular Culture: Notes Toward a Definition," *Popular Culture and Curricula* by Ray B. Browne and Ronald Ambrosetti, Bowling Green University Popular Press, 1970; 20: Excerpts from "Parameters" in *Parameters of Popular Culture* by Marshall Fishwick, Bowling Green University Popular Press, 1974; 22: "The Popular Arts and the Popular Audience" excerpted from the book *The Unembarrassed Muse: The Popular Arts in America* by Russel Nye. Copyright © 1970 by Russel Nye. Reprinted by permission of The Dial Press; 27: Excerpts from the introduction of *America Through the Looking Glass*, David Burner, Robert Marcus and Jorj Tilson, eds., Prentice-Hall, 1974. Reprinted by permission of David Burner; 31: From *Popular Culture and High Culture: An Analysis and Evaluation of Taste* by Herbert J. Gans, pp. 20 –27. © 1974 by Basic Books, Inc., Publishers, New York; 36: "Network Nexus: T.V.'s Guardians of Taste" by David Grunwald, *American Airlines Magazine*, June 1977. © Copyright 1977 by American Way, inflight magazine of American Airlines. Reprinted by permission; 41: Excerpts from *The Deejays* by Arnold Passman, Macmillan, 1971. Reprinted with permission of Macmillan Publishing Company. Copyright © 1971 by Arnold Passman; 45: "The Electronic Elite Who Share America's Taste" by Benjamin Stein. *New West*. December 20, 1976. Copyright © 1977 by the NYM Corp. Reprinted with the permission of New West Magazine; 51: "The Language of Advertising" from *Language in America* by Ronald Gross. © Ronald Gross. Reprinted by permission of the author; 55: Specified abridgment of pp. 206 –233 of *The Information Machines: Their Impact on Men and the Media* by Ben H. Bagdikian. Copyright © 1971 by The RAND Corp. By permission of Harper & Row Publishers, Inc.; 63: "Love Won't Buy You Money" by Roger Rosenblatt, *The New Republic*, 1977. Copyright © The New Republic Inc.; 67: Excerpts from "Pure Entertainment: Walt Disney Productions, Inc.," from *The Mind Managers* by Herbert Schiller. Beacon Press, 1973. Copyright © 1973 by Herbert Schiller. Reprinted by permission of Beacon Press; 72: Excerpts from "The Discovery of the Popular Culture," from *American Perspectives*, by Reuel Denney, edited by Robert E. Spiller, Harvard University Press, 1961. Reprinted by permission of the publisher from the title: *The National Image and 20th Century*. Editor Eric Larrabee, Cambridge Harvard University Press. © 1961 by the President Chancellor and Fellows of Harvard College; 77: Excerpts from "Comments on Mass and Popular Culture" by Oscar Handlin, from *Culture for the Millions?*, edited by Norman Jacobs, Van Nostrand, 1961. Reprinted by permission of American Academy of Arts and Sciences, Harvard University; 83: Excerpts from "The Concept of Formula in the Study of Popular Literature" by John G. Cawelti, *Journal of Popular Culture*, 111:3, Winter, 1969; 89: Excerpts from pp. 1 –4, 7 –8 of *Focus on the Western* by Jack Nachbar, Prentice-Hall, 1974. © 1974. Reprinted by permission of Prentice-Hall, Inc., Englewood Cliffs, New Jersey.

SECTION TWO

100: "Windows on a Made-up World" by Robert Sklar, *American Film*, July –August 1976. Copyright © 1976 by the American Film Institute. Reprinted by permission; 106: "Hollywood Harikiri: The Decline of an Industry" by William Paul, *Film Comment*, March/April 1977. Copyright © 1977 by the Film Society of Lincoln Center. Reprinted from *Film Comment*, March/April 1977 by permission. All rights reserved; 118: "Jaws in Retrospect" by Martin Dworkin. Published by permission of Transaction, Inc. from *Society*, Vol. 14, No. 4. Copyright © 1977 by Transaction, Inc.; 123: "The Scary World of TV's Heavy Viewer," by George B. Gerbner and Larry Gross, *Psychology Today*, April 1976. Reprinted by permission of Psychology Today Magazine. Copyright © 1976 Ziff-Davis Publishing Company; 128: "What TV Does to Kids," *Newsweek*, February 21, 1977. Reprinted by permission of Newsweek, Inc.; 137: Excerpts from "Roots on TV: It Touched Us All" by Peter Schillaci, *Media and Methods*, April 1977. Reprinted with permission from North American Publishing Company, 401 N. Broad St., Philadelphia, Pa. Copyright © 1977 by North American Publishing Company; 142: Excerpts from "Eyewitless News" by Ron Powers, *Columbia Journalism Review*, May/June 1977. Reprinted from the Columbia Journalism Review, © 1977; 148: Excerpts from "Millennial Dreams and Nibblers" by Robert Lewis Shayon, from *The Crowd Catchers*, Saturday Review Press, 1973. © 1973 Saturday Review Press. Reprinted by permission; 153: Excerpts from "What Is Popular Music? A Definition" by R. Serge Denisoff, from *Solid Gold: The Popular Record Industry*, Transaction Books, 1975. Published by permission of Transaction, Inc. from *Solid Gold*. Copyright © 1975 by Transaction, Inc.; 157: Excerpts from "Rock as Folk Art" by Carl Belz from *The Story of Rock*, Oxford University Press, © 1969. Reprinted by permission; 163: Excerpt from "Something's Happening and You Don't Know What It Is, Do You Mr. Jones?" by Nat Hentoff, from *The Age of Rock*, edited by Jonathan Eisen, Random House, 1969. Copyright © 1969 by Nat Hentoff. Reprinted by permission of International Creative Management; 169: Excerpts from "Singing Along with the Silent Majority" by John D. McCarthy, Richard A. Peterson, and William L. Yancey, from *Side-Saddle on the Golden Calf*, edited by George Lewis, Goodyear Publishing Company, 1972. Reprinted by permission of Dr. John D. McCarthy; 175: Excerpts from "Age of Pretty Pop: They Oughta Be in Pictures" by Robert Hilburn, *Los Angeles Times Calendar*, June 9, 1977. Copyright © 1977, Los Angeles Times. Reprinted by permission; 178: Copyright © 1975 by Robert Lipsyte. Reprinted by permission of Quadrangle/The New York Times Book Company from *SportsWorld: An American Dreamland* by Robert Lipsyte; 185: Excerpts from Michael R. Real, *Mass Mediated Culture*. © 1977, pp. 92, 93, 94, 95, 96, 103, 112, 113, 115. Reprinted by permission of Prentice-Hall, Inc., Englewood Cliffs, New Jersey; 191: Excerpts from "Sports: The Natural Religion" by Michael Novak from Chapter 2, *The Joy of Sports: End Zones, Bases, Baskets, Balls, and the Consecration of the American Spirit* by Michael Novak. © 1976 Basic Books, Inc., Publishers, New York; 196: Excerpts from "Glory, Glory, Hallelujah: The New Patriotism and Sports" by Jerry Izenberg, from *How Many Miles to Camelot*, Holt, Rinehart and Winston 1972, pp. 179 –197. Reprinted by permission of publisher; 202: "Middle America's Woodstock: The Indy 500" by Jeff Greenfield, *Saturday Review*, July 1, 1972. Copyright © Saturday Review.

SECTION THREE

214: Excerpts from "The Pseudo-Event," from *The Image* by Daniel J. Boorstin, Atheneum, 1962. Copyright © 1961 by Daniel J. Boorstin. Reprinted by permission of Atheneum Publishers; 220: Excerpts from "The Inside of the Outside," from *The Responsive Chord* by Tony Schwartz, Anchor Books, 1974, pp. 80 –88. Copyright © 1973 by Anthony Schwartz. Reprinted by permission of Doubleday & Company, Inc.; 225: Excerpts from "Political Campaigns: TV Power Is a Myth" by Thomas E. Patterson and Robert D. McClure, from *The Unseeing Eye*, G. P. Putnam's Sons, 1976. Reprinted by permission of the publisher; 233: Excerpts from "Politics in the Movies" by Gerald Mast, *The New Republic*, March 6, 1976. Copyright © The New Republic Inc.; 237: "Television and the Black Revolution," from *To Kill A Messenger*, Copyright © 1970 by William Small, permission by Hastings House, Publishers; 242: "Blacks on TV: A Replay of Amos 'n' Andy?" by J. K. Obatala, *Los Angeles Times* (Part II, page 5), November 26, 1974. Copyright 1974, Los Angeles Times. Reprinted by permission; 247: From *To Find an Image*, copyright © 1973 by James P. Murray, reprinted by

CONTENTS

PREFACE

This is the eighth in a series of books developed for Courses by Newspaper. A national program, originated and administered by University Extension, University of California, San Diego, and funded by the National Endowment for the Humanities, Courses by Newspaper develops materials for college-level courses that are presented to the general public through the nationwide cooperation of newspapers and participating colleges and universities.

The program offers three levels of participation: interested readers can follow a series of newspaper articles that comprises the course "lectures"; they can pursue the subjects in supplementary books—an anthology (or reader) and a study guide—and with audio cassettes; and they can enroll for credit at one of the 300 participating colleges or universities or through the Division of Independent Study at the University of California, Berkeley. In addition, many community organizations offer local forums and discussion groups based on the Courses by Newspaper series.

This volume supplements the fifteen newspaper articles written especially for the eighth Course by Newspaper, POPULAR CULTURE: MIRROR OF AMERICAN LIFE, by prominent scholars from around the country. The newspaper articles will appear weekly in newspapers throughout the nation beginning in January, 1978.

The efforts of many people and organizations have contributed to the success of Courses by Newspaper, and we would like to acknowledge them here. Hundreds of newspaper editors and publishers have contributed valuable newspaper space to bring the series to their readers; and the faculties and administrations of the many colleges and universities participating in the program have cooperated to make credit available on a nationwide basis.

Deserving special mention at the University of California, San Diego are Paul D. Saltman, vice chancellor for academic affairs and professor of biology, who has chaired the faculty committee and guided the project since its inception, in addition to serving as the first academic coordinator in 1973; Caleb A. Lewis of University Extension, who originated the idea of Courses by Newspaper; and the faculty committee, who contributed to the conception of this course. The members of the Courses by Newspaper staff—Cecilia Solis, Yvonne Hancher, Stephanie Giel, and Susan Rago—have been critical to the success of this year's program. In addition, Linda Rill assisted with photo research and permissions, and Susan Orlofsky with editing and research.

The authors also wish to acknowledge the help of Catherine W. White, Stephanie Pendleton, and Jim and Cindy Joslyn in making valuable suggestions for the book. The advice of Dr. George A. Colburn, Project Director of Courses by Newspaper, was cheerfully given throughout the compilation of the book and invariably proved worth listening to. Jane L. Scheiber, Editorial Director of Courses by Newspaper, was virtually a collaborator in the preparation of this volume. Her perceptive gifts as an editor helped us immeasurably.

We also wish to thank the authors of the newspaper articles—Bennett M. Berger, Ray B. Browne, Betty Friedan, Herbert J. Gans, George Gerbner, Andrew Hacker, Nat Hentoff, Nathan Irvin Huggins, Robert Lipsyte, Robert Sklar, and Alvin Toffler for their suggestions for this book and their bibliographies.

Finally, we wish to express our gratitude to our funding agency, the National Endowment for the Humanities. The Endowment, a federal agency created in 1965 to support education, research, and public activities in the humanities, has generously supported this nationwide program from its beginning. We wish particularly to thank James Kraft, program officer in the Office of Planning and Analysis at NEH, for his support and advice.

Although Courses by Newspaper is a project of the University of California, San Diego, and is supported by the National Endowment for the Humanities, the views expressed in course materials are those of the authors only and do not necessarily reflect those of the funding agency or of the University of California.

INTRODUCTION

Anything as pervasive, complex, and fascinating as popular culture demands scholarly attention. Fortunately, those who toil in the field of popular culture studies no longer feel compelled to mount a massive campaign to defend their pursuits. A glance at the contents of this book will reveal that many eminent writers and scholars have directed their analytical skills toward the examination of popular culture.

The selections in this anthology reflect a great diversity of interpretation and a wide range of opinion regarding the value, quality, and importance of popular culture in American society. This book is by no means an *apologia* for popular culture. Like most of the authors of the essays, and perhaps like most Americans, we harbor ambivalent feelings toward the subject. Our objective is neither to praise nor bury popular culture, but to try to present an interesting, critical, and comprehensive assessment of it.

The multifaceted nature of popular culture poses problems in any attempt to arrive at a final, all-inclusive definition. Norman Cantor and Michael Werthman, in their two-volume *History of Popular Culture* (1968), asserted that "popular culture is really what people do when they are not working." Other scholars have found this description to be too nebulous and have struggled to reach a definition that would somehow be both specific and general.

The introduction to Section One and the first five essays in the book offer some insight into the meaning of popular culture, but they should not be construed as the last words on the subject. Nor are they intended to be. Too much time and energy has already been expended in the search for *the* definition of popular culture. Students of popular culture should concentrate instead on what they consider to be its component parts. By examining particular issues, problems, and concerns reflected by specific areas of popular culture, we may arrive at a better general understanding of it as a whole.

The title of the book denotes our conviction that popular culture can be viewed as a "mirror" of American life. Some scholars have criticized the use of the metaphor as a methodological tool. Robert Sklar, in his article "Windows on a Made-up World" (which appears in Section Two),

rejects the applicability of the mirror concept to motion pictures. Rather than serving as mirrors that reflect "real life," the movies, Sklar contends, function largely as windows through which we gaze upon the wonderful fantasies of Hollywood.

Despite Sklar's persuasive argument and his nomination of the "window" metaphor (which, by the way, we also consider a valid and useful idea in understanding popular culture) as more meaningful in evaluating movies, we still find significance in the notion of popular culture as a mirror. For one thing, as Sklar himself acknowledges, much of popular culture *does* reflect social reality. In 1948, for example, the film *The Snake Pit* portrayed the horrible conditions of most mental institutions in this country and helped stimulate legislation for needed reform. The movies "made for television" of the 1970s have continued this trend, dealing with such prevalent social ills as rape, drug abuse, alcoholism, and runaway children and generating public interest in these problems.

Other areas of mass entertainment, notably popular music, provide graphic examples of the mirror role popular culture plays. During the height of public concern for the civil rights of black Americans, Peter, Paul and Mary recorded Bob Dylan's "Blowin' in the Wind," a song that asks, among other questions, when every human being will be "allowed to be free." The record sold over 300,000 copies in only eight days, illustrating the capacity of popular music to effectively portray existing social protest sentiment.

Many who bought the record undoubtedly cared more for the harmonizing of Peter, Paul and Mary than for the humanistic outrage of Dylan's lyrics. Nevertheless, the song did cater to feelings of discontent that were evident in certain segments of American society. "Blowin' in the Wind" simply fulfilled a traditional function of popular culture: to articulate an existing idea, attitude, or concern and, in the process, to reinforce people's convictions. By doing this so magnificently, "Blowin' in the Wind" became one of the anthems of the burgeoning civil rights movement.

In such areas of popular culture as fashions and fads, the idea of the mirror is especially appropriate. We define ourselves—who we are, what we believe in, what we value, what our priorities are—by what we eat and wear, what pastimes we are engrossed in, and what diversions amuse and distract us. While it may be impossible to say with complete certainty precisely why something is popular, our choices reveal a great deal about the nature of American life.

Even when popular culture presents "bigger-than-life" spectaculars and outright fantasies or when it appears to be reflecting a distorted or "grotesque" image of America, the looking glass metaphor is still a viable one. As Andrew Bergman observed in *We're in the Money* (1971), a study of Depression America and its films, such apparent "fantasies" as *King Kong* had a definite relevance to American life. In the case of *King Kong*, the epic of the mammoth gorilla taken from his native jungle to be exploited in the big city for profit could be, and quite often was, interpreted as symbolizing the prevailing problem of urbanization in American life.

In other words, themes inherent in *King Kong* were recognizable to Americans as mirrors of their deepest concerns and preoccupations. The recent success of *Star Wars* offers further testimony to the ability of popular culture to reflect important ideas, attitudes, and values. While *Star Wars* is considered to be science fiction, the film involves battles between the forces of good and evil, a traditional concern of our society and its media of entertainment.

Our interpretations of popular culture do not hinge merely on matters of serious social and intellectual content. We wholeheartedly agree with the view that popular culture is preeminently a collection of major capitalistic enterprises. The prevalence of a certain trend in architecture, advertising, or entertainment is often due more to business considerations than to the basic values and attitudes of the populace.

While it is true that the entrepreneurs of popular culture generally have to exploit public tastes in order to create a successful "product," there are exceptions to this rule. Some fads and crazes in popular culture apparently come into vogue simply because they are novel. And whenever something succeeds, the prevailing premise in the business world is that if one is good, ten must be ten times better. Since the question "will it

sell?" has always been the major consideration of the popular culture magnates, investing all trends with great social importance may prove to be an untenable task for the scholar. Many of the articles presented in this anthology illustrate an acute sensitivity to the problem of commercialism in popular culture. Of course, it can be argued that the United States is essentially commercialistic in all phases of its society. In this respect, popular culture is truly a mirror of American life.

In evaluating the concept of the mirror, an examination of the creators of popular culture proves especially fruitful. While some of them may despise their audience and feel alienated from the mainstream of American society, most of them are more exemplary of their culture than they would care to admit. Many of the architects of our mass entertainment speak self-righteously of "artistic integrity," but even the most avant-garde movie producer, as William Paul observes in his article on the motion picture industry (which appears in Section Two), eventually gets around to discussing box-office receipts.

Despite their protestations to the contrary, most of those involved in the mass media are in it to make a buck and are thus not much different from their fellow citizens. In fact, entertainers and creators of popular culture are quite often very representative of their society and reflect basic ideas and ideals with which the public can readily identify.

The concept of the mirror is an intricate one and is certainly not the only legitimate approach to the study of popular culture. We employ it as the unifying theme of the book because we believe it can further an understanding of the subject. Through our introductions to the readings and the introductions to each section, we have tried to achieve an internal consistency that presents the selections as a cohesive package rather than a disparate collection of articles. The study of popular culture is an interesting and immensely rewarding undertaking, and we trust this anthology will contribute in some measure to a growing awareness of who we are as a people and how the multiplicity of American life is reflected in our popular culture.

SECTION ONE:
WHAT MANNER OF
MIRROR?

The Mass-Mediated Society
Bruce Davidson/© Magnum Photos, Inc.

How, indeed, does one define "popular culture"? All around us we are seldom an eye's blink from hearing, seeing, touching, tasting, wearing, or otherwise experiencing the vast, pervasive panorama of popular culture in America. Can we encompass the totality of so complex a phenomenon in a single, discrete definition? A knowledgeable scholar, Dr. Michael Real, says that trying to define popular culture is like asking a fish to analyze water.

You are an unusual American if at one time or another during the past year you haven't stopped in at a McDonald's for a Big Mac or gone to the Colonel's for a bucket of fried chicken,

listened to Walter Cronkite encapsulate the last twenty-four hours' happenings and blithely tell you "that's the way it is," watched an old Bogart or Cary Grant movie on your television set, gone to Disneyland or another theme park, or flung a Frisbee on the beach. Maybe you've done all of these things during the same day and never thought that you were engaging in popular culture.

Two hundred years ago when this country was just shaking off its birth trauma, most of its citizens were content merely to subsist, but today Americans have both the time and the resources to spend on the gratification of their personal desires.

In 1976, two astute media investigators in San Diego, Dr. Jeffrey Kirsch and Susan Pollock, interviewed many of the leading scholars in the burgeoning field of popular culture studies. After lengthy interviews with Professors Marshall McLuhan, Russel Nye, Joseph Arpad, Arthur Asa Berger, and several others, Kirsch and Pollock also despaired of a simple explanation of popular culture. Most of the scholars agreed that it has its roots in the vitality of folk culture and the emergence of an affluent mass society. Kids surely played with balls for hundreds of years before Abner Doubleday "invented" baseball in the middle of the nineteenth century; and it takes quite an affluent society to pay Jim "Catfish" Hunter $3 million for signing up with the New York Yankees and pitch-

ing "curves" at a batter for a few months each year.

Whether for stimulation or relief from boredom, each person in a mass society chooses his or her own personal cultural accompaniment. Putting aside, for the moment, the fact that this "choice" is conditioned by skillful persuaders from the media industries, Kirsch and Pollock concluded that popular culture is "the total process by which a society enables its members to compose their own life accompaniment." In this sense, then, popular culture is an important indicator of the general quality of American society, and as such, it is extremely important to study and understand.

The purpose of the selections in this first section of this anthology is to examine both the aesthetic, ideological, and historic roots of popular culture, and the complex interaction between the producers of mass-mediated products and the consumers, the Great American Public. In subsequent sections of the book, we will examine in depth specific institutional aspects of popular culture, for example, sports, and also the manner in which social change is effected by the mass media.

Initially, it is important to recognize that the *content* of popular culture, whether it's the latest episode of "Kojak," an issue of *Family Circle* or *Penthouse*, the Sunday edition of the *Chicago Tribune*, or the most recent John Denver album, represents a corporate

perception of the public's taste.

In a giant corporation such as the Columbia Broadcasting System, the ultimate power rests with its long-time chairman (and major stockholder), William Paley. But even Mr. Paley, strategically placed as he is at the key gate in a conglomerate that includes a television network as well as book publishing and magazines, seldom exercises his power on a day-to-day basis. He sets overall policy, then relies on his handpicked lieutenants to implement his no-

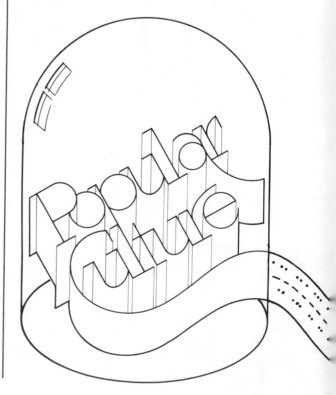

tions of the media fare Americans desire.

Although they are generally the key figures, executives like Mr. Paley still are only one of several gatekeepers through whom the content of popular culture flows. They use their power, for the most part, by naming the vice-presidents who have the responsibility for choosing station managers, or in the case of the print media, newspaper and magazine editors. In turn, these middle-management executives select the primary gatekeepers—the producers, directors, city editors, reporters, and writers. This first line of gatekeepers is responsible for the day-to-day process of providing most of the content in our popular culture.

Let there be no doubt about it, popular culture is big business. The financial world took notice when 20th Century

Fox lost most of the $50 million it invested in one year in such gigantic flops as *Dr. Doolittle* with Rex Harrison and *Star* with Julie Andrews. But in 1977 when it released the greatest box-office hit in Hollywood's history, George Lucas' *Star Wars*, 20th Century's stock price on the New York Exchange's Big Board almost doubled in a couple of weeks.

Those who sit at the helm of the popular culture mega-enterprises, such as Samuel I. Newhouse, must be not only business experts but also highly intuitive students of the Great American Public's taste. Newhouse is one of the nation's largest media owners. His twenty-one newspapers, five television stations, and three radio stations in 1970 gave him access to more than 25 percent of the homes in eleven major American markets. The concentration of such power in the hands of one man disturbs some critics of the large popular culture enterprises. Kevin Phillips, for one, is concerned lest the United States become a "mediacracy."

The popular culture business, particularly for those who own television stations, can be extremely lucrative. According to Nicholas Johnson, former member of the Federal Communications Commission, the television industry averages an 82-percent return *per year* on depreciated capital. Many Americans were appalled when the oil industry had one of its best years in

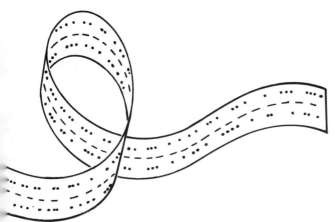

1976, but the percentage of profit in the television industry was three times as great.

If the primary mandate of the so-called media moguls, like Paley and Newhouse, is to augment corporate profits, it would be surprising if lesser gatekeepers in their organizations didn't have the same goal. There is nothing sinister about this; it is in the best tradition of the American enterprise system. Critics may complain that there is an homogenized sameness in the products turned out by the great popular cultural organizations, but generally it isn't good business policy to be too innovative or to leap too far ahead of the status quo.

The enormous growth of these corporate popular culture enterprises has been made possible largely by a corresponding growth in the amount of leisure time that Americans now enjoy. When this country was younger, the average person worked from sunup to sundown. When work was finished, he was usually too tired to do much except eat, sleep, and then wake up the next morning for more of the same. With today's shorter work week and the many labor-saving devices in the home, office, and factory, American men and women spend more hours in leisure pursuits than at work. Since 1900, the shortening of the work week alone has added about 1,100 hours a year to the average person's free time. Yet even in the early days of this country, certain patterns in our popular culture were emerging, as Professors Denney and Handlin show in their essays in this section of the anthology.

One of the dominant themes of nineteenth-century popular culture was the American dream of success. Our great-grandfathers doted on fictional characters like Horatio Alger's Mark, the Match Boy, and told themselves if Mark could do it, they could do it too. Today more Americans seem to identify with what Lawrence Chenoweth called "Schulz's confused, lonely and passive Charlie Brown" and find Alger's protagonists naive and two-dimensional.

Still, some heroes from the popular culture of early America have remained high in their appeal to our imaginations. Daniel Boone and Davy Crockett were the heroes of scores of dime novels 100 years ago and still remained the ego-ideals of television viewers just a few years ago. The development of the frontier as the nation pushed further west provided lasting figures who bridged the leap from folk to popular culture easily—Wild Bill Hickok, Calamity Jane, Billy the Kid, Doc Holliday. These and many other diverse personalities, including desperados John Dillinger and Bonnie and Clyde, became transmuted into cult stardom through the media's gatekeepers who perceived what the public wanted.

The hero is a social creation amplified and literally broadcast throughout the land in a mass-mediated culture. In the types of heroes and heroines it chooses, American society reveals some of its most basic values, beliefs, and aspirations.

For the past 100 years, the theme of violence has played an increasingly important role in American popular culture. In the 1880s Horace Greeley's *New York Tribune* voiced concern over the influence of dime novels, claiming that three boys had robbed their parents and fled to the West after reading of a similar escapade in their favorite pulp stories. Even while reading or watching more of it, Americans have continued to worry about the violent content of popular entertainment forms. Today the American Medical Association and the national Parent-Teachers Association are on record against the excessive violence they believe exists on network television shows. No other single aspect of our contemporary popular culture arouses such heated debate and emotional charges and countercharges as the issue of violence in our mass media.

Perhaps any definition of popular culture and the intricate nexus between those who produce it and the way the Great American Audience fills its leisure hours with it must seem tentative and unresolved. For popular culture is a dynamic process constantly adapting

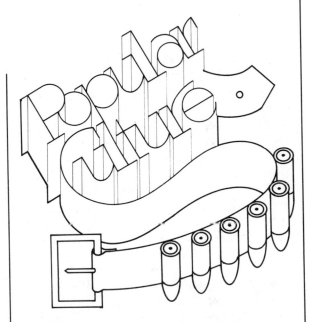

itself to our changing life styles.

Whether Walt Whitman was America's greatest poet is a matter for literary criticism to ascertain; that he was the poet-laureate of popular culture in America seems beyond dispute. When we become frustrated trying to describe popular culture in terms that will encompass all of its complexities and contradictions, we can turn again to Whitman, who put it so simply and directly:

Who are you indeed who would talk or sing to America?
Have you studied out the land, its idiom and men?
Are you really of the whole People?
Have you vivified yourself from the maternity of these States?

The long-standing debate on the aesthetic quality of popular culture has been a major stumbling block for students of "mass art" forms. The increasing pervasiveness and importance of popular culture at the turn of the twentieth century gave rise to a great deal of alarm among the custodians of "official" culture. The terms "highbrow" and "lowbrow" (and later other such coined words as "middlebrow" and "midcult") were used to distinguish the presumably more "refined" elite culture from the "crude" popular culture. The criterion of aesthetic merit was the gauge most commonly used to justify this kind of categorization.

The negative evaluation of popular culture did not impede its growth. As the twentieth century progressed, popular culture, fed by new technological advances, gradually replaced "high culture" as the pacesetter and tastemaker of American society. Until recently, the opinions of Dwight Macdonald and other elitist critics of "mass society and its culture" exerted a major influence in the academic world.

The bias of critics such as Macdonald no longer holds such sway in the intellectual community. David Manning White, one of the first to legitimize the study of popular culture, urges us to discard our prejudices and seek to understand rather than to judge. White marshals staggering evidence of the omnipresence of popular culture in his argument for serious study of the subject. He also raises some crucial questions. Does the "Great Audience" get the entertainment it wants, or is it cunningly manipulated by the mercenary media masters? Is the function of art only to edify, or should it not also provide recreational benefits? Does American popular culture lead to a dangerous conformism, or does it actually strengthen the diversity of American life?

Popular Culture: The Multifaceted Mirror
David Manning White

When such a spacious mirror's set before him,
He needs must see himself.

W. Shakespeare
Antony and Cleopatra
Act V, Scene I

Popular culture is a multifaceted, pervasive process by which most people decide what they buy, what style of clothes they wear, how they spend their leisure hours and otherwise acculturate themselves in a mass society. It is a "spacious mirror" which we enter in some ineluctable way. As the poet Rilke aptly perceived, we become a part of the mirror, while the mirror simultaneously becomes engrained in our personal life-style.

There are those who feel that it is a grotesque mirror, that the quality of American life would be augmented immeasurably if overnight every television and radio transmitter spontaneously imploded, if virtually all the presses that print our newspapers and magazines rusted to a rasping halt, and if the word "best-seller" became an anachronism. But examine their disdain for popular culture more closely and you will soon discover that their neo-elitism is showing at the intellectual seams.

These are the people who sigh when they contemplate the unwashed masses reading the *National Enquirer* and watching Carol Burnett every Saturday night, salivating over the latest Harold Robbins epic, or swelling the movie box offices for films like *Jaws* or *Star Wars*.

But it's all fitting and proper if the class-media provide the neo-elitists with their *New Yorker* magazine, or offer them a smashing lecture on pre-Columbian artifacts via an educational television channel, or the latest Bertolucci film, or a paperback edition of a recent Nabokov, Bellow, or Cheever novel.

Let's set the record straight: It isn't media per se that trouble those who denounce popular culture as much as the way other people with a so-called lower cultural IQ use these media. Given time to reflect on the proposition, even the neo-elitists are not likely to wish us all back into the days of hand-illuminated manuscripts or of an occasional troupe of traveling players to perform the man from Stratford's latest comedy.

Rather than getting into a fruitless argument over the relevance (or irrelevance) of popular culture in contemporary American society, we can serve ourselves better if we begin to understand what kind of mirror it truly is and why it flourishes in our society today.

There is a very high correlation between a man's occupation, his socioeconomic status, and what he reads, what kind of music appeals to him, what kind of motion picture is likely to get his patronage, and so forth. Of course, we have known many exceptions to this generalization, and who cannot call to mind a little round-shouldered lathe operator in Bucyrus, Ohio, who spends most of his leisure hours listening to Mozart piano concerti in the public library's music room, or a Ph.D. physicist from Cal Tech who collects only James Talley records and who reads the latest issue of *Penthouse* with a joyous visceral reaction?

Education alone is no assurance that an individual will prefer Bartok to Irving Berlin (personally, I like both of them, depending on my mood and other circumstances), but in the aggregate it is quite likely that those who are more highly educated will opt for Bartok. Even today, when college populations have nearly tripled since the end of World War II, the median number of years of school completed by Americans twenty-five years and older is still less than twelfth grade for male whites, and eighth grade for nonwhites. Only about 20 percent of our work force are in those categories designated (1) professionals, technical, and kindred workers, and (2) managers, officials, and proprietors. These are the people with greater income, education, and perhaps an interest in the more subtle and "artistic" of the popular arts. That still leaves roughly 80 percent who are clerical and sales workers, craftsmen, operatives, laborers, service workers, private household workers, farmers and their hired hands.

Only when we accept these demographic facts of life in our democracy can we appreciate how utterly naive it is to tear our togas over the low-to-middle-brow level of our popular culture and to chastise the mass-media industries for debasing the national taste. The critics of popular culture are certain that the mediocre quality of most television programs, mass magazines, or Hollywood films is due to some cabal on the part of the media managers. The gatekeepers of the media, on the other hand, often with the futile grimace of a Pontius Pilate, rationalize their products by insisting that they are giving the Great American Public what it wants. How do they know what the public wants? Easy. The proof is in the cash box. In a country where Mammon is a very potent god, money talks in convincing tones.

Would the media-managers provide us with a "better" (that is, less homogenized) brand of popular culture if the people wished it? If it could produce sufficient revenue, why not? I have known scores of writers, television producers, and publishers and talked at length with many of them. Most are cynical about the public's taste, but few are openly contemptuous. Some are ashamed of the product they say the public demands from them. Indeed, I know a perfectly delightful, urbane, compassionate television executive whose eyes dim with tears when he ponders the latest episode of a weekly situation comedy produced under his aegis. However, a sip of sixty-year-old brandy to settle his chateaubriand steak dinner does wonders to relieve such attacks of artistic conscience.

The Great Audience speaks through the dreaded "ratings" as account executives from Madison Avenue swallow another tranquilizer. And we should also keep in mind that there is tremendous competition between the various media for the attention and time of almost every American. Since the public *does show* preference for one popular culture product over another, the media managers, despite their shrewd marketing, can never be certain they are "on target."

The seemingly insatiable appetite of 225 million Americans for the varieties of popular culture means that many hundred thousands are employed in a continuous quest for salable manifestations of popular culture. Television, for example, begins its competition with the other media for the consumer's attention with the youngest tots. A recent Nielsen study indicated that pre-school children are watching television an average of fifty-four hours each week. Some years ago a statistically minded chap (whether pro television or con is not certain)

made us all gasp when he concluded that by the time a child graduates from high school he or she will have spent 15,000 hours in classrooms, but more than 18,000 hours in front of a television set.

Still, those who feared in the early 1950s, when television first became a real competitor for leisure time, that the other media would wither away from lack of attention were being unduly pessimistic. As we near the end of the 1970s, for example, we find the book-publishing industry as vigorous as at any time in our history. Any industry that sells more than $3 billion of its products is far from moribund.

The newspaper, even though its primary purpose is to inform, must also be considered an agency of popular culture. The number of daily newspapers—fluctuating only slightly from about 1,750 to 1,770—remains fairly constant, with more than 60 million copies sold each day. If we assume, conservatively, that each paper is read by poppa, mamma, and often one of the kids—although each may seek different rewards from his reading—that would give us a daily newspaper reading audience in excess of 150 million.

One of the most popular of all art forms, comic strips are the most widely read features in our newspapers. "Peanuts," for example, appears in 1,400 papers around the world. It has appeared in book form a hundred times in twelve different languages, had several television specials, and generated a virtual industry of products ranging from sweatshirts to bedsheets. Charles

Schulz's empire is estimated to be a $150-million-a-year enterprise! Strips like "Peanuts," "Blondie," and "Dick Tracy" probably have 50 to 60 million readers every day of the year. This kind of audience can't be matched even by the most fervently watched television programs. Despite rapid encroachment from television, the newspaper industry is still the titan in advertising revenue, producing record figures over the past few years.

Magazines in the United States also serve the entire spectrum of tastes. Although most of us read a few of the top fifty (whose circulation exceeds a million), there are literally thousands of magazines that emerge from the approximately 2,700 magazine publishers.

Perhaps more than any other of the mass entertainment media, with the exception of popular music, the motion picture has felt the impact of a *young* audience. Two-thirds of the audience in movie theaters today are people under twenty-five. Most Americans still love motion pictures, but see them mainly on television. Instead of paying $2.50 to see as popular a star as Robert Redford in *The Great Waldo Pepper* (1975), they wait a couple of years and see it on NBC's or CBS' movie of the week.*

Let's turn to still another major source of popular culture in America: radio, the medium whose obituary was written too soon. When national network television became a reality in the early 1950s, the word spread fast that radio would soon die. Such predictions looked good when radio's net profits, which in 1952 were $61 million, dropped to $32 million by 1961.

Then suddenly the tide changed to radio, in large part because of the young audience who responded with frenzied devotion to rock, folk rock, and soul music. Like Mary's little lamb, their radios were never far behind.

*An in-depth examination of today's movies, as well as other popular media, will be found in Section II

Radio, indeed, passed the test for survival and learned to live with its half-brother, television. At the end of World War II there were some 950 stations on the air; today there are more than 7,500 radio stations in the United States. Ninety-seven out of every 100 American homes have one or more radios, with nearly one-third of a billion sets in use, if we include automobiles and public places. Because a radio station is relatively inexpensive to establish, as compared with a television station, and can be operated with a smaller staff than a newspaper, we have a great many stations that focus on one aspect of popular culture, whether it be hard rock music, country-western and blues, show music and standard jazz, or classical music. The listener who opts for such stations knows pretty much what to expect; in fact the station is capitalizing on his expectations.

There is radio programming for every taste, and the average time spent each week listening to radio by Americans is between twenty and twenty-five hours. If that seems too high an estimate, remember that from 5 o'clock Friday afternoon until 8 or 9 A.M. Monday morning some 200 million of us are not in school or on a job. Homemakers, of course, must do their routine things over the weekend, but they are heavy users of their kitchen radios, which dispel some of the daily ennui of preparing meals, washing dishes, and so forth.

There are sixty-four "leisure" hours alone over the weekend, and even if twenty-four of them are spent sleeping, and another six in eating and brushing your teeth, there are still many hours to fill. Radio is deceptively seductive—often providing the background accompaniment to driving, studying, shopping, and working—whether broadcasting Rasputin and the Freaked Out Monks' latest ear-splitting disk, or a performance of the Chicago Symphony from Ravinia.

When we use radio to hear the best of classical and contemporary music or provoca-

Alice Cooper (left) and Leonard Bernstein in Concert. Popular culture embraces many tastes, some preferring Bernstein and the Boston Symphony at Tanglewood, Mass., others Alice Cooper on TV.
UPI Photos

tive discussions such as "Meet the Press" or the latest hourly news, we tell ourselves that we are using it for cultural enrichment, information, and maybe even for enlightenment. Properly speaking we are doing just that, but nevertheless it is *our* way of filling time, rather than building a plastic model of King Kong, reading René Descartes or Jacqueline Susann, walking with our kids in the countryside, or any of the scores of options we can choose when we are not earning a living.

And what of the time we fill watching television? Could even the most astute media soothsayer have predicted the extraordinary speed with which television became the dominant purveyor of popular culture in less than two decades? In 1947 if an American owned a television receiver he probably would have been the only one on the block, for there were only 75,000 in the entire country. Twenty years later there were 55 million homes with television in the United States, with more than 600 commercial stations and 156 educational stations. Today there is virtually a total saturation of American households.

What would Henry David Thoreau have to say about his countrymen today when most of the rooftops of his beloved Concord have dipole antennae? Would he revise his observation that most men lead lives of quiet desperation to "most Americans lead lives of frenetic excitation by soap-sellers and mind-ticklers"?

Now, I have nothing against soap per se.

I merely wonder what is happening to a country where Procter and Gamble alone spends more than $300 million for advertising, almost all of it for television. It must say something about the sensibility of a nation if it requires *twelve times* the amount paid by Thomas Jefferson for the entire Louisiana Purchase to persuade us that Ivory Soap is 99.44 percent pure.

Why has the national advertising budget risen so fast, from about $3 billion in 1945 to about ten times that amount today? The noted wit, Mr. Stan Freberg, in a University of Kansas seminar, came very close to the answer, despite his tongue-in-cheek dis-

course. Freberg suggested that the *consumer* (and to the marketing geniuses of Madison Avenue every single one of us is a viable, statistically verifiable, super-stratified consumer) has reached a point of commercial saturation. What follows is a sort of Hegelian thesis, antithesis, and synthesis, with the big corporations having to spend more and more money to snag the attention of us consumers. Our antithesis is to build more immunity "in the interest of sanity," says Freberg, and, in turn, Procter and Gamble develops newer and costlier ways of washing our rebellious minds with soap, and thus the triad begins again. We might, indeed, wonder, as Freberg did, if it really takes a 30-billion-dollar sledge hammer to drive a 39-cent thumbtack.

As I stated earlier, a number of distinguished savants believe that our popular culture should be considered something akin to the bubonic plague of the modern mind. If one leans toward this position and desires reinforcement, such arguments are stated forcefully by Dwight Macdonald, Leo Lowenthal, Irving Howe, Daniel Boorstin, Bernard Rosenberg, and the late Hannah Arendt, to name but a few. With the exception of such scholars as Russel Nye, Ray B. Browne, and Marshall Fishwick (and the members of the burgeoning Popular Culture Association), it has been difficult to find anyone from academe who will say a few kind words, let alone be a St. George for the side of popular culture; but there are a few such intrepid souls who at least try to understand this phenomenon without caressing it. The noted sociologist Edward Shils is perhaps the most conspicuous "semi-champion" of this point of view, but one also can find cogent arguments from the pens of Gilbert Seldes, Raymond Bauer, Leo Rosten, John Cawelti, Leslie Fiedler, and the late Robert Warshow.

My own view of the role of popular culture in American life will not endear me to either of the opposing sides, since I see some merit at both ends of the controversy. Does it do any good to tell ourselves that our mass culture is appreciably less violent than the *circus maximus* of Nero and his contemporaries, or that Cain slew Abel sans the influence of *Dirty Harry* or "Starsky & Hutch"? Or that Shakespeare's theatrical company competed with the bear-baiting pits a few hundred yards away in Elizabethan London, and that today Shakespeare still is being performed, whereas bear-baiting has been discarded as suitable entertainment?

Conversely, will it give us solace to realize that 99 percent of the television programs, while perhaps only 98 percent of today's novels, films, essays (including this one), and popular music from Irving Berlin to Bob Dylan probably will be completely forgotten or else be a matter of bewilderment or sniggering to our grandchildren's children?

On the other hand, can we be sure that just because something is enormously popular it will not endure? Robert Burns' poems and songs belonged to the people of his day long before the literary coterie in Edinburgh lionized and eventually ruined the poor man. John Huston's *Treasure of Sierra Madre*, like Chaucer's "Pardoner's Tale," makes the point *radix malorum cupiditas est* (the love of money is the root of evil). A hundred years from now our descendants may choose to

recognize both of these works as concise and masterful statements of human greed. Will it matter to them that Huston's version of the "Pardoner's Tale" came out of Hollywood, for by that time Hollywood itself may be only a footnote in the continuing saga of mass entertainment?

I suppose what most offends the bitter antagonists of the Great Audience culture is that each of the mass media, with their potentially enormous numbers of consumers, can *vulgarize* the arts so much faster than was possible a hundred years ago. Popular culture is not only a pervasive, salable, and ever-proliferating product; it is a natural consequence of our highly industrialized society. As the working week has diminished from seventy to sixty hours during our grandfathers' time to little more than half that for most workers today, the question of what to do with our leisure hours has become increasingly germane.

If we could take an instant audit of what every American over twenty-one was doing during any of his leisure hours we would find a broad spectrum of activity. We might find 200,000 or more of them reading the banal, pseudo-erotic novels of Harold Robbins, whose art is, generously put, neo-troglodyte, and whose work epitomizes what I mean when I refer to popular culture as a "product." Perhaps 100,000 are building cobbler's benches or canoes in their basement workshops, while 300,000 are playing golf, tennis, or just walking in the woods. Many millions, of course, are just sitting in front of their television sets with a can of

"As the working week has diminished . . . the question of what to do with our leisure hours has become increasingly germane."

beer in their hand, a little like the people in Plato's cave. The workday has been boring or tedious or nerve-wracking, and the television set is a good sugar-tit.

My point is that you can find our population doing many things to relax and trying to forget the exigencies of the working day. To be sure, most of what is going on between 5 P.M. any day and 9 A.M. may or may not have social value. Yet, would we prefer the Orwellian specter of *1984* as practiced in its current version in mainland China, where hundreds of millions of Chinese spend their nonworking hours listening to or reading the state-controlled media-dispensed propaganda? This clearly is *one* socially ameliorative way to spend leisure time; at least the state thinks it is. It may be that China is merely applying the strict rules on the dangers of popular art that Plato espoused so strongly in the tenth book of the *Republic.* Plato happens to be an excellent example of a self-appointed arbiter of the public's taste. He intended to ban Homer and Hesiod because they sometimes portrayed the gods as immoral, death as fearful, and the relationship of reward to merit as quite fortuitous. These are ideas from which youth must certainly be shielded, according to Chairman Plato.

I find myself far more in sympathy with Plato's pupil, Aristotle, who states clearly in the *Poetics* that it is not the only purpose of art to edify or teach us a moral lesson. This is not to say that Aristotle had anything against our being edified as a consequence of an artistic experience. But he thought art was under no aesthetic obligation to give us enjoyment of the "higher" sort, whatever that might be. We recognize, as did Aristotle, that the greatest art stimulates and invigorates our minds and hearts alike. But Aristotle intuited long before the days spent by millions upon millions of Americans, in factories and foundries, in punching IBM cards or selling anti-perspirant in cluttered drugstores, that man needs recreation as well as serious endeavor.

In Aristotle's book, the lower classes, too, who for a number of reasons are less likely to appreciate art of the more serious sort, are entitled to forms in which they find entertainment and even repose. His reasoning: better that they should enjoy art of some kind than be cut off altogether from aesthetic pleasure.

I am not so naive that I expect a massive leap away from Harold Robbins, Mickey Spillane, Ian Fleming, Norman Rockwell, and their ilk because the Great Audience occasionally gets exposed to a more demanding art, and then only in bits and pieces. But there are signs that our popular culture has risen, albeit slowly, and is continuing to rise. We should be patient. Any elitist worth his salt knows that it took the masses thousands of years to get as vulgar as they are.

It really is no skin off my nose if my neighbor prefers a re-run of *The Sound of Music* at 8:30 P.M. while I decide to see Fellini's *La Strada* for the third or fourth time. I may, somewhat smugly, consider myself a bit more "cultured," but if my neighbor derives enjoyment and surcease from his workaday anxieties by watching Julie Andrews, I have no more right to take him away from it than he has to enter my art theater and yell "Culture Vulture!"

I would and do have the right to protest loudly if somehow my tastes cannot be satisfied merely because there are not as many of me as there are of him. It doesn't take a very large percentage of the available audience to make a viable market. That is why we have some specialized magazines that can make money for their publishers with fewer than fifty thousand subscribers, or about one out of every four thousand people in the United States. It also explains why we now have thousands of paperback book titles to choose from. Granted, a Leon Uris novel sells millions, but it is also economically feasible to publish paperback editions of less spectacular sellers like David Riesman's *Lonely Crowd* or Hesse's *Siddhartha*.

I shall never forget overhearing a conversation some years ago between a middle-aged gentleman, whose diction and grammar were far from Oxonian, and a clerk in a paperback book store. The customer said he had recently purchased one helluva good war story by a writer named Homer, and he asked if Mr. Homer had written any new books for him to read. Without batting an eye, the heroic clerk said, "Yessir, we just got a new one by him that I think you would like. It's called the *Odyssey*." The man went out of the store, caring little whether he was reading one of the world's masterpieces. He would read a fast-moving prose translation of a timeless story that night. I wonder what the clerk told him when he came in for the third novel by Mr. Homer. "Sorry, sir, he was traveling in Greece and he died unexpectedly."

Despite the blight of commercialism, American popular culture is not a wasteland. Good and enduring movies continue to come out of Hollywood; the giant book clubs often distribute novels and nonfiction of more than ephemeral worth; there are magazines to suit the most refined sensibilities; and television, while it has yet to recapture its Golden Age of entertainment and drama, nevertheless provides us with news and informational programs of great impact and immediacy. Indeed, television may well be forcing us to reconsider the demarcation between art and reportage. That such achieve-

ment, however less than perfect, is possible at all, given the circumstances of a cultural democracy, is in itself quite remarkable. The mass media in order to survive must reflect prevailing taste and cater to public demands. Despite the strictures placed upon them by the taste of the majority, innovative and daring media managers have been able to break away, now and then, from the expected mode.

Much of the encouragement for innovation has come from the Young Audience. Today in the United States, for the first time in our history, more than half of college-age youth are engaged in higher education. If education and exposure to diverse cultural experiences are the answer to raising the level of mass taste, there is reason for considerable optimism. In our universities and colleges today there may be developing the Great Audience of selectivity and discernment that Gilbert Seldes long envisioned. One can hope that the enthusiasm and interest now being cultivated on hundreds of campuses will show up in future offices on Madison Avenue, at NBC, and at United Artists.

Whether the products of the mass media improve or deteriorate depends to a large extent on the future relations among American social, economic, political, and educational values. The mass media endemically mirror the prevailing social climate, so popular culture will be no better or worse than our society demands and therefore deserves.

The study of popular culture gained a great deal of momentum in the mid-1960s. Most of the impetus for academic examination of the field came from a few innovative scholars in English departments at midwestern and eastern universities. Russel Nye, Marshall Fishwick, John Cawelti, Carl Bode, and Ray Browne emerged as the guiding lights of the inchoate popular culture "movement" of the sixties.

Ray Browne has been particularly effective as a coordinator of the various enterprises of popular culture studies. In addition to his many books on popular culture, Browne was a founder of the *Journal of Popular Culture*, the Popular Culture Association, and the Bowling Green Popular Press. He is cur-rently chairman of the Popular Culture Department at Bowling Green State University in Ohio, the only university to date that has granted departmental status to a program of study focusing on popular culture.

In the following selection, from *Popular Culture and Curricula* (1970), Browne tackles the formidable task of defining popular culture and offers a penetrating analysis of the relationship of folk, mass, and popular cultures and the role of the mass media. Although the essay was written several years ago, Browne's preference for inclusiveness over exclusiveness is still the dominant feature of most definitions of popular culture.

Popular Culture: Notes Toward a Definition

Ray B. Browne

Popular Culture" is an indistinct term whose edges blur into imprecision. Scarcely any two commentators who try to define it agree in all aspects of what popular culture really is. Most critics, in fact, do not attempt to define it; instead, after distinguishing between it and the mass media, and between it and "high" culture, most assume that everybody knows that whatever is widely disseminated and experienced is "popular culture."

Some observers divide the total culture of a people into "minority" and "majority" categories. Other observers classify culture into High-Cult, Mid-Cult, and Low-Cult, or High-Brow, Mid-Brow, and Low-Brow, leaving out, apparently, the level that would perhaps be called Folk-Cult or Folk-Brow, though Folk culture is now taking on, even among the severest critics of popular culture a high class and achievement unique unto itself. Most of the discriminating observers agree, in fact, that there are perhaps actually four areas of culture: Elite, Popular, Mass, and Folk, with the understanding that none is a discrete unity standing apart and unaffected by the others. . . .

Many definitions of popular culture turn

on methods of dissemination. Those elements which are too sophisticated for the mass media are generally called Elite culture, those distributed through these media that are something less than "mass"—that is such things as the smaller magazines and newspapers, the less widely distributed books, museums and less sophisticated galleries, so-called clothes-line art exhibits, and the like—are called in the narrow sense of the term "popular," those elements that are distributed through the mass media are "mass" culture, and those which are or were at one time disseminated by oral and non-oral methods—on levels "lower" than the mass media—are called "folk."

All definitions of such a complex matter, though containing a certain amount of validity and usefulness, are bound to be to a certain extent inadequate or incorrect. Perhaps a workable definition can best be arrived at by looking at one of the culture's most salient and quintessential aspects—its artistic creations—because the artist perhaps more than any one else draws from the totality of experience and best reflects it.

Shakespeare and his works are an excellent example. When he was producing his plays at the Globe Theater, Shakespeare was surely a "popular" author and his works were elements of "popular" culture, though they were at the same time also High or Elite culture, for they were very much part of the lives of both the groundlings and the nobles. Later, in America, especially during the nineteenth century, all of his works were well known, his name was commonplace, and he was at the same time still High art, Popular (even mass) art and Folk art. In the twentieth century, however, his works are more distinguishable as parts of various levels. *Hamlet* is still a play of both High and Popular art. The most sophisticated and scholarly people still praise it. But *Hamlet* is also widely distributed on TV, radio and through the movies. It is a commonplace on all levels of society and is therefore a part of

"...Popular Culture is all those elements of life which are not narrowly intellectual or creatively elitist..."

"popular culture" in the broadest sense of the term. Other plays by Shakespeare, however, have not become a part of "popular" culture. *Titus Andronicus*, for example, for any of several reasons, is not widely known by the general public. It remains, thus, Elite culture. . . .

Aside from distribution another major difference between high and popular culture, and among popular culture, mass culture and folk culture, is the motivation of the persons contributing, the makers and shapers of culture. On the Elite or sophisticated level, the creators value individualism, individual expression, the exploration and discovery of new art forms, of new ways of stating, the exploration and discovery of new depths in life's experiences.

On the other levels of culture there is usually less emphasis placed upon, and less accomplishment reached in, this plumbing of reality. Generally speaking, both popular and mass artists are less interested in the experimental and searching than in the restatement of the old and accepted. But there are actually vast differences in the esthetic achievements attained in the works from these two levels, and different aspirations and goals, even within these somewhat limited objectives. . . .

The popular artist [according to Hall and Whannel] is superior to the mass artist because for him "stylization is necessary, and the conventions provide an agreed base from which true creative invention springs." It is a serious error therefore to agree with Dwight Macdonald (in *Against the Ameri-*

can Grain) that all popular art "includes the spectator's reactions in the work itself instead of forcing him to make his own responses." . . .

It is also unfair to give blanket condemnation to mass art, though obviously the accomplishments of mass art are less than those of "higher" forms. Liberace does not aspire to much, and perhaps reaches even less. His purposes and techniques are inferior, but not all his, or the many other workers' in the level, are completely without value.

All levels of culture, it must never be forgotten, are distorted by the lenses of snobbery and prejudice which the observers wear. There are no hard and fast lines separating one level from another. . . .

All elements in our culture (or cultures) are closely related and are not mutually exclusive one from another. They constitute one long continuum. Perhaps the best metaphorical figure for all is that of a flattened ellipsis, or a lens. In the center, largest in bulk and easiest seen through is Popular Culture, which includes Mass Culture.

On either end of the lens are High and Folk Cultures, both looking fundamentally alike in many respects and both having a great deal in common, for both have keen direct vision and extensive peripheral insight and acumen. All four derive in many ways and to many degrees from one another, and the lines of demarcations between any two are indistinct and mobile.

Despite the obvious difficulty of arriving at a hard and fast definition of popular culture, it will probably be to our advantage—and a comfort to many who need one—to arrive at some viable though tentative understanding of how popular culture can be defined. . . .

A viable definition for Popular Culture is all those elements of life which are not narrowly intellectual or creatively elitist and which are generally though not necessarily disseminated through the mass media. Popular Culture consists of the spoken and printed word, sounds, pictures, objects and artifacts. "Popular Culture" thus embraces all levels of our society and culture other than the Elite—the "popular," "mass" and "folk." It includes most of the bewildering aspects of life which hammer us daily.

Such a definition, though perhaps umbrella-like in its comprehensiveness, provides the latitude needed at this point, it seems, for the serious scholar to study the world around him. Later, definitions may need to pare edges and change lighting and emphasis. But for the moment, inclusiveness is perhaps better than exclusiveness.

"Popular" is a word that can be defined in many ways, often depending on the predilection of who is doing the defining. There seems to be a lingering stigma, equating "popular" with "vulgar," "ephemeral," and (forgive us, our Puritan fathers) "enjoyable." To be "popular" also has the connotation that you are somewhat "loose," like the pretty gal who keeps getting telephone calls all the time from strangers asking her for a date.

Undeniably, the image purveyors of Madison Avenue have contributed to the overkill of the word with their incessant fear-provoking messages that unless your teeth are gleaming white and your body smells like a gentle wind whispering through a grove of lilacs, you will not be "popular," that is, desirable.

But there are other parameters of popular culture that need to be explored, and this is what Professor Marshall Fishwick attempts in this excerpt from his book, *The Parameters of Popular Culture*. Fishwick, one of the pioneers in the academic study of popular culture, speaks with the eloquence and passion of a poet in pleading for an unbiased examination of the words "popular" and "culture."

Parameters

Marshall Fishwick

Just what are the parameters of popular culture? Shall we begin with a short, acceptable definition of "popular culture"? Impossible. The words, considered either singly or jointly, seem like elastic bands that stretch in many directions. There are 21 "definitions" of the verb *pop* in the 1970 *Random House Dictionary*—to say nothing of the noun, adjective, abbreviations, and link words (popcorn, pop-eyed, popgun, etc.). . . .

There are, of course, dominant ideas or points in the many descriptions and attempted definitions of popular culture. "Pop" usually means one of three things in contemporary usage:

1. New, faddish, "in." To be "popular" is to be "top ten," a pace-setter. (The operative word is ephemeral—in today, out tomorrow.)
2. Vernacular, folksy, earthy. To be "popular" is to by-pass the elite and appeal to the ordinary man who is rooted in real life. (One detects some reverse snobbism and anti-intellectualism here.)
3. Universal-electronic-instant. To be "popular" is to be plugged in, via film, television, tape. (Here the appeal is to technology and McLuhan's Age of Circuitry.)

Common denominators in the three meanings emerge. Pop is an unflinching look at the real world today; a fascination with and acceptance of our mechanized, trivialized, urbanized environment; a mirror held up to life, full of motion and madness. It is rooted in new factors—physical and social mobility, mass production, abundance, anxiety. Pop challenges conventional boundaries and eliminates walls between art and non-art, high and low culture. What we confront is not so much a fixed definition as a fluid approach—Einstein's answer to Aristotle. . . .

Despite the stress on nowness and newness, Pop has a long, complex history. Not enough has been discovered and recorded about prior pop; what was "popular" in ancient Greece, Imperial Rome, medieval Europe, colonial Africa. There is still much to be done in piecing together American precedents. Emerson, we remember, asked us to "sit at the feet of the familiar, the low." His sometime gardener, Henry Thoreau, loved "the music of the telegraph wires." Walt Whitman shouted his barbaric yawp from the rooftops of the world, urging us to

Unscrew the locks from the doors
Unscrew the doors from their jambs.

"I am not a bit tamed," he bragged. "I too am untranslatable." So he posed, shouted poetry at the sea, rode on the Broadway horse-car, pounded the open road. . . . His unique mixture of concrete and abstract, adoring and absurd, anticipated today's Pop Revolution. . . .

For most people sights and sounds penetrate quicker than words: the Pop Revolution is more visual than verbal. The mind is not so much a debating society as a picture gallery. Our icons are no longer in church but on the tube—the NBC peacock, the CBS Big Eye, the cliché-ridden ad. Classical rules are abandoned. Paintings move, movies stand still. Films are reel illusion, as real life nudges out fiction. Goodbye, Gutenberg. The mourning becomes electric, as the world itself is an art object. . . .

The new generation is no longer willing to die for communism, capitalism, or any other ism. Instead they want to be tuned in. We should remember that when Lenin sparked the 1917 Revolution he shouted not only "Bolshevism!" but also "Electricity!" He turned on the light and shocked a backward peasantry into the Electric Age. By 1970 the whole world was wired for sound. Anyone who would lead must face the Big Light; must live or die by his "image." The nineteenth century took its toll on workers' bodies; the twentieth on their minds. In place of the illusion of progress is the illusion of technique. The abrasive process of rubbing information against information accelerates. Instead of simple sequence there is radical juxtaposition. Political science has become instant alchemy. "Don't *tell* us about politics. *Be* political."

In short, seek meaning through movement. From the trips to the frontier to the "trips" of hippiedom, Americans have followed this formula. Daniel Boone, Buffalo Bill, Teddy Roosevelt, Timothy Leary, and Matt Dillon went thataway. They took with them weapons of violence and seeds of the new style. Characters in novels by Cooper, London, Hemingway, and Bellow did too. We are the Huck Finns, not the Siddhartha. Instead of watching the river flow by, we cross it.

"Instant" intrigues us. Mom thaws out instant meals to supplement instant coffee, instant soup, and instant sex. "Nobody has time any more to start from scratch," Arlene Dahl claims in *Always Ask a Man*. "We can't wait for the coffee to perk, the soup to simmer, or physical attraction to grow into love. Who has time to waste on preliminaries these days? Besides, you can always switch to another brand.". . .

American society remains, in theory and in fact, a wilderness shared. Our waterfalls and Watergates are over-whelming. On we sail, probing the water, the land, the society. Who knows if we shall ever catch up with Moby Dick; or if, once we have done so, he will turn majestically and destroy us all?

A delightful song from Lerner and Lowe's hit musical *Camelot* posits the question, "What do the common folks do?" The great Flemish artist, Peter Breughel, asked the same question in the fifteenth century, then went out and painted what he saw, and we, his fortunate heirs, can see what medieval popular culture looked like. So vivid is his art that we can almost hear, smell and feel both the joys and the anguish of being a peasant in Breughel's time.

High and folk art have coexisted since the days of the Egyptians, despite the Cassandra-like critics who dolefully predicted the demise of high art because of the erosive quality of popular art. The Gresham's Law of Culture, that is, that bad art would always drive out good, has been a maxim for centuries.

Yet, not every person who lived in Pericles' Golden Age of Greece went to Athen's great amphitheater to see Sophocles' tragedies. If we were to study the diversions of the artisans or slaves in that society, or the Romans who went to the Colosseum to enjoy the *circus maximus* instead of Terrence's comedies, we would appreciate that the roots of popular culture have been with us from earliest civilizations.

Professor Russel Nye's book, *The Unembarrassed Muse*, is the definitive history of popular culture as it developed in the United States. In his cogent introduction to that book, reprinted here, Nye provides a most succinct overview of the historical development of popular culture, and at the same time helps us to define its contemporary meaning.

The Popular Arts and the Popular Audience
Russel Nye

The term "the popular arts" cannot be used accurately to describe a cultural situation in Western civilization prior to the late eighteenth century. Certainly large numbers of people before that time found pleasant and rewarding ways of cultural diversion, but not until the emergence of mass society in the eighteenth century—that is, until the incorporation of the majority of the population into society—could either popular culture or popular art be said to exist.

Obviously, there had always been two artistic traditions—the high and low comedy of Greece, the drama and circuses of Rome, medieval cathedral plays and street fairs, Renaissance court-drama and tavern farces—separated by lay and ecclesiastical controls. The appearance of a predominantly middle-class civilization in the Western world, accompanied by the decrease in size and importance of the so-called "elite" and "lower" classes, drastically changed the cultural pattern. The eighteenth century thus saw the establishment of a triple artistic tradition—the folk and high art of the past, plus a new popular level of art (although the lines of demarcation were never so clear cut). Prior to the eighteenth century the serious artist created for a relatively small minority on whom his subsistence depended. Though Sam Johnson looked for patron, he succeeded without one, for by his time the elite no longer could legislate culturally for the powerful middle class.

The primary condition for the emergence of popular culture was a great leap in population growth in Europe and the Americas, and the subsequent concentration of people into cohesive urban or near-urban units with common social, economic, and cultural characteristics. The result was the creation of a huge market for entertainment, with identifiable desires and responses. The existence of what is now called "the entertainment industry" can be easily recognized as early as 1750, when marketable cultural goods began to be manufactured in quantity to meet the needs of this mass public, to the profit of those who produced them.

After revolution broke the domination of cultural standards by the upper classes, the spread of education and literacy through the great middle class and below created a new audience which represented the tastes of the population at large. Control of the means of cultural production and transmission passed from a previously privileged elite to the urbanized, democratized middle classes. By the middle of the nineteenth century nearly everyone in the United States (except slaves and Indians) was minimally literate; by the middle of the twentieth three-quarters of American adults possessed a high-school education or better. This mass society had much more leisure time, much more disposable income, and it needed a new art— neither folk nor elite—to use the one and fill the other.

Popular culture was also a product of modern technology and its new techniques for duplicating and multiplying materials (high-speed presses, cheaper paper, new ways of graphic representation) along with much more efficient methods of production and dis-

tribution. Print became pervasive in nineteenth-century society, as machines widened and cheapened the public's access to the printed page. The twentieth century opened other channels of cultural communication to even larger audiences by introducing quite revolutionary methods of reproducing and transmitting sound and image—the phonograph, film, radio, television. Print is no longer the chief means of contact between artist and public, for the mass of today's population is accessible in a variety of ways. The average American between his second and his sixty-fifth year spends three thousand entire days, almost nine years of his life, watching television; by the time the average five-year-old enters kindergarten, he has spent more time before the family television set than the average college student has spent in classrooms over a four-year span.

The growth of a large popular audience, increasingly accessible through the mass media, caused in turn a demand for artists to satisfy its cultural needs. To these artists success lay not in pleasing a rich patron and his small, aristocratic, cultural circle, but in satisfying an increasingly broad "popular" audience. By the middle of the eighteenth century a large number of artists, especially novelists and dramatists (genres most adaptable to mass consumption) aimed their work directly at this new, general audience. The popular artist had to make his own tradition by investigating his market, calculating its desires, and evolving devices (many of which he adapted from folk art) for reaching it. He became a kind of professional (personified clearly, for example, by Daniel Defoe in England), who created for profit the kind of art that the public wanted.

The appearance of a *popular* artistic tradition, therefore, derives from a shift—initiated in the eighteenth century and completed during the nineteenth—from the patronage of the arts by the restricted upper classes to the support offered by a huge, virtually unlimited, middle-class audience, within the context of great technological, social, and political change. Modern mass society was fully formed by the middle of the nineteenth century; the modern mass media, in various stages of development, already provided the dominant forms of communication. Popular culture developed with it. The twentieth century established both more securely.

Although rather clear boundaries lie between popular and folk art on the one hand, and elite art on the other, the line between the first two is vague and easily crossed. The folk artist is usually satisfied with somewhat more anonymity; he is less concerned with aesthetic context, and less with specifically aesthetic purpose, though he wants to satisfy his audience, as does the popular artist. His art, however, tends to be thematically simple and technically uncomplicated, its production—the folk song, the duck decoy, the tavern sign, the circus act—not so strongly influenced by technological factors.

Popular art is folk art aimed at a wider audience, in a somewhat more self-conscious attempt to fill that audience's expectations, an art more aware of the need for selling the product, more consciously adjusted to the median taste. It is an art trying to perfect itself, not yet complete, not yet mature.

Elite art is produced by known artists within a consciously aesthetic context and by an accepted set of rules, its attainment (or failure) judged by reference to a normative body of recognized classics. The subjective element—that is, the presence of the creator or performer—is vital to its effectiveness. Elite art is exclusive, particular, individualistic; its aim is the discovery of new ways of recording and interpreting experience. Technical and thematic complexity is of much greater value in elite art than in folk or popular art; in fact, technique may become a vehicle for thematic expression, or may simply become an end in itself.

Popular art, aimed at the majority, is neither abstruse, complicated, or profound.

"...popular art has been an unusually sensitive and accurate reflector of the attitudes and concerns of the society for which it is produced."

To understand and appreciate it should require neither specialized, technical, nor professional knowledge. It is relatively free of corrective influences derived from minority sources; its standards of comprehension and achievement are received from consensus; it must be commonly approved, pervasive in the population, "popular" in the sense that the majority of people like and endorse it and will not accept marked deviations from its standards and conventions. More individualized than folk art, but less so than elite art, popular art tends to be more dependent than either on the skill of the performer.

Popular art confirms the experience of the majority, in contrast to elite art, which tends to explore the new. For this reason, popular art has been an unusually sensitive and accurate reflector of the attitudes and concerns of the society for which it is produced. Because it is of lesser quality, aesthetically, than elite art, historians and critics have tended to neglect it as a means of access to an era's—and a society's—values and ideas. The popular artist corroborates (occasionally with great skill and intensity) values and attitudes already familiar to his audience; his aim is less to provide a new experience than to validate an older one. Predictability is important to the effectiveness of popular art; the fulfillment of expectation, the pleasant shock of recognition of the known, verification of an experience already familiar—as in the detective story, the Western, the popular song, the Edgar Guest poem.

Popular art must be adaptable to mass production, and to diffusion through the mass media. It is irretrievably tied to the technology of duplication; to the popular artist the machinery of production and distribution may be as important—or more so—to what he does than either technique or content. Popular art, therefore, must be produced under conditions which make it possible to reach the widest possible audience in the most efficient way, a fact of life which the popular artist must accept as one of the stipulations of his craft.

Popular art assumes its own particular kind of audience, huge, heterogeneous, bewilderingly diverse in its combination of life styles, manners, interests, tastes, and economic and educational levels. This audience is much less self-conscious than an elite art audience; its standards are less clearly defined, its expectations less consistent and integrated. The audience for elite art possesses commonly held aesthetic and intellectual standards and has its own specialized idiom of appreciation and criticism. But those who respond to the popular arts are not sure why. Their standards are never precisely formulated or articulated and they are flexible and impermanent to a much greater degree than those of the audience for folk or elite art.

The relation of the popular artist to his audience is unique. The elite artist knows that his audience views his art in a context of certain predispositions; he anticipates success or failure within a definable framework of theory and achievement. His audience is acutely aware of him as an individual, knowing that his primary concern is the interpretation of his individual experience, and that he is personally involved with the content and technique of his product. The popular artist, however, works under no such set of rules, with a much less predictable audience, and for much less predictable rewards. His relationship with his public is neither direct nor critical, for between him and his audience stand editors, publishers, sponsors, directors, public relations men, wholesalers, exhibitors, merchants, and others who can and often do influence his product.

The elite artist is governed by traditional conventions of genre and technique, and knows that he will be judged by them. Since his accomplishment is measured by comparison with what others have done or are doing at his artistic level, he clearly understands the objectives and standards set for him by his critics and fellow artists. The popular artist, however, is subject primarily to the law of supply and demand; his aim is to win the largest possible audience in the marketplace. Neither what others have done, nor what critics say must be done, will necessarily guarantee success. The criterion of his success is contemporary, commercial, measured in terms of the size and response of his public. He competes not with his medium, nor with a preconceived set of critical standards, nor even with other popular artists, but with the audience under whose indirect control he must work—a notoriously fickle audience of unknown size and composition.

The popular artist must communicate with his audience through the mass media—with their interminably recurrent need for materials, unalterable publication deadlines, and vast amounts of empty space and time to be filled—which tends to depersonalize him, to remove him from close involvement with his art. The novelist writing for the little magazine or the prestige publisher, and the Western specialist writing for the mass-circulation weekly stand at completely different positions in relation to their materials and audiences, because they reach their audiences through media which make quite different demands and impose quite different conditions upon them.

The elite and popular arts are also distributed to their audiences in quite different ways, which in turn influence their product. Galleries, concerts, the quality press, the hardback book trade, academic discussion, self-improvement clubs and societies are not for the popular artist; he finds his public via the newsstand, the movie screen, the television, the paperback. His audience sees him less as an individual than as its own surrogate; his personal vision takes on meaning and effectiveness only when it reflects a wider, majority experience. He expresses not only what he feels, but also what many others feel.

The popular audience expects entertainment, instruction, or both, rather than an "aesthetic experience." To create for such an audience means that the popular artist cannot take into consideration the individualities and preferences of minority groups. Since the popular arts aim at the largest common denominator, they tend to standardize at the median level of majority expectation. The popular artist cannot disturb or offend any significant part of his public: though the elite artist may and should be a critic of his society, the popular artist cannot risk alienation.

The popular artist, then, hopes to do the very best he artistically can within the rigorous limits set by his situation. His accomplishment is measured by his skill and effectiveness in operating within the boundaries of the majority will and the requirements of the mass media. Since he hopes to make money, he aims at one thing—the largest possible audience—and whether it be a best seller, a high program rating, a four-star feature, or a "golden disc," his talents (which may be considerable) are directed toward mass response.

This does not mean that what the popular artist does is not worth doing, or personally unsatisfying, or aesthetically bad, or commercially cheap. It merely means that he must develop certain kinds of specialized skills to accomplish it, for his product must pay the medium and show a profit. And since popular art, to be successful, must be immediately popular, the artist must use those forms and media to which his audience has easiest access—movies, radio, television, the phonograph record, the magazine, the paperback book, the popular song, the newspaper, the comic book, and so on—and which it can most easily understand.

The fact that the mass audience exists, and that the popular artist must create for it, are simply the primary facts of life for the popular arts. Popular art can depend on no subsidy, state, or patron; it has to pay its way by giving the public what it wants, which may not always agree with what the artist may feel to be the most aesthetically apt. Satisfying a large audience involves no less skill than pleasing a smaller or more sophisticated one; popular artists can and do develop tremendous expertise and real talent. A best-selling paperback is not *ipso facto* bad; a song is not necessarily worthless because people hum it; a painting is neither bad because many look at it with pleasure nor good because few do.

Sometimes, with skill and talent alone, a popular artist may transmute mediocre material into something much better than it is, something even good; the gradual improvement over the years of standards of performance in the popular arts provides sufficient proof of this. A brief glance at the almost unbelievable banalities and ineptitudes of early movies, radio, television, fiction, or popular theater, in comparison with today's products, makes it abundantly clear that contemporary popular artists have developed tremendous technical skill, and that their sophistication and subtleties of performance are much greater than those of their predecessors. The distance between the movies of William S. Hart or Mary Pickford (or even of some Chaplin), between the comedy of Gallagher and Shean or Amos and Andy, between the music of the Wolverines or Paul Whiteman, and today's equivalents is incredibly wide. Over the years, the simple literalness of Tom Mix and Edward G. Robinson has become the symbolic, multileveled popular art of *High Noon* and *Bonnie and Clyde*.

Resistance to the study of popular culture has been particularly strong in the field of history. Although theoretically concerned with the entire spectrum of human experience, the historical profession has the dubious distinction of being one of the last of the social sciences and humanities to consider popular culture a legitimate area of inquiry. There have been some notable exceptions within the ranks of historians, ranging from Moses Coit Tyler, writing in the nineteenth century about newspapers, to Arthur Schlesinger Jr. and John Higham in the 1960s, contributing salient interpretations of television and sports.

In the 1970s, however, many of the young historians, profoundly influenced by growing up in the "mass-mediated society," have eagerly endorsed the study of popular culture. For instance, in 1973 doctoral students John Pendleton and James Joslyn created a course titled "American Popular Cultural History" at the University of California, Santa Barbara. They were aided in the development of the course by Roderick Nash, a young intellectual and environmental historian who ser[ ] faculty sponsor and one of the lecturers for the class. Through his many books and articles, Nash has established himself as a leading historian of popular culture from 1900 to 1930. Milton Plesur, of the State University of New York at Buffalo, and Fred MacDonald, of Northeastern Illinois University, among others, have fashioned similar popular cultural history courses in the seventies.

David Burner, Robert Marcus, and Jorj Tilson have attempted to show their fellow historians the broad expanse of popular culture that demands historical scrutiny in their book, *America Through the Looking Glass* (1974). The following selection, from the introduction to the book, offers a succinct statement on the importance of popular culture in understanding the American experience. The authors also examine the concept of the mirror and conclude that while popular culture may often give an inaccurate, distorted, even "grotesque" view of American life, the images are more recognizable to the masses than the traditional "kings-and-battles" view of history.

America Through the Looking Glass

David Burner
Robert Marcus
Jorj T. Tilson

American popular culture is the mirror of American life; it is, in fact, the way most people see themselves. Like other mirrors, this one can give a true picture, a distorted one, or even a grotesque image. But we examine this reflection of American life, because it gives the only view that would be fully recognizable to the common men and women of the nation's past whose experience constitutes our history.

Culture is, quite simply, the subjective resources that members of a group possess: the body of beliefs, practices, rituals, goals, patterns of behavior that people have available to cope with life. It is the "inside" of which society or social structure is the "outside." No analysis of the activities of a people would be complete without examining both the objective structure of society—the institutions and actual relationships among people—and the culture, the way experience is subjectively organized.

In American history the backbone of every textbook is its account of the nation's institutions. Students come away with a shadowy vision of the people of the past "responding" to the frontier, to industrialism, to the rise of a welfare state, and to the country's role in world politics. The past becomes what happened to people, not what people did or who they were. An introduction to their culture, to their sense of the world, to their amusements, customs, and passions is an obvious first step toward righting this balance.

The study of popular culture is a relatively recent intellectual discipline that has only begun to affect historical studies. It grew up since the 1930s, principally as a branch of literary criticism. Some custodians of high culture, convinced that they could no longer simply avoid the subject, embraced the distinction between serious and popular culture—in short to prevent the infection from spreading. Others applied the canons of serious criticism to popular culture to discover that popular entertainers like Charlie Chaplin were in fact artists or that tragedy, a traditional theme of high culture, could be found in popular media. Still, so long as esthetic standards dominated inquiry, the second-class character of popular culture could only be confirmed. And the emphasis on contemporary materials left historians with little of value to use when they sought to describe popular culture in the past.

The historical study of ideas often reinforced the tendency to ignore or isolate popular culture. Much intellectual history

studied culture in the old nineteenth-century sense—the best that has been thought and felt. This, however, does little toward recapturing the way most people in the past encountered the world. The theory of virtual representation—that the elites of society can speak for the lowly—has long since vanished from political thought and ought to quit the cultural scene as well. The culture of the great and powerful is not the culture of the masses. Even the greatest works of art—Dante's poetry or Shakespeare's plays—do not speak for an age; they speak for less than that—a class or a group or a tendency, and they speak for more, transcending their age and touching the concerns of humanity in some way general and timeless. As humanists, we study them without worrying about what they tell us of the past. As historians, we study them as we would any other cultural artifact, for what they say about the man or woman who created them and the audience they reached. They provide a valuable entrée to one part of the past, not some royal road to broad insight.

Another discipline that has restricted inquiry into popular culture is the study of folklore. Like the literary critic, the folklorist saw popular culture as an alien force, undermining folk expression. He defined folklore as culture passed directly by word of mouth without the intermediaries of print or electronic media. Only such culture could be genuinely of the people. Popular culture using folk themes became known as "fakelore"—a pejorative term if there ever was one. Popular culture, then, became whatever was neither high culture nor folk culture, something both inferior and inauthentic; and most scholars gave it a rather wide berth. Only in the last few years have folklorists realized the artificial limits of their definition, recognizing that much vital folk culture moves in and out of print and electronic media without ceasing to be authentically of the common imagination.

Most of these problems of definition disappear when one focuses on historical rather than esthetic questions. Viewed historically, popular culture means any form of expression or custom that achieves popularity among a large group of people. It can include the high culture created by a single self-conscious artist (e.g., Shakespeare, whose plays were a staple of touring companies a century ago) and the folk artifacts that enter media such as print or phonograph records. Once into the consciousness of a substantial group both become indistinguishable parts of the community's cultural endowment. Transformed into popular culture, they function no differently from the products composed commercially for popular audiences.

In short, popular culture and all culture is a process, not a specific kind of product. Students of high culture call this process "tradition"; folklorists speak of "the folk process." Both mean something living and evolving out of the imaginations of specific groups of people. Still, popular culture, because of its low academic pedigree and its concentration on the present, achieved a far more limiting definition than is implied in the image of a free-flowing process. Most people, their gazes narrowed to the electronic media, the professional entertainer, and the mass-produced popular book, magazine, or comic, envision popular culture as a consumer item created by professionals for a passive audience.

This static definition does not at all conform to most historical experience and even eliminates a good deal of contemporary culture from consideration. Much popular cul-

ture was created wholly or in part by the people who enjoyed it. Transmission by the folk process meant a continuous modification of what was inherited. Even the transmission of commercially produced popular entertainment was once a more active process. Sheet music, for example, was printed for playing on the piano and singing at home. Similarly, in transmitting the culture of home economics, the cooking, and housekeeping, and childrearing books, and even the sex manuals that dot the American past and clot the American present assume a more active role on the part of the ultimate consumer than, say, the motion picture. Rituals such as quilting bees, barn raisings, Fourth of July fireworks, cookouts, coffee klatches, garage sales, dormitory bull sessions, bar hopping, and neighborhood cancer fund drives reflect as much popular culture as listening to *Amos 'n' Andy* or watching *All in the Family*. The whole world of how-to-do-it books is a continuing index to the popular mind. Popular culture, then, is not simply mankind as a vast audience: it is whatever provides materials for people to use in their daily lives—to use to give meaning to their experience.

Popular culture so defined encompasses the whole cycle of human life from midwifery and childrearing practices through marriage rituals and success images to the art of tombstone inscriptions. Most beliefs about hygiene and health come through the conduit of popular culture augmented by, perhaps, less science than we like to think.

"Most beliefs about hygiene and health come through the conduit of popular culture augmented by, perhaps, less science than we like to think."

Humor becomes a part of the culture as do religious practices and beliefs. Instruction comes in schoolbooks, etiquette manuals (extremely influential in the nineteenth century), and how-to-do-it books of every description (perhaps even more prevalent a hundred years ago than now). Even political life once had much the form of popular entertainment and then as now helped to mold people's perception of the world. Domestic architecture and fashions in clothing fixed some of the most basic parts of people's imaginations, teaching particular standards of beauty, of order, of seemliness. A wide range of materials addressed to both children and adults affected the meanings people found in work, the views they took of the environment, their visions of people they had never seen, or their stereotypes of people they encountered daily.

Among the most important *gatekeepers* in a mass-mediated society are the men and women involved in the making of its popular culture. Storytellers of the past transmitted or embellished regional folktales, ballads, or art forms. Today they reach a vast audience by writing television or motion picture scripts, composing songs like "I'm Dreaming of a White Christmas" and "Moon River," or painting the cover art for a magazine like *McCalls'* with five million readers. These storytellers and their employers, the story sellers, as sociologist Herbert Gans terms them, are largely responsible for the form and content of American popular culture. The question that intrigues many observers is just how much the collaborative efforts of these so-called tastemakers truly affect the Great American Public. In this yet unresolved debate, one side argues that the successful makers of popular culture are those who intuitively understand what the public wants and then proceed to supply it in abundance. The opposing view holds that the public doesn't really know what it wants, and therefore its tastes are shaped by the sophisticated sellers of mass culture.

Dr. Gans, one of the most prolific writers in the field of popular culture studies, deals with this seeming paradox in his book, *Popular Culture and High Culture*. In this excerpt, he suggests that most Americans don't care too much about the popular culture they get.

Popular Culture's Defects as a Commercial Enterprise

Herbert Gans

The criticism of the process by which popular culture is created consists of three related charges: that mass culture is an industry organized for profit; that in order for this industry to be profitable, it must create a homogeneous and standardized product that appeals to a mass audience; and that this requires a process in which the industry transforms the creator into a worker on a mass production assembly line, requiring him or her to give up the individual expression of his own skill and values.

For example, [Leo] Lowenthal writes:

The decline of the individual in the mechanized working processes of modern civilization brings about the emergence of mass culture, which replaces folk or "high" art. A product of popular culture has none of the features of genuine art, but in all its media popular culture proves to have its own genuine characteristics: standardization, stereotypy, conservatism, mendacity, manipulated consumer goods.

Dwight Macdonald puts it more sharply:

Mass Culture is imposed from above. It is fabricated by technicians hired by businessmen; its audience are passive consumers, their participation limited to the choice between buying and not buying. The Lords of *Kitsch*, in short, exploit the cultural need of the masses in order to make a profit and/or to maintain their class rule.

Implicit in these charges is a comparison with high culture, which is portrayed as noncommercial, producing a heterogeneous and nonstandardized product, and encouraging a creative process in which an individual creator works to achieve his or her personal ends more than those of an audience.

Differences Among Cultures

Systematic evidence to evaluate the three charges is scarce, but the differences between popular and high culture as economic institutions are smaller than suggested. To be sure, popular culture is distributed by profit-seeking firms that try to maximize the audience, but then so is much of high culture, at least in America, where government subsidies and rich patrons are few. Although much has been written about the intense competitiveness and cynical marketing ethos of Hollywood and Madison Avenue, a study of art galleries, magazines, and book publishers appealing to a high culture public would show similar features. Indeed, pressures to deceive the customer and to cut corners in relationships with competitors may be even more marked in some high culture firms, for example, in the art world, if only because their market is smaller, making it necessary to struggle harder to get business.

One major difference between popular culture and high culture is the size and heterogeneity of the total audience. High culture appeals to a small number of people, probably not more than half a million in the whole country, whereas a popular television program may attract an audience of over 40 million. Because the popular audience is larger, it is also more heterogeneous, and although the high culture public prides itself on the individuality of its tastes, it is in fact more homogeneous than the publics of popular culture. Given the size of the audience, popular culture is often mass-produced, but so is much of high culture, for example, its books, records, and films. A few high culture users are rich enough to buy original paintings, but most, like the buyers of popular art, must be satisfied with mass-produced prints.

In order to produce culture cheaply enough so that people of ordinary income can afford it, the creators of popular culture, faced with a heterogeneous audience, must appeal to the aesthetic standards it holds in common, and emphasize content that will be meaningful to as many in the audience as possible. Whether the resulting culture is, however, more homogeneous than high culture can be questioned. Popular culture is more standardized, making more use of formulas, stereotypical characters and plots, although even high culture is not free from standardization. For example, many recent "serious" novels have made the theme of the artist as a young man, borrowed originally from Joyce and D. H. Lawrence, into a formula, featuring a stereotypical young man striving to develop his identity as an artist. Westerns may resemble each other more than high culture drama of a similar genre, but Westerns are as different from family comedies as high culture drama is from high culture comedy. Conversely, the differences within a given genre are no smaller in popular culture than in high culture; there are as many varieties of rock as of baroque chamber music, even though

"...popular culture is distributed by profit-seeking firms that try to maximize the audience, but then so is much of high culture..."

scholars only study—and thus publicize—the variations in the latter. Likewise, formal and substantive differences abound in popular art, although they are less visible than those in high art, which are discussed by critics and classified into schools by academics. In many ways, the different schools in high culture are equivalent to the different formulas in popular culture, for both represent widely accepted solutions to a given creative problem.

Since each taste culture is sensitive only to its own diversity and judges the others to be more uniform, a careful comparative study would be needed to say whether there is actually more diversity in high culture than in popular culture. The same observation applies to the amount of originality, innovation, and conscious experimentation. Both cultures encourage innovation and experimentation, but are likely to reject the innovator if his innovation is not accepted by audiences. High culture experiments that are rejected by audiences in the creator's lifetime may, however, become classics in another era, whereas popular culture experiments are forgotten if not immediately successful. Even so, in both cultures innovation is rare, although in high culture it is celebrated and in popular culture it is taken for granted. High culture being more timeless than popular culture, its classics are constantly revived for contemporary audiences, but since the late 1960s, when nostalgia began to be profitable, popular culture classics have also been revived, usually in modernized forms.

Differences Among Creators
Finally, the differences between the motives, methods, and roles of the creators are also fewer than has been suggested. A number of studies have indicated that creators are communicating with an audience, real or imagined, even in high culture, and that the stereotypes of the lonely high culture artist who creates only for himself or herself,

and of the popular culture creators who suppress their own values and cater only to an audience, are both false. Many popular culture creators want to express their personal values and tastes in much the same way as the high culture creator and want to be free from control by the audience and media executives. Conversely, "serious" artists also want to obtain positive responses from their peers and audiences, and their work is also a compromise between their own values and those of an intended audience. Some high culture creators, particularly those working on a freelance basis, may put their own values before that of the audience, and accept a smaller audience in the tradeoff, whereas many popular culture creators, at least those who are employees, must produce for a large audience and cannot make this tradeoff. (Whether these reactions are functions of culture or of occupational position within the culture-producing agency remains to be studied.)

Even so, popular culture creators also try to impose their own taste and values on the audience, and many see themselves as popular educators, trying to improve audience taste. For example, when I interviewed some writers of popular television series several years ago, they pointed out that they were always trying to insert their own values into their writing, particularly to make a moral or didactic. point. If and when producers objected—as they sometimes did—the end result was usually a compromise, for the producer cannot get along without the writer, and writers, like their high culture peers, are reluctant to compromise their own values. In films and plays, where the production pace is more leisurely and the budget more flexible, the writer who cannot work out a compromise is replaced by another, and sometimes, several writers—and directors—are employed before the film or play opens. In high culture, on the other hand, creators who cannot produce for an audience are simply ignored, and their product vanishes into museums, libraries, and scholarly studies.

One of the major reasons for the conflict between writers and producers has to do with the class and educational differences between popular culture creators and their audiences, which do not exist—or at least not as often—in high culture. Many popular culture creators are better educated than their audiences and are upper-middle-class in status, so that when they create, say, for a lower-middle-class audience, some differences in values and tastes are inevitable. Because creators are of higher status than their audiences, they try to impose their own tastes, but because the product they create must reach the largest possible audience, producers, whose jobs depend on the rating or the box office results, must stop them from doing so. When the audience for a given television series (or movie) is heterogeneous, for example in class or age, the writer's taste may appeal to part of that audience but not to another's, and much of the producer-writer conflict is over which part of the audience—or more correctly, the audience as they imagine it to be—is to be given priority. When the audience is more homogeneous, the gap between the creator and the audience—and the producer—is much smaller, and in many cases, creators share the tastes of their audience. Indeed, the most popular creators come from much the same socioeconomic and educational background as their audience and therefore share its taste, much like the real or idealized folk-artist who created folk culture for his audience. In high culture, the creator-audience gap is much smaller, if only because the audience is smaller, more homogeneous, and usually of the same educational and class background as the creator.

Nevertheless, some distance must always exist between creators and their audiences, because creators look at culture differently than its users. Creators make culture their work, whereas users do not, and can rarely have as much interest or ego-involvement

"A creator needs an audience as much as an audience needs a creator, and both are essential to the product."

in a cultural product as the person who created it. For creators, culture is often the organizing principle of their lives, whereas users are more likely to treat it as a tool for information or enjoyment. This difference between creators and users . . . leads to different perspectives toward culture which exist in popular culture as well as high culture and are a more important cause of the alienation of the artist from the audience than value or taste differences between them.

The critics of mass culture are creator-oriented; they argue that differences of perspective between creators and users should not exist because users must bend to the will of creators, taking what is given them, and treating culture from the creator's perspective. Whether users have any right to their own perspective, and to having that perspective affect the creation of culture is, of course, a question of values, and . . . they have that right, because culture cannot exist without them. A creator needs an audience as much as an audience needs a creator, and both are essential to the product.

Moreover, the freedom of the popular culture creator to ignore user perspectives is not as limited, and that of the high culture creator not as limitless as is often thought. In fact, a recent study of Hollywood studio musicians suggested that the men who perform the background music for the movies found their work more creative and their working conditions freer than when they played in symphony orchestras. In all the mass media, creative people who are successful are generally free to do what they want or think is right, provided they stay within the acceptable formats and do not antagonize important elements in the audience, but this is also the case in high culture. Of course, successful creators are free in part because they have accepted, consciously or unconsciously, the basic goals and policies of the firms and institutions within which they work, and in both high and popular cultures, young innovators face many obstacles unless and until they can prove that their innovations will be accepted.

Actually, the freedom of the creators depends less on whether they are in high or popular culture than on whether they are working in an individual or group medium. A novelist can create a finished product by himself, but playwrights, filmmakers and musicians are inevitably involved in group enterprises, and their work is often changed by other group members who also partici-pate in creating the finished product. Because it is older and intended for a smaller audience, high culture is more often communicated through the individual media, but artistic conflict between the playwright and the director is as likely in a high culture play as in a popular one. In popular culture, there may be more conflict over which sectors of the total audience are to be reached, but this is a function of audience size and heterogeneity; and when the occasional high culture work becomes popular, there is the same pressure on the creator to change it so as to attract the popular audience. Even so, popular culture creators fight as intensely for their own ideas as high culture creators, and thinking of the former as opportunistic hacks out to give an audience what it wants is an unfair and inaccurate surrender to a facile stereotype.

Most mass-mediated entertainment (as well as news) is the end product of a chain of gatekeepers, the majority of them with diverse personalities and experience. Gatekeepers, simply defined, are individuals who are directly involved in relaying, transferring, or censoring the content of some kind of mass communication.

For example, when the writer of an episode for "Maude" depicts her as considering an abortion, the "gatekeeper" above him, perhaps the producer, has to accept or reject his story line for the week. On the basis of his perception of the audience, the producer decides whether or not to go with it. Even if he personally may not have any qualms about Maude's having an abortion, he weighs the question of how much the audience may be outraged or delighted by her actions. How many might write to the show's sponsors and threaten to boycott their products? Although, in the end, one top gatekeeper must make the "go" or "no-go" decision, those in the chain below him are well aware of their chief's biases and predilections and act accordingly.

David Grunwald gives us a fascinating portrait of three of the most powerful gatekeepers in American popular culture. Although few Americans would recognize their names, these three television network vice-presidents have the final decisions on what 100 million or more Americans will watch at home on any evening. Of course, there is the ultimate gatekeeper, the audience. If they tune off "Maude" or switch from Harry Reasoner to Walter Cronkite, they, indeed, have turned thumbs down on all the previous gatekeepers.

Network Nexus:
TV's Guardians of Taste

David Grunwald

Television is a home medium designed to appeal to audiences of diverse tastes and interests ... the Company recognizes its obligation to maintain the highest standards of taste and integrity in all its programming. In general, programs should reflect a wide range of roles for all people and should endeavor to depict men, women and children in a positive manner, keeping in mind always the importance of dignity to every human being.

—*NBC Broadcast Standards*
for Television

At CBS he is called vice president of Program Practices. At ABC and NBC he is called vice president of Broadcast Standards. The critics call Van Gordon Sauter, Alfred R. Schneider and Herminio Traviesas censors.

They are the pointmen of television, the holders of possibly its most thankless job, the ones who decide what can go on the air and what can't, the ones who get all the flak. But then, it's easy to take potshots at them, just as it's easy to take potshots at television itself.

This year the theme is violence. There is too much on the air, the critics cry. *Newsweek* features an eight-page cover story on how television affects kids, how the "Kojacs" and "Barettas" numb children's minds. Viking publishes children's writer Marie Winn's indictment, *The Plug-In Drug*, suggesting that quality makes no difference, the mere act of watching alone may adversely affect kids.

Forgotten in all the hue and cry is that television is a business, a mass medium, an entertainment service designed to deliver viewers to the advertisers. If people don't watch, ratings suffer, advertisers go elsewhere, and the networks go down the tube.

"Television is by and far the most conservative of the mediums of mass communication in this country," says CBS's Sauter. "The relationship people develop with television is unprecedented in our society. There's never been anything like it before in our experience, and we don't wholly understand it."

"We have to be very careful that we do not shock a large group of people when we come as guests into their homes," says NBC's Traviesas. "There is a puritanical streak in this country," he adds. "It doesn't change."

"We have to serve various masters: the advertisers, who pay for the programs in a free enterprise system; the viewers, who are really the ultimate people in control, because if they don't watch, the programs won't be there; the affiliates, which are the means of distribution," says ABC's Schneider. "If I said no to everything that the major pressure and special-interest groups said not to put on the air, I would have to go black."

"The worst thing that we could be called in doing this job is a censor, and yet I know that is the easiest way to explain it," admits Traviesas. In truth, the word is to some extent a misnomer. He and his counterparts are there not to censor thought but rather to review all network entertainment programming (Sauter also reviews sports while Schneider reviews nonlive sports) and commercials submitted for network airing, concerned that the programming doesn't alienate large blocs of viewers and that commercials are honest and in good taste. While some, particularly television writers and producers, contend that the number of viewers easily offended is quite small, Traviesas feels that over 50 percent of the audience is "concerned about how far we go in story materials."

"We represent what we perceive to be the interests of our viewers," says Sauter. "Having lived in countries where censorship is a real and sometimes very lethal quality, I certainly don't want to think of myself as a censor. If indeed this department ends up functioning as a censor and we become a Dr. No—well, then we are really inhibiting the creative process and probably being of no service whatsoever to the viewers."

Over the course of a year, each network reviews close to 50,000 commercials and some 2,800 hours of programming. "Our main concern," says Schneider, "is not with the thwarting of creativity or the prohibition of the expression of creative ideas, but rather the treatment in which those creative ideas are handled with respect to time and scheduling, to appropriateness of composition of audience, and to some kind of evaluation of where we are in the culture of this country."

"We are involved in an unscientific, highly subjective field. It's a matter of individual judgment," says Sauter. "There is no magic meter that you strap a script to, push a button, and the meter tells you it's in good taste, it's in bad taste. There's no meter that tells you that the script is too violent, not violent." Quite simply, says Schneider, we're "on a teeter-totter between the use of the medium to create new ideas, to make people think, and the concerns of so many people saying, 'That's inappropriate for me or my children.'"

One key factor is the nature of television itself. Unlike magazines and newspapers, it

> "Parents are there to parent. If they don't want their children to see a certain kind of program, they should turn off the television set..."

is not targeted to a specialized and/or regional group of readers. Unlike movies and the theater, it does not require an extra effort to see, but sits there in the home, its programming easily available to the whole family. And because of that easy access, viewing in many households is not at all selective.

It is only during the day that viewing is primarily a solitary affair. And what can be handled during the day—the trials and tribulations of soap opera life—presents problems at night. Prime time, explains Sauter, is "fundamentally a family situation where the person who watched the television set alone during the day is watching the set with a husband, boyfriend, father, lover, sister, brother, whatever, and the same themes could and would create in many households a very awkward environment, and the viewers would become uncomfortable with it."

What commercial television strives for, says Schneider, is "to have a diversity of presentation so that there is at some point, at some time within the broadcast day or week, something for everyone's taste, from pure escapist entertainment to the thoughtful presentation of provocative, significant issues that the country has to deal with."

Not surprisingly, there are some touchy areas that constantly cause problems: language, eroticism, religion, minority groups' images, controversial themes, violence. "We've got to reflect what we feel is now acceptable," explains Traviesas. "We are still getting complaints about bikini-clad young ladies." As for nudity and religious humor,

those just aren't done. Even the ethnic humor once displayed on "Laugh-In" is less common now.

"Part of my job is to listen to groups—not to be pressured into something, but to be concerned when enough of them are telling us that we are doing something that is hurting them in front of the viewing audience," continues Traviesas. "This type of outcry is constant and growing. It almost becomes a joke as to whether the next time we make fun of somebody with a beard they will organize."

And language. "Even words like 'hell' and 'damn' I try to avoid in the first ten or fifteen minutes, especially of a ninety-minute or two-hour show, until that audience out there knows the character that's going to say it" so that "when they say it, they don't even know it happens," says Traviesas. "But if you start right up front with it, then they start saying, 'There they go again, using those words all over the place.' "

As for violence, it seems to depend on the nature of the program and who's watching. Schneider says there were very few complaints about the violence shown on "Roots," which in certain respects, he contends, was more violent than the programs people complain about: the "Starsky & Hutches," the "Police Stories." "Why is violence in that program acceptable?" Probably because of the context, the "emphasis upon the why of the violence rather than the violence itself."

"We are virtually at a point now in our action-adventure programming where we can't take any more violence out of them," says Sauter. "If we did, they would cease to be in the genre of action-adventure programs and the content of the broadcasts would fail to meet the very legitimate expectations of the audience for that type of broadcast."

But it is because of the violence on television that so many parents are critical, worried about the possible impact on their children. Says Sauter, "Parents are there to parent. If they don't want their children to see a certain kind of program, they should turn off the television set or tell the child not to watch it." Schneider agrees, but concedes there is a problem with "the absentee parent, the parent who is out at work, who's not at home with the child."

Still, Sauter contends, "Television can't structure all its programming under the assumption that out there somewhere some children are watching. If we did, we'd radically alter the nature of television programming for the worse." Adds Schneider, "The parent cannot expect me to totally take over his responsibility when he's not there."

"The fundamental question," Sauter maintains, "is do the values inherent in television reflect the values of the American people? Do they represent the more positive aspects of our national experience or do they represent the least desirable aspects of our national experience? Do they contribute to the preservation of our values, or do they in some fashion diminish them?"

Sauter feels that people watch too much television and aren't selective enough in what they choose to view. The audience is diverse, the programming is diverse. If they don't like a program, they shouldn't watch it. "There's no sense in sitting there getting upset and complaining about something you don't like. There are other options available."

In the end, it boils down to taste. "There's no way of defining good taste," says Traviesas. "There are certain things that I do on 'Saturday Night Live' that according to my tastes, my personal lifestyle, I find very difficult to accept. But, boy, that audience, that young audience watching it just loves it."

The radio "disk jockey" epitomizes the role of the gatekeeper in popular culture. By deciding which records to play, the "deejay" wields enormous power in the popular music panoply. Together with radio programmers and record reviewers, the disk jockey actively influences, at times even determines, the tastes of the radio-listening audience. "Despite the artists' dues paying and record-company mixing and hype," observed popular music sociologist R. Serge Denisoff, "it all comes down to getting a deejay to play that record so a sufficient number of people can hear it." Small wonder that many disk jockeys feel confident enough to refer to themselves as "the emperor" or "your leader."

The disk jockey emerged as a prominent cultural gatekeeper in the 1930s. Pioneer deejays such as Al Jarvis and Arthur Godfrey, by emphasizing their personalities as much as the music they played, transformed themselves from radio announcers into full-fledged celebrities.

The rise of rock 'n' roll in the mid-fifties provided new dimensions for the disk jockey as a significant popular cultural figure. Once a crucial part of the pop music establishment, the deejay could now play the role of cultural revolutionary. Cleveland disk jockey Alan Freed was a case in point in the early fifties. By playing black rhythm-and-blues music (which he called "rock 'n' roll") for a listening audience composed of a large number of white teenagers, Freed helped facilitate the development of rock 'n' roll as a new force in popular music.

The "payola" or "play for pay" scandals of 1959/1960 tarnished the image of the deejay somewhat. Yet they also served to highlight the position of power the disk jockey commanded, since so many record producers were willing to play the bribery game for a shot at success. Despite the payola hullabaloo, most deejays, including "American Bandstand" impresario Dick Clark, managed to emerge relatively unscathed from the ordeal. A rough estimate in the early 1970s indicated that some twenty or thirty thousand Americans made their living spinning platters and filling the rest of the air time with humor and a variety of verbal pyrotechnics.

Arnold Passman's book, *The Deejays* (1971), examines the phenomenon of the disk jockey in a critical, satirical, and often irreverent manner. Is the radio jock merely "an electronic extension of the countless traveling salesmen and medicine men who crisscrossed America during its expansion," asks Passman, or is he more akin to the shamans of primitive tribal culture?

The Deejays
Arnold Passman

As commercial radio in the U.S. closes a half-century of scatter-shot development, its prominence in the lives of every American has been suggested by [Marshall] McLuhan. Building from the message of the electric light as total change ("pure information without any content to restrict its transforming and informing power"), he says of "the little box":

The uniting of radio with phonograph that constitutes the average radio program yields a very special pattern quite superior in power to the combination of radio and telegraph press that yields our news and weather programs.

The disc jockey, "the impresario of the love court," . . . is the servant and sorcerer of this media mix, which makes up at least 80 percent of all broadcast time in the United States. And the growth of radio since the Depression may be directly traced through his evolution. The fact that the notion of the jock as a serious element of American life is not a common one makes it all the more fundamental to take a look at what's been happening.

A lotus of questions opens up in dealing with the deejay—an occupation that speaks directly to Freud's belief in the primacy of language, an axiom that, even in his time, was beginning to fall on deaf ears. And there are as many opinions about disc jockeys ("nobody listens to radio, but *everybody* can tell you what you said yesterday"), and the sheaf of forms radio takes, as there are products they must sell. A big one is music.

For instance, formula or format radio began in the early fifties as an extension of "The Lucky Strike Hit Parade," a weekly national program of the ten best-selling songs. Cigarette manufacturers had flocked to a top-tunes format in emulation of "The Hit Parade" to satisfy the defiant growing pains of susceptible youth—kids who were spiralingly younger, but more mature, by the time radio extended the formula around the clock over a decade ago.

The great popularity of "The Hit Parade" from 1935 to 1958 (its decline, however, began in 1950) caused music people many headaches, mainly because of its two-to-three-week time lag in on-the-air reportage. Its full-time successor swelled out of the midlands to meet the life-and-death challenge of network television with a barrage of the leading record purchases, not always adequately derived.

Known initially as "Top 30," "40," or "50," modern radio has perpetuated its conservative liturgy with a tight playlist at the lower figure (anywhere from the mid-twenties to the mid-thirties generally). It's still the same old "Top 40" ("today's American Academy"), but today it's more of less.

More than fifteen years after its rise, formula radio remains one of the more controversial products of mass communication, having been called everything from "a great, new art form" to "America's Rapid Rancid System.". . . More music and less talk is increasingly making radio an economically dictated, mechanical medium. This, in fact, *is* meeting the demands of the listening audience. But these programmers would seem to be running computers, and the live, informal immediacy of the jock, his reputed strong point, has long been, fitfully, on its way out. Why shouldn't he be also?

Barney Pip is a jock in his mid-thirties, although his audience has been led to believe he is in his post-teens. On the air he blows unnerving blasts on a trumpet, which he really can't play. But he calls himself "The World's Greatest Trumpeter," and he uses a falsetto voice, versions of which can be heard on many "Top 40" stations. Said Pip, who is very bright and sensitive and knows exactly where he's at:

As far as the computer and my job, the audience I work with demands the truth because machines don't lie. So, if humans are going to start fooling around, they *can* be replaced by machines.

So, if the truth comes off a little straight sometimes, then that's a value judgment on my part, rather than go that free-form route where somebody couldn't latch onto it, and say, "Well, it is the truth and it isn't the truth, and I have my own outlook and if I want the truth I'll go to a machine instead of him then.

After three hundred years, modern science now finds its electronic *cum* computer self turning on itself and returning man to the primeval state on the hairpin road of evolution. With the flux fest that is radio as constant companion, how key a voice in the evolving electronic sound is the immediate but ephemeral spoken word (McLuhan calls the spoken word "the most emotional form of communication") sandwiched around the music (another "most"—and increasingly, with stereo FM, headphones—and drugs)? . . .

The word "jockey" is a surprisingly basic one to Western man. Aside from its ready definition of a horse-supported man in a race, it also refers to "a man of the common people"—and "to bring, put, etc., by skillful maneuvering; to trick or cheat; or manipulate trickily."

The label can be traced from Jacques (French for peasant), and the Battle of Hastings gave it to the Scotch as Jock (nickname for man or fellow). John, the most common of men's names, means "Jehovah is most gracious," and its Italian, Giovanni, shorthanded to "Johnny," is the stem for "zany," which defines a clown's attendant who mimics his master's act. . . .

What primordial memories (*and new ones*) does the disc jockey call up? Is the microphone to the deejay what the rattle was to the shaman? The antennae his totem? How true does the jock run to archetype? Does he responsively sound prototypal motifs—walk as on a tightrope . . . , the line of intersection of the Trivial and Tragic Planes? . . .

Despised more than admired, the disc jockey is a curiously scaled member of an indiscernible *nouveau* vulgar elite. The standards for true qualification are loose and not really subject to greatly concerned definition. Still, this cell of inestimable sound purveyors (there are twenty thousand to thirty thousand in the United States, and, perhaps, a like number in the rest of the world), their lives sparked with insecurity and turmoil, bears striking witness to the times in which the deejay was born—the chaotic and totalitarian twentieth century.

Such a profession would seem to find ego at the crossroads—directing traffic from the hip? It has to be some ego that can believe an audience would rather hear its voice (warm as it may be) than music, and nearly every survey suggests that he say what he has to say and get out of the way. . . .

The jock is himself not a musician in his performances, but his orchestrating and interruptions run the full range of communication. The success or failure to "get across" is a constant puzzle and source of fulmination to himself and all around him. . . .

However, the ultimate concern is with a far greater commitment, an ominous pervasiveness of seemingly somewhat lesser stature. The omnishepherding disc jockey ("aside" from those select but shaky "hit" leaders who function as powerful advance pitchmen for the high-powered popular-music industry) surrounds the public with

"... much of what becomes fashionable in the United States ... has its inception in the playing of popular music on radio stations."

the demand of words and music (BUY!)—to act, lest it burn in the eternal hell-fire of depression.

An electronic extension of the countless traveling salesmen and medicine men who crisscrossed America during its expansion, the "faceless" deejay—a 24-hour tout with "Average Joe" purse-suasion the likes of which the world has probably never seen before—may be the pop propagandist who is the American Dream—or a nightmare of a Knight Mercantile.

What makes this commercial conditioning more complex, however, is the role of the better disc jockeys. These are the Perelmaniacal "wake-up" mountebanks, those with the highest ratings generally, although the long-lasting, looping, and ricocheting morning "satirist" has seen his audience begin to fragment.

These anchor men seem to have as point of departure from their lesser *frères* a humorous approach. The comic style is something not at all viewed as rigid, and usually seen as anathema to propaganda. Its intent is entertainment, but quite often—because of its tenuous reliance on the unexpected—it may represent an irreverent and incisive tack. . . .

In an immediate sense, much of what becomes fashionable in the United States—and, as a result, in the world today—has its inception in the playing of popular music on radio stations. The popular music of a culture is powerful medicine ("It's amazing," says a Noel Coward character, "how

potent cheap music is"), and the disc jockey is smack dab in the middle, perhaps the mint, of the psychedelic movement as it mushrooms out of the electronic and molecular revolutions. He represents the thrust of a definite cultural pluralism, not unlike, perhaps, the proliferation of Oriental cults in early Christian Rome.

Carl Haverlin is a man who has lived every year of the twentieth century. From 1947 to 1964, he was president of Broadcast Music, Inc., a licensing organization that was thirty years old the fall of 1969. BMI was established by the independent radio operators to challenge the narrowing monopoly the New York-nuanced American Society of Composers, Authors and Publishers (ASCAP) had on U.S. popular music.

The new source for backwater composition took the light off Broadway and made it shine from throughout the country. Said Haverlin:

And the music flows back to us, as witness The Beatles. It's a vast democratization, a world democratization. It's the tempo of the Nigerian drum, and it's worldwide.

From the deejay's playing of a record, it may be only a step to Ed Sullivan, "American Bandstand," Radio Luxembourg, The Beatles, fashions, slang, truly great wealth for the performers (although not as much for most as most people believe), and a decided pervasiveness of our lives. An envelopment, which, it can be shown, has most of its recalcitrant roots (as did millennial Spain—the forerunner of the Renaissance—in its Moorish incantation, which was blasted into being by the Roman colonization of Asia Minor and North Africa) in the life of the black man and the teen-ager, from where it has rapidly filtered into advertising, the subteen, and the culture at large.

Radio was utterly explosive to the preliterate South, as it still is. But it has yet really to get its black and white residents to make music together—to share their blues. Nevertheless, Egmont Sonderling, the white owner of six AM, four FM, and two television stations, whose radio stations in New York, Washington, Memphis, and Oakland comprise the largest single group of Negro-oriented stations in the country, noted:

Negro radio stations are the only true media of communication between black and black, and black and white, because we are there twenty-four hours a day. No other medium can say that.

Likewise, as the share of the audience slithers from a slice to a sliver (the New York City market has upwards of fifty radio stations, and the audience for "Top 40" at night dropped from nearly 50 percent to 15 percent during the late sixties), the deejay has something for everybody. And he who entertains us receives our most grateful and heartfelt approval. ("If Homer bores his au-dience he will not be invited to dinner again.") This has always been reflected in the image of the happy-go-lucky traveling salesman (the detached amusement of Madison Avenue?) whose witty, worldly, yet very personal approach resulted in, if not always a sale, certainly a "score."

In the vernacular, "to score" means "making it" *any way*, ranging from "illicit" success in business (from swindling to a drug purchase) to getting laid through charm alone. Radio has pushed the great myth of the magical traveling man to unquestioned heights in the form of the drifting disc jockey—science fiction's privateers. Just to hear them in constant battle may be precisely the role of the great, unwinding American public, and to get involved.

In his film *Annie Hall* (1977), Woody Allen refers to Los Angeles as a city in which "the only cultural advantage is being able to turn right at a red light." Others have criticized the city for its "plastic" environment and people, its "empty values," and its faddishness.

Despite the unfavorable opinion of Los Angeles held by many people, the city is, in the words of Benjamin Stein, "the hub of a media empire." The creative elite of mass entertainment, especially television, exerts enormous control over the attitudes, values, and images transmitted to the American public. And because they are such products of their environment, in Stein's estimation, they essentially present a very biased, Los Angeles view of life.

The handful of leading creators of television fare have, in effect, become powerful tastemakers in American society. This is not a new phenomenon in popular culture. As early as the turn of the twentieth century, editors of mass circulation magazines were regarded as individuals who could set cultural standards and influence public taste. The omnipresence of television has simply intensified the tastemaker role of popular culture.

The audience, of course, can reject the messages and images put forth by the makers of mass entertainment. The violent reception that greeted the motion picture *Exorcist II: The Heretic* is a case in point. Many of those watching the film were so outraged by what they considered the ludicrous or phony aspects of the movie that they reacted by laughing, jeering, or throwing popcorn at the screen. The producers, in turn, responded by reediting the film to try to make it a credible picture.

Television, motion pictures, and other forms of entertainment may project slanted or distorted views of American society and may produce incredulous or laughable "creations," but the audience is the final gatekeeper and can always turn their TV sets off or walk out of the movie houses.

The Electronic Elite
Who Shape America's Taste

Benjamin Stein

When I think of businessmen, I think of what Kennedy's father told him about them—'They're all sons-of-bitches.' I think of them as cannibals, eating their own," says Jim Brooks, producer of *The Mary Tyler Moore Show*, creator of *Rhoda*, major Hollywood TV writer. "Businessmen," Brooks adds, "commit a fraud when they say they're interested in anything but profit."

Allan Burns, co-producer of *The Mary Tyler Moore Show*, co-creator of *Rhoda* and, like Brooks, a major TV personality, agrees. "Big business," he says firmly, "is the enemy. My personal enemy. They scare me because of how big they are. Some of these companies have armies in foreign countries. It's frightening."

Meta Rosenberg, executive producer of *The Rockford Files* and Universal honcho, agrees, but with a twist. "Any bigness is dangerous," she says. "And, of course, there's a link between big business and the Mafia. That's not true of all businesses, just big business."

Stanley Kramer, motion picture producer and director with a list of credits as long and shiny as anybody's in Hollywood, has recently turned to television for several dramas based on real-life incidents, including an acclaimed account of the trial of Julius and Ethel Rosenberg. He also has some strong views about businessmen, views similar to Meta Rosenberg's: "When I think of business, I think of power." Put together with the military, Kramer says, "business results in a dangerous complex which means that things are done for profit instead of idealism." Kramer adds that "the Mafia is part of the whole corporate entity now."

Jerry Thorpe, producer of movies made for television and former producer of *Harry O*, sees businessmen as "ambitious, self-destructive and repressed, sometimes so repressed that they have violence within them."

Of course, it's nice for me to know what my neighbors here in Los Angeles think, but what these folks have to say about businessmen is interesting infinitely beyond the views of five successful people. Brooks, Burns, Rosenberg, Kramer and Thorpe sit astride the greatest media empire of all time, the American television networks, deciding, with others, what goes on the air. They decide, along with astonishingly like-minded others, what image of the world will go out over the airwaves to the national community in front of the television set.

That means that if they don't like businessmen, the 96 percent of Americans who watch television will see businessmen who are not fun people.

Proper-looking, well-dressed men with suburban mansions and well-coiffed wives will turn out to be murderers and dope dealers, at least on TV adventure shows. If a banker appears on a TV comedy show, he's definitely going to cheat someone and steal his money.

The people who make prime time television have absolute power over what images flicker on the cathode ray tube. Since all prime time (except for a rare special event) comes from Los Angeles, the views of just a few people here decide what is going to appear on television in the way of views of the American experience. That means that L.A. is the hub of a media empire that decides *what people will look at* and *what people on TV will look like.*

Michael Shamberg, 32-year-old vice-president of TVTV, Inc., an L.A.-based production company, sums it up succinctly. "If you want to see the people who decide what TV will look like, you should look only in L.A. This is where it's all happening—media content, media style, everything."

Al Burton, head of new projects at Norman Lear's T.A.T. Communications, Inc., puts it this way: "The people in the TV community here in Los Angeles may not figure out every detail of what goes on the TV screen in advance, but it sure comes out of their heads."

And so it happens: Meta Rosenberg has ambivalent feelings about small towns. "Small towns can have a greater sense of community than large cities, which is good. On the other hand, corruption can permeate a small town simply because it is small. In large cities," she adds, "people and corruption are dissipated. In small towns, there are less strong feelings opposing corruption. In a big city, there are strong countervailing forces."

You can be sure that Jim Rockford, Rosenberg's creation, is going to find his way to a small town and become the victim of a large plot by everyone in the small town aimed at covering up something ghastly.

In fact, the cliché of the evil small town

luring and ensnaring the clean-cut city slicker has become visible almost every night on TV adventure shows. Again, listen to what people in Hollywood have to say about small towns.

Stanley Kramer says that "small towns are extremely reactionary. In pursuit of the American dream, they endanger America."

Even David Begelman, the extraordinarily diplomatic head of Columbia Pictures (which has a major TV production subsidiary), notes that small towns are "alien places." He explains, "They're difficult to get used to unless you were born there. They're markedly different, with different kinds of people than people in the cities. They react differently."

Allan Burns sees small towns as "definitely not wholesome places to live." Burns, an advocate of gun control, also agreed that small towns probably were not in favor of gun control. "You have to consider the redneck population."

Jerry Thorpe gave another reason besides political and social aversion to small towns for the constant depiction of small town evil-doers at war with innocent city folk. "It's an easy way of generating melodramatic conflict," Thorpe says, "and people here are always interested in melodramatic conflict."

So, again, we have the nation's heartland depicted as the exclusive domain of Snopes-like characters intent on using that strong sense of community to cover up something loathsome.

Another instance: When asked whether she thought that people in the government knew what they were doing, Meta Rosenberg laughed and said, "Absolutely not." She adds, "I'm sure there are some fine people in the lesser jobs in government, but, frankly, the more we learn about government, the more we are unnerved."

Stanley Kramer sees the federal government as "a grossly incompetent piece of machinery." (Kramer notes that he has boundless admiration for the Constitution.)

Both Burns and Brooks agree that government is "generally incompetent, even though it's full of well-meaning people."

The predictable result is that when the federal government narcs muscle in on Kojak's turf, they'll make hash of it. If a federal welfare official comes to see someone in a sitcom, he'll be an easily fooled meathead. The only shows in which people from the federal government look good are shows for children. Everywhere else, the heroes of the show spend half their time cleaning up the feds' mess.

All of these views—about small towns, businessmen, the federal government—are held to an astonishingly homogeneous extent by people in the TV creative community. They enable that community to get its views across, however unwittingly, with a degree of uniformity that makes the L.A. message far more persuasive than it would be if it were contradicted by other messages on other shows.

The explicitly political and social views of the L.A. TV people are less interesting, though, than the L.A. ethos, the L.A. experience that comes across on the tube. The political and social views could just as easily come from another place, say, New York. But the look of things on TV is ineluctably and indelibly the look which comes only from the cultural center known as L.A. It is the Los Angelization of America on the TV screen.

Take hair, for instance. There is a certain way that people in Southern California and especially Los Angeles wear their hair. It looks lanker, straighter and neater, especially on men. Think of the men walking around Beverly Hills, with every hair neatly in place, and you've just about got it. People in the East, where the winds blow, or where, more importantly, men walk instead of drive, simply do not look like that. But if you see a television show like *Kojak*, set in New York, or *All's Fair*, set in Washington, the men look as if they might have just stepped out of a salon on Camden Drive in Beverly Hills.

The same goes for women. Take a look at the girls on *Charlie's Angels*, a soft-core show on prime time. One of the girls has a hairdo that must take days to prepare. When that show recently showed women in a Louisiana prison farm, their hair was only slightly less elegant.

Stanley Kramer, who has been everywhere and done everything, gave another superb example of the L.A. vision at work in the world. He was asked what the two best things in America were. First, he said, is the access to information. The second best thing in all of American life is that "almost everyone has a vehicle, a car."

In Los Angeles an artist who has written and directed and produced movies about heroism, treason, man's love of his fellow man, youth and age, and every sublime topic in the entertainment catalogue, believes that having a car is the second best thing about the society that he describes as "the last bastion of freedom on earth."

Nor is Kramer unusual or bizarre. The importance of the automobile to Los Angeles culture cannot be overrated. Jerry Axelrod, president of Southwest Leasing Corporation, has an endless series of anecdotes about the fixation of the rich and powerful of Los Angeles on their cars. "There are people who literally cannot rent an apartment, but who will scrimp and save to have a [Mercedes] 450 SL. They sleep in their cars."

This is seen on TV adventure shows with a vengeance. Everyone (with a few generic exceptions) has a shiny new car on cops and robbers shows. Bad guys, good guys, secretaries, businessmen, rich men, poor men—everyone has a new car. And a lot of time is spent watching people go back and forth in those cars. An extravagantly large amount of time is spent watching car chases with squealing tires as the detective chases the bad guy down Topanga Canyon. The exception to the new car allotment is that certain TV detectives are given a used car as a sign that the character is highly idiosyncratic. Columbo, who always appears rumpled and dirty, drives a rumpled and dirty Peugeot convertible. Harry Orwell, a similarly outlandish character, used to drive an Austin Healy Sprite. (At some points in *Harry O*, when Harry was considered particularly around the bend, he did not drive at all. Instead, he took a bus. But that was always considered the equivalent of going in drag.)

There is, in the instance of automobile worship, a direct transference, like the time Charlton Heston was transferred from one airplane to another in *Airport '75*—only in this case, it is a transfer from reality to fantasy.

The example of colors is equivalently fascinating. Look at the colors you see on *The Blue Knight*. As Bumper walks down the street there is an assortment of pastel pool halls, orange bars, black-painted massage parlors and other hues which do not look as if they exist in real life. Then look beyond *The Blue Knight*. Soon you will notice that every show which involves outdoor backdrops uses colors that don't look like they bear any relation to colors here on earth.

"But cars, hair and colors are not as full an expression of the L.A. experience and vision brought to the TV screen as space."

"Those weird colors," says Larry Wilson, a free-lance art designer lately associated with the University of California, "are the colors of the seamy parts of Hollywood or Alvarado Street or Western Avenue. They are the colors of the poor, old sections of Los Angeles, the cheery colors that bums in the L.A. area wake up to."

So much for that mystery.

But cars, hair and colors are not as full an expression of the L.A. experience and vision brought to the TV screen as space. Generally, people who live in bigger, more spacious residences are happier than those who live in more cramped circumstances. Space goes with grace and freedom and comfort. Lack of space goes with squalor, anxiety and despair.

A simple for-instance—the brave family in *Good Times* struggles to laugh despite a crowded and ungenerous apartment living area. It is clear that their basic circumstance is sad. Likewise with *Sanford and Son*, who laugh despite adversity in an almost hysterically full shack.

Real elegance, the life of *McMillan*, for instance, means living in an apartment that you could get lost in. Even better than that is living in the land of Mary Tyler Moore, where even a small apartment is so furnished and decorated that it gives that spacious look. Best of all is to have a little land, as the poor but deliriously happy Waltons do.

On the crime shows, the happy people all live in the suburbs and the pathetic, anxiety-ridden people all live in either small houses or apartments. (It has nothing to do with guilt or innocence though—the guilty usually live in the biggest and fanciest houses.)

Jerry Thorpe has part of the explanation. For him, crowded places "are not wholesome places." He adds that "crowding breeds crime and poverty and dissatisfaction and unemployment." In a word, says Thorpe, "high-density places breed bad things." Thorpe believes that, "of course, space is very important to people. If possible, I like to show people in spacious surroundings." He agrees with the idea that this viewpoint is widely shared among his co-executives, and therefore shows up in television.

Meta Rosenberg also likes a more spacious atmosphere. "I like quieter places than cities, less tense places. It's better if it has a slower pace." In a good environment (by which she means a non-city environment), Rosenberg believes "tension and pressures come from within. In a big city like New York or Chicago, tension and pressures come from outside."

Stanley Kramer has similarly negative feelings about crowded parts of cities. When he thinks of them, he thinks of ghettos, "of places which no longer work as communities. They're unpleasant; the air is bad; the transportation is bad; they're dangerous." Kramer adds that when he sees cities, he thinks that "the outer shell of sophistication is a façade. It doesn't show the city as it really is." Even though the cities may make a kid tough, Kramer believes that "you may not want your children to grow up in one."

Allan Burns sees New York City (as an example of crowded places) as "a frantic place where you wouldn't want to raise your children," even though he also sees it as an intellectually stimulating place. Jim Brooks, who also finds that he "thinks better" in New York, adds that "New York City is definitely not a wholesome place."

All of this reaction against a very crowded place by people in Los Angeles (many of whom are from that very crowded place, New York City) takes the form of a spread-out, uncrowded life in Los Angeles. The houses in the hills, the huge bungalows on the Westside of Los Angeles, the boats and trips to the desert are all part of a way of life that rejects crowding.

And, again, this view of the benefits of open spaces makes its appearance in television shows, where happy and sad are seen as open and crowded.

There are other examples. People in high positions in TV have an extremely high degree of affection for the police. "The police are in my employ. They're there to help me. They're almost always polite," is Meta Rosenberg's representative reaction. That's because, as the TV people say, in Beverly Hills, where most of them live, "the police are nice to you if you have a Mercedes and are well-dressed" (Meta Rosenberg's words).

That feeling of friendliness towards the police makes itself seen on TV in the form of friendly and respectful police. (The police on television, according to Larry Wilson, look like male models, which, he says, is also what Beverly Hills police look like.)

But all of the examples boil down to a few simple truths. There is a coherent set of views among TV creative people. The people quoted here are extraordinarily articulate and representative of their colleagues. Purposely or not, those people put across on TV their views of life. Most important of all from the standpoint of Los Angeles is that the views of life on television are L.A. views. They arise from the L.A. experience and the L.A. vision of what is and what should be. When America watches itself on TV, it sees itself through Los Angeles eyes.

None of this means that there is anything like an agreement among TV creative people to depict life in a certain way. Far from it.

Apparently, all of this uniformity of views has come about without any kind of coordination. Again, it may be that the experience of rising to a responsible position in TV production demands a certain type of person who has had a certain type of experience and has certain widely shared views.

Perhaps living in Los Angeles imposes a certain set of values beyond the values that shaped Los Angeles. Almost certainly that is true of the worship of the automobile. But, in any event, the people I talked to all seemed surprised that their views were so similar to other creative people's views. Moreover, they all are clearly uncomfortable with their role as arbiters of what the people shall see, and especially of how the American people see themselves.

The quintessential example of that embarrassment appeared in an interview with two rich and successful TV writers of situation comedies. Each writer has been doing major comedy work for more than 30 years. They now produce a new situation comedy. One day they complained of the pressures of their work. When a visitor reminded them that their work gave them the power to shape what hundreds of millions of people see on TV each week, one of them shrugged his shoulders and said. "So? It's not my fault."

"That's right," the other said. "What can you do?"

John Wanamaker, the department store magnate, put it this way: "I know half the money I spend on advertising is wasted, but I can never find out which half." Not that conceptualizing an ad that catches the attention (and hopefully triggers a buying response) of the potential millions exposed to it isn't difficult. Aldous Huxley insisted that it was easier to write ten passably effective sonnets than one effective advertisement that "will take in a few thousand of the uncritical buying public."

As Ronald Gross points out, there is hardly a scintilla of difference between two competing cigarettes or facial tissues (which we generically call *kleenex*, even though it's a brand name). That's where the advertising expert, that mischievous Loki in the Valhalla of popular culture, comes in. He fabricates something about the product, and it usually has nothing to do with the product itself. The subject matter of most ads, Gross shows us, is what most people have in common, such as their basic conditioned fear of smelling bad.

Ads add us, and if we knew exactly how and why, maybe, just maybe, we would have a different kind of society, one that would have a different, perhaps better kind of popular culture.

The Language of Advertising
Ronald Gross

The language of ads is language used to sell, language on the make. Its charms and its dangers, like those of the good-hearted whore whose most ambitious goal is a fur coat, are real but not of ultimate consequence. No man was ever importantly ruined by his infatuation for a whore: it's the mistresses we really love who rend our lives. So with language: the trivial choices between brands which the advertisers frantically seek to influence are of little significance beside the political and religious credos with which the ideologists ravish our minds and hearts.

Veblen, knowing this, dismissed advertising language as a mere "trading on the range of human infirmities." When F. R. Leavis surveyed the subject in 1934 in *Culture and Environment*, he concurred with Veblen. The ads he examined appealed mainly to petty greed, mean fears of social inferiority, anxieties about health, etc.

In the past twenty years the advertisers' repertoire of incantations has been augmented by some fumbling applications of behaviorism and Freudianism, the chief stratagems being repetition and sexual suggestiveness. But the ultimate aim is still merely to wheedle out of us a few greasy quarters or dollars. The ultimate consequences of switching from one toothpaste to another, or even from one automobile to another, are hardly momentous in themselves.

Why, then, is it worthwhile to scrutinize the language of advertising? Because the pathologies of language evident in advertising are now carrying over into other, more important, areas of our lives. As Galbraith points out, the breeding of delusory "images" has spread from the area of marketing to that of domestic and foreign policy, and thus colors our entire national life with a hue of unreality.

In a time like ours, when the mind is under constant semantic siege, every man must undertake what Daniel Boorstin calls "the task of disenchantment." Advertising language is not a bad place to start, though when we have penetrated its stratagems and discerned its obfuscations, we shall only be started on the road to mastery of the language environment.

Ads add. On that fact rests the entire semantic interest of advertising. If ads just gave us information about products, they would be of no use whatever to the semanticist, the cultural critic, or the social scientist. But precisely because ads bear only the flimsiest relationship to their ostensible subjects—the products—they are interesting.

Why do ads add? For the simplest possible reason—want of anything else to say about the product. There being no significant difference between two competing cigarettes or rolls of toilet paper, advertisers must fabricate a subject matter for their advertisement other than the product itself. What shall it be?

The answer is dictated by the major constraint under which the copywriter works: that his words must influence the largest possible number of people. The subject matter, then, will be what most people have in common—their basic fears, anxieties, and hopes. In short, our style of life, our values.

What ads add is *us*. Around the anonymous commodity—the bare roll of toilet paper, the unbranded cigarette, the purely chemical motor oil—the adman weaves his congeries of emotions. His raw materials are not the product's characteristics, but our own drives and aspirations. People must be made to want this object, not for what it is, but for what language can endow it with, for what it can be made to *mean*. The ad, in short, is a Rorschach blot onto which advertisers contrive to make us project some of our most pervasive and controlling attitudes. Advertising generally constitutes a vast collective Rorschach, an inchoate medium onto which advertiser and consumer project one another's fantasies and fears.

What better materials could there be for studying the patterns of appeal, persuasion, and ingratiation which operate in one's culture, the hopes, fears, and anxieties which haunt its inhabitants, than to look into these works of impure artifice? Before we put down the plethora of advertising which affronts us on every side, then, we should seize out of it those insights about the temper and the fever of the society in which we live. To close our eyes to these figments is to remain even more in the dark about the fears and hopes which drive our fellow countrymen in their groping toward some kind of human satisfaction.

Shelley's pronouncement that "Poets are the unacknowledged legislators of the world" seems preposterous to us because we think of poetry as being what's in books of poems. But semanticist S. I. Hayakawa has pointed out that advertising copywriters are the sponsored poets of our time, the laureates of a consumer society. Thus Shelley's dictum becomes merely a noble restatement of the documentary accounts of advertising one finds in Vance Packard, et al. The advertisers, not in their overt messages and their "power" to shape consumer preferences but in the underlying vision of man and of human life which they purvey, certainly shape attitudes and aspirations in just such a way. Shortly after the 1967 summer riots in the Negro ghettos, Bayard Rustin wrote in *The New York Times Magazine*: "If those Negro youths who rioted thought that a man was nothing if he didn't have an alpaca sweater

> "Far from being bold mind-shapers, advertisers are timid to an appalling degree."

and suede shoes—who taught them that?"

But here again, we must make an important distinction. Poets—and of course Shelley would include among them Plato and Kant and Marx—give us new images of man and of life, which widen our sensibilities. Advertisers help reinforce such images, but they do not create them in their important aspects. Rather, they slavishly search out pre-existing models to follow. Far from being bold mind-shapers, advertisers are timid to an appalling degree.

For example, motivational research revealed a few years ago that most people brush their teeth only once a day, "at the most pointless moment possible in the entire twenty-four-hour day from the dental-hygiene standpoint." Here was a small but real opportunity for advertisers. Armed with this intelligence they could have combined public usefulness with profit-making by trying to educate the public to their brand as well as to better habits which would detract from no one's profits. Rather than undertaking such a modest exercise in changing behavior, however, the agencies—snapping up the fact that people only brushed their teeth to get the crummy early-morning taste out of their mouths—elevated "tingly-taste" flavor and "clean mouth" breath-sweetening to No. 1 on their list of copy points.

The distinction between the overt effects of advertising language and the far more important side effects can be seen most clearly if we look at the interesting case of "good ads." Here the overt message is widely agreed to be beneficial, yet the underlying assumptions are pernicious. And their perniciousness derives from the same source as it does in all American advertising: the basic system of ideas which governs our society and economy. *The most basic dire effect of advertising, in short, lies in its affirmation of "the American way of life."*

Consider the prime example of "good ads": those dull, worthy campaigns of the Advertising Council. Financed by the industry, and operating through free space donated by the media, the council self-righteously advances behind its musty colophon of a quill pen crossed over a drawn saber, pressing on us that most repellent of commodities, good advice. When and as unfilled advertising space permits, the council reminds us to attend church, use the litter baskets, and retrain ourselves as automation gobbles up our jobs. Surely nothing could be more innocent.

But the whole business is something more than a bore: it is also a subtle medium for obfuscating some important public issues and reducing the likelihood of needed action. Not consciously, I imagine—that would credit the people behind the enterprise with more savvy than they probably have. But unconsciously, subliminally, and by default.

Take a recent ad. It shows an electric circuit, suitably baffling to the layman. "What are you going to do," asks the copy, "when this circuit learns your job?" The implication is clear: get off your ass, you sluggard. Retrain thyself—prepare. We're doing you the service of giving you fair warning—but you'd better get a move on.

But why, one might ask, is the responsibility fixed so unerringly on the individual worker? Don't the businessman, the union, and government have any identifiable responsibility to prospective displaced workers when that circuit is installed? One can't imagine signs directed at businessmen which said: "What will happen to your workers when this circuit takes their jobs?" Again, intervention by the government to provide jobs for those displaced by automation is neglected as a possible remedy. Suddenly, in this campaign, the individual worker seems to have taken on all the responsibility for the epochal industrial transformation which our society is fumbling through.

Of course, a single car card can't do everything. "This is just one approach to the problem." But if you recall the council campaigns from the past few years, a somewhat sinister pattern emerges quite clearly. First, there's a problem: the streets are filthy; there's a ghastly death toll on the highways; colleges need more money.

Now, each of these problems is complex and has many possible and probably partial solutions. For instance, filthy streets might be remedied by greater expenditures for public sanitation services; deaths on the highway suggest that cars might be structurally unsafe; higher education's needs perhaps require federal aid to universities.

In the council's campaigns, however, such solutions are consistently neglected in favor of pinning the responsibility for action on the individual citizen: don't litter the streets; drive safely; give to the college of your choice. Clearly, each of these will contribute to the end desired. Equally clearly, however, other changes are mandatory—changes which challenge powerful vested interests in the society. Ralph Nader made it clear, for example, that the development and adaptation of a safer car by the automobile industry is a quicker and surer way to reduce traffic deaths than is the gigantic campaign to teach people to drive more carefully.

Such solutions don't commend themselves to the Advertising Council. Rather, it hammers away at the unprovocative, anonymous individual—if he'd just shape up, things would be fine. This country could solve its problems handily, the council ads seem to suggest, if it weren't for that sloppy, lazy, stingy, frivolous, uncivic, obdurate element—its people.

While no man was ever importantly ruined by a whore, the practice of debauchery on a continuous, society-wide basis certainly would have a demoralizing effect. And this is the important thing to say about the language of advertising. Although the choices which the advertisers seek to shape with their words are trivial, the side effects which permeate our society are ominous. They amount to nothing less than unremitting reinforcement, through ubiquitousness and repetition, of a demeaning conception of man, life and the world.

Popular culture in the United States is a much bigger business than most people realize. We may find it hard to believe that it costs nearly $250,000 for a one-minute television commercial inserted into a movie like *Gone with the Wind*, but it's true. Media stars like Johnny Carson or Paul Newman probably earn more than $1 million a year, and somebody has to pay for that. Someone also has to pay—however indirectly—for the more than $30 billion spent each year to advertise the products we wear, eat, drink, drive, and wash our faces and teeth with, for in a mass-mediated society we are being bombarded with these "buy *me*" messages hundreds of times each day. That someone is we, the consumers.

To show a profit at year's end, the industries that produce our popular culture (like any other industry) must attract our attention, and when they do, it is usually at the expense of a competing medium. Our time is their sustenance.

Sometimes we pay for our popular culture directly, as when we buy a book or go to a theater to see a movie, and here again we are paying more and more. The day of the 25-cent paperback book seems more like ancient history than a mere three decades ago, and it costs five to six times as much to see a first-run movie today than right after World War II.

As Ben Bagdikian clearly shows in this excerpt from his book, *The Information Machine*, the American consumer also pays for the news, and that cost too will be rising. Although the selection was originally published in 1971 and some of the data have changed, Bagdikian's conclusions remain valid today.

Who Pays for the News?
Ben Bagdikian

The most innocent view of the economics of news is that the consumer pays his daily dime for his paper and gets broadcast news free.

That is not true, of course. One way or another, the consumer pays more for the systems that bring him his daily news than he does for his telephone service. . . .

Deciding who pays for news is not simple. If news proprietors went to the wholesale market at dawn to buy large quantities of information and retailed it to consumers later in the day, the transaction would be relatively simple. But almost all news is distributed along with unrelated products—merchandising information, entertainment, etc.—that have their own costs and benefits. Today the average consumer cannot select and pay solely for his daily news. In general, no systematic daily news is distributed unless it is associated with other activities whose primary objective is to collect large audiences for the purpose of selling merchandise.

Newspapers get from 70 to 75 percent of their revenues from merchants who buy space in the papers to advertise their goods. Broadcasters get practically 100 percent of their revenue from advertisers. Because the carriers of daily news—newspapers, radio, and television—receive about half of all advertising money spent in the United States, the present and future level of advertising is important.

All advertising expenditures have paralleled general economic activity, at least in this century. In 1867 gross national product was $6.7 billion, of which only $50 million, less than 1 percent, was spent on advertising. But since then both GNP and advertising money have grown substantially, and while the percentage of all money in the country allotted to advertising has declined from a high in the 1920's, the great increases in the absolute level of both have meant continuous expansion of advertising money.

Year	GNP ($ billions)	Advertising ($ millions)	Advertising as % of GNP
1920	$ 89	$ 2,935	3.5%
1930	91	2,607	2.8
1940	100.6	2,087	2.0
1950	284.6	5,710	2.0
1960	503.8	11,932	2.4
1969 (est.)*	850	18,800	2.1

Source: From *Statistical Abstract of the United States, 1968;* estimated 1969 from *U.S. Industrial Outlook, 1969,* Department of Commerce, p. 313.

Ed. note: The preliminary figure for 1975 for GNP was $1,516.3 billion, and for advertising, $28,320 million. Advertising as a percentage of GNP was thus about 1.9 percent. (*Statistical Abstract of the United States, 1976*).

In the 1960s advertising as a percentage of GNP has averaged 2.2 percent. In 1969 this produced $18.8 billion in advertising money, or $306 per household.

Estimates of further GNP for the next 30 years show continuing increases, barring catastrophe. By 1985, according to Wiener and Kahn, GNP should have reached about $1.5 trillion, and by the year 2000 about $2.9 trillion. If the same percent goes into advertising, this would mean that the present expenditure of $306 of advertising per household would rise to $400 by 1985 and to $630 in the year 2000. (There would be about 82 million households in 1985 and 101 million in 2000.)

At present, newspapers get 29 percent of all advertising money, television 17 percent, and radio 6 percent. This means that advertising associated with daily news carriers is spent at the rate of $89 a year per household for newspapers, $52 for television, and $18 for radio. (The news carriers did not receive all of this money, since advertising agencies and others lie between most advertisers and mass outlets.)

Who ultimately benefits from this advertising money is a matter of some contention. Advertisers and media operators like to describe advertising as a "subsidy" that supports the news, since it represents three-quarters of revenues for newspapers and 100 percent for broadcasting. In this view, the citizen gets his printed news at less than a third of its real cost and his broadcast news free.

Money spent on advertising is added to the cost of the product which the consumer pays. Conventional wisdom claims that advertising does not cost the consumer anything and might even save him money, since it stimulates mass sales and mass production which so lower the prices of goods that whatever is spent on advertising is more than made up by the lowered cost of the merchandise.

Many economic authorities on advertising do not agree with this view. They believe that, while advertising can produce increased sales of some items at particular times, and thus influence the flow of cash within the economy, it does not have a significant effect on the overall amount of money spent on goods and services. In this view, if there were no advertising, the gross national product would not change significantly and consumer money now spent in response to ads would be spent on other things. Absence of advertising due to media strikes, for example, does not increase savings. In this view, advertising money is not a "subsidy" for the news but a "hidden tax."

Whether subsidy or hidden tax, it means that "Who pays?" must be refined to "Who handles the money?" The consumer may pay for the advertising in the news media, but he does not control the allocation of the money. Ten billion dollars a year is spent on advertising in newspapers, television, and radio, but neither the news proprietors nor the news consumers have much control over this 90 percent of the economy of the American daily-news media.

Furthermore, allocation of the money is decided by advertising agencies and merchandisers solely on the basis of what they believe will most efficiently sell their goods. Consumers of the end product might make different decisions if they controlled their medium's economy.

The only way the consumer can control the spending of the $10 billion in his news media is to withhold his purchases of advertised goods or of media carrying the advertising. He can refuse to buy a newspaper or to listen to broadcasting. But both newspapers and broadcasting are multifunction media and there are not many consumers who will dismiss an entire medium over dissatisfaction with a part of it.

The consumer has slightly more influence over his printed news since he makes direct payments to the newspaper. But even this is limited. He pays only 25 or 30 percent of the cost. Furthermore, in 96 percent of communities there is only one paper, and the consumer must make the choice between the only local paper or none. . . .

Advertising is the major source of income for daily papers, approximately 72 percent. Using estimates for 1969, daily newspapers received about $4 billion in advertising revenues, but this was the net advertising revenues. The advertisers themselves paid about 20 percent more than this, in advertising-agency fees, production and other costs, or

about $5 billion for placing ads in daily papers. On the assumption that the consumer ultimately pays for the total cost of these ads, this comes to a cost spread to all 1969 households of $83 per household. Thus, the total ultimate cost of placing daily and Sunday newspapers into homes, spread equally to all households, comes to $37 paid directly by the consumer and $83 via advertising, or about $120 a year.

On the surface it would seem easier to calculate who pays for broadcasting, since all its revenue comes from advertising. This gives the impression, encouraged by commercial broadcast operators, that radio and television are "free."

There is, of course, the cost of advertising, which for television in 1969 was about $3.3 billion (spent by advertisers; broadcasters received less after agency and other processing costs). Spread over every household this comes to $55 per household (97 percent of all households have television sets).

However, unlike newspapers, television cannot be received unless the consumer makes an investment in special equipment. In the last ten years consumer spending on television sets, antennae, and repairs has averaged about $2.6 billion a year. Using the average number of households during this same ten-year period, this comes to about $47 a year paid by each household for the purchase and maintenance of television receiving equipment.

Radio-advertising spending was about $1 billion a year, or $16 per household. In recent years, the cost of car, home, and portable radios, with associated equipment and repairs, has run to about $10 a year per household.

Total direct payments by consumers for radio and television equipment, repairs, and maintenance come to about $57 a year.

Consumers spend much more for equipment to receive broadcasting than producers spend to transmit it. In the 1946–1966 period consumers paid $26.5 billion for television sets, while broadcasters paid $1.2 billion for physical assets in transmitting and studio equipment. Unlike most consumers, broadcasters could deduct their physical investment from taxes. During that period the industry ended with a depreciated value of physical assets of $661 million. So, for every net dollar spent by the television industry in physical equipment to transmit to the consumer, the consumers spent $40 to receive the message.

So advertisers spent $83 per household on newspapers and subscribers about $37, for an annual total of $120. Advertisers spent $55 per household on television, and consumers spent $47 to receive broadcasts, for an annual total of $102. Radio-advertising spending was $16 per household and consumers spent $10 for equipment and repairs, for a total of $26.

This compares with other annual costs for household communications as follows:

Telephone	$225
Newspapers	120
Postal service	116
Television	102
Periodicals	44
Books	42
Radio	26
Phonograph records and tapes	13

(The above figures are not payments made annually by a "typical" or "average" household. They are the total receipts for each activity divided by the total number of households in the country. Most of the activities are organized around household spending; using expenditures on that basis permits projections for future total income and future numbers of households.)

Thus, $688 a year is spent per household for incoming and outgoing communications, of which the primary carriers of daily news represents a third. Disposable personal income is expected to increase by 41 percent by 1985 and by 117 percent by the year 2000. If household communications takes the present proportion of income, it would mean that in fifteen years each home would spend $970 and in thirty years, $1,400. . . .

The future of advertising and merchandising will be important. The simplest consideration is whether advertising will continue to supply its present share of money going into news systems.

Changing population characteristics and communications techniques could produce radical changes in how advertising money is spent among the various news media. Advertisers deciding that new methods of presenting information are more effective could reduce or eliminate their spending in older media.

There is some experience with this already. In the 1935–1945 period the relationships of the major advertising media did not change radically. There were some changes, many flowing from World War II when there were massive population changes and limited outlets for consumer spending. After the war there was an enormous increase in money spent on advertising. As the country once more became a consumer-oriented economy, advertising became a growing activity, eclipsing all other single factors as a source of revenue for the media. In the 1945–1950 period all kinds of advertising increased, but in 1950, when television began to grow, there were obvious shifts. Television's electronic cousin, radio, suffered the most, dropping in its absolute revenues as well as its percentage of the market. Magazines benefited only slightly from the added availability of advertising money, with business papers and outdoor advertising even less so. Direct mail and newspapers, along with television, faithfully followed the upward surge in all advertising, which paralleled the gross national product. At no time was the dominance of newspapers as the leading medium of advertising challenged, though television, at a lower absolute level, had a faster rate of growth.

This seems to say two things.

First, the introduction of a new medium may win over attention and money from those most like it, rather than those very different. Radio suffered noticeably with the introduction of television, to a much greater degree than radio was able to affect newspaper revenues when it entered the commercial scene fifteen years earlier. Even more dramatic was the reaction of the motion-picture industry to television. It is not a significant carrier of advertising, but it is an important mass medium. Movie receipts grew significantly even during the Depression and spectacularly in the 1940–1946 period, when it reached the level and growth rate of newspaper advertising receipts. But when television began to be observable in neighborhood bars and other centers in 1947, motion pictures went into a radical decline. They did not begin a recovery until the 1960s and that was chiefly as a supplier to the television industry.

Second, a new actor on the advertising-communications scene seldom enjoys a quick and conclusive triumph over his elders. The new challenger does not stride onto the stage and fling the old stars into the pit. Instead, the stage seems to enlarge, and the old actors remain with the new, all sharing the expanded space, though with changed relationships. . . .

A radical change in production methods and costs for newspapers could change its sources of income. Advertising, for example, becomes less important as a share of total revenue as papers become smaller in pages and in circulation. Advertising produces the largest portion of newspaper revenues, but it also requires some of the heaviest costs. Since advertising represents 61 percent of all pages printed in daily papers, it represents the most expensive peak production equipment and labor costs. Advertising is more expensive to handle than news. In a newspaper where it costs $3.23 to process a thousand characters of text matter from typewriter to printed paper, it costs $10.81 for a thousand characters of classified ads. . . .

Calculations made in the RAND study by Dr. James N. Rosse estimate that if newspapers eliminated all advertising, including the plant and manpower now devoted to the selling, composition, and printing of ads, and instead delivered newspapers consisting solely of the present quantity of news, the subscriber would pay from 65 to 75 percent more for his newspaper than he does today. . . .

However, advertising is more than a convenient source of cash flow for a newspaper. It is a positive attraction to a large number of readers, as sources of product and price information in daily transactions. In 1940 Marshall Field established an adless paper in New York City, *PM*. It never attracted enough subscribers willing to pay 100 percent of the cost to make it self-supporting. But, just as significant, it discovered that its socially conscious readers demanded merchandising information. *PM* assigned reporters to compile daily listings of bargains in major New York City retail outlets.

Far more likely to change the nature of advertising in the news media is the development of ability by the consumer to do some of his shopping electronically, and to order onto his screen or on his facsimile document the specific information he wants. . . .

If, suddenly, the consumer were asked to pay directly for his full newspaper or for all of television programming that he watches every day, the added conscious cost might produce resistance. He might then become more concerned about one of the character-

THE MEDIA GOLIATH

CBS

1976 Fortune 500
rank: 102
1976 Total Sales:
$2.23 billion

PRINCIPAL OPERATIONS:

Broadcasting:
—owns five TV stations (New York, Los Angeles, Philadelphia, Chicago, St. Louis); seven AM radio stations and seven FM radio stations

Records:
—includes labels of Columbia, Epic, Portrait

Columbia Group
Record and tapes club;
musical instruments
(e.g., Steinway pianos, Leslie speakers, Rogers drums organs);
67 Pacific Stereo retail stores;
Creative Playthings (toys)

Publishing:
Holt, Rinehart and Winston;
Popular Library (mass-market paperback)
W. B. Saunders—professional
NEISA—Latin American and Spanish books

Magazines:
Field and Stream
Road and Track
Cycle World
World Tennis
Sea (to be combined with *Rudder*)
PV4
Popular Gardening Indoors
Astrology Your Daily Horoscope
Astrology Today
Your Prophecy
Psychic World
Popular Crosswords
Popular Word Games
Special Crossword Book of the Month
New Crosswords
Giant Word Games
The National Observer Book of Crosswords
Popular Sports: Baseball
Popular Sports: Grand Slam
Popular Sports: Kick-Off
Popular Sports: Touchdown
Popular Sports: Basketball
Fawcett Publications:
Mechanix Illustrated
Woman's Day
Rudder

THE NEW YORK TIMES COMPANY

1976 Fortune 500
rank: 394
1976 Total Sales:
$451.4 million

PRINCIPAL OPERATIONS:

Newspapers:
New York Times
International Herald Tribune (33.3%)
Six dailies and four weeklies in Florida:
Gainesville Sun
Lakeland Ledger
Ocala Star Banner
Leesburg Daily Commercial
Palatka Daily News
Lake City Reporter
Fernandina Beach News-Leader
Sebring News
Avon Park Sun
Marco Island Eagle
Three dailies in North Carolina:
Lexington Dispatch
Hendersonville Times-News
Wilmington Star-News

Magazines:
Family Circle
Australian Family Circle
Golf Digest
Golf World
Tennis
US
(Sold some eight professional magazines to Harcourt Brace Jovanovich in 1976)

Broadcasting:
WREG-TV, Memphis, Tenn.
WQXR-AM/FM, New York City

Books:
Quadrangle/NYT Book Co.
Arno Press, Inc.
Cambridge Book Co.

TIME INC.

1976 Fortune 500
rank: 217
1976 Total Sales:
$1.038 billion

PRINCIPAL OPERATIONS:

Publishing:
Time, Fortune, Sports Illustrated, Money, and *People* magazines account for 35% of total revenue
Time-Life Books
Little, Brown
New York Graphic Society (Alva Museum Replicas)
Minority interests in publishers in Germany, France, Spain, Mexico, and Japan

Films and Broadcasting:
Time-Life Films
TV production and distribution, multimedia, TV books
Home Box Office
Manhattan Cable TV
WOTV—Grand Rapids, Mich.

Newspapers:
Pioneer Press, Inc.—17 weekly newspapers in suburban Chicago
Selling Areas-Marketing, Inc. (distributing marketing information)
Printing Developments, Inc. (printing equipment)

Other:
Forest Products:
Temple-Eastex, Inc. (pulp & paperboard, packaging, building materials, timberland)
AFCO Industries, Inc. (interior wall products)
Woodward, Inc. (bedroom furniture)
Lumberman's Investment Corporation
Sabine Investment Company

RCA

1976 Fortune 500
rank: 31
1976 Total Sales:
$5.32 billion

PRINCIPAL OPERATIONS:

Electronics—Consumer products & services (25.6% of total sales)
Electronics—Commercial products & services (12.8% of total sales)

Broadcasting:
NBC: owns one TV station in Chicago, Los Angeles, Cleveland, New York City, Washington, D.C., and one AM and one FM station in Chicago, New York, San Francisco, Washington, D.C. (17.8% of total)

Publishing:
Random House (Random House, Alfred A. Knopf, Pantheon, Ballantine Books, Vintage, Modern Library) (17.6% of total)

Other:
Banquet Foods; Coronet (carpets); Oriel Foods (U.K.); Vehicle Renting & Related Services (e.g., Hertz); Gov't Business

GULF & WESTERN

1976 Fortune 500
rank: 57
1976 Total Sales:
$3.39 billion

PRINCIPAL OPERATIONS:

Manufacturing (25% of total sales)

Leisure Time:
Paramount Pictures—motion picture production & distribution; TV exhibition & series production.
Owns: Oxford Films (distribution of non-theatrical films), Magicam, Inc. (rents camera systems), Future General Corp. (research, special effects services)
Cinema International (49% interest)—owns or operates four theaters in London, one in Amsterdam, two in Egypt, 17 in Brazil, 10 in other parts of South America, 19 in South Africa
Famous Players Ltd. (51% interest)—owns or operates some 300 theaters in Canada, one in Paris, and owns 50% of a French company operating 35 theaters in France
Sega Enterprises, Inc.—coin-operated amusement games

Publishing:
Simon and Schuster—includes Fireside and Touchstone quality paperbacks; and mass-market paperbacks from Pocket Books, Washington Square Press, Archway (14% of total sales)

Other:
Natural Resources—zinc and cement (5% of total)
Apparel Products—apparel, hosiery, shoes
Paper and building products (11% of total)
Auto replacement parts (8% of total)
Financial services—consumer and commercial financing, life insurance, casualty insurance (19% of total)
Consumer and agricultural products —sugar; Minute Maid (citrus); livestock; Consolidated Cigar; Schrafft Candy Co. (14% of total)

A sample of conglomerates in the communications industry

TIMES MIRROR COMPANY

1976 Fortune 500 rank: 232
1976 Total Sales: $964.7 million

PRINCIPAL OPERATIONS:

Newspapers:
Los Angeles Times, Newsday, Dallas Times Herald (Tex.), L.A. Times-Washington Post News Service (joint)

Magazine and Book Publishing:
New American Library
Signet, Signet Classics, Mentor, Meridian paperbacks
Abrams art books
Matthew Bender law books
Year Book medical books
C.V. Mosby medical, dental, and nursing books and journals
Outdoor Life
Popular Science
Golf
Ski
The Sporting News
Ski Business
How to
The Sporting Goods Dealer

Television:
KDFW-TV, Dallas, Tex.
KTBC-TV, Austin, Tex.
Owns two newsprint mills, 10 wood products mills, and 320,000 acres of timberland

Other:
Information Services
Cable Communications
Directory Printing

THE WASHINGTON POST COMPANY

1976 Fortune 500 rank: 452
1976 Total Sales: $375.7

PRINCIPAL OPERATIONS:

Newspapers:
Washington Post, Trenton Times and Sunday Times-Advertiser, International Herald Tribune (30%)
Washington Post Writers Group (syndication and book publishing), L.A. Times-Washington Post News Service (50%)

Magazines:
Newsweek

Books:
Newsweek Books

Broadcasting:
WTOP-TV, Washington, D.C.
WJXT-TV, Jacksonville, Fla.
WPLG-TV, Miami, Fla.
WFSB-TV, Hartford, Conn.
WTOP-AM, Washington, D.C.

Other:
Robinson Terminal Warehouse Corp. (newsprint storage)
Bowater Mersey Paper Co., Ltd. (49%, Canada)

GANNETT

1976 Fortune 500 rank: 426
1976 Total Sales: $413.2 million

PRINCIPAL OPERATIONS:

Newspapers:
Pacific Daily News (Agana, Guam)
Sunday News, Enquirer and News (Battle Creek, Mich.)
Bellingham Herald, Sunday Herald (Bellingham, Wash.)
Evening Press, Sun-Bulletin, Sunday Press (Binghamton, N.Y.)
Idaho Statesman (Boise, Idaho)
Courier-News (Bridgewater, N.J.)
Burlington Free Press (Burlington, Vt.)
Courier-Post (Camden, N.J.)
Public Opinion (Chambersburg, Pa.)
"Today" (Cocoa, Fla.)
Commercial-News (Danville, Ill.)
Star-Gazette, Sunday Telegram (Elmira, N.Y.)
El Paso Times (El Paso, Tex.)
Fort Myers News Press (Fort Myers, Fla.)
News-Messenger (Fremont, Ohio)
Honolulu Star-Bulletin, Star-Bulletin & Advertiser (Honolulu, Hawaii)
Herald Dispatch, Huntington Advertiser, Herald Advertiser (Huntington, W. Va.)
Ithaca Journal (Ithaca, N.Y.)
Journal and Courier (Lafayette, Ind.)
State Journal (Lansing, Mich.)
Marietta Times (Marietta, Ohio)
Chronicle Tribune (Marion, Ind.)
Nashville Banner (Nashville, Tenn.)
Valley News Dispatch (New Kensington-Tarentum, Pa.)
Niagara Gazette (Niagara Falls, N.Y.)
Daily Olympian (Olympia, Wash.)
Pensacola Journal, Pensacola News, Pensacola News-Journal (Pensacola, Fla.)
News-Herald (Port Clinton, Ohio)
Times Herald (Port Huron, Mich.)
Palladium-Item (Richmond, Ind.)
Times-Union, Democrat & Chronicle (Rochester, N.Y.)
Morning Star, Register-Republic, Register-Star (Rockford, Ill.)
Capital Journal, Oregon Statesman (Salem, Ore.)

Sun-Telegram (San Bernardino, Calif.)
New Mexican (Santa Fe, N.M.)
Saratogian (Saratoga Springs, N.Y.)
Daily Citizen (Tucson, Ariz.)
Daily Press, Observer Dispatch (Utica, N.Y.)
Daily Times (Mamaroneck, N.Y.)
Daily Argus (Mount Vernon, N.Y.)
Standard-Star (New Rochelle, N.Y.)
Citizen-Register (Ossining, N.Y.)
Daily Item (Port Chester, N.Y.)
Journal-News, Nyack (Rockland, N.Y.)
Daily News (Tarrytown, N.Y.)
Reporter-Dispatch (White Plains, N.Y.)
Herald-Statesman (Yonkers, N.Y.)
Review Press-Reporter (Bronxville, N.Y.)
Suburban Newspaper Group (10 weeklies) (Cherry Hill, N.J.)
Fairpress (Fairfield, Conn.)
Times (Melbourne, Fla.)
Butler County News, North Hills News Record (semi-weekly) Herald (New Kensington, Pa.)
Commercial News (Saratoga Springs, N.Y.)
Taos News (Taos, N.M.)
Star Advocate (Titusville, Fla.)

Broadcasting:
WBRJ (Radio) (Marietta, Ohio)
WHEC-TV (Rochester, N.Y.)
WKFI (Radio) (Wilmington, Ohio)

Other:
Louis Harris & Associates and Louis Harris International

KNIGHT-RIDDER

1976 Fortune 500 rank: 295
1976 Total Sales: $677.5 million

PRINCIPAL OPERATIONS:

Newspapers:
Aberdeen American News
Akron Beacon Journal
Boca Raton News
Boulder Daily Camera
Bradenton Herald
Charlotte Observer
Charlotte News
Columbus Enquirer
Columbus Ledger
Detroit Free Press
Duluth News-Tribune
Duluth Herald
Gary Post-Tribune
Grand Forks Herald
Journal of Commerce
Lexington Herald
Lexington Leader
Long Beach Independent
Long Beach Press-Telegram
Macon Telegraph
Macon News
Miami Herald
Pasadena Star-News
Philadelphia Inquirer
Philadelphia Daily News
St. Paul Pioneer Press
St. Paul Dispatch
San Jose Mercury
San Jose News
Seattle Times
Tallahassee Democrat
Walla Walla Union-Bulletin
Wichita Eagle
Wichita Beacon
Arcadie Tribune (Calif.)
Temple City Times (Calif.)
Monrovia Journal (Calif.)
Duartean (Calif.)
Buena Park News (Calif.)
La Mirada Lamplighter (Calif.)
Huntington Beach Independent (Calif.)
Anaheim-Fullerton Independent (Calif.)
Orange County Evening News (Calif.)
Broward Times (Fla.)
Coral Gables Times and Guide (Fla.)
Florida Keys Keynoter (Fla.)
North Dade Journal (Fla.)
Union Recorder (Ga.)

Other:
Commercial Terminals of Detroit, Inc.
Commodity News Services, Inc. (Kansas City, Mo.)
Knight-Ridder Newspaper Sales, Inc. (New York)
Knight News Services, Inc. (Detroit, Mich.)
The Observer Transportation Co. (Charlotte, N.C.)
Portage Newspaper Supply Co. (Akron, Ohio)
Twin Cities Newspaper Services, Inc. (St. Paul, Minn.)

istics of these media—they contain a great deal of material that no one consumer is interested in. Newspapers especially are collections of minority-appeal materials—foreign news, sports, dress patterns, comic strips, stock-market reports, travel features, pet care, state-house politics, advice to the lovelorn, car ads, lingerie ads, fashion predictions, crossword puzzles, news from Congress, descriptions of local dinner parties, etc. Because the conscious price of this collection is small . . . there is considerable tolerance and even attraction toward the mixed package whose various parts can be easily scanned and rejected. But if somehow the advertisements were placed free and the consumer paid the whole amount, which would be about thirty cents a day, he might wish to reject some of the things he and his family almost never look at. Or he might reject all the ads, paying for a paper containing only news. . . .

Today, the average American household pays directly and indirectly about $120 a year for newspapers. Of this, about 69 percent is for advertising, or $83 for daily printed ads, and 31 percent for subscriber payments, or $37. If household income rises as expected, and is divided among the media the way it is today, then in 1985 each household will pay $121 a year for daily printed advertising information or 34 cents a day, compared to the 23 cents a day each household spends today. For news and other daily non-advertising, each household would spend $52 a year, or 14 cents a day, compared to the 10 cents paid today. The daily payments in the year 2000 would be 48 cents a day for printed advertising information, and 22 cents for other daily printed information.

Today, each household pays 28 cents a day for all its television programming, including advertising and news. In 1985, if the predictions and shares of market by the media hold, this would become 40 cents a day in 1985 and 61 cents a day in the year 2000. . . .

The answer to "Who pays?" is, of course, the consumer. But what he pays for indirectly now he may have a choice of paying for directly in the future. He will probably have to do it if for no other reason than to protect himself from the growing avalanche of information. The capacities of future information systems will be so much greater that the selection of what is wanted and what is not will be an absolute necessity. It will probably be through the favorite mechanism of a cash economy, by the consumer paying for what he wants and refusing the rest.

If anyone ever doubted that book publishing has become Big Business, with all the calculated risks and rewards of the corporate milieu, the $1.9 million paid in 1977 to an unknown writer, Coleen McCullough, for the mass-market paperback rights to her novel, *The Thorn Birds*, should be convincing. Or the reported $2 million that Little, Brown and Company is going to pay Henry Kissinger for his memoirs. In a time when conglomerates sometimes bring together strange bedfellows, it shouldn't be too surprising that the three major television networks own major publishing operations, including books, magazines, and specialty publications. CBS, for example, owns both Holt, Rinehart and Winston, book publishers, and such magazines as *Field and Stream* and *World Tennis*, while RCA, of which NBC is part, is heavily involved in book publishing through its subsidiary, Random House.

Roger Rosenblatt, literary editor of *The New Republic*, admires those writers who can come up with the best-sellers that make nice-plus figures in the conglomerate earnings. He shows us that the sequel to Erich Segal's *Love Story* follows a formula for American best-sellers that has worked for sixty years. With movie rights and other subsidiaries, Mr. Segal stands to make at least $2 million, or about the same as Kissinger. Where else but in the popular culture environment of America could a couple of Ph.D.s from Harvard do as well?

Love Won't Buy You Money
Roger Rosenblatt

E rich Segal's *Oliver's Story* begins with Oliver Barrett still grieving over the death of his wife Jenny. Phil Cavilleri, Jenny's father, tells Oliver to get married, but Oliver buries himself in his work, defending the civil liberties of "what in lawyer's slang we call 'screwees.'" Unable to fall in love again, Oliver consults a psychiatrist who listens as Oliver recounts his guilt about descending from a family which was one of the "pioneers in sweatshop labor," but does not cure Oliver. Of more help is Marcie Nash, née Binnendale, beautiful, athletic, divorced heiress to a chain of department stores, who talks dirty and seeks love herself. Oliver almost falls for Marcie but a trip to Hong Kong disillusions him when he discovers that Marcie employs children in her sweatshops. They part, and Oliver leaves his New York law firm to accept a partnership in his father's investment house.

I resent this—not Oliver's partnership; I resent the success this novel is going to have. In 1969, when *Love Story* was at so high a peak that a banner was strung across Broadway saying "New York Loves *Love Story*," I was feverish to write a sequel, something more moderate, more broadly appealing. I hit on the *Like You A Lot Story*, in which the lovers would be coeds at Tulane, the heroine's disease pyorrhea, and the memorable maxim, "liking you a lot ordinarily means never having to say 'excuse me.' " To my disgust it went nowhere.

There's a genius to writing best sellers. Whether Segal, Harold Robbins, Irving Wallace or any other popular novelist actually *plots* his fiction according to an understanding of mass preferences, certainly that understanding is clear—in the frantic million-dollar bids for paper rights, in the lines of impatient millions around movie houses, perhaps most dramatically in the amazing public grapevine which by its mysterious structure will now carry word of Oliver's fate as it did of Jenny's onto buses, trains; into waiting rooms, diners and English classes where teachers will snicker with envy at another smash. Some grand American chords are touched in popular fiction, as surely if not as deeply as in serious literature. Lots of people called *Love Story* junk, and cried their eyes out.

One reason is probably that books like *Love Story* and *Oliver's Story* give *pleasure*, which sounds like precious little until one considers what small pleasure (pure and quick, not morally transforming) there is in most modern novels. Another, that these books are stories, not screams, riddles or suicide notes. A third, that no demands are made on the reader to explore his life beyond the depth established in the novel. Read of Raskolnikov, and you dive to the dark places of the heart reluctantly. Read of Oliver Barrett and pain bobs on the surface; your cry is a *good* cry.

But the reasons for *Oliver's Story*'s particular assured success are more precise than these. Knowingly or not, Segal has followed a formula for best sellers with this book, the same formula used in the early World War I years, 1914–1916, in a dozen novels including Somerset Maugham's *Of Human Bondage*, Booth Tarkington's *Penrod* and

The Book Business. Of the more than 40,000 new book titles each year, some will be best-sellers that earn more than $2 million for their authors.
Martin Trailer/Photophile

Seventeen, Mary Roberts Rinehart's *K*, and (no kidding) in Edgar Rice Burroughs's *Tarzan of the Apes*. Those novels answered a need of their times by expressing concretely some amorphous though strong public feelings. So be it for *Oliver's Story*, and what this says about current public feelings is not encouraging.

The characteristics of American best sellers between 1914–1916 are described neatly in a fine study of popular fiction called *Books for Pleasure* by Suzanne Ellery Greene (Popular Press, 1974). Line up these characteristics with *Oliver's Story*, and we see why Segal will grow richer:

no villains—technically child labor in Hong Kong is a villain in *Oliver's Story*, but Oliver thinks of it as one of many injustices, such as the war in Southeast Asia, that he'd like to set right some time.

the search for order is realized in personal happiness or stability—Oliver just wants to be happy. There are no abstract conflicts.

the value of feeling and intuition—Oliver senses that he and Marcie will never be two; his father senses difficulty; Phil has a feeling about Marcie, etc.

naiveté and ingenuousness of the hero—Oliver is impetuous.

shunning the big city—Oliver's retreat to Boston is like going back to rural America, the controlled and simple life.

Anglo-Saxon superiority—implied in all

Barretts, new and traditional. Oliver recoils from such notions, thereby emphasizing his superiority.

class dialect and colloquialisms—Oliver's social class is Harvard '64. He and Marcie talk dirty to show poise.

political connection between hero and outer world is slight—Oliver admits to dreaming of becoming president, but says lately he'd rather teach his kids to ice-skate.

little or no mention of ethnic groups—unless you count the Chinese in China as ethnics. Oliver has a mild yen for Joanna Stein, a Jewish doctor; and he often "lifts a glass" with Stanley Newman or Gianni Barnea. Phil Cavilleri phones occasionally and visits once.

parents are responsible for hero's innate nobility—quarrel as they may, Oliver is his father's son (Tarzan's parents were also aristocrats). It even turns out that Mr. Barrett is kind to mill workers.

education is good and necessary—Oliver lectures Marcie on the Treaty of Nanking.

virtue of Nature—here shown in hero's athleticism and anti-materialism.

tension between generations, yet parent and child reconcile—done.

love is pre-marital—much of *Oliver's Story* is an extended date, covering Ipswich, Denver, "21" and Howard Johnson's.

hero displays natural skills—hockey, jogging, tennis, the law.

selflessness of hero—"Be a little selfish, Oliver," says senior partner, Mr. Jonas. "You've earned it."

age is disparaged, and youth is seen as a time to be tortured and envied—done.

nationalism, a major theme—a mill worker tells Oliver that Mr. Barrett is under great pressure.

"Why?"

He looked at me and spoke two syllables: "Hong Kong."

I nodded.

He continued. "And Formosa. And they're starting now in South Korea. What the hell."

"Yeah, Mr. Francis," I replied. "That's wicked competition."

simplicity of prose style—"I waited, while the mountains sat in silence, offering no comment."

There are other corresponding elements, but that's enough to make a case. If the same ingredients that made best sellers 60 years ago will make them today, how far have we come? According to these characteristics the American reader of 1914 was solidly interested in his own welfare and circle of friends, did not theorize abstractly about world events, did not question democracy, felt no broad economic or political reponsibilities, cherished privacy, trusted intuition, and celebrated himself. Since that's a pretty fair summation of where we are now, Segal has read us right.

Then there's that final element of our fascination with money, which Segal has also read right, and in the right proportions. The idea of class as social division was an element in the best sellers of World War I, but in the '20s the possession of money determined class. Here Segal has it both ways. As Fitzgerald said of Daisy in *Gatsby*, "her voice was full of money"; so Oliver of Marcie: "she was dressed in money." The more Oliver and Marcie deny the importance of money, the more magical it seems, particu-larly as they deny it in mansion after mansion. Money talks, shines, changes bad to good, has its own intrinsic beauty. Few scenes in American movies are as happy as the last one in *How to Marry a Millionaire* when Lauren Bacall ogles her boyfriend's enormous roll of bills. Few figures of American fiction are as joyful as Walt Disney's Scrooge McDuck, whooping up coins in his money bin.

As Segal and other popular novelists have discovered, money even accounts for more best sellers than love, which is why Oliver can lose his two girls, but hold on to his cash, and still delight his readers. That he plans good deeds with his riches is commendable—"I mean the companies we help to float create new jobs"—but the nice thing is he *has* the stuff. Moreover he is finally a *businessman*, at once the rarest sort of hero in American fiction, and the one in whom we've wished most to believe. For in him are wed capitalism and virtue, the love story we have longed for since the first sale to the first Indian.

If this analysis is correct—and I'm counting on it—I think I know how to beat Segal to the next bundle. I'll call it *Ghost Story*. In it Oliver has forsaken Annie Gilbert, the distant cousin whose name he deliberately drops on the last page of *Oliver's Story*, because—are you ready?—Jenny returns from the dead. Oliver, unable to find love again, is money-crazy; he needs love to temper avarice. One night as he is about to sign a corrupt contract, his hand is stayed. He looks up, and there entering from the moonlight through the French doors, standing on the Tabriz carpet beside the Mies chair, and holding a viola, is the only woman who ever mattered. "Hello, Preppy," she says.

Start bidding.

Novelist Ray Bradbury reportedly once suggested to Walt Disney that he run for mayor of Los Angeles, and the reply was, "Ray, why should I run for mayor when I'm already king?" It would be difficult to dispute that Disney, indeed, was the king, emperor, and grand-panjandrum of all-American entertainment.

Disneyland and its younger brother, Disney World, are probably the popular culture capitals of the United States, if not the entire world. More people visit these twin memorials to Disney's entrepreneurial genius than Washington, D.C. The 20 million or more who make an annual pilgrimage to these entertainment meccas in Anaheim, California and Orlando, Florida are paying (with hundreds of millions of dollars)

homage to Disney's vision.

Just as a plastic model of Abraham Lincoln became a very popular feature in Disneyland, perhaps someday Walt's heirs will construct a talking statue of Disney himself, fabricated from thousands of wires, transistors, and human-like plastic. If Moscow can have its mausoleum of Lenin as one of the great attractions for the masses, should Anaheim have less?

Professor Herbert Schiller, in this excerpt from his book, *The Mind Managers*, examines the industrial dimensions of the Disney entertainment conglomerate. His findings substantiate why they called the former Missouri farm boy the "Henry Ford of the entertainment business."

Pure Entertainment: Walt Disney Productions, Inc.

Herbert Schiller

In 1972 *Fortune* magazine confirmed what had been suspected for a long time—that the Walt Disney entertainment empire is one of America's largest industrial enterprises, ranked 502nd in the nation with sales exceeding $175 million. In fiscal 1972, sales increased spectacularly to $329 million, reflecting the huge revenues derived from Disney World, the new entertainment park in Orlando, Florida.

To American businessmen this came as no surprise. Indeed, years earlier, they had voted Disney, along with Henry Ford, Andrew Carnegie, John D. Rockefeller, Jr., and

other illustrious capitalists as one of the ten greatest men of business in American history. The citation noted that, "while making millionaires of himself and business associates, the Missouri farm boy was entertaining children and grown-ups with wholesome, clean cartoons and live movies . . . " In their opinion, "Walt Disney was a modern day Hans Christian Andersen with business ability." One writer, marveling at the technical ingenuity and size of the exhibits in Disneyland, declared that they "establish [Disney] as the Henry Ford of the entertainment business."

The business, under Disney's direction, reached out to a fabulous and unprecedented kind of market. The eyes and ears, the minds and the bodies, of tens of millions of human beings annually encounter some Disney message or product. Richard Schickel, the biographer of the Disney saga, reported: "In 1966 Walt Disney Productions estimated that around the world 240,000,000 people saw a Disney movie, 100,000,000 watched a Disney show every week, 800,000,000 read a Disney book or magazine, 50,000,000 listened or danced to Disney music or records, 80,000,000 bought Disney-licensed merchandise, 150,000,000 read a Disney comic strip, 80,000,000 saw Disney educational films at school, in church, on the job, and 6.7 million made the journey to that peculiar Mecca in Anaheim, insistently known as 'Walt Disney's Magic Kingdom' in the company's press releases and more commonly referred to as Disneyland."

However inflated by puffery or double-counting, the spread of the Disney influence is impressive. It continues to grow. In 1971–1972, for example, the two entertainment parks, Disneyland in California and Disney World in Florida, attracted 20.3 million customers, "more than the total number of people who attended all National League baseball games played during the same period, and almost twice as many as attended all the NFL football games played during the 1971 season" (*Wall Street Journal*, 8 December 1972).

Disney is not an exclusively domestic entertainment phenomenon. The company's products swell the stream of international communications. As early as the 1930s, Disney comic and story books appeared in . . . twenty-seven [languages] and were distributed worldwide. The show "Disney on Parade," which attracted audiences totaling over 7 million persons, in the United States and Canada, has also performed in Australia, Japan, New Zealand, and Mexico City. A two-year European tour commenced in 1972. . . .

There are also record clubs, book clubs, and weekly magazines for new readers, as well as encyclopedias that are sold globally.

The corporate structure that manages this vast assemblage of entertainment and popular culture is a model of modern conglomeratization. It oversees domestic and international distribution subsidiaries, a music publishing company, an educational materials company, a research and design affiliate, one enormous unit to manage the newly opened Florida complex, and another to run the hotels in the area. There are also real estate development and communications services affiliates. What makes these enterprises so profitable—first half earnings in 1972 jumped 50 percent over the preceding year—is the skillful utilization of a systems approach to entertainment and especially to the use of the mass media. The company carefully selects one medium to promote its activities in other media, which in turn creates additional interest in the original promotion.

For example, the media preparations preceding and immediately subsequent to the opening of Disney World on October 1, 1971, resembled the logistical planning of D-Day—the difference being that the Disney onslaught was directed at people's minds. The company's annual report observed that "the opening was handled by almost unprecedented newspaper and national magazine coverage, including cover stories in *Look* and *Life*, and major sections in such other magazines as *Time*, *Newsweek*, *Paris Match*, *Epoca*, *Esquire*, *Forbes* and *Business*

Week.'' Most important of all, "An estimated 52,000,000 people across the United States were introduced to Walt Disney World during a 90-minute NBC Television Special on October 29th."

The effectiveness of television to focus attention on other Disney entertainment and business promotions has been understood and effectively applied by the Disney management since the beginning of television. Disneyland was financially linked in the beginning with ABC-Paramount Theatres, Inc. ABC bought 34.8 percent of the shares of Disneyland, Incorporated, and Walt Disney agreed to produce a weekly TV show, *Disneyland,* for ABC for seven years. Said Disney at the time, "I saw that if I was ever going to have my park, here, at last, was a way to tell millions about it . . . with TV."

When Disneyland opened on July 17, 1955, there was a 90-minute ABC-TV Special, on which dozens of celebrities appeared at the site guided by Disney himself. Disneyland became an instant hit, and so did the weekly TV program.

The company's television revenues are modest in comparison with its other activities—$8 million in 1971, while films accounted for $64 million and total revenues were $175.6 million—but TV is essential for the advertising it affords Disney's films, amusement parks, and commercial products. "The Wonderful World of Disney," now [1973] in its nineteenth season, and its eleventh on NBC, remains in the "top twenty" shows; according to the Nielsen TV index, the show's first seven episodes in 1972 reached a total audience of more than 19,000,000 homes.

The interwoven promotions of TV programs, the amusement centers, and new and old films in turn heighten interest in the printed materials of the Disney complex. In foreign markets, the printed products sometimes precede the films and TV programs, and generate demand for these other items. In any case, the way in which film, TV, and print are managed to promote Disney creations and products derived from these creations is a source of envy and admiration in the marketing field. *TV Guide*, for example, discussing a television show that was successfully generating commercial product tie-ins, noted [in July 1972]: "The first, and still the most successful, film merchandiser is the Disney studio, which ... first began to move Mickey Mouse watches, comic books and related products by the millions in the 30s. Presently, Donald Duck joined the parade. . . . Today [they] do $11,000,000."

Business Week [in July 1965] had earlier called attention to Disney's adept timing. "The pattern set with Mickey Mouse is followed with the Beatles and James Bond merchandising today. Long before other movie men realized that paperback books help the sale of pictures, Disney Studios was timing comic book distribution to picture release."

Disney's recognition of the associative effects of imagery and the interrelatedness of modern communications is further attested to in Schickel's observation that, "no Disney character is allowed to appear on products with unpleasant connotations for children, such as medicines."

The Disney empire deals largely, though no longer exclusively, in imagery. More recently, as the enterprise has prospered, real estate operations, hotel construction and management, transportation, and communications services have been added to the company's interests. Whereas at Disneyland motel and hotel concessions were from the start granted to outside interests, at the new Disney World the company retains ownership and control of these ancillary but very profitable activities.

Nevertheless, film, television, print materials, and the entertainment parks (themselves thousand-acre assemblages of imagery) remain the dominant elements in Walt Disney Productions. Communications—in all the media—are the entertainment empire's main products. What, then, are the messages that flow from the dozens of feature-length films, the continuing weekly TV shows, the thousands of comic and story books, the educational materials, the records, and the amusement parks themselves?

Just as the Disney management finds it profitable to use a systems approach to sell its products, the best way to understand the message it is selling is to adopt a systems analysis approach to the product—that is, to take the Disney machine as an entity, and to examine its many outputs as *elements in a totality* with some common features. Approached in this way, the message becomes the dominant factor, and the media that carry it appear secondary. It should never be forgotten, however, that repetition and cross-media reinforcement are crucial factors in disseminating the message.

Max Rafferty, a former Superintendent of Public Instruction in California and a very conservative gentleman, has referred to Disney as "the greatest educator of this century." If greatness is equivalent to degree of impact, Rafferty may be closer to the truth than many have ever imagined. Disney from the beginning claimed to be offering entertainment and nothing else. It was as simple as that. His obituary in the *Los Angeles Times*, the newspaper which covered his successes so enthusiastically, significantly repeated this theme: "*His characters knew no politics*, and received affection from the young at heart *of whatever political persuasion or ideology* [emphasis mine]." . . .

Disney was a powerful educator. Since his

death, Walt Disney Productions has become an even more influential shaper of minds, because it is able to disseminate its entertainment to more people in more ways than had been possible earlier. . . .

Obviously, the character and nuances of the message may differ from medium to medium, from product to product, and from one setting to the next. With these qualifications in mind, it is accurate, I believe, to articulate the transcendent Disney message, transmitted by film, tape, and comic book, in movie, story, and record, in the great outdoors and in suburban scenarios, thus: *behold a world in which there is no social conflict.* There is plenty of violence. There are some "bad guys," but they are individuals, not representatives of significant social divisions. The world is a happy place and the American middle class experiences the world at its best. . . .

All of this is accomplished with incredible technical virtuosity in photography, engineering, and construction, as well as a perfectionist insistence on verisimilitude in the details of whatever is being presented—a wildlife scene on film, an audio-animatronic model of Abraham Lincoln at Disneyland, or a TV production of Winnie-the-Pooh. . . .

There is no doubt that Disney is a very successful part of the North American business system.

As stated earlier by Russel Nye, the convergence of several important factors in the late nineteenth century precipitated the rapid growth of popular culture. Industrialization, urbanization, and the influx of millions of immigrants from Southern and Eastern Europe profoundly altered the cultural life of the nation. This social milieu proved to be especially conducive to the development of new media such as the motion picture. Even a poor immigrant, unable to speak English, could afford to frequent the movie houses and could easily follow the superficial story line.

Older areas of popular culture were also affected by the rapid changes in American society in the late nineteenth and early twentieth centuries. Sports, which once symbolized an orderly, pastoral American way of life, became increasingly aggressive, with football and boxing rivaling baseball in popularity. Many newspapers, eager to expand their circulations, began catering to the urban immigrant masses with sensationalized stories, comic strips, and an increasing reliance on nonverbal representation in advertising.

Reuel Denney's cogent essay, "The Discovery of the Popular Culture," analyzes these and other major trends. Denney also examines, in great detail, the evolution of critical response to the culture of the masses. In so doing, he offers some valuable insights into the subject of "change and continuity" in popular culture.

The Discovery of the Popular Culture

Reuel Denney

Not until almost the second quarter of the twentieth century was there an adequate critical response to an American popular culture which depends as much on aural and visual media as upon the printed page. The preparation for that response, nonetheless, had been made in previous decades. In the period 1880–1950 the response of critics and interpreters of popular culture to increasing mass-duplication and mass-distribution of symbols returned again and again to certain major questions. At least six of these questions had been more or less implicit throughout the nineteenth century, and became explicit between 1880 and World War I.

A question about democratic man: Was he losing his way by standardizing so much of his imaginative life at the low level suggested, for example, by yellow journalism?

A question about democratic-industrial culture: Was the United States leading the Western world in a leveling process that threatened to go too far—as in the banality and vulgarity of some of its schoolbooks?

A question about social structure: Could society survive such a rapid transfer of power from the rich and the better-educated to those who were as yet both poor and uneducated? What should the relation be between mass and elite?

A question about the American communications system: What effects on language, tradition, and character would be caused by massive immigration from countries that not only spoke a foreign language, but lived by a different ethos?

A question about the New World and the Old: How did American popular culture affect the terms of America's relation to its European past?

A question about the relation between city and farm: Was the decline of agrarian occupations changing the nature of American society?

To these questions, already standardized in one form or another before World War I, the period since 1920 has added others. Many of them were in the air as early as Van Wyck Brooks's pivotal publication of *America's Coming of Age* in 1915; not until after 1920 did they become more widely recognized as "topics." Here are three of the most salient.

A question about industrialism and mass-marketing in relation to social character: To what degree is the American economy of surplus compelled by its own nature to expand consumer motives as fast as possible?

A question about the relation between new communications trades, the elites that practice them, and the products they produce: Would all symbols degenerate as the result of their manufacture not by creative individuals but by industrial teams, not necessarily by personalities pledged to their work, but by anonymous craftsmen? Would the producers degenerate also?

A question about the place of our popular and industrial culture in a sequence between the older industrial cultures (Britain, for example) and the newer industrial cultures (Japan, for example): What could we actually transmit from old to new? What were the merits and demerits of our role as an agent of transmission? . . .

With [the increasing] urbanization [of America] came a broadening of the critical perspective on popular culture as the waves of "new" immigration after 1885 brought greater racial variety to the American public and its critics. Long before 1885, however, the immigrant Germans, one of the first large non-English speaking groups to come over, had made the forum and the press bilingual. And if the Irish had not made it bilingual, they had made it at least bicultural; they used the English language, as they used the political institutions of the country, in ways that were shockingly new. As the post-1885 immigration from central and southern Europe made itself felt, the impacts were even more noticeable. In 1895 about half of the total population of cities such as New York and Chicago spoke broken English, if much English at all. The rise of the foreign language press has been studied by [sociologist] Robert Park and others, but it is not easy to find systematic interpretations of the way in which immigrants influenced the press when the American English-language journals began to incorporate immigrants as readers, and began to be influenced by that readership.

This was only the first step in a gradual process of deverbalization of the forum. Some of the first steps in that direction were changes in the *use of language itself.* Joseph Pulitzer demanded that his reporters produce "color." And, during the seventies, eighties, and nineties, according to [historian] Richard Hofstadter, there was "an increasing disposition on the part of editors to use the human-interest story, the crusade, the interview, and the stunt or promotional device." While these strengthened the resources of journalism and publicity, they generally did so at the price of spoon-feeding the public a diet of sensations expressed in stereotyped language aimed at low levels of education. In the end such editorial policies led to the substitution of a word for a sentence and a picture for a word wherever a gain in attention could be anticipated. Lloyd Morris believed that the journalistic war between Pulitzer and Hearst (in the largely "foreign" city of New York) in

1895 was the seedbed of such journalistic innovations as the supplement, the magazine section, the big Sunday edition, and the comic strip. It is not an exaggeration to say that the deverbalization of the forum began as a result of the presence of the immigrants in the cities, in the growth of journalistic forms which could be followed, as children still follow them, *either* by word or by picture—as, for example, the cartoon strip or the picture-emphasizing advertisement.

The invasion of the forum by nonverbal modes of communication reached a climax between 1900 and 1920 when the movies lit up the cafes and little stores where they were first shown. Later, television was to command a larger audience—but this audience was already familiar with the audiovisual medium for which TV provided a new channel of transmission. Probably no future revolution in mass-communications techniques will ever occur under conditions so strongly favoring the appeal of a story that can be followed through its picture content alone as the movie revolution. For it was only around 1920, at the end of the period, that foreign languages began to decrease as the household tongue of millions of city dwellers.

Perhaps an even more important result of the influx of this new immigration was a change in American social structure which tended to decrease the influence of the elite and to increase that of the mass. One result was that the nature of the relation between American culture and its parental culture in Europe began to change in ways that led to new self-definitions on both sides of the Atlantic. Before World War I, we sent to Europe as tourists those who stood at the top of our society. At the same time, at least until the reaction to immigration that appeared with the legislation of 1917–1924, we took from Europe those who were at the bottom of Europe's social structure. World War I, however, introduced a massive contact between Americans of all origins and Europeans of all

"...the nature of the relation between American culture and its parental culture in Europe began to change in ways that led to new self-definitions on both sides of the Atlantic."

origins. Europeans who would earlier have pointed out to Americans the derivative status of the American culture were now more likely to point, by contrast, to some of the few ways in which America had achieved a degree of cultural autonomy. Many Europeans praised not American architectural styles imported from the Old World, but bridges on the East River; not American symphony orchestras, but jazz; not plays modeled on Mayfair, but musical reviews manufactured in Manhattan. . . .

Critical responses to the popular culture after World War II were dominated by the spread of television, which regenerated on a new level many of the issues that had appeared when movies and radio were first making their power felt. The terms of the investigation of the new media, however, had shifted. A trend that began with such studies as that of the movies by the Payne Fund Studies, under the direction of sociologists, had developed in force. Building on the work of the 1930's, a variety of investigators began to tackle highly specific problems, problems in which the effort was to see how the uses and the effects of the mass media might be related to some theory of social structure. Leo Lowenthal studied changes in the ideal-types of the successful man in American magazine biographies, noting a shift from the producer-hero to the consumer-hero. Robert Merton studied the myth-making talents of the wartime bond saleswoman and radio singer Kate Smith. W. Lloyd Warner and William Henry investigated the appeal made by the fantasy of soap opera to women in different social classes. Martha Wolfenstein and Nathan Leites carried the psychoanalytic analysis of film to a new level of interest.

Studies of the popular culture by the social sciences were shaped by the interests of particular disciplines. The more behavioristic psychologists were interested in the learning processes generated by the modern mass media; psychologists of a more Freudian bent were concerned with processes of identification with film and TV heroes and heroines. Sociologists showed a continued interest in the way in which the popular culture played a part in reinforcing the "collective representations" of class and mobility patterns of American life. Anthropologists were interested in the processes by which the popular culture embodied or reflected cultural norms and values. Social psychologists continued to occupy a central place in popular culture studies because of their concern with such problems as the effect of communications on the formation, organization, and cohesion of social groups. . . .

In some degree, the postwar discussion of the popular culture had also been stimulated by articles on popular mythology and propaganda in Dwight Macdonald's periodical, *politics*, in the early 1940's. In this publication, the values of popular culture were attacked in terms inherited from the broad criticism of popular culture by Marxists in the 1930's. The terms of the debate thus engendered are best summarized in the 1954 exchange between Dwight Macdonald and British historian Denis W. Brogan. Macdonald continued his attack on the popular culture as the product of a sick society; Brogan retorted with the observation that it was no different in the eighteenth century—the problem was not a typically modern problem at all, but has always been with us.

The attitudes and interests of those who wrote in more essayistic terms about the popular culture in the 1940's and early 1950's must be considered as a unit; they seem to arrange themselves between these two poles of opinion. Their interests, at the same time, were highly individualized. Leslie Fiedler, observing the concern of certain middle-class people about the popular culture, wondered why they feel this way. Could it be because they wish to make popular culture so excellent that there will be no need to admit the existence of a "high culture"? Apparently these people dream of a "one-class" society. Milton Klonsky renewed the attack on the products of popular culture on the ground that they are not the product of an "organic" imagination, being fabricated by industrial teams. Louis Kronenberger attacked many aspects of the popular and middle-brow culture not so much because of its own particular traits as because it is employed by a middle-class (which should know better) to protect itself from reflection and self-knowledge. Marshall McLuhan approached the whole topic by way of an historical and humanistic interest in the forms of popular art and rhetoric. He argued that, before making judgments of particular products, such as the TV commercial, one had to define its place in a new universe of perception generated along non-print "non-linear" principles by the new media.

During the 1940's and the early 1950's, the discussion was carried along within an international framework that encompassed some of the Europeans who wrote on the popular culture. André Malraux, for example, argued that the main fault of the vulgar popular culture was that it got in the way of attempts on the part of the elite of the Western world to get on with the job of reforming and transvaluating their own ethos. George Orwell also approached the problem with an eye on the processes by which elites are dissolved and reconstituted. He was especially interested in the effects that the popular arts and their myths had upon the historical tradition, and the transmission of the tradition to new generations and new social classes. One of his main objections to the popular arts and fiction of the period 1920 to 1950, roughly, was that they seemed to him to pass on to rising orders of society the vices (sadism, for example) but not the virtues (magnanimity, for example) of a declining aristocratic order.

In 1950, the interest in historical continuity and in the crosscultural method were made to work together in a new analysis of the mass culture and its communications habits by David Riesman in *The Lonely Crowd*, a work he wrote in collaboration with Nathan Glazer and me. The work drew heavily on suggestions by Freud as to the process of personality formation and the suggestions of Max Weber as to the dominance of the Protestant ethos in Western industrialism. The profusion of the popular culture of movies, advertisements, and song was seen as one part of a general economic development: the shift from emphasis on production to emphasis on consumption, occasioned by unforeseen abundance. All other things being equal, unfavorable responses to the popular culture might be a reflex of the older production-oriented types of social character. All other things being equal, favorable responses might be a reflex of the newer consumption-oriented types of social character.

Beginning in the late 1940's, I began to explore the importance of the various genres of art and rhetoric employed by the mass media. My conclusion was that the mass media are a dumping ground for the artistic theories elaborated in the production-minded, late nineteenth century under the labels of realism and naturalism. By employing actuality techniques, the mass media marketed fantasy packaged in the form of "documentation." This tendency reinforced, and is reinforced by, the industrial organization of the studios and networks and their associated guilds and crafts. "Literalism" becomes the order of the day in the mass media, and all standards of critical and popular evaluation are compromised by failure to take into account the differences in the appeals and effects of fictional and nonfictional forms.

One of the major controversies among popular culture scholars is: To what extent has the development of the mass media of communication altered the nature of popular culture? Marshall McLuhan interprets the emergence of the new electronic media in revolutionary terms. His oft-quoted declaration, "the medium is the message," suggests his basic argument, that the power of popular culture to transform people's lives stems from the technological apparatus rather than the subject matter. To the McLuhanites, a cowboy story in a dime novel is fundamentally different from a movie or television Western because of the nature of the media involved.

Eminent historian Oscar Handlin sides with those who believe the mass media has all but obliterated the nature of popular culture as it existed in the nineteenth century. Handlin points out that popular culture was essentially a conglomeration of many individual subcultures, often tied to a specific ethnic group. The advent of the electronic media, he asserts, did not create a cohesive culture of the masses, but rather had a disruptive effect on the many homogeneous popular cultures. The popular artist, for instance, once came from the same milieu as his audience and had a strong rapport with the people he entertained. The mass media, on the other hand, rely on professional performers who are packaged and sold to the mass culture consumers.

Handlin's essay, "Comments on Mass and Popular Culture," was originally presented at the highly influential seminar on popular culture held at the Tamimont Institute in June 1959. Cosponsored by *Daedalus*, the journal of the American Academy of Arts and Sciences, the seminar brought together scholars, broadcast executives, and artists who contributed immeasurably to Othe study of popular culture by their papers and discussion.

Comments on Mass and Popular Culture
Oscar Handlin

The question of the uses of culture... offers a strategic point for analysis of the differences between those forms of expression communicated by the mass media and all other popular varieties of art. For, although no society has been devoid of culture, that which we now associate with the mass media appears to be unique in its relationship to the way of life of the people. A brief consideration of the function of culture will illuminate the character of that uniqueness.

Until the appearance of those phenomena which we now associate with the mass media, culture was always considered incidental to some social end. Men did not build architecture or compose music in the abstract. They constructed churches in which to worship or homes in which to live. They composed masses and cantatas as parts of a sacred service. The forms within which they built or composed were important in themselves, but they were also intimately related to the functions they served for those who used them. . . .

By 1900 almost everywhere in the Western world the term culture had acquired a distinctive connotation, just as the term Society had. Society no longer referred to the total order of the populace in a community, but only to a small self-defined segment of it. And culture no longer referred to the total complex of forms through which the community satisfied its wants, but only to certain narrowly defined modes of expression distinguished largely by their lack of practicality.

In the process of redefinition, culture lost all connection with function other than that of establishing an identification with that narrow society which had made itself the custodian of the values attached to the arts. The châteaux of Fifth Avenue were not erected to meet men's needs for homes, any more than the rare books of the tycoons were assembled to satisfy their desire for reading matter. Architecture, literature, art, and music, as defined by society and its intermediaries, became, rather, primarily the symbols of status.

That very fact, indeed, served Society as the justification of its aristocratic pretensions. "Changes in manners and customs," an influential manual explained, "no matter under what form of government, usually originate with the wealthy or aristocratic minority, and are thence transmitted to the other classes. . . . This rule naturally holds good of house-planning, and it is for this reason that the origin of modern house-planning should be sought rather in the prince's mezzanine than in the small middle-class dwelling" [Edith Wharton and Ogden Codman, Jr., *The Decoration of Houses* (New York: Charles Scribner's Sons, 1897), p. 5].

By the end of the nineteenth century, therefore, Americans could readily identify a miscellaneous congeries of artistic forms as their culture. The citizens of the Republic and foreign observers had no difficulty in recognizing what was American music, literature, or painting, for an elaborate apparatus of critical institutions—museums, orchestras, journals, and universities—existed to pass judgment on what belonged and what did not. These institutions and the impresarios who controlled them had the confidence and support of Society, that segment of the community which assumed that wealth or birth gave it leadership.

Outside the realm of the official culture as defined by Society there persisted other, but excluded, modes of action and expression. The peasants of Europe, the workers of the industrial cities, the ethnic enclaves of the United States did not share the forms of behavior, the tastes and attitudes of the would-be or genuine aristocracy, although they often acknowledged the primacy of the groups above them. But peasants, laborers, and foreigners did retain and employ in their own lives a complex of meaningful forms of expression of their own. At the time these were commonly characterized as popular or folk culture. Thus in the early decades of this century, it was usual to refer to popular music, popular literature, and popular art, set off and distinct from *the* music, *the* literature, and *the* art of Society.

That designation was misleading, in so far as it carried the implication that popular culture was as coherent and uniform as the official culture. In actuality, popular culture, in America at least, was composed of a complex of sub-cultures. The mass of the population of the metropolitan cities, the Negroes, the farmers of the Great Plains, and other groups which together constituted the bulk of the American population had no taste for the music played by the Philharmonic or the novels approved by Thomas Bailey Aldrich or the paintings certified by Duveen. These people sang and danced, they read, and they were amused or edified by pictures. Only, what they sang or read or looked at was not music or literature or art in the sense defined by Society, and therefore was explained away by the general designation, popular.

Superficially, popular culture differed from the defined culture in the lack of an accepted set of canons or of a normative body of classics. A vaudeville song or a piece of embroidery or a dime novel was accepted or rejected by its audience without comparison with or reference to standards extraneous to itself. But this surface difference sprang from a deeper one. Popular, unlike defined, culture retained a functional quality in the sense that it was closely related to the felt needs and familiar modes of expression of the people it served. Popular songs were to be danced to, vaudeville to be laughed at, and embroidery to be worn or to cover a table.

The development of mass culture—or more properly speaking of the culture communicated through the mass media—has had a disturbing effect upon both popular and defined cultures. The consequences for the latter are the easier to distinguish, for it left not only vestiges but a record of its past which makes possible ready comparisons with the present.

It is far more difficult to make similar comparisons in the case of popular culture. Precisely because it lacked a canon, it also lacked a history. It was not only displaced by later forms; its very memory was all but obliterated. As a result we know very little about the culture that until recently served the people who now consume the products of the mass media. And that gap in our information has given rise to the misconception that the "mass culture" of the present is but an extension of the popular culture of the past.

Yet if that popular culture did not produce its own record, it can be pieced together from fragmentary historical materials which reveal that the mass media have had as deep an impact upon popular as upon official culture. The Ed Sullivan show [was] not vaudeville in another guise any more than "Omnibus" [was] a modernized Chautauqua. Television, the movies, and the mass-circulation magazines stand altogether apart from the older vehicles of both popular and defined culture.

An examination of the popular theater, of vaudeville, of the popular newspapers, especially in the Sunday supplements, and of the popular literature of the 1890's reveals four significant elements in the difference between the popular culture of that period and that communicated by the mass media of the present.

In the first place, popular culture, although unstructured and chaotic, dealt directly with the concrete world intensely familiar to its audience. There was no self-conscious realism in this preoccupation with the incidents and objects of the everyday world. Rather, this was the most accessible means of communication with a public that was innocent in its approach to culture, that is, one that looked or listened without ulterior motive or intent.

In the second place, and for similar reasons, popular culture had a continuing relevance to the situation of the audience that was exposed to it. That relevance was maintained by a direct rapport between those who created and those who consumed this culture. The very character of the popular theater, for instance, in which the spontaneous and the "ad lib" were tolerated, encouraged a continuous and highly intimate response across the footlights. So too, the

---

"Popular, unlike defined, culture retained a functional quality in the sense that it was closely related to the felt needs ... of the people it served."

---

journalism of the American ethnic sub-groups maintained an immediate awareness of the needs and problems of their readers. In general, furthermore, in all media, the writers and actors sprang from the identical milieu as their audience did, and maintained a firm sense of identification with it.

In the third place, popular culture was closely tied to the traditions of those who consumed it. A large part of it was ethnic in character, that is, arranged within the terms of a language and of habits and attitudes imported from Europe. But even that part of it which was native American and which reached back into the early nineteenth and eighteenth centuries, maintained a high degree of continuity with its own past.

Finally, popular culture had the capacity for arousing in its audience such sentiments as wonder and awe, and for expressing the sense of irony of their own situation which lent it enormous emotional power. Men and women shed real tears or rocked with laughter in the playhouses of the Bowery, as they could not in the opera or the theater uptown. The acrobats and the animals of the circus evoked wonder as the framed pictures of the museum could not. The difference was the product of the authenticity of the one type of culture and the artificiality of the other.

Out of American popular culture there emerged occasional bursts of creativity of high level. Instances may be found in the work of Charlie Chaplin, in some of the jazz music of the decade after 1900, and in that strain of literary realism developed by novelists and dramatists whose experience in journalism had brought them into direct contact with popular culture.

In total perspective, however, popular culture was not justified by such by-products so much as by the function it served. Millions of people found in this culture a means of communication among themselves and the answers to certain significant questions that they were asking about the world around them. Indeed, it was the perception of this

function that attracted the avant-garde in the opening decades of the twentieth century. Those creative spirits, repelled by the inert pretensions of official culture, often found refreshing elements of authenticity in the popular culture of their times. Bohemia, too, was a kind of ghetto in which the artist, equally with the Italian or Negro laborer, was alien, cut off from respectable society. In fact some of the Bohemians were inclined to idealize popular culture in revulsion against the inability of the official culture to satisfy their own needs.

In the light of these considerations, it is possible to begin to assess the effects of the mass media on the character of popular culture. To some extent the impact of the new media is simply a product of their size. The enormous growth of these media has been of such an order as to involve immediate qualitative changes. The transformation of an audience, once numbered in the thousands, to one of millions profoundly altered all the relationships involved. More specifically, the impact of the mass media has altered the earlier forms of control; it has deprived the material communicated of much of its relevance; and it has opened a gulf between the artist and the audience.

A good deal of the familiar talk about the degree to which advertisers or bankers or interest groups control the mass media is irrelevant. There has been a genuine change in the character of the control of these media as contrasted with the situation of fifty or sixty years ago. But it has taken a more subtle form than is usually ascribed to it.

What is most characteristic of the mass media today is precisely the disappearance of the forms of control that existed in the popular culture of a half-century ago. No one can decide now (as Hearst or Pulitzer could in 1900) to use a newspaper as a personal organ. Nor could any TV or movie executive, advertiser, agent, or even a large sector of the audience dictate the content of what is transmitted through these media. The most they can do is prevent the inclusion of material distasteful to them.

The only accurate way of describing the situation of the mass media is to say they operate within a series of largely negative restraints. There are many things they cannot do. But within the boundaries of what they may do, there is an aimless quality, with no one in a position to establish a positive direction. In part this aimlessness is the product of the failure to establish coherent lines of internal organization; in part it flows from the frightening massiveness of the media themselves; but in part also it emanates from a lack of clarity as to the purposes they serve.

The inability to exercise positive control and the concomitant inability to locate responsibility heighten the general sense of irrelevance of the contents of the mass media. It would, in any case, be difficult for a writer or performer to be sensitive to the character of an unseen audience. But the problems are magnified when the audience is numbered in the millions, in other words, when it is so large that all the peculiarities of tastes and attitudes within it must be canceled out so that all that remains is an abstract least common denominator. And those problems become insoluble when no one has the power or the obligation to deal with them.

In the world of actuality, Americans are factory workers or farmers, Jews or Baptists, of German or Irish descent, old or young; they live in small towns or great cities, in the North or the South. But the medium which attempts to speak to all of them is compelled to discount these affiliations and pretend that the variety of tastes, values, and habits related to them do not exist. It can therefore only address itself to the empty outline of the residual American. What it has to say, therefore, is doomed to irrelevance in the lives of its audience; and the feedback from the consciousness of that irrelevance, without effective countermea-

"...the impact of the mass media...has opened a gulf between the artist and the audience."

sures, dooms the performer and writer to sterility.

The critics of the mass media are in error when they condemn its products out of hand. These media can tolerate good as well as bad contents, high as well as low art. Euripides and Shakespeare can perfectly well follow the Western or quiz show on TV, and the slick magazine can easily sandwich in cathedrals and madonnas among the pictures of athletes and movie queens.

What is significant, however, is that it does not matter. The mass media find space for politics and sports, for science and fiction, for art and music, all presented on an identical plateau of irrelevance. And the audience which receives this complex variety of wares accepts them passively as an undifferentiated but recognizable series of good things among which it has little capacity for choice, and with which it cannot establish any meaningful, direct relationship.

The way in which the contents of the mass media are communicated deprives the audience of any degree of selectivity, for those contents are marketed as any other commodities are. In our society it seems possible through the use of the proper marketing device to sell anybody anything, so that what is sold has very little relevance to the character of either the buyers or of the article sold. This is as true of culture as of refrigerators or fur coats. The contents of the magazine or the TV schedule or the newspaper have as little to do with their sales potential as the engine specifications with the marketability of an automobile. The popularity of quiz shows no more reflects the desires of the audience than the increase in circulation of *American Heritage* or *Gourmet* reflects a growing knowledge of American history or the development of gastronomic taste, or, for that matter, than the efflorescence of tail fins in 1957 reflected a yearning for them on the part of automobile buyers. All these were rather examples of excellent selling jobs.

The mass media have also diluted, if they have not altogether destroyed, the rapport that formerly existed between the creators of popular culture and its consumers. In this respect, the television playlet or variety performance is far different from the vaudeville turn, which is its lineal antecedent. The performer can no longer sense the mood of his audience and is, in any case, bound by the rigidity of his impersonal medium. The detachment in which he and they operate makes communication between them hazy and fragmentary. As a result, the culture communicated by the mass media cannot serve the function in the lives of those who consume it that the popular culture of the past did.

Yet the latter was no more able to withstand the impact of the mass media than was official culture. The loose, chaotic organization of popular culture, its appeal to limited audiences, its ties to an ethnic past attenuated with the passage of time, all prevented it from competing successfully against the superior resources of the mass media. Much of it was simply swallowed up in the new forms. What survived existed in isolated enclaves, without the old vitality.

The most important consequences of this change were the destruction of those older functional forms of popular culture, the separation of the audience from those who sought to communicate with it, and the paradoxical diminution of the effectiveness of communication with the improvement of the techniques for communication. Thus far the result has been a diffusion among the audience of a sense of apathy. The intense involvement of the masses with their culture at the turn of the century has given way to passive acquiescence. Concomitantly, the occasional creative artist who wishes to communicate with this audience has lost the means of doing so. At best his work will be received as one of the succession of curious or interesting images that flicker by without leaving an enduring impression upon anyone's consciousness.

Thus there is passing a great opportunity for communication between those who have something to say and the audiences who no longer know whether they would like to listen to what there is to be said.

The architects of popular culture must work within the constraints of time and space. Newspaper and magazine writers have to tailor their articles to suit maximum word requirements. Producers of television programs have to conform to an even tighter format. Popular musicians can, and do, compose lengthy songs, but chances are slim the numbers will receive much airplay (at least on the AM stations) if they exceed three minutes. The creators of motion pictures have a bit more flexibility, but any movie over two-and-a-half or three hours risks playing to empty theaters.

The space and time limitations of popular culture are largely dictated by the consumer of media products. We have more leisure time than ever before, but there are also more varieties of leisure activities competing for our time. On any given evening, one may want to scan the local newspaper, read a couple of articles in *Time* or *People*, catch a sporting event on television, and listen to a new album. The popular culture merchants realize the plethora of entertainment available to Americans and structure their offerings so as not to demand too much of their customers' time.

They know full well the sales pitch has to be short and sweet to succeed in business.

The restrictions inherent in popular culture make simplification inevitable. To achieve simplicity, the popular arts employ "formulas" that serve a dual purpose: They facilitate comprehension of the material and they satisfy the audience psychologically. By combining familiar subjects and settings with identifiable characters and a predictable course of events, popular culture can wrap up a fairly complex set of circumstances in a nice, neat, compact package.

John Cawelti, a leading figure in the popular culture studies movement of the past decade, views the concept of formula as a valuable theoretical tool in understanding the nature of popular literature and other aspects of mass entertainment. Cawelti offers some particularly interesting insights into the ideas of "conventions" and "inventions" in popular culture, noting that the former "assert an ongoing continuity of values," while the latter "confront us with a new perception or meaning which we have not realized before."

The Concept of Formula in Popular Literature

John G. Cawelti

Students of popular culture have defined the field in terms of several different concepts. When scholars were first interesting themselves in dime novels, detective stories, etc., they thought of them as subliterature. This concept reflected the traditional qualitative distinction between high culture and mass culture. Unfortunately it was really too vague to be of much analytical use. Even if one could determine where literature left off and subliterature began, a distinction that usually depended on the individual tastes of the inquirer, the term suggested only that the object of study was a debased form of something better. Like many concepts that have been applied to the study of popular culture, the idea of subliterature inextricably confused normative and descriptive problems.

Four additional concepts have come into fairly wide use in recent work: a) the analysis of cultural themes; b) the concept of medium; c) the idea of myth; and d) the concept of formula. I would like to deal briefly with the first three, mainly by way of getting to a fuller discussion of what I consider the most promising concept of all.

The analysis of cultural, social, or psychological themes is certainly a tried and true method of dealing with popular culture. In essence, what the analyst does is to determine what themes appear most often or most prominently in the works under analysis and to group different works according to the presence or absence of the themes he is interested in. Unfortunately, there is a certain vagueness about the concept of theme. Such various things as the ideal of progress, the oedipal conflict, racism, and innocence have all been treated as themes. In effect, a theme turns out to be any prominent element or characteristic of a group of works which seems to have some relevance to a social or cultural problem. Though the vagueness of the concept can be cleared up when the investigator defines the particular theme or set of themes he is interested in, the concept of theme still seems inadequate because it depends on the isolation of particular elements from a total structure. This not only tends to over simplify the works under investigation, but to lead to the kind of falsifying reduction that translates one kind of experience into another. Thus, a story of a certain kind becomes a piece of social rhetoric or the revelation of an unconscious urge. No doubt a story is or can be these things and many others, but to treat it as if it were only one or another social or psychological function is too great a reduction. What we need is a concept that will enable us to deal with the total structure of themes and its relationship to the story elements in the complete work.

The concept of medium has become notorious through the fascinating theories of Marshall McLuhan, Walter Ong and others who insist that medium rather than content or form as we have traditionally understood them ought to be the focus of our cultural analyses. This concept seems to have a particular application to studies in popular culture because many of the works we are concerned with are transmitted through the new electric media which McLuhan sees as so different from the Gutenberg galaxy, the media associated with print. The concept of medium is an important one and McLuhan is doubtless correct that it has been insufficiently explored in the past, but I am not persuaded that more sophisticated studies of the nature of media will do away with the need for generalizations about content. I am sure that we will need to revise many of our notions about where medium leaves off and content begins as the new studies in media progress, but for the present, I would like to forget about the idea of medium altogether with the explanation that I'm concerned with a different kind of problem, the exploration of the content of the popular media. . . .

While a large proportion of popular culture can be defined as stories of different kinds, this is certainly not an exhaustive way of defining popular culture. Just as there are other arts than fiction, so there are works of popular culture which do not tell stories. With additional qualifications the concepts I am seeking to define are applicable to the analysis of other expressions of popular culture than those embodied in stories, but to keep my task as simple as possible, I have chosen to limit myself to the discussion of stories.

The most important generalizing concept which has been applied to cultural studies in recent years is that of myth. Indeed, it could be argued that the concept of formula which I will develop . . . is simply another variation on the idea of myth. But if this is the case, I would argue that distinctions between meanings of the concept of myth are worth making and naming, for many different meanings can be ascribed to the term. In fact, the way in which some people use the term myth hardly separates it from the concept of theme, as when we talk about the myth of progress or the myth of success. There is also another common meaning of the term which further obfuscates its use, namely myth as a common belief which is demonstrably false as in the common opposition between myth and reality. Thus, when a critic uses the term myth one must first get clear whether he means to say that the object he is describing is a false belief, or simply a belief, or something still more complicated like an archetypal pattern. Moreover, because of the special connection of the term myth with a group of stories which have survived from ancient cultures, particularly the Greco-Roman, the scholar who uses the concept in the analysis of contemporary popular culture sometimes finds himself drawn into another kind of reductionism which takes the form of statements like the following: "The solution of the paradox of James Bond's popularity may be, not in considering the novels as thrillers, but as something very different, as historic epic and romance, based on the stuff of myth and legend." But if the retelling of myth is what makes something popular why on earth didn't Mr. Fleming simply retell the ancient myths?

Because of this great confusion about the term myth, I propose to develop another concept which I think I can define more clearly and then to differentiate this concept from that of myth, thereby giving us two more clearly defined generalizing concepts to work with. Let me begin with a kind of axiom or assumption which I hope I can per-

"All cultural products contain a mixture of two kinds of elements: conventions and inventions."

suade you to accept without elaborate argumentation. All cultural products contain a mixture of two kinds of elements: conventions and inventions. Conventions are elements which are known to both the creator and his audience beforehand—they consist of things like favorite plots, stereotyped characters, accepted ideas, commonly known metaphors and other linguistic devices, etc. Inventions, on the other hand, are elements which are uniquely imagined by the creator such as new kinds of characters, ideas, or linguistic forms. Of course it is difficult to distinguish in every case between conventions and inventions because many elements lie somewhere along a continuum between the two poles. Nonetheless, familiarity with a group of literary works will usually soon reveal what the major conventions are and therefore, what in the case of an individual work is unique to that creator.

Convention and invention have quite different cultural functions. Conventions represent familiar shared images and meanings and they assert an ongoing continuity of values; inventions confront us with a new perception or meaning which we have not realized before. Both these functions are important to culture. Conventions help maintain a culture's stability while inventions help it respond to changing circumstances and provide new information about the world. The same thing is true on the individual level. If the individual does not encounter a large number of conventionalized experiences and situations, the strain on his sense of continuity and identity will lead to great tensions and even to neurotic breakdowns. On the other hand, without new information about his world, the individual will be increasingly unable to cope with it and will withdraw behind a barrier of conventions as some people withdraw from life into compulsive reading of detective stories. . . .

This brings us to an initial definition of formula. A formula is a conventional system for structuring cultural products. It can be distinguished from form which is an invented system of organization. Like the distinction between convention and invention, the distinction between formula and form can be best envisaged as a continuum between two poles; one pole is that of a completely conventional structure of conventions—an episode of the Lone Ranger or one of the Tarzan books comes close to this pole; the other end of the continuum is a completely original structure which orders inventions—*Finnegan's Wake* is perhaps the best example of this, though one might also cite such examples as Resnais' film *Last Year at Marienbad*, T. S. Eliot's poem "The Waste Land," or Beckett's play *Waiting for Godot*. All of these works not only manifest a high degree of invention in their elements but unique organizing principles. . . .

I would like to emphasize that the distinction between form and formula as I am using it here is a descriptive rather than a qualitative one. Though it is likely for a number of reasons that a work possessing more form than formula will be a greater work, we should avoid this easy judgment in our study of popular culture. In distinguishing form from formula we are trying to deal with the relationship between the work and its culture, and not with its artistic quality. Whether or not a different set of aesthetic criteria are necessary in the judgment of formal as opposed to formulaic works is an important and interesting question, but necessarily the subject of another series of reflections.

We can further differentiate the conception of formula by comparing it to genre and myth. Genre, in the sense of tragedy, comedy, romance, etc., seems to be based on a difference between basic attitudes or feelings about life. I find Northrop Frye's suggestion that the genres embody fundamental archetypal patterns reflecting stages of the human life cycle, a very fruitful idea here. In Frye's sense of the term genre and myth are universal patterns of action which manifest themselves in all human cultures. Following Frye, let me briefly suggest a formulation of this kind—genre can be defined as a structural pattern which embodies a universal life pattern or myth in the materials of language; formula, on the other hand is cultural; it represents the way in which a culture has embodied both mythical archetypes and its own preoccupations in narrative form.

An example will help clarify this distinction. The Western and the spy story can both be seen as embodiments of the archetypal pattern of the hero's quest which Frye discusses under the general heading of the mythos of romance. Or if we prefer psychoanalytic archetypes these formulas embody the oedipal myth in fairly explicit fashion, since they deal with the hero's conquest of a dangerous and powerful figure. However, though we can doubtless characterize both Western and spy stories in terms of these universal archetypes, they do not account for the basic and important differences in setting, characters, and action between the Western and the spy story. These differences are clearly cultural and they reflect the particular preoccupations and needs of the time in which they were created and the group which created them: the Western shows its nineteenth-century American origin while the spy story reflects the fact that it is largely a twentieth-century British creation. Of course, a formula articulated by one culture can be taken over by another. However, we will often find important differences in the formula as it moves from one culture or from one period to another. For example, the gunfighter

> "...formula...is cultural; it represents the way in which a culture has embodied both mythical archetypes and its own preoccupations in narrative form."

Western of the 1950's is importantly different from the cowboy romances of Owen Wister and Zane Grey, just as the American spy stories of Donald Hamilton differ from the British secret agent adventures of Eric Ambler and Graham Greene.

The cultural nature of formulas suggests two further points about them. First, while myths, because of their basic and univeral nature turn up in many different manifestations, formulas, because of their close connection to a particular culture and period of time, tend to have a much more limited repertory of plots, characters, and settings. For example, the pattern of action known generally as the Oedipus myth can be discerned in an enormous range of stories from *Oedipus Rex* to the latest Western. Indeed, the very difficulty with this myth as an analytical tool is that it is so universal that it hardly serves to differentiate one story from another. Formulas, however, are much more specific: Westerns must have a certain kind of setting, a particular cast of characters, and follow a limited number of lines of action. A Western that does not take place in the West, near the frontiers, at a point in history when social order and anarchy are in tension, and that does not involve some form of pursuit, is simply not a Western. A detective story that does not involve the solution of a mysterious crime is not a detective story. This greater specificity of plot, character, and setting reflects a more limited framework of interest, values, and tensions that relate to culture rather than to the generic nature of man.

The second point is a hypothesis about why formulas come into existence and enjoy such wide popular use. Why of all the infinite possible subjects for fictions do a few like the adventures of the detective, the secret agent, and the cowboy so dominate the field?

I suggest that formulas are important because they represent syntheses of several important cultural functions which, in modern cultures, have been taken over by the popular arts. Let me suggest just one or two examples of what I mean. In earlier more homogeneous cultures religious ritual performed the important function of articulating and reaffirming the primary cultural values. Today, with cultures composed of a multiplicity of differing religious groups, the synthesis of values and their reaffirmation has become an increasingly important function of the mass media and the popular arts. Thus, one important dimension of formula is social or cultural ritual. Homogeneous cultures also possessed a large repertory of games and songs which all members of the culture understood and could participate in both for a sense of group solidarity and for personal enjoyment and recreation. Today, the great spectator sports provide one way in which a mass audience can participate in games together. Artistic formulas also fulfill this function in that they constitute entertainments with rules known to everyone. Thus, a very wide audience can follow a Western, appreciate its fine points and vicariously participate in its pattern of suspense and resolution. Indeed one of the more interesting ways of defining a Western is as a game: a Western is a three-sided game played on a field where the middle line is the frontier and the two main areas of play are the settled town and the savage wilderness. The three sides are the good group of townspeople who stand for law and order, but are handicapped by lack of force; the villains who reject law and order and have force; and the hero who has ties with both sides. The object of the game is to get the hero to lend his force to the good group and to destroy the villain. Various rules determine how this can be done; for example, the hero cannot use force against the villain unless strongly provoked. Also like games, the formula always gets to its goal. Someone must win, and the story must be resolved.

This game dimension of formulas has two aspects. First, there is the patterned experience of excitement, suspense, and release which we associate with the functions of entertainment and recreation. Second, there is the aspect of play as ego-enhancement through the temporary resolution of inescapable frustrations and tensions through fantasy.... Thus, the game dimension of formula is a culture's way of simultaneously entertaining itself and of creating an acceptable pattern of temporary escape from the serious restrictions and limitations of human life. In formula stories, the detective always solves the crime, the hero always determines and carries out true justice, and the agent accomplishes his mission or at least preserves himself from the omnipresent threats of the enemy.

Finally, formula stories seem to be one way in which the individuals in a culture act out certain unconscious or repressed needs, or express in an overt and symbolic fashion certain latent motives which they must give expression to, but cannot face openly. This is the most difficult aspect of formula to pin down. Many would argue that one cannot meaningfully discuss latent contents or unconscious motives beyond the individual level or outside of the clinical context. Certainly it is easy to generate a great deal of pseudo-psychoanalytic theories about literary formulas and to make deep symbolic interpretations which it is clearly impossible to substantiate convincingly. However, though it may be difficult to develop a reliable method of analysis of this aspect of formulas, I am convinced that the Freudian insight that recurrent myths and stories embody a kind of collective dreaming process is essentially correct and has an important application on the cultural as well as the universal level, that is, that the idea of a collective dream applies to formula as well as to myth. But there is no doubt that we need to put much more thought into our approach to these additional dimensions of formula and about their relation to the basic dimension of a narrative construction.

My argument, then, is that formula stories like the detective story, the Western, the seduction novel, the biblical epic, and many others are structures of narrative conventions which carry out a variety of cultural functions in a unified way. We can best define these formulas as principles for the selection of certain plots, characters, and settings, which possess in addition to their basic narrative structure the dimensions of collective ritual, game and dream. To analyze these formulas we must first define them as narrative structures of a certain kind and then investigate how the additional dimensions of ritual, game and dream have been synthesized into the particular patterns of plot, character and setting which have become associated with the formula. Once we have understood the way in which particular formulas are structured, we will be able to compare them, and also to relate them to the cultures which use them. By these methods I feel that we will arrive at a new understanding of the phenomena of popular literature and new insights into the patterns of culture.

While popular culture has felt the transforming effects of the mass media, themes such as heroism, success, and adventure remain the cornerstones of our entertainment. Despite the anti-hero trend of the past forty years, most Americans continue to thrill to the exploits of strong, courageous, resourceful individuals who master their environment and heroically "save the day" during a time of crisis. The disaster films of the past few years are attractive largely because they reaffirm our faith in the heroic fiber of individuals who can surmount even the "towering infernos," earthquakes, and *Poseidons* of our lives.

Although materialism has been denounced from all quarters of American society, most of us still admire the "self-made man" who symbolizes the attainment of the American Dream. Much of the popularity of television game shows stems from the "get rich quick" mentality that continues to loom large in the American mind. And one need only casually observe the surfeit of action-packed books, movies, and television programs to realize that the element of adventure is firmly ingrained in contemporary mass entertainment.

Themes such as heroism and adventure are attractively encapsulated in that characteristically American genre—the Western. The use of conventions in popular culture is nowhere more glaring than in the Western. From Owen Wister's novel, *The Virginian* (1902), and primitive movies such as *The Great Train Robbery* (1903) through the Gunsmokes and Bonanzas of the fifties and sixties to the John Wayne and Clint Eastwood films of the 1970s, the Western has endured by relying on stereotypical characters, stock plots and routine dialogue, and an occasional spark of brilliance. Cultural climate and historical context, of course, must be taken into account in evaluating the significance of the Western to a particular time period. But much of the appeal of the Western is derived from its ability to exude a sense of tradition, a "continuity of values," to use John Cawelti's phrase.

Jack Nachbar brings to his study of the Western an acute analytical eye and an important sense of historical perspective. Nachbar is reminiscent of the excellent film critic Robert Warshow, who thoroughly enjoyed the subject of his scrutiny but always maintained a high level of intelligent and objective investigation.

Focus on the Western

Jack Nachbar

It's now a quarter of a century since Westerns took up my whole life. There were, first of all, in those pleasant postwar years in Minneapolis, endless summer hours of "playing cowboys." Whenever it rained we read or traded our Western comic books. I remember especially liking Monte Hale and "Rocky" Lane comics because their movies never came to our theater. Three times a week supper was bolted to catch "The Lone Ranger" on the radio. All these activities, of course, were just killing time, trivial warm-ups for Saturdays, when we would gather an hour before the box office opened in front of the Nokomis Theater, only three blocks away, in order to be the first neighborhood bunch to shove our twelve cents at the cashier and have our choice of seats to watch a Western serial, invariably featuring Zorro or the James Brothers, and to see a matinee Western, with Johnny Mack Brown or Sunset Carson, whom we disliked, or Charles Starrett, Whip Wilson, or Hopalong Cassidy, whom we liked, or, on very special days, Roy Rogers, who was always shown with ten extra cartoons and whom every one of us adored. Sometimes we would be lucky and the regular feature would also be a Western like *Colorado Territory* with Joel McCrea or *Fighting Man of the Plains* with Randolph Scott, which we would always sit through twice, making our time at the Saturday movies about eight hours, not a second of which ever occurred to us was useless or wasted or boring. So predictably ritualistic were the gunplay, fistfights and riding on the screen and so religious was my attendance that once, when I got to the theater a few minutes late and alone to see *Calamity Jane and Sam Bass*, I unthinkingly betrayed my Catholic school upbringing and genuflected by the side of my seat. I saw nothing incongruous about this until a couple of my pals told each other out loud what I'd done and began to giggle. None of this ever struck me as in any way "meaningful." It was simply what I liked to do and what everybody I knew liked to do. It was not until long into my adulthood that it occurred to me that it was because of the very ordinariness of my boyhood cowboymania that Westerns were significant, that the same Saturday ritual commonly experienced by millions of children and adults in thousands of theaters in all parts of the country for three generations hinted at something important about the collective mind of twentieth-century America.

Risking the charge of overstatement,

Westerns, especially Western movies, are thus far the single most important American story form of the twentieth century. Consider, for example, how Westerns have dominated and influenced the U.S. film industry. Edwin S. Porter's one-reel *The Great Train Robbery* (1903) was not only the first narrative Western, but was also the U.S.'s first big box-office hit. When the first nickelodeon opened in Pittsburgh in 1905, its initial attraction was *The Great Train Robbery*, and the successful combination of broad physical action and the suspense of the chase that characterized *The Great Train Robbery* has come to characterize most American movies since. "Broncho Billy" Anderson, the screen's first Western hero, was the first performer to have his name be the central attraction of the movies in which he appeared. From Anderson therefore came that bedrock of Hollywood production, the "star system." Hollywood itself owes its status as the American Mount Olympus largely to the needs of Western film production. Richard Dale Batman in "The Founding of the Motion Picture Industry" points out that the first film companies to migrate to California—Selig, Bison, Essanay, and Biograph—went, not as popularly believed, to escape prosecution for patent violations, but because California offered good shooting weather and because its scenery offered perfect locations in which to film Westerns. Finally, before television in the mid-1950's gunned down one of the staples of Hollywood security, the cheaply made "B" feature, Westerns were overwhelmingly the most prolific of Amer-

ican movies, most years comprising between 25 and 30 percent of American-made features. Garth Jowett points out that even during the 1950's, when the feature production of Westerns was dramatically dropping off, Westerns still comprised one-half of American-made historical films.

It is little wonder that, because they have been so popular, so almost unavoidable, Westerns came to define for all classes of white Americans their traditional ethics, values and sources of national pride. It was appropriate, for example, when John Wayne created an ideological defense of the Vietnam War in *The Green Berets* (1968) that Western imagery helped carry the political message. The Green Beret outpost is named Dodge City. Only a bit more surprising are bits of casually reported news that demonstrate that Westerns still hold the imagination of some of the world's elite. Henry Kissinger confessed to Italian reporter Oriana Fallaci in 1972 that the source of his charisma while negotiating the Vietnam settlement was his being analogous to American Western heroes riding into town to face the baddies alone. The image of the negotiations, Kissinger concluded, was "a Wild West tale, if you like." A similar response occurred in the summer of 1973 at the Nixon-Brezhnev summit. At one point in the meetings, as the Russian and American leaders flew over the Grand Canyon, Nixon asked Brezhnev if he had ever seen such country. NBC News showed Brezhnev answering that Yes, he had seen such scenes—in John Wayne Westerns. The two world leaders grinned at one another in what was obviously a pleasurably shared remembrance and then playfully began making the gestures of the stereotyped movie gunfight. . . .

The central image in Western movies is the European-American's three-centuries-long confrontation with the immense North American frontier. This relationship between the new land and the European, and the results of that relationship, were seminally defined by historian Frederick Jackson Turner in 1893 in a paper he presented before the American Historical Association entitled "The Significance of the Frontier in American History." American development, argued Turner, is explained by "an existence of an area of free land, its continuous recession, and the advance of American settlement Westward." Turner concluded that as the European continually confronted the land on an imaginary line between frontier and civilization, the experience tempered traditional European ideas of interdependent social classes and autocratic government toward American ideals of individualism, classlessness and democracy. The validity of the Turner thesis has been questioned by some historians who cite the realities of cold historical data. But its acceptance for several decades after its initial presentation as the definitive interpretation of American development demonstrates that Americans desired and believed it to be true. Turner did not define American history so much as he defined for European-Americans the central myth of their history. At the same time the Turner thesis was most universally accepted, Western movies attained their greatest popularity. The relationship is in part coincidental. . . . Nevertheless the relationship between the Turner thesis and Westerns is an intimate one. Turner announced in his paper that the primal American ex-

perience was over; as of 1890, census reports showed that the frontier was officially closed. Western movies, with their historical time customarily fixed between 1860 and 1890 and their location in the sparsely settled areas West of the Mississippi, are thus a perpetual re-enactment of the last moments of the white man's settlement of the wild American landscape. Just as Turner cited facts, dates and other historical data to define the essential American experience, nearly all of the thousands of Western films symbolically celebrate that experience by ritualistically recreating its essence over and over in dramas depicting in heroic terms the civilizing of the final American frontier. Besides their importance as an influence on the American film industry, Westerns have, even more crucially, affected American thought by perpetuating a psychic confidence and belief in the myth of American national identity, as defined by Frederick Jackson Turner, for more than half a century after Turner himself declared as finished forever the possibility of physically renewing that identity on new American frontiers. . . .

Westerns may indeed be American history, . . . but history provides Westerns with no more than their "mores and milieu." The "real" West is only the physical environment of Western movies; at their heart Westerns present the "idea" of the West, history not as it in fact occurred but how it is imagined to have occurred.

Frederick Jackson Turner presented his thesis in 1893 to the American Historical Association, which was meeting that year inside the grounds of the Columbian Exposition in Chicago. It is said that while Turner spoke before his fellow historians, Buffalo Bill Cody, whose Wild West Show had not been allowed on the Exposition grounds, was presenting his Indians, cowboys, horses and covered wagons to sellout crowds only a few blocks away. By an uncanny coincidence, Turner, the seminal articulator of the American myth, and Cody, the nineteenth century's foremost embodiment of that myth, were thus nearly within hailing distance of one another in a city on the great prairie which more than any other symbolized the center, the heart of America, at an Exposition that symbolized the beginnings of modern America, and neither saw the other, nor, probably, knew or cared that the other was there. As much as *Stagecoach* and *Shane* are archetypes of white America's taking of the land, that moment of two great men converging at such a culturally important crossroads but ignoring one another is an archetype for American cultural studies. The continuing pattern, until recently, has been one in which historians, social scientists and students of the humanities passed over the work, customs and entertainment of the masses as trivial and, for most part, insignificant. It was not until Turner's presentation of his thesis, for example, that most historians even began to acknowledge an element of cultural significance in the three-centuries-long settlement of the frontier. It is not surprising that the crudity of the first movies, including Westerns, made them intellectually suspect and therefore that, with the exception of a few sociologists who worried that movies were destroying the morals of American children, the educated left movies to the recent immigrants, the poor and the young.

Developments of the last twenty-five years lead to the hopeful conclusion that, at least in the study of the American frontier, heirs of the popular tradition of Buffalo Bill and the intellectual tradition of Turner may finally begin talking to one another. Scholars . . . are detailing the rich importance of such popular materials as Puritan Indian captivity narratives, dime novels and pulp magazines. On the other hand, sincere fans of Westerns, such as the Western Collectors of America, are apparently becoming more aware that Western films are historically significant artifacts and are meticulously gathering accurate data and compiling detailed filmographies about B-Western stars and Western subgenres such as "trio-Westerns" and Western serials. . . .

Westerns, by their sheer omnipresence were the center of my life and of the life of the entire nation twenty-five years ago. In many ways, through their continuing ability to reflect current social and political attitudes, they still are.

SECTION TWO: POPULAR CULTURE AND AMERICAN INSTITUTIONS

The development of sophisticated media of communication has transformed the entertainment of the masses into major social institutions. Motion pictures, television, popular music, and spectator sports are particularly important as both mirrors and molders of American life. They often show us who we are and what we stand for, they occasionally titillate our imaginations with "bigger-than-life" displays, they influence our behavior and our life-style patterns, and they almost always give us momentary respites from everyday routine.

Movies, sports, and popular music emerged as major components of American society in the early twentieth century. By the 1920s all three commanded huge audiences and wielded enormous power to affect people's lives. Movie stars such as Douglas Fairbanks and Rudolph Valentino symbolized the ultimate in romantic life-styles, and millions of young Americans looked to them as guides in matters of love and sex. The Babe Ruths and Lou Gehrigs of baseball and the titans of football, boxing, and other sports functioned as cherished heroes. Black musicians such as Louis Armstrong and his white counterparts, George Gershwin and Paul Whiteman, catered to the superficial exuberance of the twenties and helped the decade earn the tag "the jazz age."

Television came on the scene decades later, but it certainly had as much, if not more, of an impact on American life.

Less than 200,000 families had television sets in 1948, but the industry expanded rapidly during the next two years, and the 1950 census reported that five million families owned one of the new electronic boxes. By the early sixties some 90 percent of American homes enjoyed at least one television set. The new medium of popular culture, like movies, popular music, and sports before it, quickly assumed institutional stature in American society. Social commentator Max Lerner went so far as to label television a "psychological necessity" for many Americans.

The number and magnitude of the attacks on motion pictures and television suggests their importance in American life, if only as subjects of spirited debate. Movies were condemned soon after they

94

originated. Censorship of films began in 1907 in Chicago, and two years later New York established a board of censors that was particularly watchful for what it termed "gruesome or suggestive acts, undue violence, and acts which arouse rather than minimize passion."

The motion picture serial, with its concentration on action and violence, elicited strong condemnations from public leaders. The warden of a Pennsylvania penitentiary, in a statement supporting the movement to censor movie serials in 1915, declared, "I do not think, I know that criminals are made in the picture houses. I study the cases of those who come to me. I ask the men how they were started on the paths that brought them to me and they say through the motion picture."

The belief that movies have the power to drastically shape people's lives gained academic respectability in the 1930s. Books with such titles as *Movies and Conduct* (1933) and *Our Movie-Made Children* (1934) used the techniques of social science to illustrate the influence of film content on the thought and behavior of millions of Americans. With the advent of television, academic interest in motion pictures declined somewhat, but in recent years the medium has again become a major subject of scholarly examination. The articles on motion pictures in this anthology exemplify the fresh, incisive quality of contemporary film studies.

Much of the criticism leveled at television merely echoed the verbal assaults on motion pictures. The question of what effects violent subject matter had on the audience, especially the young viewers, seemed to be of paramount concern to those who attacked television. In the 1950s numerous groups of parents and academic investigating teams monitored television programs in an effort to document their objections to television content. A 1953 University of Illinois study of one week of television in New York City, for example, revealed that 3,421 acts and threats of bloodshed were recorded, an average of over six instances of violence per hour. When children's shows were isolated, the incidence of violence rose to a rate of thirty-six times per hour.

Congressional investigations of television and other forms of mass entertainment became commonplace in the fifties. So did the ever-increasing study of popular culture by psychologists and psychiatrists. The consensus of those trained in the workings of the mind was that violence in the media, especially on television, could encourage one to "act out" aggressive tendencies. The 1972 report of the Surgeon General's Scientific Committee on Television and Social Behavior reaffirmed this position, concluding that television violence did not have a cathartic effect but rather tended to arouse aggressive feelings. The report admitted, however, that the findings were not scientifically proven facts. And so the debate rages on, with the American Medical Association adding new fuel to the fires of controversy by claiming in 1977 that television violence constituted "an environmental health risk."

The idea of the "gatekeeper" in popular culture is instructive in the current furor over the content of mass entertainment. While it may be true that a select few actually determine what we see on television, for instance, the power of this elite is far from absolute. The audience is essentially the final gatekeeper and can change media content by refusing to watch certain programs or by organizing protest campaigns.

The National Parent-Teacher Association illustrated how effective this could be. The organization informed the networks that they were being placed on six-months' "probation" as of July 1, 1977. If the media moguls failed to make a "substantial response" to the public outcry against violence, the PTA threatened to boycott sponsors and local stations and initiate test cases in the courts that could bring about governmental action in regulating media content. Shortly after the PTA announced its plans, several major sponsors decided to disassociate themselves from programs that were deemed "too violent." It remains to be seen whether this signals a new trend in popular culture or simply a temporary expedient to pacify an irate public.

Scene from *Woodstock* (1969).

It is tempting to conclude from the recent emergence of "media protesters" that the movie and television industries have been grossly out of touch with the needs, desires, and values of the American people. Yet there appears to be ample evidence to suggest the opposite interpretation: Popular culture simply "gives the people what they want." Motion pictures, television, popular music, and sports can be viewed as "cultural indicators" or as "social barometers." This is especially evident during times of national crisis.

In both world wars, motion pictures responded enthusiastically to the needs of the country. Films helped to bolster morale, stimulate patriotism, and reaffirm the American view of the war. The government unashamedly utilized the propaganda value of movies and also called upon leading movie stars to spearhead war bond drives and to entertain the troops.

Popular music fulfilled similar functions, but it also had the advantage of being able to react very quickly to new developments and produce records that capitalized on prevailing concerns and issues. Songs such as "Remember Pearl Harbor" and "Goodbye Mama, I'm Off to Yokohama" came out very shortly after the Japanese attacked the United States on December 7, 1941. Popular musicians also "did their part" for the war effort. Perhaps the most striking example was swing band leader Glenn Miller,

who joined the army in 1942 and organized a "swinging" military band. After his death in a plane crash in 1945, he was hailed as both a great musician and a national hero.

The sports world contributed a great deal to maintaining social stability during wartime. The familiar ritualistic patterns of sporting events offered a sense of order and continuity in an otherwise insecure and tumultuous time. Many sports heroes also served in the military.

Baseball slugger Ted Williams spent three years in the armed services, a stint that robbed him of the playing time that could have increased his superstar batting statistics even more. While millions of Americans made much greater sacrifices, popular cultural celebrities such as Williams received the publicity and functioned as symbols of the selfless and noble war effort.

The relationship between television and war is colored by the fact that the medium really emerged during a time when traditional warfare had been dramatically altered by the dawn of the atomic age. The conflicts in Korea and Vietnam received substantial coverage by television, but the purpose of the reporting was not to aid the war effort. Since these were "undeclared" wars, television tended to adopt a kind of neutral stance, with newscasters and correspondents trying their best to respond to the desire of the American people for "the true story." Since the military often released statements, particularly in the case of Vietnam, which contradicted the "reality" presented on television, the medium actually contributed to public cynicism and frustration over the "limited wars."

The articles in this section offer a wide range of interpretations of movies, television, popular music, and sports as major social institutions. Despite the problems that beset the movie industry, films continue to reflect the ideas, attitudes, and preoccupations of Americans and have come to be regarded by many as an art form that may eventually serve as a bridge between popular and elite culture. Regardless of such epithets as "vast wasteland" and "boob tube," television functions as one of the most powerful tastemakers in American society. Popular music, long regarded as intellectually simplistic or as irritating noise, has demonstrated its capacity to articulate and initiate major social movements such as the counterculture. And the sports world, which is currently suffering from an obsession with the almighty dollar, remains an integral part of our culture, with popular spectacles such as the Super Bowl offering valuable insights into the nature and quality of American life.

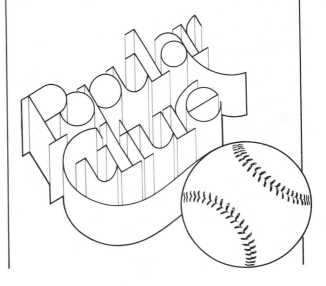

Hortense Powdermaker, the noted cultural anthropologist, called Hollywood "the dream factory," and perhaps she put her finger on the element of motion pictures that made them so important an aspect of American popular culture. Since the earliest days of movies, people have gone to the theater to evade, if only for a couple of hours, the realities of everyday living.

During the 1930s when America was in the stranglehold of the Depression, the Dream manifested itself in the pure escape musicals of Busby Berkeley, as his beautiful girls and handsome men danced across the lavish sets.

Robert Sklar argues that the Dream factory isn't too particular about which kind of fantasies it is selling. If one disaster picture like *Airport* was a hit at the box office, it indicated that Americans in the 1970s would continue to buy this momentary surcease from larger underlying anxieties, such as possible nuclear war. So give them the likes of *The Towering Inferno* or *The Poseidon Adventure*.

Did Hollywood in its Golden Age reveal the American popular imagination, indeed, our national soul, as Sklar suggests? Shall we even again see the day when millions of Americans of all ages, races, regions, classes, religions, and ethnic origins join in a national congregation before their idols, the Gables and Garbos, the Bogarts and Bergmans? Quoth the raven, "Nevermore."

Windows on a Made-Up World

Robert Sklar

Once upon a time, old movies just disappeared—the Hollywood studios didn't want them competing against their new pictures. Then a few turned into "classics," playing revival houses and cinema societies. More recently, in the last decade or so, they have become required viewing in a thousand college film courses, and fodder for almost as many reappraisals of directors and stars out of Hollywood's past. And now those survivors of the studio vaults, so we are told, have an even more significant future in store. They can serve as keys to unlock the meaning of the American cultural past, mirrors of the way we used to live, reflections of who we were, artifacts by which to decipher the mind and soul, not to say the social and economic order, of days gone by.

But wait a moment. Anyone who tries to use old movies as mirrors is liable, like Lewis Carroll's Alice, to slip right through the looking glass. We would be woefully mistaken if we accepted accounts of that topsy-turvy world as accurate pictures of past cultural and social reality. This is not to say movies don't have messages, for they are crammed with information, symbols, signals, and signs, overt and covert. There are compelling reasons to discover the most effective ways of understanding those messages. But first of all we need to find a more transparent metaphor than mirror. The main reflection the critic is likely to see in the silver screen is his own fantasy.

Let's take an example to see how the mirror metaphor works. Forty years ago, in 1936, economic depression still gripped the country. Millions remained unemployed; and Franklin Roosevelt's New Deal was on trial in his first reelection bid. What were the prominent films coming out of Hollywood? According to *Film Daily*'s ten best poll, the Academy Awards, and the New York Film Critics' choices, they included *The Great Ziegfeld, Mutiny on the Bounty, Mr. Deeds Goes to Town, Anthony Adverse, Dods-worth, San Francisco, The Story of Louis Pasteur*, and *A Tale of Two Cities*. Some memorable, some forgettable, but only one, Capra's *Mr. Deeds*, has anything to do with Depression America as a subject.

Historical costume pictures, some would say, by their very success, tell a great deal about the American mind of 1936—they show that movie audiences wanted escape from social reality and immersed them-selves in past adventures. But others would say it's the wrong list from the year's pictures. Take *Modern Times, Fury, My Man Godfrey, Libeled Lady, Winterset, The Pet-rified Forest, Wife Versus Secretary*. What a different version one would get of con-temporary American life through Holly-wood's eyes.

If the mirror metaphor is to survive, these objections suggest it's a miraculous mirror indeed, a composite of all the mirrors in the fun house: Here convex, here concave, here clear, here cloudy, adding up to hundreds of tiny mosaic images, one for every picture Hollywood made. No one is going to create order out of such bewildering variety with-out resorting to the subjective selectivity that is standard and necessary for film crit-icism—a selectivity far more problematic when the stated aim is to reveal cultural reality through old films.

Change the metaphor, however, and it's possible to make a big step in the right di-rection. Instead of calling movies mirrors, call them *windows*. Instead of a reflection, a vista—as many window images, to be sure, as mirror images, but with critical differ-ences between the two ways of seeing. When you are looking through a window, you're looking *at* something, and though each im-age may be separate, all share the same characteristic: They are products of an in-dustry. Movies may indeed reveal something to us about the cultural past—of course, they do—but first of all, they are windows on a created world, the world that Holly-wood made.

Hollywood's made-up world naturally depended on audience approval for sur-vival—it could never stray too far from the expectations, needs, hopes, and fantasies of its paying customers. Still, from a very early point in movie history, and through the hey-day of studio filmmaking between the world wars, the movie industry was considerably freer of box-office pressure than one is likely to guess. True, many studios experienced economic difficulties, and serious chal-lenges came from religious and political groups. But Hollywood's product was sur-prisingly well insulated by its distribution structure. Block booking, later outlawed by the Supreme Court, guaranteed playdates for a studio's films even before they were made; overseas bookings often provided a healthy margin of profit for films which barely broke even at home.

Under the circumstances, Hollywood had the opportunity to create a screenworld that reflected its own—its personal, corporate, and communal aspirations, ambitions, and feelings. As Harry Cohn used to boast, the feelings that mattered most in judging pic-tures were those of his own rear end. Iso-lated from political and financial centers (unlike British and European film indus-tries), held at arm's length by the local Southern California community, the movie colony developed an intensely insular view of itself. What went into movies mirrored the realities of life not in America but in Hollywood; and the two were so different in degree as to be different in kind.

Hollywood's realities were money, power, and good looks, in no necessary order. The top producers, directors, and stars, though never as wealthy as robber barons, ranked among the country's highest-paid salaried employees. Even the Depression hardly dented their four- and five-figure weekly pay checks. To get to the top, and stay there, was the prime motive of nearly everyone in the movie business. That good movies were made was proof that talent more often than not was a necessary ingredient of a money-making formula. But there were more atheists in foxholes than idealists in Hollywood.

Getting and keeping money and power dictated the way movies were made, and producers were at the center of the machinations that dominated the creative process. They possessed, as a rule, neither good looks nor talent, but they held both under long-term contracts. What gave the movie-making game its bite was the producers' constant effort to enhance their fortune and might by manipulating their gilt-edged chattels. This led, for example, to the practice of assigning multiple writers and rewriters to scripts, and to the farming out of contract stars to other producers as a disciplinary measure. It was more important that a writer be controlled than a good script accepted, for a star to be chastised than a part perfectly cast.

What we call Hollywood's Golden Age—from the introduction of sound to the advent of television—was, curiously, the period when producers dominated moviemaking most completely. Their eyes rarely strayed from the bottom line. And if movies in the early Depression years became remarkably sexier and more violent, it wasn't because American culture had grown more sexually free or more brutal, it was to increase shock and titillation values to counter declining attendance. Those historical costume pictures that won all the honors in 1936—biographies of Ziegfeld and Pasteur, dramatizations of Dickens's French Revolution and the Bounty mutiny—were made less to feed a putative audience longing for escapism than to gratify producers' desires for prestige and respectability.

Given these realities, it may sometimes seem a wonder that Hollywood created so many marvelous movies, indeed so much enduring art. One reason was that it had such a rich foundation of art and entertainment to build upon. The Western world's heritage of make-believe, of story and drama, of comedy and dance, was available for the camera to copy—and sometimes to enhance.

Those windows on the world that Hollywood made are also windows on novels, stories, and plays from many lands and languages, and on genres, myths, and formulas that were creaky with age when Hollywood was still a cow pasture.

It's hard to talk about old movies as mirrors of our cultural past without asking: Aren't old novels, old magazines, old vaudeville skits, old sermons, old textbooks, mirrors too? Hollywood didn't invent the cowboy or the private eye; *Stagecoach* and *Holiday* did not originate as screenplays, nor for that matter did *The Godfather* or *Barry Lyndon*. Which mirror is more clear, the original or Hollywood's? Does the Garbo *Camille* of 1936 reflect Depression-era America better than its 1915, 1917, 1921, and 1927 predecessors mirror the World War I years or the Roaring Twenties—or are they all reinventions of an imagined nineteenth-century Paris?

That noise you hear is the movie mirror shattering, strewing the premises with thousands of gleaming shards. Most of the movies' codes, symbols, conventions, and genres belong to a vast stream of entertainment forms across the centuries—clowns and lovers, murderers and heroes—we've always had them, and always will. Of course, images and emphases change in different eras and cultures; but why should movie messages be considered more important, vivid, accurate, or pervasive than others? Hardly anyone has asked that question—let alone indicated effective ways to answer it.

The assumption (before television) had generally been that movies surpassed all other media in mass appeal: Therefore movie images quantitatively were more important. Yet even that truism is open to doubt. Certainly movies had a larger total audience than, say, fiction, but there's a distinct possibility—though the data is notoriously incomplete—that the handful of top bestselling mass market novels had a readership equal in size to the big box-office movies. Maybe the books of Zane Grey or James M. Cain, rather than Tom Mix oaters or films noir, are where we should be looking for the clues to American cultural past.

No, those novels don't reflect any better. The mirror, like Humpty-Dumpty, can't be glued together somewhere else. And our windows on the movie world, having shown that movies reveal principally the industry that produced them and the expressive forms they adopted and developed, also make clear how far removed they are from cultural "reality." Movie windows enable us to cast eyes on many delights, as who would deny; but one favor they withhold is an accurate portrayal of American life.

Accurate portrayal? No need to belabor the point. Library shelves groan under new books proclaiming that blacks, women, and Indians almost never received their due as

---

"Movie windows enable us to cast eyes on many delights, . . . but one favor they withhold is an accurate portrayal of American life."

---

human beings from the movies. Race and sex stereotyping in movies is impossible to defend, but it's worth pointing out that the movies' worst offenses were more than matched by every other information and entertainment medium, including the schools, the churches, and the halls of Congress. Why always single out the movies, as if they somehow mattered more? You'd think people believed that movies had had a greater influence than any other source on how American culture defines and understands itself.

Many do believe it. This is why some have found comfort in imagining movies to be mirrors: The concept provided a convenient solution to two vexing mysteries. One was the basic nature of a motion picture's enormous influence, its uncanny power over our reason to convince us two-dimensional pictures were more real, more true to some fundamental essence, than quotidian life itself. The other was the nature of our shared experience in the dark, where millions of Americans of all ages, races, regions, classes, religions, and ethnic origins came together in silent congregation before flickering idols on the screen. The only answer commensurate to such unity and power was that movies mirrored the American popular imagination; indeed, the national soul.

Given what we've learned about the flaws in such a view, let's try a radically different solution. Paraphrasing Gertrude Stein, a screen is a screen is a you know what. What it reflects is light from a projector bulb, diffused by a moving reel of film.

It may seem to reduce drastically the movies' cultural significance, to assert they do not reveal reality, or the American past, or the popular mind. But that doesn't have to be the case at all. The essential step toward what I believe is a more accurate, useful, and penetrating approach is to regard movie messages not as descriptive statements *about* a culture, but as expressions *to* the people of a culture. Their significance comes from their power to create on screen a world unlike any experienced outside the theater, yet a world audiences could relate to as a separate realm, with styles and values one could sometimes import into one's own.

This power had many sources. On a psychological level, the power came from the impact of larger-than-life images, and the medium's capacity to move freely across space and time, giving audiences heightened senses of existence and imaginative will. On a sociological level, it came from the composition of the movie audience, rooted in early twentieth-century urban working class and immigrant peoples who found in movies a way of acquiring values and styles distinct from those of a repressive and disdainful "official" American culture. On an economic and political level, it came from the struggle for supremacy within the industry, won by a group of immigrant entrepreneurs who turned into mighty moguls, the producers who stamped their shrewdness and sentimentality indelibly into the pattern of motion picture content.

From this background, movies in America took their unique form. They drew on the legacy of literature and drama, of genre and convention, but reshaped that material in their own fashion. They created a remarkable comic style, aggressive and exaggerated, grossly disrespectful toward authority; and they received truth, vividly physical, and speaking directly to the feelings of working people and immigrants as no medium before had done. It flowered with Chaplin and the Keystone Kops, reached another peak in the early 1930s in the Marx Brothers and Mae West, and appears to thrive once again in Robert Altman's films, most notably in *Nashville*.

They proved an unmatched medium for showing the fantastic—ghosts, devils, zombies, and witches; prehistoric monsters; trips to the stars and into the bloodstream. The folktales, myths, and superstitions that modern industrial life was swiftly under-

mining by its rational processes found their salvation in the movies, and retain a vigorous life right through *The Exorcist* and *Jaws*.

Movies became our century's principal purveyor of notions about sex and romantic love—separately and together. From their very beginnings they overstepped the bounds of propriety in American culture, providing a glimpse of a woman's undraped ankle when it was the most daring one could imagine; and they've kept up the pace until now it appears that pornography has finally exhausted the imagination, if not the organs, of sex. Even on a more chaste visual level, where love and marriage were the object, the movies gave lessons no other curriculum provided.

And they presented stark and sometimes ugly images of violence, crime, war, and death. This had always been art's function, from the brutal candor of Homer's language to Shakespeare's corpse-littered stages. But in movies the realism of the screen image, and the vast visual resources at the medium's command, seemed always to arouse more controversy—and no more so when it was not the death and violence and wars of royalty they portrayed, but of common people, crooks and gangsters, the outcasts, rebels, and misfits of society.

Anarchic comedy, grotesque fantasy, risqué sex, crude violence—I don't mean to imply these constitute the sum of American movies, that Andy Hardy never lived (on the MGM lot); nor to suggest that movies were constantly at odds with the virtuous, correct, and accepted American values. Of course not. A great deal of "standard" American culture was glorified and reinforced in the movies. But I am impressed at how much the forbidden, the improper, the disapproved, made and still make up movie content, and how so many of the most memorable "classic" films fall into one or more of these categories.

This, I think, is the final nail in the crate in which we're packing away the movie mirror. Movies didn't make up their content out of whole cloth—moviemakers knew their audience had a taste for comedy, fantasy, sex, and violence, and even some knowledge of those facets of life—but they constantly invented and exaggerated. Movies didn't reflect life; they were bigger than life. They made certain real aspects of their culture more vivid and important at the expense of slighting other themes. They made a world, and to incalculable degrees audiences accepted the validity of that world and adopted many of its gestures and expressions, and some of its views of life. But it's still the movies' world, not our own. Movies are not about us, not mirrors reflecting us; they are about themselves. They reveal not life as it was lived, but their interpretation, their messages to us about it.

There remains unresolved one important question about art, what it is and does—and it's no contradiction to talk about art in the same breath as Hollywood. Ezra Pound called artists antennae of the race, forecasters of the future, seers who grappled with emerging elements of culture and consciousness. In the vast range of quality and content among American commercial movies, some speak to us prophetically (as do also some avant-garde and independent films)—not simply because we will adopt their views like next fall's fashions, but because they express something, perhaps unrecognized, perhaps unpopular, about who we are and where we are headed.

A principal task of film critics and historians is to identify those prophetic films—easier, of course, in hindsight, when we know a little better what we have become. As an example from recent years I nominate Robert Altman's 1970 film *Brewster McCloud*. At a time when profound changes in cultural mood were hardly becoming clear, the film expressed in tragicomic metaphor the fate of youth's desire to *soar*, in a rich and satiric texture of allusions to sexual and political issues of our time. When we go to old movies we see the past, the movies' past; and on some rare moments we may glimpse the culture's future.

The movies are clearly one of America's greatest popular art forms, but in Hollywood they're called "the industry" or "the movie business" and correctly so. From their earliest nickelodeon days, the movies have been closely associated with the mundane world of money. William Paul puts it more bluntly: Talk to even the most intellectual directors, screenwriters, or actors about the latest popular hit, from *Rocky* to *Star Wars*, and sooner or later the conversation will get around to budgets, grosses, publicity campaigns. Production costs and box-office receipts invariably determine the kinds of films that get into production.

Mr. Paul also casts a jaundiced eye at talk about the "new Hollywood" and the often-discussed rise of artistic freedom in American films. He sees the new Hollywood fully as crass and commercial as in the days of "King" Cohn and Louis B. Mayer. If anything, the new Hollywood operates under economic restrictions more stringent, with artistic options more limiting, than anything in the bad old Hollywood.

"The industry" is in a difficult competitive situation vis-à-vis television. Where moviegoing used to be a family habit, it's now a television habit—at home. Today, it is estimated that about 50 percent of moviegoers are between the ages of sixteen and twenty-four; at least two-thirds of them are under thirty. A 1974 study by the National Advertising Bureau shows that 41 percent of the American adult population never goes to the movies. In 1946, money spent on movies amounted to 20 percent of total expenditures by Americans for recreation; by 1972, movie revenue brought in only 2.6 percent of the recreation dollar.

Small wonder, then, that Hollywood's corporate minds are concerned, or that William Paul is worried that "the industry" is committing harakiri.

Hollywood's Harakiri
William Paul

The old Hollywood had one real advantage over the new: there was greater economic security. Whatever its fluctuations from year to year, an assured audience of regular moviegoers kept Hollywood financially happy for close to forty years. The number of moviegoers peaked just after the Second World War, and it's been pretty much downhill ever since, but even in the Fifties—the beginning of the old Hollywood's decline—there remained a large audience that went to the movies with faithful regularity and minimal selectivity. The regular moviegoers provided Hollywood with a guarantee of a steady income, and even though some pictures got reputations as flops, the net takes for most films throughout this period provided surprisingly little variety.

Nowadays, it's possible to net more than ever before: whereas any film in the Fifties that took in more than six million dollars would have been considered a "blockbuster," *Jaws* has already returned over $100 million to Universal. But as much as potential profits are up, so are potential losses: every year, a fair number of low-budget films—those costing $1–2 million or so to make—take in only a couple of hundred thousand at the box office. In today's market, a studio is likely to find itself in the red if it doesn't turn out one or two blockbusters a year.

An article on new Hollywood production in the *New York Times* last year had a "Wall Street movie analyst" explain the phenomenon of runaway hits like *The Sting* and *Jaws* by saying that Hollywood has "learned—relearned—how to make the mass audience film again." "Relearned . . . again" suggests that Hollywood had forgotten how to make this kind of film twice before but in point of fact Hollywood never really did know how. The audience for the old Hollywood film was easily as large as the audience for *The Towering Inferno*—probably larger—but production schedules in the past rarely tried to appeal to all segments of that audience at once, the way the contemporary blockbuster is supposed to do.

The old studio bosses didn't have the kind of demographic studies that studios now use, but most of them had begun their careers in theatrical exhibition, and as a result they knew something about varying audience tastes. Every studio tacitly recognized differences in audiences by diversifying its product into a variety of genres: westerns, women's weepies, war films, gangster films, musicals, etc. Certain genres might have achieved a greater popularity in some periods—musicals in the early Thirties, for example—but this hardly put an end to production in other genres. By contrast, Hollywood product of the Seventies has been characterized by the big-budget multicharacter action film to the exclusion of much else.

To a large degree the genre system of the old Hollywood can be regarded as a logical response, aesthetic issues aside, to economic necessity: it was a means of insuring a steady flow of new product to satisfy the demands of a large and varied audience. If audiences were going to attend movies with any kind of regularity—and the economic health of any business depends on steady patronage—then they would have to receive some assurance in advance of what they were going to see. Genres with well-defined conventions had two overlapping purposes: they acted as a means of streamlining production, and they provided a guarantee to audience expectations. In the bargain, they led to the only genuinely classical art form in the twentieth century. The most intriguing paradox of American movies is that while they were technologically the most advanced art of the century, aesthetically they were the most reactionary.

The move away from the classical cinema in the last fifteen years was as economically determined as was the classical cinema itself. The marked business changes that America's major film companies underwent after their period of relative stability led to equally dramatic changes in the form and substance of American films. The western, once considered the bread-and-butter product of the industry, has virtually disappeared; other genres have had their conventions weakened or otherwise used with an extreme degree of self-consciousness. A sociologically-minded critic might want to regard the sense of confusion and uncertainty that has become so characteristic of American films in the last decade as an appropriate response to Vietnam or Watergate, but I think it's more accurate to see in it a reflection of the financial instability of the movie business itself.

While the regular moviegoing audience has all but disappeared, a small number of films manage to score phenomenal box office successes every year. These successes have convinced the businessmen that the mass audience is still out there somewhere, and that maybe, if only the right formula could be found, its attendance could become more of an assured thing again. But no one is sure just what *the* formula is. Old

Hollywood relied on a varied but conventional product to attract its mass audience. New Hollywood looks to lists of "bankable" stars—trend-spotting, demographic studies—all of which adds up to a clear admission of failure, a loss of the intuitive certainty about its audience that old Hollywood had: what brought the audience into a theater, what it wanted when it got there, what would surprise it. . . .

Commercial Success

Hollywood has just had three of the most successful years in its entire history. Commercially, that is. From the aesthetic viewpoint, it wouldn't be too difficult to argue that this has been the worst period since the years before 1908 when D. W. Griffith began making his adventurous short films for the Biograph Company, films that now look both more experimental and more accomplished than any of the great cinematic breakthroughs that critics seem to find every couple of months in the current product. Whatever the actual relationship of commercial health to aesthetic health, this is far from being the first period of good money and bad films in the history of Hollywood. The real novelty in the current situation is Hollywood's decision to make major cutbacks in new film production. With all that money flowing in like waters bursting through a dam at floodtide, and old box-office records being overturned with imposing regularity, major production is already down . . . by five to twenty-five percent of last year's activity. If movies are bringing in more money than ever before, why cut back the number of movies being made?

In June of 1975, when *Jaws* opened, it had been booked by Universal into about 500 theaters for a minimal twelve-week run; during this entire time, Universal didn't open any other films. Another "movie analyst" quoted in the *Times* article on production explained this: "Universal feels it would be foolish to produce more pictures and com-

pete with themselves." That's a bit like having General Motors decide to produce only one kind of car. If you wanted to buy a new GM car, then you'd buy *the* car. There were in fact a number of small communities where, if you wanted to see a movie that summer, you had *Jaws* to choose from. . . .

However real the product shortage has become, complaints about it often amount to little more than grousing about a shortage of blockbusters. Theater owners know from experience that some films can fill their theaters every night of the week, and, in between wondering why Hollywood doesn't make more of them (as if Hollywood didn't want to), they'll frequently overlook any film that doesn't have superhit potential. Theaters themselves are wary of "small" films and are liable to cancel a booking in the middle of a run because it isn't performing as well as a fourth rerun of *Blazing Saddles* might. Producing companies can exert indirect pressure on theaters by threatening—anything more overt would be illegal—to book future product of the classier sort elsewhere if current run-of-the-mill items don't get a fair playoff. But they don't directly control theaters showing their films, which is why they have ample reason for being nervous about risking theatrical release on some "small" films. Nowadays movie companies lack the certainty they once had: that a film going into production would get released.

The seeds for the change that grew into the current situation were planted in 1948 when the Justice Department, following one of the largest antitrust actions in the nation's history, denied major movie-producing companies the right to own large chains of theaters. Considering the extraordinary growth in conglomerates in the intervening period, a number of them involving movie companies, the blow for free enterprise that this decision was supposed to strike was little more than aimless flyswatting. As far as I know, the U.S. to this day remains the only country in the world where direct corporate ties between major distributors and major theater chains are prohibited. In fact, the largest theater chain in Canada is still owned by Paramount Pictures.

Prior to the Justice Department action, the major movie companies owned only seventeen percent of the theaters in the country, but in terms of actual revenues that seventeen percent comprised a powerful block since it accounted for seventy percent of the first-run theaters in the ninety-two largest cities. Theater ownership had a clear enough economic advantage in providing the producing company with a guaranteed first-run playoff of its product, thus assuring a base minimal return on its investment. How much the filmmakers themselves had to benefit from a guaranteed playoff and how much the lack of that guarantee might in turn affect the kinds of movies produced has become clear only in the last decade, when movie companies frequently decided not to release "shaky" product at all, thereby eliminating the further losses that would be incurred by the costs of ad campaigns, prints, and booking arrangements. Lamont Johnson's *A Visit to a Chief's Son*, for example, was completed well over three years ago, but still has not played in theaters even though Johnson has attracted a critical following.

By describing the present evils I don't mean to minimize the real harms of the theater monopolies in the past. Independent theaters and small chains existed at the mercy of the big circuits. Non-theater-owning companies like Universal and Columbia, as well as independent producers, always found themselves in a defensive position to the major studios. It's significant that United Artists, a non-studio company that was organized solely to handle the films of independent producers, became one of the most commercially successful movie distributors in the Fifties after a not particularly illustrious past. But, whatever the improvements it created in these companies, the divorce decree came at the worst possible time for

the theater-owning studios since a new competitor in the form of television had just started making claims on Hollywood's audience.

Most of the aesthetic changes in films of the Fifties can be directly traced to the double economic impact of the divorce decree and the competition of television: the introduction of wider screens that decisively shifted the emphasis in film drama from face to space and further diminished the power of the spoken word; the rising budgets in A-pictures which made physically more ambitious productions possible; the scrapping of B-pictures until they returned as "TV movies" in the Sixties; and a marked relaxation of artist restraints through both a weakening of the censorship code and the rise of independent producing companies headed by such former slaves to the old system as actors and directors.

As important as these changes were, producing schedules pretty much continued along the same lines, with a variety of genres designed to appeal to the wide variety of audiences. "Movies are better than ever," Hollywood's defensive slogan of the Fifties, was really just a way of telling audiences they could still see pretty much the same old thing at the same old place but in somewhat bolder, more lavish packaging than television could provide.

If the product itself was still reasonably the same, the booking patterns in the early Fifties also continued mostly along the same lines as in the past, partly from inertia, partly from the security of transacting business with familiar faces. That most producing companies at the time persisted in regarding theaters as the chief means of exhibiting their product accounts in large part for the out-and-out panic that characterized Hollywood's initial reaction to television. Only Columbia Pictures, probably because it had owned no theaters, had the foresight to get into television production right away, setting up its Screen Gems TV production unit in 1950. It wasn't until 1955 that other Hollywood studios began to discover television, and discover it not just as a supplement to theatrical exhibition, but in many cases as a good competitor to it.

From its first tentative forays into television, Hollywood soon launched a full-fledged invasion that by the late Fifties was powerful enough to shift the seat of television production from New York to Hollywood. And in the process Hollywood as a center of theatrical film production was irrevocably changed. The takeover of Universal Pictures in the early Sixties by MCA, previously a talent agency and television film producer, can be regarded as emblematic of the changes in Hollywood throughout the Sixties. Agents as makers of deals and packagers of independent productions gradually found themselves in a greater position of power than they had ever enjoyed under the old studio system. And television, the erstwhile enemy that once bedeviled Hollywood's profits, was quickly being transformed into Hollywood's savior.

Hollywood vs. New York

When D. W. Griffith first brought his film company to California in 1910, he was in search of sunshine and more spacious locations. At the time New York was still the center of film production, offering its burgeoning theatrical competitor an almost bottomless pool of action talent, although talent in the long run wasn't enough to keep film companies in the East. For some of the earliest producers, the move to the West Coast was a financial necessity, a way of escaping the Patents Trust that had a stranglehold on film production in the East. But for Griffith and those who came after him, the chief advantages of California were climate and landscape.

If the reasons for the West Coast shift of movies in the Teens were mostly physical, then the reasons for television's shift in the Fifties might be described as metaphysical, signifying as it did a change in the very essence of television. Television began on the East Coast in the late Forties and remained dominated by the East Coast until the mid-Fifties. Almost from the beginning there was some film production for TV in Hollywood—situation comedies like *I Love Lucy* and *My Little Margie*, and half-hour dramatic series—but with the sole exception of Columbia Pictures the major studios had nothing to do with this production. For the most part, the really prestigious product of the period—live television drama and the big variety shows—originated in New York. By 1957, however, the most acclaimed directors of live TV drama—Penn, Mulligan, Ritt, Frankenheimer—were all in Hollywood working on their first feature films. TV by this time had changed from an essentially live medium to a canned one, with film completely dominating the programming. The decisive movement away from New York in the mid-Fifties was really dictated by a changing conception of television itself, a shift from TV as theater to TV as movies.

What finally attracted the Hollywood studios into television after their initial fright was the realization that TV was not a competitor but a potential buyer for their wares. If TV was a competitor to anything, it was to the movie theaters themselves, and the movie producing companies no longer had corporate ties to them. With large numbers of theaters being turned into supermarkets and bowling alleys at the time, it wasn't too hard to see TV as the wave of the future. If the Hollywood studios wanted to stay in business at all, then television was clearly going to be the best way.

Warner Brothers entered TV production in the 1954–1955 season and within a year became the chief supplier to ABC, producing six one-hour series that helped put ABC for the first time in a genuinely competitive position against CBS and NBC. By 1959, activity on the Warners lot in Burbank was dominated by TV production, a situation toward which other Hollywood studios were beginning to move. But actual production for TV was only one inning in this whole new ballgame. TV threw another major source of income Hollywood's way, and an income that required absolutely no expenditures in new film production. In the late Fifties the major movie companies flooded TV with classy pre-1949 feature films that gave both network-affiliated and independent stations a relatively inexpensive way of filling daytime and latenight broadcasts with first-class productions. By 1959, Screen Gems, the Columbia Pictures subsidiary set up to handle new series production and distribution of old movies to TV, was doing better business than the rest of the corporation. By the Sixties, most major movie companies had become dependent on TV for their own fiscal health.

In 1955, close to two-thirds of all American homes had TV sets. In 1959, the Federal Communications Commission estimated that an extraordinary 85.8 percent saturation of the potential TV market had been reached. Considering these numbers, the effects of TV on theatergoing probably should have peaked in the early Sixties. Yet, throughout the decade, theater audiences continued to grow smaller and smaller. The effects of TV as a novel source of entertainment might well have worn off by 1960, but an important change in programming that put recent theatrical releases into prime-time slots made TV more than a novelty. Television in effect came to mean movies, and

theaters now found themselves competing with TV for the same audience by means of the same product.

At the beginning of the era of the prime-time network movie, the only real advantage left to theaters was time—the five-or-so-year period between theatrical premiere and TV playoff that could act as incentive for getting people out of the house. But by the end of the Sixties even this advantage had been substantially weakened. Now the period of time between initial release and TV showing has become so short that the majority of films shown on TV are broadcast within one or two years of their theatrical release. When Paramount sold *Love Story* to ABC, the film had not finished all of its theatrical engagements in the Mid-West.

If Hollywood movie companies helped change the nature of television in the Fifties, TV itself produced far-reaching changes in theatrical features in the Sixties. There was, and still is, too much money to be made in theatrical release for the movie companies to turn their backs on theaters completely. But, by making recent theatrical features the cornerstone of its network programming, TV increased the pressure on the theatrical film to possess some unique quality that could make people want to pay for it rather than wait the year or so to see it for free.

Bigger Is Better

In the Fifties, Hollywood tried to lure audiences back into theaters by proving that bigger was better: the bigger screen sizes introduced by Cinerama in 1952 and CinemaScope in 1953, and, frequently, bigger budgets. There was also something of a relaxation of censorship—brought about partly by Otto Preminger's successful attacks against the ludicrously limiting regulations of the Production Code with *The Moon Is Blue* in 1953 and *The Man with the Golden Arm* in 1955—but for the most part the difference between theatrical and television production was more one of style than of content.

The lure of wider screens did have good effect for a couple of years, producing a temporary increase in audiences that is usually referred to as the "CinemaScope rebound." But audience size soon resumed its downward trend, and the big screens of the Fifties eventually gave way to the small screens in small theaters of the late Sixties. Recent theater design—both for new theaters and the duplexing of old theaters—seems aimed chiefly at recreating the TV experience, and probably with good reason. Whereas most Americans during the Fifties had been moviegoers before they were television viewers, by the late Sixties the reverse was true.

The movies themselves began to reflect television styles, an aesthetic development that probably serves as the best demonstration of Hollywood's economic dependence on TV. It wasn't only the generally soft-focus style and hazy color definition (reminiscent of a cathode ray tube) which characterized theatrical movies in the late Sixties. In addition, they were overrun by a plague of zoom shots, telephoto lenses, and rack focus shots. Since all three of these devices rely on an artificial distortion of space for their effects, they can be regarded as completely reversing the wide-screen aesthetic of the Fifties that held spatial integrity as the key to film expression, a style that the American cinema had been moving towards since the "deep focus" films of the late Thirties and early Forties, such as Orson Welles' *Citizen Kane*.

Throughout the late Sixties, Hollywood began to think more and more of theatrical and television production as activities that were similar, yet in some way opposed. The chief problem facing those involved in new film production is determining just what that opposition is—or, rather, what the differences are that will lure audiences into theaters. As the style of theatrical films increasingly imitated television technique throughout the Sixties, the most important

Waiting in the Cold for *The Exorcist*. This controversial film, regarded by some as obscene and profane and by others as brilliant, drew record crowds in 1974. UPI Photo

distinctions between the two developed in the area of content, especially as all censorship in feature films virtually came to an end. Explicit sex, violence, and language have become the primary means of distinguishing theatrical from television production, elements that in most films are easily exciseable, thereby guaranteeing a viable television career even after theatrical release. Indeed, it has become common practice in Hollywood to shoot two versions of a feature, providing "cover" scenes for material television might consider objectionable.

While the new freedom is preferable to the old restraints, Hollywood's inclination to differentiate between theatrical and television production has given rise to a peculiar kind of reverse censorship that in turn has placed new restraints on filmmakers. If a new project doesn't contain explicit sex, language, or violence it's likely to be dismissed as television fare and transformed from a feature film into a "movie of the week." One prominent screenwriter assures me that the only way to convince prospective buyers that a script is intended for theatrical rather than TV production is to end every third line of dialogue with "fucking asshole."

High Stakes

The seemingly greater freedom of contemporary theatrical films has led some critics to claim that this is, artistically, one of the best times in the history of American films. While it is true that the average director nowadays is less likely to be interfered with

than he might have been in the past, it's na-ive to imagine that the demise of the studio system has taken off all controls. Since the Sixties, the changing economics of theatri-cal distribution has put more pressure on Hollywood to find out just what makes the big hits big. Of the top one hundred films on *Variety*'s list of "All-Time Film Rental Champs," films that have netted $14 mil-lion or more, only *ten* were made before 1960. And of those ten, seven were made in the Fifties. Even taking inflation into ac-count—a 1958 dollar is worth fifty cents to-day—this still represents a major change.

As staggeringly impressive as these higher profits may be, they can't be taken as signs of true economic health, since they repre-sent hit status for an increasingly smaller number of films. Between ten and fifteen films have completely dominated the in-come of the major movie companies for practically every year in the last decade. In 1975, according to the charts in *Variety*, the top fifteen films had a combined domestic rental (monies returned to the producing companies from the U.S.-Canada market) of $395,750,000. The next 64 films (comprising films that earned at least $2 million, in most cases somewhat below the minimum nec-essary to break even) had a combined rental of only $293,299,000, which is over $100 million less than the top fifteen alone. In other words, of the top seventy-nine films (in 1975) a mere fifteen accounted for fifty-seven per cent of the total income.

The logic suggested by these kinds of fig-ures has led Hollywood more and more to focus its interest on the top grossers of the year. Investment in film production may have been something of a gamble in the past, and the risk might have increased substan-tially with the disappearance of a regular audience in the Fifties, but the stakes have also increased, almost a hundredfold in fact. With the kind of money that can now be made, it's only natural for Hollywood to look for ways of improving the odds. In the mid-Sixties, following the phenomenal suc-cesses of *Mary Poppins* (1964), *The Sound of Music* (1965), and *Doctor Zhivago* (1965), it was thought that the surest way of bettering the odds was by giving the public more of the same. All the major movie companies poured large amounts of their production money into reserved-seat spectaculars, mostly big-budget musical sons and daugh-ters of *The Sound of Music*. The net result of these new production schedules was that all the companies were in the red by the early Seventies. Paramount, which quickly saved itself by coming up with the first two super-blockbusters of the Seventies (*Love Story* and *The Godfather*) was one of the worst hit, with over $60 million invested in only four movies, three of them musicals (*Paint Your Wagon*, *On a Clear Day You Can See Forever*, *Darling Lili*, and *Catch-22*).

The economic disasters of 1969–70 chas-tened Hollywood to the extent that practi-cally all major companies put ceilings of three to four million on the budgets of new productions. But the putting-all-your-eggs-in-one-basket mentality that had contrib-uted to the disaster had taken hold, and Hollywood was still busy looking for *the* hit genre. The success of *Easy Rider* in 1969 led to a large number of low-budget, youth-oriented features, almost all of them bombs. But even in this bad period—easily the worst in Hollywood's history—there were always a couple of films a year that did extraordi-nary business, occasionally, as in the case of *The French Connection* (1971), taking the movie company responsible for it com-pletely by surprise. But if 20th Century-Fox hadn't expected much from *The French Connection* before it was released, its suc-cess (when combined with that of Warners' *Dirty Harry* of the same year) became the answer to Hollywood's prayers. Once again production was concentrated in one genre; over the next few years, cops and more cops shot violently across the screens.

Star Wars Star. C3PO, the robot from *Star Wars*, adds his footprints to those of other film celebrities in the cement in front of Hollywood's Chinese Theater.
UPI Photo

The spectacular commercial successes of isolated films like *The Godfather* made Hollywood forget its chastening of 1970. Hopes buoyed and budgets climbed—so much so that, by the time Francis Ford Coppola made his sequel to *The Godfather* in 1974, he was given almost twice as much money to play around with. With the successes of *Airport* (1970) and *The Poseidon Adventure* (1972), a hopelessly hooked junkie Hollywood, the same Hollywood that swore off big budgets forever, returned to them with the big-budget disaster cycle that the dismal flop *The Hindenburg* of [1976] largely brought to a close. But even with the failure of a number of these films, budgets continue to rise, and rise with a vengeance: several films currently in production have announced budgets of $15 to $20 million, astronomical figures even by the inflated standards of a few years ago. The search for *the* big-budget genre continues, with war films (*Apocalypse Now, A Bridge Too Far*) and science fiction

(*Star Wars, Close Encounters of the Third Kind*) the current favorites.

Is this any way to run a business? Well, as far as business goes, it might very well be. There is at least a kind of business logic behind it—although it's a logic that might prove faulty. After an upturn for two years, movie attendance dipped somewhat in 1976. The big budgeters just weren't bringing audiences into the theaters, although, as is always the case now, there was at least one superhit: the low-budget *One Flew Over the Cuckoo's Nest*. Still, one suspects that Hollywood looks at 1976 as a transition year between types of big-budget genres. After all, if you're turning out one product that can give you a return of $50 to $100 million and another that can give you $5 to $10 million, you obviously concentrate on the first, perhaps even to the exclusion of the second. Only this kind of thinking can help explain Paramount's supposed disappointment with the $8.2 million take of *Nashville* in the U.S. and Canada, even though the film cost only $2.2 million to produce, and, by Hollywood's usual accounting, broke even at $5.5 million. Considering the amount of money that *can* be made in this business, practically any film that takes in less than $10 million has got to be considered disappointing. . . .

High Cost of Movies

Of course, rising ticket prices coincided with a period of rising prices in general, and I have heard a number of Hollywood spokesmen defend the higher prices as a reflection of overall inflation. But the fact is that ticket-price inflation has been well ahead of general inflation in practically every year for the past twenty years. An article in *Variety* a few years ago showed that in the period from 1956 to 1972, when the overall U.S. cost of living index rose 53.9 percent, ticket prices jumped up an astounding 160 percent. Back in 1932, when Hollywood finally began to feel the effects of the Depression for real, first-run theaters in New York ran ads announcing a price roll-back from fifty cents to thirty-five cents. Such a simple working of supply and demand disappeared almost completely in the Sixties, when a decreasing demand peculiarly led to an increase in prices that in turn not only helped to decrease the demand further but transformed the very *nature* of the demand. Since ticket prices were advancing far ahead of general inflation, theatrical movies had to take on the connotation of "special event," even though very few of them were capable of living up to that new expectation.

There are some people in Hollywood who would like to reverse this trend. Gilbert Cates, a director who has worked entirely in intimate, distinctly non-"event" films (*I Never Sang for My Father*; *Summer Wishes, Winter Dreams*), has called for a general roll-back in first-run prices, at the very least on an experimental basis, in an attempt to develop a regular moviegoing audience again. An executive I've spoken to at one of the major film companies also expresses the feeling that the high prices have had a negative effect, especially hurting "small" films. But, he adds, most people in the business feel that you can always charge a lot of money for a movie people want to see and can't get them into a theater at any price for a movie they don't want to see. This either/or type of thinking automatically rules out any middle-range kind of movie, and its accuracy has been belied by the success of the dollar theaters. The dollar theaters have, in fact, proven to be the last bastion of the nondiscriminating filmgoer, people who go to *the* movies rather than to *a* movie. The dominant mood in Hollywood, however, clearly favors seeing how much money can be milked out of the current market; there's little concern for how this policy will affect future business.

One of the oddest side effects of the hit-flop mentality that Hollywood and the theaters have nurtured in their audiences is the phenomenon of repeat viewers. Regular moviegoers of the old Hollywood generally considered it sufficient to see a film once: once you knew the ending, what was the point of going again? Besides, even if there were would-be repeaters, few films stayed around long enough to give them a chance. Now, a lot of the high grosses are dependent for their income on repeat viewers, a fact that Universal exploited in its ads for *Jaws*. With the disappearance of conventional genres, these repeat viewers confirm what the genre system always implied, namely that audiences have an almost limitless capacity for familiar material. But they also prove that at the ridiculously advanced prices of first-run theaters an audience is less likely to take risks in what it chooses to see....

A number of filmmakers and critics I've talked to think the new big-budget bubble will finally burst just as the last one did in 1970, and the "small" film will then be able to stage its triumphant comeback. The less than spectacular grosses of *Lucky Lady*, *The Hindenburg*, and *Barry Lyndon* [in 1976] and of *King Kong* in [1977] seem to be preparing the way for the change. But will a few big-budget stinkers really reverse Hollywood's direction?

The economic disaster of 1970 produced a lot of official proclamations of change, but in the final analysis things didn't change very much. In the bleak early Seventies, following the indulgent extravagances of the Sixties, Hollywood pronounced the star system dead. It was the movie itself, so the thinking went, that brought audiences into the theater, not the stars. *Summer of '42* and *American Graffiti* were small films without stars that scored major successes in this period. But, even so, by 1974 the star system had returned with a vengeance, making it increasingly difficult to interest studios in projects for anyone but the "Golden Dozen," twelve stars that Hollywood considers "bankable," sure box-office draws. Because of this new situation, certain stars are able to demand $1 or $2 million per film.

For all the successes of a few small films, it was finally the more predictable successes of big films and big stars that carried Hollywood bookkeeping back into the black. *One Flew Over the Cuckoo's Nest* and *Rocky* are unlikely to change the trend. Now, more than ever before, Hollywood is on the lookout for the "pre-sold" project, the films that come with a formula for guaranteed success—films based on runaway bestsellers and hit plays, or films with stars who in themselves are so big that they generate their own publicity.

Big losses sustained over a couple of years could possibly force Hollywood to cut back its budgets again, but it is less likely that audiences would also cut back their expectations of theatrical films. Unless there is a radical change in the economic relationship of audience to artist, it seems to me unlikely that the "event" mentality that the movie companies and theaters have nurtured in their audiences will give ground. This radical change could come in the form of Home Box Office on cable television, or of video cassettes for home use—new forms of distribution that, if profitable enough, could take movies entirely out of the realm of theatrical exhibition, creating, in effect, a new medium. I lay no claims to clairvoyance. I hope the industry will find better ways of keeping theatrical exhibition alive. But it takes no great prophetic powers to see that the direction the film companies are moving in right now indicates disaster for the art form and, in the long run, I suspect, for the industry itself.

The Latin adage, "There is no disputing a person's taste," seems as apt to today's popular culture as it did to Nero's brand of mass entertainment. As William Paul pointed out in his essay on Hollywood's decline as an industry, the studios are always hoping for that one blockbuster that will make them look good with their conglomerate bosses. In 1977 it was *Star Wars*, expected to gross over $200 million for an ecstatic 20th Century-Fox.

Did the Great American Public make George Lucas, the producer-director of *Star Wars*, a very rich young man for his ingenious comic-book version of science fiction because 1977 was a vintage year for pure escapism? Take the previous all-time champions at the box office, *The Sound of Music*, *Godfather I* and *II*, and, of course, *Jaws*, and what thematically did they have in common, if anything?

Martin S. Dworkin, in his perceptive analysis of the success of *Jaws*, both as a book and as a movie, gives us a case study of how Peter Benchley's novel became one of the most successful popular culture "products" of all time. His portrait of Edgartown, Massachusetts, where *Jaws* was filmed, will not endear him to the citizens of that resort town, but Dworkin makes his point: The shark meant money for all concerned. And in a world where money is the symbol of success, *Jaws* met the test with awesome beauty.

Jaws in Retrospect
Martin S. Dworkin

J*aws* was well on its way as an authentic popular culture phenomenon before a foot of film was shot. It had developed a momentum of its own in the public consciousness, apart from the hype: the professionally pumped-up campaigns that fill the print, sound, and image media with overtly paid advertising and nominally free publicity, covertly purchased opinions and invented news. In fact, the book made noise in culture business circles even before it was in print, *Publishers Weekly* announcing in January 1974 that "Peter Benchley has written a major novel, one that has created virtually unprecedented prepublication excitement."

This was only one of many signals of anticipated commercial success; by late 1975 it would be clear that the signals had been grossly underestimated. The cloth edition had led the *New York Times* listings of bestsellers for forty-four weeks in 1974; Bantam's paperback was rounding 9.2 million copies in print in November 1975; and one report from overseas was that "with more than two million copies sold, and the November printing of 300,000 cleaned out in two days flat, *Jaws* is outpacing all other titles in the 26-year history of the British paperback house, Pan." Earnings of the film had far exceeded those of any other in film history (opening June 20, 1975 in 464 theaters in the United States and Canada, the film took in almost $37 million in its first seventeen days), with foreign distribution still to come.

In what had begun as a year of disappointing movie theater business, following the record volume of 1974 (*The Exorcist*, *The Sting*), the box-office score was counted with manifest glee by the general press and entertainment trade papers. A spin-off paperback "diary" of the making of the film, *The Jaws Log*, raced to completion in less than three weeks by Carl Gottlieb, who had adapted Peter Benchley's screenplay for production (and also, like Benchley, appeared in the film) and went through seven printings, totaling more than one million copies, in four months. There was an eruption of tie-in promotions and the inevitable unauthorized imitations: *Jaws* T-shirts, *Jaws* towels, *Jaws* drinking cups, *Jaws* great white shark pendants, as well as shark's-teeth gewgaws for wearing, for keyrings, and for charms to hang over the windshield.

Jokes about sequels started early. Parodies passed from wistful speculation to physical presence as if overnight, as T-shirts appeared emblazoned with the now ubiquitous, instantly recognizable ideograph of the rising shark's head and mouth. The figure of the huge shark's head menacing the tiny swimmer (from the jacket design by Alex Gotfryd, symbolizing the horrific opening incident of the book and the film) has become one of the most widely disseminated and quickly assimilated pictographs of our culture, a part of the popular speech-within-language that somehow evokes immediate comprehension, apparently without instruction or deliberate inculcation.

With no word of command, or even entreaty, from the image commissars of Hollywood, Madison Avenue, CBS's "Black Rock" building in New York, the Pentagon in Washington, or that plush hotel penthouse in Las Vegas where six men sit at a green baize table and run everybody's business, newspaper and magazine cartoonists by the score (in the United States and beyond) simultaneously took up the *Jaws* shark-and-swimmer motif. The oil and energy interests immediately had their innings too, taking the *Jaws* motif for their own symbol of menace. And in a kind of feeding frenzy of their own, editorial cartoonists extended the *Jaws* metaphor, with no end of possible applications in sight. In the United States the response to the book and the film, with their attendant publicity, whether contrived or fortuitous, aroused concern on behalf of sharks—predictably exercising marine biologists and the ecology minded, but also involving serious fishermen and others worried about far more dangerous monsters.

Even to complain about exaggerations in the book and the film is to pay tribute to their impact, pointing to the many levels of meaning and attitudes that are evoked. Deep analysis could probe the primordial, universal terror of sharks, those quintessential predators, supreme in an element in which humans are inevitably alien, dependent for moment-to-moment survival on some kind of contact with air and land. The book and the film could be precisely located on maps of popular culture, using reference points in such traditional genres of literature, drama, and cinema, whereby people frighten themselves for their own entertainment. Studies could be made of persistent attention to sea monsters in fiction generally and films in particular—with ineludible (and here quite pertinent) allusion to the classic, *Moby Dick*. There would, however, have to be sufficient recognition that there is something different this time, and something different about this time, in accounting for the extraordinary grasp of this shark story on the public consciousness.

For one thing, this shark, a great white, is supposed to be twenty-five-feet long, uncommonly large for this species, to be sure, but not impossible—and without science fiction interventions of nightmare fears of atomic radiation, naive or evil researchers fooling around with genetic mutations, or cracks in the earth's crust letting loose prehistoric leviathans from subterranean worlds. This gigantic shark, then, comes on as real, and it catches people in a situation of utmost relaxation and vulnerability: on vacation from the world of diurnal labors and dangers, nakedly or near nakedly playing in the benign sea off a summer resort. Of course, to talk this way is to be fully aware of the modes of story telling, the writing of the book, and the cinematography of the film. Their impact cannot be considered as a result only of the significance of sharks in our imaginings—although this is quite a factor.

Benchley's writing may be judged as good enough, especially in dealing with the shark, to be a major—even the principal—element in accounting for the response to the book. This observation is made with all due awareness of what some critics noted were slippages into slickness in dealing with people, and in establishing events as accidental in working out the plot. *Jaws* was written and rewritten, edited and promoted, to be a popular book, and it has become just that multiplied many times over. The film was even more deliberately manufactured to be merchandised to a mass audience, and the ringing of box-office cash registers, the loudest such sound in the history of the movies, effectively drowns out most questions and criticisms. A few persist, nevertheless, and not out of any propensity to cavil with success, or to put down popular sentiment as one measure—at the least—of what is important. Indeed, it is because *Jaws* was so popular that there is point in asking why it is not a better film.

With so much acceptance of the book going for it, why did the film have to seek a lower level of import? With a sufficiency of the sensational inherent in the presence and action of the shark, why was it necessary to exaggerate it to fill out the entire content of the film, downplaying or wholly eliminating aspects of the human dramas that make up the deeper story to be told? Not at issue here is any abstract principle of inflexible fidelity to the text of the book, something fundamentally impossible in considering transformations from the one medium into the other. Little is lost, for example, as far as the film is concerned, in deleting a subsidiary plot in

the book involving adultery, or in compressing several characters into a single person, or in adding certain incidents (such as a panic of a crowd of bathers at a beach). But a lot is lost in reducing to background and flattening the several personifications of the corruption of the resort town, that comes to only one expression in the stupid venality of the good citizens who fear the shark chiefly as a menace to summer business.

This theme of corruption had worked in the book as the context of crisis within which the characters were developed as persons. In the film the context is only perfunctorily presented, and the characters are made superficial, unambiguous figures of simplistic melodrama. The players of the chief roles—Roy Scheider as the police chief, Robert Shaw as the shark hunter, and Richard Dreyfuss as the young ichthyologist—go through their motions well enough, but there is little depth in the personae they must portray; they end up being hardly more than straight men to the shark. In the central instance of the police chief there is as little to understand in his early pusillanimous retreat before the collective irresponsibility of the townspeople, as there is in his final, dogged pursuit of the monster.

What director Steven Spielberg has brought in is a film that stresses action, involving special effects of great complexity, photographed with technical virtuosity, and slick, sophisticated editing for maximum suspense and climactic shock. Spielberg's film [brought] in tidal waves of money, favorable response from reviewers ranging from superlative wringing to stunned indulgence, and praise from film professionals. The film [was] a blockbuster, as they love to say in the trade; why worry about possibilities that it could have been better? Well, first and last of all because it could have, and ought to have, been; and, in between, because a better film would have been at least as successful.

An interesting and significant sidelight to the story of the making of *Jaws* is that something analogous to the drama of the town in the book—that was all but left out of the film—was going on in the actual town where it was made. "Amity," the summer resort in the novel, on the south, Atlantic Ocean shore of Long Island (apparently somewhere in the Hamptons), was confected out of Edgartown, the old, once and now again world-famous whaling port that is the shire town of the island of Martha's Vineyard, Massa-chusetts. The coming of *Jaws* to Edgartown exacerbated a lot of long-festering abrasions over questions of development and crowding on the island, which is roughly triangular in shape, some twenty miles long by nine miles at its widest point, with a population of some six thousand in winter (when it is actually rated as a "depressed area") that bloats to forty-thousand-plus in summer (when it boasts a lot of wealthy and/or famous people in residence). The summer people are considered as "off-islanders" to their dying days by the locals, even if they have come to their property on the Vineyard for three generations and pay the bulk of the taxes; they have no voting rights and little effective voice in basic geopolitical affairs. These affairs can be fought over in combats the more fierce, deeply involving personal, day to day business and social relationships, because of the face-to-face New England town meeting type of local democratic government that is the Vineyarders' pride—and their despair.

A large majority of the summer people and a good many of the natives are worried that development already has gone too far in spoiling the very resources of beaches, multicolored clay cliffs, woods, trails, fields, and ponds that are the island's chief attractions—as well as in overbuilding and overcrowding its small, in many ways uniquely characteristic, New England villages. In this view the island has had far too much notoriety.

A lot of people thought that selling the *Jaws* filmmakers on Edgartown and the island as the location site was just more exploitation, for it would bring in a lot of money (at a fair estimate, at least $1.5 million) to local businesses and to individuals who would appear in the film. The leading local entrepreneur and development booster—a man with interests in real estate, hotels, restaurants, a boatyard, a hamburger and ice cream stand, and nobody knows what else—made the big pitch to get the filmmakers to come—thereby further endearing himself as either resident benefactor or chief vandal, as one's viewpoint prescribed. It was considered some kind of justice that he appears in a nonspeaking role in the film, as one of the scabby selectmen who are worried more about losing holiday trade than they are about the deadly killer in their home waters. There was even some talk that he was being considered a "natural" for the part of the culpably dim-sighted mayor of "Amity"; but this talk was only a rumor, again either friendly or derisive, since the role had been actor Murray Hamilton's from the beginning.

As if in a crazy, fun-house mirror, the film *Jaws* was to Edgartown what the shark was to "Amity": an immense, pervasive presence, impelled by forces of elemental power, challenging the people to more than daily virtue and even heroism, defeating all but the very few by the sheer magnitude of the temptations proffered: easy money; instant, if barely momentary, glory on screen; hail-fellow fraternity with real Hollywood professionals, worldly and glamorous; summer season sex, with illusions of romance, with genuine movie stars. The whole thing was stretched out past the planned completion in the spring, through the height of the season, deranging everything until well after Labor Day, dividing the population—permanent or vacationing—in such ways as to aggravate old enmities and foster new ones.

Games of local politics were played to the hilt in raising obstructions, hugely expensive in time and money, to the filmmakers and their local allies—and in evading them. Money changed hands, above and under tables, leaving whiffs of chicanery and scandallike sulphurous fumes out of openings to Avernus. In one instance the actual chief of police was found to be on the filmmakers' payroll, against rules of probity and the articles of the town government. In the succeeding tumult over his deposition there were many cries of holier-than-thou hypocrisy and factional vengeance.

Many of the islanders made their own films and photographs of the moviemaking, and two years later were still putting on highly successful showings of a composite program, *Inside Jaws*. A slightly jaundiced account—with drawings and photographs—written by Edith Blake, of the staff of the island newspaper the *Vineyard Gazette*, was published locally by Lower Cape Publishing, and later picked up by Ballantine for mass paperback distribution, selling 225,000 copies in the first three weeks.

These actions could be taken as signs of a therapeutically cathartic attitude on the part of the islanders. But their own ambiguity in exploiting and celebrating what they want to disdain suggests that it will take more to get what *Jaws* meant to the island out of its system. Benchley had written to his publisher, in his first prospectus for the book, that he wanted the shark to signify "a peculiar natural disaster—not an earthquake or a flood . . . but a continuing, mysterious devastation that, as time goes on, loses its natural neutrality and begins to smack of evil." The book may not have risen all the way to this grand, Melvillian purpose; the film does not even try. And what the shark symbolizes everywhere, by now, may be only money, after all.

A few years ago a deranged sniper on top of a University of Texas tower was shooting down forty-six people with a high-powered rifle. A young nun on a lower floor chanced to look out a window and saw what was happening, and at first looked upon the spectacle with an almost passive, lackadaisical response before it occurred to her, "My God, this is not television; those are real people getting shot out there."

Do the media of popular culture inure us to real violence? Is the social cost of television programs like "Baretta" or "Starsky & Hutch" too high? During the past year both the American Medical Association and the National Congress of Parents and Teachers stated in unequivocal terms that they wanted a cleansing of violence from television. The A.M.A. gave $25,000 to Nicholas Johnson's vigorous National Citizens Committee for Broadcasting to partially support a study on TV violence. When the study's findings were reported, the A.M.A. then asked ten of TV's biggest advertisers to withdraw their commercials from the most violent programs.

Even though two firms, Eastman Kodak and General Motors, gave in to the various pressures and withdrew their advertising from violent shows, one shouldn't expect a quick, drastic change in television's prevailing patterns.

In their noted study of television's heavy viewer, Drs. Gerbner and Gross report that by mobilizing fear, the medium has replaced the church as the toughest means of social control. As they see it, the effects of TV's symbolic world extend much further than whether its violence leads viewers to aggressive acts.

The Scary World of TV's Heavy Viewer
George Gerbner
Larry Gross

Many critics worry about violence on television, most out of fear that it stimulates viewers to violent or aggressive acts. Our research, however, indicates that the consequences of experiencing TV's symbolic world of violence may be much more far-reaching.

We feel that television dramatically demonstrates the power of authority in our society, and the risks involved in breaking society's rules. Violence-filled programs show who gets away with what, and against whom. It teaches the role of victim, and the acceptance of violence as a social reality we must learn to live with—or flee from.

We have found that people who watch a lot of TV see the real world as more dangerous and frightening than those who watch very little. Heavy viewers are less trustful of their fellow citizens, and more fearful of the real world.

Since most TV "action-adventure" dramas occur in urban settings, the fear they inspire may contribute to the current flight of the middle class from our cities. The fear may also bring increasing demands for police protection, and election of law-and-order politicians.

Those who doubt TV's influence might consider the impact of the automobile on American society. When the automobile burst upon the dusty highways about the turn of the century, most Americans saw it as a horseless carriage, not as a prime mover of a new way of life. Similarly, those of us who grew up before television tend to think of it as just another medium in a series of 20th-century mass-communications systems, such as movies and radio. But television is not just another medium.

TV: The Universal Curriculum
If you were born before 1950, television came into your life after your formative years. Even if you are now a TV addict, it will be difficult for you to comprehend the transformations it has wrought. For example, imagine spending six hours a day at the local movie house when you were 12 years old. No parent would have permitted it. Yet, in our sample of children, nearly half the 12-year-olds watch an average of six or more hours of television per day. For many of them the habit continues into adulthood. On the basis of our surveys, we estimate that about one-third of all American adults watch an average of four or more hours of television per day.

Television is different from all other media. From cradle to grave it penetrates nearly every home in the land. Unlike newspapers and magazines, television does not require literacy. Unlike the movies, it runs continuously, and once purchased, costs almost nothing. Unlike radio, it can show as well as tell. Unlike the theater or movies, it does not require leaving your home. With virtually unlimited access, television both precedes literacy and, increasingly, preempts it.

Never before have such large and varied publics—from the nursery to the nursing

"With virtually unlimited access, television both precedes literacy and, increasingly, preempts it."

home, from ghetto tenement to penthouse—shared so much of the same cultural system of messages and images, and the assumptions embedded in them. Television offers a universal curriculum that everyone can learn.

Imagine a hermit who lives in a cave linked to the outside world by a television set that functioned only during prime time. His knowledge of the world would be built exclusively out of the images and facts he could glean from the fictional events, persons, objects and places that appear on TV. His expectations and judgments about the ways of the world would follow the conventions of TV programs, with their predictable plots and outcomes. His view of human nature would be shaped by the shallow psychology of TV characters.

TV Hermits
While none of us is solely dependent upon television for our view of the world, neither have many of us had the opportunity to observe the reality of police stations, courtrooms, corporate board rooms, or hospital operating rooms. Although critics complain about the stereotyped characters and plots of TV dramas, many viewers look on them as representative of the real world. Anyone who questions that assertion should read the 250,000 letters, most containing requests for medical advice, sent by viewers to "Marcus Welby, M.D." during the first five years of his practice on TV.

If adults can be so accepting of the reality of television, imagine its effect on children.

By the time the average American child reaches public school, he has already spent several years in an electronic nursery school. At the age of 10 the average youngster spends more hours a week in front of the TV screen than in the classroom. Given continuous exposure to the world of TV, it's not surprising that the children we tested seemed to be more strongly influenced by TV than were the adults.

At the other end of the life cycle, television becomes the steady and often the only companion of the elderly. As failing eyesight makes reading difficult, and getting around becomes a problem, the inhabitants at many nursing homes and retirement communities pass much of the day in the TV room, where the action of fictional drama helps make up for the inaction of their lives.

To learn what they and other Americans have been watching we have been studying the facts of life in the world of evening network television drama—what that world looks like, what happens in it, who lives in it, and who does what to whom in it. We have explored this world by analyzing the content of the situation comedies, dramatic series, and movies that appear in prime time, between 8 and 11 P.M.

The Simple World of TV Plots

Night after night, week after week, stock characters and dramatic patterns convey supposed truths about people, power and issues. About three-fourths of all leading characters on prime-time network TV are male, mostly single, middle- and upper-class white Americans in their 20s or 30s. Most of the women represent romantic or family interests. While only one out of every three male leads intends to or has ever been married, two out of every three female leads are either married, expected to marry, or involved in some romantic relationship.

Unlike the real world, where personalities are complex, motives unclear, and outcomes ambiguous, television presents a world of clarity and simplicity. In show after show, rewards and punishments follow quickly and logically. Crises are resolved, problems are solved, and justice, or at least authority, always triumphs. The central characters in these dramas are clearly defined: dedicated or corrupt; selfless or ambitious; efficient or ineffectual. To insure the widest acceptability (or greatest potential profitability) the plot lines follow the most commonly accepted notions of morality and justice, whether or not those notions bear much resemblance to reality.

In order to complete a story entertainingly in only an hour or even a half hour, conflicts on TV are usually personal and solved by action. Since violence is dramatic, and relatively simple to produce, much of the action tends to be violent. As a result, the stars of prime-time network TV have for years been cowboys, detectives, and others whose lives permit unrestrained action. Except in comic roles, one rarely sees a leading man burdened by real-life constraints, such as family, that inhibit freewheeling activity.

For the past four years, we have been conducting surveys to discover how people are affected by watching the world of television. We ask them questions about aspects of real life that are portrayed very differently on TV from the way they exist in the real world. We then compare the responses of light and heavy viewers, controlling for sex, education, and other factors.

Anyone trying to isolate the effects of television viewing has the problem of separating it from other cultural influences. In fact, it is difficult to find a sufficiently large sample of nonviewers for comparison. For this article we have compared the responses of light viewers, who watch an average of two hours or less per day, and heavy viewers, who watch an average of four or more hours per day. We also surveyed 300 teenagers in the 6th, 7th, and 8th grades, among whom the heavy viewers watched six hours or more per day.

The Heavy Viewer

Since the leading characters in American television programs are nearly always American, we asked our respondents: "About what percent of the world's population live in the United States?" The correct answer is six percent. The respondents were given a choice of three percent or nine percent, which obliged them either to underestimate or overestimate the correct percentage. Heavy viewers were 19 percent more likely to pick the higher figure than were the light viewers.

We next took up the subject of occupations, since the occupational census in prime time bears little resemblance to the real economy. Professional and managerial roles make up about twice as large a proportion of the labor force on TV as they do in the real world. To find out if this distortion had any effect on viewers, we asked: "About what percent of Americans who have jobs are either professionals or managers—like doctors, lawyers, teachers, proprietors, or other executives?" When forced to make a choice between either 10 or 30 percent (the correct figure is 20 percent), the heavy viewers were 36 percent more likely to overestimate.

One might argue, correctly, that heavy viewing of television tends to be associated with lower education and other socioeconomic factors that limit or distort one's knowledge about the real world. But when we controlled for such alternative sources of information as education and newspaper reading, we found that although they did have some influence, heavy television viewing still showed a significant effect. For example, while adult respondents who had some college education were less influenced by television than those who had never attended college, heavy viewers within both categories still showed the influence of television. We obtained similar results when we compared regular newspaper readers with occasional readers or nonreaders.

The only factor that seemed to have an independent effect on the responses was age. Regardless of newspaper reading, education, or even viewing habits, respondents under 30 consistently indicated by their responses that they were more influenced by TV than those over 30. This response difference seems especially noteworthy in that the under-30 group on the whole is better educated than its elders. But the under-30 group constitutes the first TV generation. Many of them grew up with it as teacher and babysitter, and have had lifelong exposure to its influence.

Diet of Violence

Anyone who watches evening network TV receives a heavy diet of violence. More than half of all characters on prime-time TV are involved in some violence, about one-tenth in killing. To control this mayhem, the forces of law and order dominate prime time. Among those TV males with identifiable occupations, about 20 percent are engaged in law enforcement. In the real world, the proportion runs less than one percent. Heavy viewers of television were 18 percent more likely than light viewers to overestimate the number of males employed in law enforcement, regardless of age, sex, education, or reading habits.

Violence on television leads viewers to perceive the real world as more dangerous than it really is, which must also influence the way people behave. When asked, "Can most people be trusted?" the heavy viewers were 35 percent more likely to check "Can't be too careful."

When we asked viewers to estimate their own chances of being involved in some type of violence during any given week, they provided further evidence that television can induce fear. The heavy viewers were 33 percent more likely than light viewers to pick such fearful estimates as 50–50 or one in 10, instead of a more plausible one in 100.

While television may not directly cause the results that have turned up in our studies, it certainly can confirm or encourage certain views of the world. The effect of TV should be measured not just in terms of immediate change in behavior, but also by the extent to which it cultivates certain views of life. The very repetitive and predictable nature of most TV drama programs helps to reinforce these notions.

Victims, like criminals, must learn their proper roles, and televised violence may perform the teaching function all too well [see "A Nation of Willing Victims," *Psychology Today*, April 1975]. Instead of worrying only about whether television violence causes individual displays of aggression in the real world, we should also be concerned about the way such symbolic violence influences our assumptions about social reality. Acceptance of violence and passivity in the face of injustice may be consequences of far greater social concern than occasional displays of individual aggression.

Throughout history, once a ruling class has established its rule, the primary function of its cultural media has been the legitimization and maintenance of its authority. Folk tales and other traditional dramatic stories have always reinforced established authority, teaching that when society's rules are broken retribution is visited upon the violators. The importance of the existing social order is always explicit in such stories.

We have found that violence on prime-time network TV cultivates exaggerated assumptions about the threat of danger in the real world. Fear is a universal emotion, and easy to exploit. The exaggerated sense of risk and insecurity may lead to increasing demands for protection, and to increasing pressure for the use of force by established authority. Instead of threatening the social order, television may have become our chief instrument of social control.

If the philosopher Plato were living today, he probably would be the leader of those who denounce television. He would probably say that the 2,000 or more hours spent each year in front of the tube by the average American are dooming us to lives spent before screens that are poor mirrors of reality. Like the people in the cave, might we not eventually lose our ability to differentiate between what is shadow and what is substance?

As noted in the previous article by Gerbner and Gross, heavy viewers of television are making many wrong assumptions about American society. Plato would say that the people in the cave had their legs and necks chained from childhood. If, in his words, they could "only see before them, being prevented by the chains from turning their heads," then, indeed, their curiosity to search for the truth behind the shadows on the wall would be immobilized. As a nation, have we become so hooked on the images of television that we have lost the freedom to step outside the cave?

Harry Waters, in a 1977 cover story for *Newsweek*, examined a controversy that has raged for several years, and that shows no immediate signs of abating: What is television doing to the children of America? If the first five years of life are inordinately important in the individual's intellectual growth, what are we to say when confronted with the statistic that children under five watch nearly twenty-four hours of TV each week? Perhaps Walt Whitman provided the answer when he wrote,

> *There was a child went forth every day,*
> *And the first object he look'd upon, that object he became.*
>
> *And that object became part of him for the day,*
> *Or for many years or stretching cycles of years.*

What TV Does to Kids
Harry F. Waters

His first polysyllabic utterance was "Bradybunch." He learned to spell Sugar Smacks before his own name. He has seen Monte Carlo, witnessed a cocaine bust in Harlem and already has full-color fantasies involving Farrah Fawcett-Majors. Recently, he tried to karate-chop his younger sister after she broke his Six Million Dollar Man bionic transport station. (She retaliated by bashing him with her Cher doll.)

His nursery-school teacher reports that he is passive, noncreative, unresponsive to instruction, bored during play periods and possessed of an almost nonexistent attention span—in short, very much like his classmates. Next fall, he will officially reach the age of reason and begin his formal education: His parents are beginning to discuss their apprehensions—when they are not too busy watching television.

The wonder of it all is that the worry about television has so belatedly moved anyone to action. After all, the suspicion that TV is turning children's minds to mush and their psyches toward mayhem is almost as old as the medium itself. But it is only in recent years—with the first TV generation already well into its 20s—that social scientists, child psychologists, pediatricians and educators have begun serious study of the impact of television on the young. "The American public has been preoccupied with governing our children's schooling," says Stanford University psychologist Alberta Siegel. "We have been astonishingly unconcerned about the medium that reaches into our homes. Yet we may expect television to alter our social arrangements just as profoundly as printing has done over the past five centuries."

The statistics are at least alarming. Educators like Dr. Benjamin Bloom, of the University of Chicago, maintain that by the time a child reaches the age of 5, he has undergone as much intellectual growth as will occur over the next thirteen years. According to A.C. Nielsen, children under 5 watch an average of 23.5 hours of TV a week. That may be less than the weekly video diet of adults (about 44 hours), but its effects are potentially enormous. Multiplied out over seventeen years, that rate of viewing means that by his high-school graduation today's typical teen-ager will have logged at least 15,000 hours before the small screen—more time than he will have spent on any other activity except sleep. And at present levels of advertising and mayhem, he will have been exposed to 350,000 commercials and vicariously participated in 18,000 murders.

The conclusion is inescapable: after parents, television has become perhaps the most potent influence on the beliefs, attitudes, values and behavior of those who are being raised in its all-pervasive glow. George Gerbner, dean of the University of Pennsyl-vania's Annenberg School of Communications, is almost understating it when he says: "Television has profoundly affected the way in which members of the human race learn to become human beings."

A Question of Air Pollution

Unquestionably, the plug-in picture window has transmitted some beneficial images. [The] showing of "Roots" [in January 1977], for example, may have done more to increase the understanding of American race relations than any event since the civil-rights activities of the '60s. And the fact that 130 million Americans could share that experience through the small screen points up the powerful—and potentially positive—influence the industry can have on its audience. In general, the children of TV enjoy a more sophisticated knowledge of a far larger world at a much younger age. They are likely to possess richer vocabularies, albeit with only a superficial comprehension of what the words mean. Research on the impact of "Sesame Street" has established measurable gains in the cognitive skills of pre-schoolers. And many benefits cannot be statistically calibrated. A New York pre-schooler tries to match deductive wits with Columbo; a Los Angeles black girl, who has never seen a ballet, decides she wants to be a ballerina after watching Margot Fonteyn perform on TV.

Nonetheless, the overwhelming body of evidence—drawn from more than 2,300 studies and reports—is decidedly negative. Most of the studies have dealt with the antisocial legacy of video violence. Michael Rothenberg, a child psychiatrist at the University of Washington, has reviewed 25 years of hard data on the subject—the 50 most comprehensive studies involving 10,000 children from every possible background. Most showed that viewing violence tends to produce aggressive behavior among the young. "The time is long past due for a major, organized cry of protest from the medical profession in relation to what, in political terms, is a national scandal," concludes Rothenberg.

An unexpected salvo was sounded ... when the normally cautious American Medical Association announced that it had asked ten major corporations to review their policies about sponsoring excessively gory shows. "TV violence is both a mental-health problem and an environmental issue," explained Dr. Richard E. Palmer, president of the AMA. "TV has been quick to raise questions of social responsibility with industries which pollute the air. In my opinion, television ... may be creating a more serious problem of air pollution." Reaction was immediate: General Motors, Sears Roebuck and the Joseph Schlitz Brewing Co. quickly announced they would look more closely into the content of the shows they sponsor.

The AMA action comes in the wake of a grass-roots campaign mobilized by the national Parent-Teacher Association. The 6.6 million-member PTA recently began a series of regional forums to arouse public indignation over TV carnage. If that crusade fails, the PTA is considering organizing station-license challenges and national boycotts of products advertised on offending programs.

"The Flickering Blue Parent"
In their defense, broadcasting officials maintain that the jury is still out on whether video violence is guilty of producing aggressive behavior. And they marshal their own studies to support that position. At the same time, the network schedulers say they are actively reducing the violence dosage. "People have said they want another direction and that's what we're going to give them," promises NBC-TV president Robert T. Howard. Finally, the broadcast industry insists that the responsibility for the impact of TV on children lies with parents rather than programmers. "Parents should pick and choose the shows their kids watch," says CBS vice president Gene Mater. "Should TV

be programed for the young through midnight? It's a real problem. TV is a mass medium and it must serve more than just children."

But the blight of televised mayhem is only part of TV's impact. Beyond lies a vast subliminal terrain that is only now being charted. The investigators are discovering that TV has affected its youthful addicts in a host of subtle ways, varying according to age and class. For deprived children, TV may, in some cases, provide more sustenance than their home—or street—life; for the more privileged, who enjoy other alternatives, it may not play such a dominating role.

Nonetheless, for the average kid TV has at the very least preempted the traditional development of childhood itself. The time kids spend sitting catatonic before the set has been exacted from such salutary pursuits as reading, outdoor play, even simple, contemplative solitude. TV prematurely jades, rendering passé the normal experiences of growing up. And few parents can cope with its tyrannical allure. Recently, Dr. Benjamin Spock brought his stepdaughter and granddaughter to New York for a tour of the Bronx Zoo and the Museum of Modern Art. But the man who has the prescription for everything from diaper rash to bed-wetting could not dislodge the kids from their hotel room. "I couldn't get them away from the goddamned TV set," recalls Spock. "It made me sick."

Small wonder that television has been called "the flickering blue parent." The after-school and early-evening hours used to be a time for "what-did-you-do-today" dialogue. Now, the electronic box does most of the talking. Dr. David Pearl of the National Institute of Mental Health suspects that the tube "has displaced many of the normal interactional processes between parents and children ... Those kinds of interactions are essential for maximum development." One veteran elementary-school teacher in suburban Washington, D.C., has noticed that her students have grown inordinately talkative when they arrive for class. "At home, they can't talk when the TV is on," she says. "It's as if they are starved for conversation."

The Passive Generation

Even more worrisome is what television has done to, rather than denied, the tube-weaned population. A series of studies has shown that addiction to TV stifles creative imagination. For example, a University of Southern California research team exposed 250 elementary students—who had been judged mentally gifted—to three weeks of intensive viewing. Tests conducted before and after the experiment found a marked drop in all forms of creative abilities except verbal skill. Some teachers are encountering children who cannot understand a simple story without visual illustrations. "TV has taken away the child's ability to form pictures in his mind," says child-development expert Dorothy Cohen at New York City's Bank Street College of Education.

Parenthetically, nursery-school teachers who have observed the pre-TV generation contend that juvenile play is far less imaginative and spontaneous than in the past. The vidkids' toys come with built-in fantasies while their playground games have been programed by last night's shows. "You don't see kids making their own toys out of crummy things like we used to," says University of Virginia psychology professor Stephen Worchel, who is the father of a 6-year-old. "You don't see them playing hopscotch, or making up their own games. Everything is suggested to them by television."

Too much TV too early also instills an attitude of spectatorship, a withdrawal from direct involvement in real-life experiences. "What television basically teaches children is passivity," says Stanford University researcher Paul Kaufman. "It creates the illusion of having been somewhere and done something and seen something, when in fact you've been sitting at home." New York Times writer Joyce Maynard, 23, a percep-

tive member of the first TV generation, concludes: "We grew up to be observers, not participants, to respond to action, not initiate it."

Conditioned to see all problems resolved in 30 or 60 minutes, the offspring of TV exhibit a low tolerance for the frustration of learning. Elementary-school educators complain that their charges are quickly turned off by any activity that promises less than instant gratification. "You introduce a new skill, and right away, if it looks hard, they dissolve into tears," laments Maryland first-grade teacher Eleanor Berman. "They want everything to be easy—like watching the tube." Even such acclaimed educational series as "Sesame Street," "The Electric Company" and "Zoom" have had some dubious effects. Because such shows sugar-coat their lessons with flashy showbiz techniques, they are forcing real-life instructors into the role of entertainers in order to hold their pupils' attention. "I can't turn my body into shapes or flashlights," sighs a Connecticut teacher. "Kids today are accustomed to learning through gimmicks."

For the majority of American children, television has become the principal socializing agent. It shapes their view of what the world is like and what roles they should play in it. As the University of Pennsylvania's Gerbner puts it: "The socialization of children has largely been transferred from the home and school to TV programmers who are unelected, unnamed and unknown, and who are not subject to collective—not to mention democratic—review."

What does TV's most impressionable constituency learn from prime-time entertainment? No one can really be sure, but psychologists like Robert Liebert of the State University of New York, one of the most respected observers of child behavior, don't hesitate to express sweeping indictments. "It teaches them that might makes right," Liebert says flatly. "The lesson of most TV series is that the rich, the powerful and the conniving are the most successful."

131

The View from the Victims

Whatever the truth of that, the tube clearly tends to reinforce sex-role stereotypes. In a Princeton, N.J., survey of sixteen programs and 216 commercials, it was found that men outnumbered women by three to one and that females were twice as likely to display incompetence. By and large, men were portrayed as dominant, authoritative and the sole source of their family's economic support. "These roles are biased and distorted, and don't reflect the way a woman thinks or feels," complains Liebert. "And it's just as bad for blacks."

It may, in fact, be even worse for blacks. Not only do black children watch more TV than whites, but they confront a far greater disparity between the illusions of videoland and the reality of their own lives. Two yet-to-be-published studies conducted by University of South Carolina psychology professor Robert Heckel found that young black viewers regard whites as more competent than blacks, and model their conduct accordingly. In one study, black children were shown a TV film of an interracial group of

peers choosing toys to play with—and then given the same toys to pick from themselves. All the blacks selected the toys chosen by whites in the film, even though many of those toys were smaller or inferior in quality. "On TV, the competent roles tend to go to whites, particularly young white males," explains Heckel. "Thus black children regard whites as someone to copy."

A classic example of such racial imprinting is Rowena Smith, a 14-year-old Los Angeles black who remains glued to the tube from school recess to 11 each night. Rowena's favorite TV characters are CBS's Phyllis and her teen-age daughter. "They get along so good," she sighs. "I wish me and Mom could talk that way." When Rowena was scolded for getting her clothes dirty, she indignantly told her mother that "the kid in the Tonka truck ad gets dirty all the time." Rowena's first awareness of the facts of non-TV life came after she ran away for two days—and her mother gave her a licking. "When TV shows runaways," she complains, "they don't show the part about being beaten." Nowadays, Rowena is more skeptical about television, but she has become increasingly concerned about her 8-year-old brother. He wistfully talks about getting seriously injured and then being reassembled like the Six Million Dollar Man. "This kid really *believes* TV," sighs his sister. "I gotta keep an eye on him 24 hours a day."

Indeed, call on the children themselves to testify and the message comes through clear—and sometimes poignantly. A vidkid sampler:

Fourteen-year-old, Los Angeles: "Television is perfect to tune out the rest of the world. But I don't relate with my family much because we're all too busy watching TV."

Eleven-year-old, Denver: "You see so much violence that it's meaningless. If I saw someone really get killed, it wouldn't be a big deal. I guess I'm turning into a hard rock."

Nine-year-old, San Francisco: "I'd rather watch TV than play outside because it's boring outside. They always have the same rides, like swings and things."

Fifteen-year-old, Lake Forest, Ill.: "Sometimes when I watch an exciting show, I don't blink my eyes once. When I close them after the show, they hurt hard."

Thirteen-year-old, Glastonbury, Conn.: "When I see a beautiful girl using a shampoo or a cosmetic on TV, I buy them because I'll look like her. I have a ton of cosmetics. I play around with them and save them for when I'm older."

Ten-year-old, New York: "It bugs me when someone is watching with me. If your friend is bored, you have to go out or make conversation. That's hard."

It would be preposterous, of course, to suggest that television alone is responsible for everything that is wrong with America's young. Permissiveness at home and in school, the dispersion of the extended family, confusion over moral standards and the erosion of traditional institutions—all help explain why Dick and Jane behave as they do. Moreover, any aspect of child psychology is enormously complex, especially when it comes to measuring cause and effect. There is always the temptation among social scientists to set up their experiments in a way guaranteed to reinforce their preconceptions. Nevertheless, there is one thrust of reliable study—into video violence—that has produced an unmistakable pattern of clear and present danger.

Paranoia and Propaganda

The debate over the link between TV violence and aggressive behavior in society has had a longer run than "Gunsmoke." Today, however, even the most chauvinist network apologists concede that some children, under certain conditions, will imitate antisocial acts that they witness on the tube. Indeed, a study of 100 juvenile offenders commissioned by ABC found that no fewer than 22 confessed to having copied criminal techniques from TV. Last year, a Los Angeles judge sentenced two teen-age boys to long jail terms after they held up a bank and kept 25 persons hostage for seven hours. In pronouncing the sentence, the judge noted disgustedly that the entire scheme had been patterned on an "Adam 12" episode the boys had seen two weeks earlier.

Convinced that they have proved their basic case, the behavioral sleuths on the violence beat have switched their focus to less obvious signs of psychic dysfunction. They are now uncovering evidence that the tide of TV carnage increases children's tolerance of violent behavior in others. In one experiment, several hundred fifth-graders were asked to act as baby-sitters for a group of younger kids—shown on a TV screen—who were supposedly playing in the next room. The baby-sitters were instructed to go to a nearby adult for assistance if their charges began fighting. Those who had been shown a violent TV film just before taking up their duties were far slower to call for help than those who had watched a pro-baseball telecast. "Television desensitizes children to violence in real life," observes University of Mississippi psychology professor Ronald Drabman, who helped conduct the study. "They tolerate violence in others because they have been conditioned to think of it as an everyday thing."

Beyond that, some researchers are finding that TV may be instilling paranoia in the young. Three years of tests directed by Gerbner, who is perhaps the nation's foremost authority on the subject, established that heavy TV watchers tend to exaggerate the danger of violence in their own lives—creating what Gerbner calls a "mean-world syndrome." As for children, he reports that "the pattern is exactly the same, only more so. The prevailing message of TV is to generate fear."

And now a word about the sponsors. The late Jack Benny once quipped that television is called a medium because nothing it serves up is ever well-done. But as the child watchers see it, the not-so-funny problem with TV commercials is precisely that they are so well put together. "Everybody has had the experience of seeing a 2-year-old playing on the floor, and when the commercial comes on, he stops and watches it," notes F. Earle Barcus, professor of communications at Boston University. "TV ads probably have more effect on children than any other form of programming."

Junk Food for Thought

The hottest battle involves the impact of child-directed commercials on their audience's eating habits. More than 70 percent of the ads on Saturday and Sunday-morning "kidvid" peddle sugar-coated cereals, candy and chewing gum. Laced with action-packed attention grabbers and pitched by an ingratiating adult authority figure, such messages hook children on poor eating habits long before they develop the mental defenses to resist. "This is the most massive educational program to eat junk food in history," charges Sid Wolinsky, an attorney for a San Francisco public-interest group. "We are creating a nation of sugar junkies."

Research has also established that as the kids grow older their attitudes toward commercials move from innocent acceptance to outrage about those ads that mislead and finally to a cynical recognition of what they perceive as adult hypocrisy. According to a study by Columbia University psychology professor Thomas Bever, TV ads may be "permanently distorting children's views of morality, society and business." From in-depth interviews with 48 youngsters between the ages of 5 and 12, Bever concluded that by the time they reach 12, many find it easier to decide that all commercials lie than to try to determine which are telling the truth. Concludes Bever: "They become ready to believe that, like advertising, business and other institutions are riddled with hypocrisy."

Who is to blame and what, if anything, can be done? The networks argue that the number of violent incidents portrayed on TV had declined by 24 percent since 1975. That figure has been challenged, but there is little question that the networks have instituted some reforms. The number of "action-adventure" series has decreased of late; and the weekend-morning kidvid scene is gradually being pacified. Such superhero cartoon characters as CBS's "Superman" and NBC's "Granite Man" have been replaced with gentler fare; ABC even canceled "Bugs Bunny" and "Road Runner" because of their zap-

and-whap antics.

There is also considerable merit to the broadcasters' argument that parents are to blame if they don't regulate their children's viewing habits. By the time the Family Hour experiment was struck down by the courts last year, it had already proved unworkable because so many parents refused to cooperate. Nielsen found that 10.5 million youngsters under the age of 12 were still hooked to the tube after 9 p.m., when the Family Hour ended. And a recent Roper study reported that only two-fifths of the parents polled enforced rules about what programs their children could watch. "Parents who take active charge of most of the elements of their children's upbringing allow a kind of anarchy to prevail where television viewing is concerned," says Elton Rule, president of ABC, Inc.

The Public Strikes Back

In rebuttal, public-interest groups point out that TV stations have been granted Federal licenses to ride the public airwaves—a highly lucrative privilege that carries a unique responsibility. In addition to the nationwide pressure being exerted by the AMA and the PTA, local organizations like the Lansing (Mich.) Committee for Children's Television have persuaded local stations to drop gory shows from their late-afternoon schedules. But no one has achieved more reform than the activist mothers of Action for Children's Television, based in Newtonville, Mass. ACT is largely credited with persuading the networks to reduce time for commercials on children's weekend shows from sixteen to nine and a half minutes an hour, to halt the huckstering of vitamins on kidvid and to end the practice of having the hosts deliver the pitches. ACT's ultimate—perhaps chimeric—goal is to rid kidvid of all advertising. "We feel it is wise to separate children from the marketplace until they are ready to deal with it," explains Peggy Charren, ACT's indefatigable president.

The shrewdest reform movement is aimed at persuading network programmers and advertisers that violence really doesn't sell. J. Walter Thompson, the nation's largest advertising agency, has begun advising its clients to stop purchasing spots on violent series—pointing out that a sampling of adult viewers revealed that 8 percent of the consumers surveyed had already boycotted products advertised on such shows, while 10 percent more were considering doing so. To help viewers identify the worst offenders among the shows, the National Citizens Committee for Broadcasting now disseminates rankings of the most violent series. At last body count, the bloodiest were ABC's "Starsky & Hutch" and "Baretta," NBC's "Baa Baa Black Sheep" and CBS's "Hawaii Five-O."

On the brighter side, some educators have begun harnessing commercial TV's power in positive ways. The movement first took hold a few years ago in Philadelphia's school system, which started tying reading assignments to TV offerings. For example, scripts for such docu-dramas as "The Missiles of October" and "Eleanor and Franklin" were distributed to more than 100,000 Philadelphia students in advance of the TV dates.

From Violence to Social Values

The children watched the shows while following along in the scripts, and discussed them in class the next day. The program has worked so well—some pupils' reading skills advanced by three years—that 3,500 other U.S. school systems are imitating it. [In February 1977] WBNS-TV, the CBS affiliate in Columbus, Ohio, [transmitted] four hours of classroom programing each day aimed at 96,000 local students whose schools [were] closed due to the natural-gas shortage.

Prime Time School TV, a nonprofit Chicago organization, has come up with the most innovative approach: PTST uses some of TV's most violent fare to implant positive social values. In one seven-week course, pupils were given questionnaires and told to fill them out while watching "Kojak," "Baretta" and the like. The questions, which were subsequently kicked around in class, dealt with everything from illegal search and seizure to forced confessions. "One boy told us that we had ruined television for him," reports PTST official Linda Kahn. "He couldn't watch a police show any more without counting the number of killings." Says PTST president William Singer: "We are saying that there are alternatives to merely railing against television, and this is just one of them."

Life Without the Tube

Unfortunately, the options available to the individual parent are considerably more limited. A few daring souls have simply pulled the plug. Charles Frye, a San Francisco nursery-school teacher and the father of five boys, decided he would not replace his set after it conked out in 1972. Frye's brood rebelled at first, but today none of them voices regret that theirs is a TV-less household. Fourteen-year-old Mark fills his afternoon hours with tap-dancing lessons, Sea Scout meetings and work in a gas station. Kirk, his 13-year-old brother, plays a lot of basketball and football and recently finished *Watership Down* and all four of the Tolkien hobbit books. "I know of no other children that age who have that range of interests," says their father.

Short of such a draconian measure, some parents are exercising a greater degree of home rule. Two years ago, the administrators of New York's Horace Mann nursery school became distressed over an upsurge of violence in their students' play. Deciding that television was to blame, they dispatched a letter to all parents urging them to curb their children's viewing. "After we sent the letter, we could see a change," recalls Horace Mann principal Eleanor Brussel. "The kids showed better concentration, better comprehension, an ability to think things through." Sheila Altschuler, one of the mothers who heeded the school's request, noticed that her 4-year-old son began making up his own playtime characters instead of imitating those on the tube. "If I didn't feel it was kind of freaky, I wouldn't own a set," allows Altschuler. "But these days it's a matter of conformity. Kids would be outcasts without TV."

Clearly, there is no single antidote for the vidkid virus. For the children of the global village, and their progeny to come, TV watching will continue to be their most shared—and shaping—experience. Virtually all the experts, however, agree on one palliative for parents of all socioeconomic levels. Instead of using TV as an electronic baby-sitter, parents must try to involve themselves directly in their youngsters' viewing. By watching along with the kids at least occasionally, they can help them evaluate what they see—pointing out the inflated claims of a commercial, perhaps, or criticizing a gratuitously violent scene. "Parents don't have to regard TV as a person who can't be interrupted," says behavioral scientist Charles Corder-Bolz. "If they view one show a night with their kids, and make just one or two comments about it, they can have more impact than the whole program."

Reduced to the essentials, the question for parents no longer is: "Do you know where your children are tonight?" The question has become: "What are they watching—and with whom?"

As *Newsweek* columnist Meg Greenfield so aptly pointed out, the last publishing event in the United States comparable to *Roots* happened 125 years ago with the printing of Harriet Beecher Stowe's *Uncle Tom's Cabin*. On the eve of its publication in 1851, Mrs. Stowe wrote to her editor saying she hoped she had presented slavery "in the most lifelike and graphic manner possible." Then, as if she could see 100 years ahead, she wrote: "There is no arguing with *pictures*, and everybody is impressed by them, whether they mean to be or not."

There are some remarkable similarities between *Uncle Tom's Cabin* and Alex Haley's *Roots*. Both are romantic and melodramatic; Lucy and Kunta Kinte alike are little more than stereotypes. And yet both works possess an emotional benefit that evoked the most extraordinary public response.

Uncle Tom's Cabin, as a popular culture phenomenon, brought wide-ranging social effects in the emotion-charged America a decade before the Civil War. One wonders what the effect of *Roots* might have been fifteen years ago when the civil rights movement was at its peak. Whatever its long-range influence may be, *Roots* has elicited new interest by whites in the history of their black countrymen. Several colleges reported that courses in Afro-American history were oversubscribed and that most of the new students were white. The series also had a great impact on ancestor hunting. The National Archives in Washington, D.C. has never known such activity, as thousands of Americans now want to know where they came from. Most important, perhaps, *Roots* may persuade the ruling princes of television that the Great American Public expects further programs of this magnitude.

Roots on TV:
It Touched Us All
Peter Schillaci

For a week that was reminiscent of television's Golden Age, 80 million of us watched the epic series *Roots*. Abandoning the tired company of Kojak and McCloud, *Police Story* and *Switch*, we cast our lot instead with Kunta Kinte, Fiddler, Kizzy, Bell, and Chicken George. We may, as a culture, never be the same.

There was an uncanny symmetry to the event. Information which author Alex Haley gleaned from the *griot* in his ancestral native Gambian village of Juffure was passed on to a total audience of 130 million by the new tribal medium of television. Both media communicate a strong sense of unity with a larger body present not physically but psychically. The channel was ABC, but the voice was that of Alex Haley, whose million-copy bestseller reached more people in one week of television than it may in 25 years of total readership.

Already, the forces of sociological and media research are churning away at the phenomenon of *Roots*, promising an analysis more extensive than that lavished on Orson Welles' Martian Invasion radio broadcast. The difference is that one brought fear, the other a kind of mystical understanding. *Roots* was, in my opinion, an intensely conciliatory experience. I say this as one who raged, trembled, wept, and laughed at each sequence along with millions of others. When these emotions subsided there was a deep sense of common humanity—as if a demon had been exorcised. And this feeling might be worth analyzing.

The black and white viewers alike shared the experience, each from their different backgrounds. For blacks, the tracing of *Roots* was a proud pilgrimage back to origins known conceptually but never experienced personally. Africa, far from being a primitive world inhabited by half-clad savages in perpetual conflict, emerged as a land of exotic, almost romantic charm. The continent of Haley's Gambian village was the center of a rich social and cultural life, of a people beautifully adapted to their environment, with a strict set of moral codes and educational standards which worked. Part of the cohesive force of this society was the fervent practice of Islam, with its dietary code, doctrine of universal brotherhood, and the unifying focus of monotheism. How many of us were surprised to find a black repelled by the idea that the captive who shared the slave ship chains was a "pagan"? Knowledge of this rich cultural background added to slavery a previously unknown dimension: cultural rape.

Slavery itself appeared in *Roots* as an evil more hideous than we imagined, but it was also portrayed as an evil which blacks overcame and survived, against all odds. For the first time, one could be proud of one's origin in slavery, the same way that survivors of the Nazi holocaust manifest an esprit which makes them living testimony to the indestructibility of the human spirit. Further-

more, to portray slavery as encountered by Kunta Kinte—an "African nigger," as the American-born blacks called him—put a different cast upon the "peculiar institution" of slavery. Through his proud eyes, the shuffling deference of the plantation slaves, their mixed blood, and their lack of rebellion were intolerable. So he served as a gadfly, a living witness to their origins, reminding many, like Fiddler, that "eating in the big house" did not constitute the good life. One of the most moving scenes in *Roots* is that in which the young Kunta, still in chains, sends back to his family a cricket, the bearer of his love and of his wonder that these domesticated blacks—carrying the distinctive features of Mandinka and Fulani, Wolof, Hausa, and Yuruba—are unable even to read their race in their own faces.

Ultimately, the inheritance passed along to blacks by *Roots* is the precious gift of identity; a history, a cultural heritage marred as most are by violence, oppression and failure, but enduring. People can hardly summon the courage to "get somewhere" without having a pretty good sense of who they are and where they've come from. No identity is complete without a past and a future emanating from a solid present. Somehow, *Roots* got it all together for the blacks.

What did it do for the "toubob"? Arguments about bringing white guilt out into the open are unconvincing. Although it may be true that almost every black is an ex-slave, not every white is an ex-slaveholder. Most of our ancestors arrived in the great waves of immigration *after* slavery had been dissolved in blood by the Civil War. But while each of us has our own roots to look into, *Roots* is our story as well, a part of our personal history. In some strange way, slavery bound white and black together. Every chain manacles the forger as well as the chained—even crime binds criminal and victim together in an enigmatic embrace.

The whites in *Roots* are tormented by their brown-skinned possessions, living re-

"Roots": A Television Phenomenon. The ending of the Civil War means the beginning of a new life of freedom for Tom and his wife Irene, played by Georg Stanford Brown and Lynne Moody, in the last of eight episodes of "Roots."

minders of a compromising mutual dependency. The range of white attitudes toward slaves is, even within the limited perspective of an ex-slave storyteller, almost as broad as the range of the more virtuous black characters. And although this range extends from psychotic cruelty to merely unacceptable bias, it is the ambivalence of the white masters, not their aggression, which emerges as the ultimate cruelty. Owners such as Massa Waller—the hard working, compassionate doctor—generated a trust which was inevitably betrayed. It was Missy Anne's careless affection which sent Kizzy (whom she had thoughtlessly taught to read and write) off to be sold. And Anne's reaction is an indignant cliché about "not trusting the niggers."

The historical sweep of *Roots* takes in the Civil War, but only as an event on the fringes

of the slave experience. For the descendants of Kunta Kinte, emancipation was just a word that meant legal dependency had been supplanted by economic dependency—a situation which defines the white/black scenario to this day. Both before and after the legal chains were broken, the limited perspective of the slaves—a cultivated ignorance of where they were and what "rules" they were to follow in this cruel game—emerges as a revelation in *Roots*. That Kunta Kinte should attempt four times to escape, should suffer beatings and mutilation, and still survive to pass along the seeds of his original freedom is only part of his victory. That this spark should be carried strong and clear through Kizzy to Chicken George and Tom, and on to Alex Haley, is a triumph which black and white alike cheered, and which we all relished as our own.

What about *Roots* as a media phenomenon? In Paddy Chayefsky's film *Network*, the hard-charging vice president played by Faye Dunaway experiences an orgasm while reciting to bed-partner Bill Holden the percentages and audience shares of her new programming ideas. By this criterion, there must have been a surge of ecstasy at ABC the week of January 30—especially by the executives who had the courage (audacity?) to schedule *Roots*. The difference, however, is that instead of the biting satire of a broken-down anchorman's success as a mad prophet, *Roots* starred a black African trying to hold onto his identity within the institution of slavery.

Comments on *Roots* missed the significance of the media phenomenon by playing the same numbers game as the networks—51.1% of all TV sets, 36,380,000 homes, 71% share of audience, totalling a history-making 130 million viewers, etc., etc. What few noted was the intelligently conceived and beautifully placed ad campaign which introduced *Roots*. Most so-called "educational" specials or series are dropped into the void like a penny in a pauper's cup—left to rattle around on their own. Furthermore, the decision to schedule eight *consecutive* broadcasts, three of them two hours long, gave audiences credit for an attention span greater than that of a three-year-old. The result was a unique *build* in audience, raising the numbers day-by-day through a phenomenal word-of-mouth groundswell. The daily scheduling switched actors and jumped time periods without losing audiences—and it reminded us of how tiresome the stock characters of weekly sitcoms have become.

All of this made *Roots* a unique media event, not merely because it was a serialized drama of some substance—*Upstairs, Downstairs* and *Rich Man, Poor Man* had, among others, led in this direction—but because it was so extraordinarily successful. To explain this aspect of *Roots*, one has to acknowledge the widespread interest in ethnicity among Americans. I myself, without knowing Haley's work, had completed in October a family tree which I had prepared with the help of my sister's research for our parents' fiftieth wedding anniversary. I anticipated that the family elders would love it, but wasn't prepared for the enthusiasm of people three generations younger, each of whom had to have his or her personal copy.

Roots caught this interest with perfect timing, sending millions scurrying into their familial past for grandparents great to the fifth and sixth power. They'll find help coming in Alex Haley's new book, *Search*, which will detail the techniques and lucky guesses that marked his 12-year, half-million-mile research into his own past. Most of us, how-

ever, will have a running start on Haley, who had only the name Kunta Kinte and a few words of Mandinka to go by. I plan to continue working on my own family tree, extending it back a few generations more by consulting my own *griot*, a great aunt and verbal historian of almost 90 years who lives in a small Sicilian town that once served as a thermal spa for the Carthaginians. This time I'll bring a tape recorder.

Where will the *Roots* phenomenon lead Americans, and especially educators, in the future? The most immediate consequence will be a growing academic respectability as credit courses on the book/television show are generated in some 250 colleges and universities. Black studies, recognized as one of the most spectacular flops among educational fads, will probably take on new life and new directions—no longer of interest to blacks alone. In this respect, *Roots* rejected the sanitized history of slavery—what *Time* called the "Magnolias and Banjos" of *Gone With the Wind*, and the recently popular "Blacks as Devastated Victims"—replacing it with a proud portrait of strong survivors who relied on an extended family of great cohesiveness and who, in their running war with slavery, used every weapon from flight to insurrection in wearing down the owners. Other American ethnics, disenchanted with the Melting Pot theory, are trying to restore their language, culture, and history in similar courses. For them, too, U.S. history must be rewritten, and new myths substituted for old. . . .

Roots may well have its greatest impact on America by encouraging more innovative television programming. Nobody sits around the tube discussing the latest episode of *Starsky & Hutch*, or the embarrassing subservience of somebody's "angels." But they did discuss *Roots*—in bars and living rooms, colleges and coffee shops. Pressure from a newly enticed audience (even Alex Haley plans to buy a TV set!) may determine the shape of things to come. Despite critics such as Richard Schickel who, in one of his more obtuse moments, called *Roots* a "middle-brow *Mandingo*," the series will set the style for new programming. If only on the level of fine black acting talents, the telecast was a revelation. Why has there been no serious black drama to engage the creativity of John Amos (lately of *Good Times*), Lou Gossett, Jr., Cicely Tyson, Leslie Uggams, and new-comer LeVar Burton—a mixed but impressive gallery of black talent?

Much more is certain to take place as a result of the *Roots* phenomenon. Thirty mayors declared January 24–30 "Roots Week," thereby opening up the way for what I hope is a more substantial event than the St. Patrick's and Columbus Day parades of the past. Meanwhile, we have been left with some striking scenes and images to reflect upon: the nightmare horror of the slave ship (which caused an 80% drop-out rate among extras recruited by the film producers in Savannah, Ga.); the crushing indignity of the slave auction; Kunta Kinte's first submission under the whip to his "toubob" name, Toby; Fiddler's quiet death after playing some songs *he* wanted to hear; and Chicken George leading the Kinte clan in prayer after reaching freedom in Tennessee. Those who entered the experience of these episodes need have no fear that *Roots* will exacerbate race relations. By inviting all to share the pain and humiliation of his family history, Alex Haley has allowed us to share in its unique success—survival as a proud, free people. The roots he discovered are our own.

In the early 1950s, when television was still evolving its general patterns of programming, the role of newscasting didn't differ much from radio, except in one significant respect. Network radio, in the years between 1939 and 1949, had some outstanding electronic journalists, such as Elmer Davis, H. V. Kaltenborn, William L. Shirer, and, of course, Edward R. Murrow. It would take network television several years before their news operation could begin to match radio's excellence.

With the exception of Ed Murrow, who, during the cult of incredibility ushered in by Senator Joseph McCarthy, stood as stalwart and lonely as Horatio at the bridge, most of the personalities in television news were (and still are) hardly more than pleasant, competent readers. Murrow and his close associate, Fred Friendly, became too outspoken and strident for their employer, CBS, and few in the uncritical audience of viewers seemed to mind very much when they were eased out of commercial television.

Local news on television stations has never reached even the undistinguished level of the networks. Most of the time it has been a bland product that hoped to attract enough commercials to justify its expense to the station. In recent years, even this has begun to change, and not particularly for the better.

Ron Powers, a Pulitzer Prize-winning television critic, is deeply troubled by the increasing trend of local TV news programs toward show business. He deplores this "eyewitless news," with the news teams in their matching sport coats and coiffures grinning their way through the news. Far too often, it is hardly more than a synthetic package that relies on the pseudo-events of PR gimmicks. There are, of course, a few television stations that compete favorably with other journalistic media in their communities, but the trend toward "cybernetic twinkies," as Powers calls them, continues, unfortunately, to thrive.

Eyewitless News
Ron Powers

If Edward R. Murrow, the patron saint of TV news, had visited the earth in 1976 and traversed the nation, searching for refinements of his legacy, here are some of the strange and wondrous sights he would have seen:

At WLS-TV, the ABC-owned station in Chicago, there is a filmed report by the station's weatherman, John Coleman. Coleman is standing beside a highway in North Dakota. He holds an envelope toward the camera. He says, "In this envelope are a group of never-before-published pictures of flying saucers. Are these the real thing? Or . . . are these hoaxes?"

At KNXT, the CBS-owned station in Los Angeles, a woman reporter in a wet suit plunges into a tank of water. She begins playing with a porpoise.

At KTTV, an independent in Los Angeles, co-anchormen Chuck Ashman and Charles

Rowe are reading the night's lead stories. The lead stories include an item about a bill in the Tennessee legislature advocating a state fossil and another item about a misprint in an *Azusa Herald* article announcing the appointment of Mary Hartman to the planning commission.

At WMAL-TV in Washington, a woman reporter named Betsy Ashton is announcing a story on Howard Hughes's will. She is sitting in a cemetery.

At KSTP-TV, the NBC affiliate in Minneapolis, comedienne Judy Carne pops into the newsroom during the newscast and begins playing with sportscaster Tom Rather's ears.

At WKYC-TV, the NBC-owned station in Cleveland, reporter Del Donahue is broadcasting from inside a lion's cage. The "angle" is that Donahue is "learning how" to train a lion. Donahue sits down upon the supine lion's haunches. The beast, which lacks a sense of humor, springs up and begins to maul Donahue, who suffers cuts requiring sixty stitches before he is pulled to safety by the real trainer. Journalism is served in the end, however: WKYC's camera records the entire grisly episode, and it is shown on several NBC stations—as a news event.

Murrow would have seen rank upon rank of "news teams" in matching blazers and coiffures like so many squadrons of "Up With People" teenagers, all displaying standardized wry smiles behind their *Star Trek* desks. He would have seen news teams that begin their evening's duty by strutting on camera en masse. (At WABC-TV in New York, they sort of *cascade* onto the set, like the Angelic Messengers taking the stage for Part Three of the *Dybbuk Variations*.)

He would have been puzzled by full-page newspaper ads that trumpet a news team as though it were a new kind of low-tar cigarette, and by TV "promo" commercials that show anchorman, weatherman, sportscaster, and principal reporters riding around in cowboy suits on white horses or passing inspection dressed up like doughboys. (Los Angeles's KABC has a reported yearly budget of $1.4 million for this type of advertising alone.)

What the hell, Murrow might understandably have asked, has all this got to do with *news*?

He would have seen news, all right—in a manner of speaking. (And the manner of speaking would have been strange, indeed, to Murrow's ears.) TV journalists in 1976 not only entertained, they covered "serious" news as well. That is, it would be safe to say that on any given nightly TV newscast in 1976, a viewer would be exposed to the three or four most important stories that graced the front pages of the local newspaper. Most large-city TV news departments offered, in addition, a noble-sounding catalog of secondary news services: consumer tips; perhaps a mini-documentary, in several parts, on some civic issue; an "action" reporter who was a conspicuous participant in the stories he or she covered; often a minority advocate, handsome/beautiful and vaguely ethnic, along the lines of Geraldo Rivera; an "ombudsman" reporter who checked out complaints made against local businesses and services.

But there was something missing at the core. Amidst all the self-consciousness, the preening, the ingratiation, and the bonhomie, Murrow might have noticed that in very few cases was there a sense of *mission* about the TV newscasts: a sense of continuity in the life of the city (or "market") covered; a palpable willingness to perform the vigorous, adversary, check-on-government, intervening role that American journalism has traditionally performed.

There was little feeling of real partnership with the viewer, only a vague, disguised condescension. There was little evidence that any of the coiffed anchorpersons or "action" reporters or "ombudsmen" on the

"...local stations create and choreograph entire news programs...toward the end of gratifying the audience's surface whims, not supplying its deeper informational needs..."

air shared—or were even aware of—the Jeffersonian notion that an informed public will make its own best decisions if given the facts on which to make them.

To put it in practical terms: Had Murrow stuck around a station, chosen at random, for six or eight weeks (or months or years), chances are that he would not have seen one piece of journalism, initiated by that station, that sent a corrupt politician to jail. Or that resulted in widespread and lasting structural reform. Or that forced a change in official policy. Or that prepared citizens for an impending crisis (inflation, municipal bankruptcy, educational funding, energy shortages, labor negotiations).

He would, however, have witnessed unending reports on sex fantasies. And runaway wives. And U.F.O.s. And celebrities. And fires. And murders. And accidents.

And, oh yes, the weather and sports. . . .

The blueprint [for audience building], which is painstakingly thorough, offers procedural recommendations for virtually every second of an electronic newscast. A few of its major requirements are instructive as they relate to the newscast just described:

A high story-count, with a short amount of time devoted to each story. . . .

The use of "visuals," preferably film footage, wherever possible. Film footage creates "audience interest" and adds "color and vitality" to a TV newscast. . . .

A "team atmosphere," emphasizing warmth and friendliness, among the principal news personalities.

Use of an "action" reporter to create a feel-

ing of the station's "involvement" with the community. . . .

Simple stories; an effort to stay away from the "stiff and formal" approach; a style that is easy to understand. . . .

When local stations create and choreograph entire news programs along guidelines supplied by researchers—toward the end of gratifying the audience's surface whims, not supplying its deeper informational needs—an insidious and corrosive hoax is being perpetrated on American viewers through a system that implicitly asks, and has been granted, their trust. The hoax is made more insidious by the fact that very few TV newswatchers are aware of what information is *left out* of a newscast to make room for the audience-building gimmicks and pleasant repartee.

When evidence of these and similar intrusions into the conventional journalistic process is presented to television audiences, two things could happen.

The audiences could, by their indifference, indicate an endorsement of developments—and, by extension, indicate that their traditional requirements of American journalism have broken down under the imperatives of technology, marketplace primacy, and the inertia of public will. It is the fundamental aim of journalism to arm the citizen intellectually to make decisions about how to protect his well-being. If the citizen feels powerless, in a mass society, to exercise personal control over his well-being in the first place, then perhaps cybernetic news, news as nonfiction entertainment, is the wave of the future, an index of human evolution. The diminishing percentage of active voters among those eligible to vote is a statistic that lends credence to this possibility.

Or, a minority of citizens within the mass audiences—a minority that perhaps may not be persuasive on the scale of TV's competitive viewing requirements, but which nonetheless contributes leadership to neighborhoods, communities, cities, and the nation—could assert its proprietorship over the airwaves and demand reform. This minority has already been effective, on a grass-roots level, in several areas of broadcast policy-making. The most notable example is the success of Action for Children's Television, a Boston-based group of concerned parents who have raised the standards of Saturday morning programs and commercials aimed at young children. Other citizen-interest groups with effective watchdog credentials include the communications office of the United Church of Christ and the Washington-based National Citizens Committee on Broadcasting, headed by the former citizens'-advocate commissioner of the F.C.C., Nicholas Johnson.

Such organizations are of interest not only as referral sources for those interested in protesting cybernetic news, but also as prototypes for new groups that could be formed specifically for that purpose. A monitoring project undertaken for the DuPont-Columbia survey by the American Association of University Women analyzed the news content of half-hour news programs of 262 local TV stations across the country. Similar monitoring projects could be organized within a given community by church, P.T.A., or other civic groups. The newscasts of a certain station could be taped and transcribed over a given period—a week or a month—and the content could then be collated and compared with that of local newspapers, or the group's own personal knowledge of

©1977 Bernie Lansky, *San Diego Union*

what is (and is not) happening within the community.

What would be done with the results of these surveys?

Representative Lionel Van Deerlin, a Democrat from California, is the chairman of the Communications Subcommittee of the House Interstate and Foreign Commerce Committee. This subcommittee could be called upon to open an investigation of the news-gathering and reportorial practices of local television stations.

The aim of any congressional hearings on TV news, of course, should not be to prescribe standards of broadcast journalism. Government-imposed standards would be as inimical to the integrity of TV news as are the standards suggested by consultants and researchers—more so, because they would carry the censoring force of a totalitarian stamp.

Short of suggesting standards, however, the hearings would offer for public scrutiny the organization and administration of television news. If there is widespread delegation of programming reponsibility by television stations, in direct opposition to the provisions of the Communications Act of 1934, the public has a right to know of it—and has the right also to challenge the licenses of such stations. If it is now to the economic advantage of station managers to *hire* news consultants, perhaps it should be a matter of even greater advantage *not* to hire them.

And what, after all, does constitute the ideal newscast?

There is no easy answer.

I have implied a somewhat narrow function of "news": to monitor and report on the conduct of public officials and others who exercise power over private citizens so as to assure openness, accountability, and the intelligent administration of community life. This sort of information, traditional wisdom has it, assures people of a clearer basis on which to make their political choices.

Obviously, this definition doesn't begin to encompass the full range of subjects and interests that "news" media in America have traditionally presented. Nor should it. Human beings are curious—randomly curious, illogically curious, morbidly curious. The news apparatus of a community should reflect that curiosity; in fact, it always has. Even *The New York Times* has its "People" column, and *The Wall Street Journal* is not above gossiping occasionally.

The determining factor in the quality of a news-gathering agency, then, is its shared relationship with the community it serves. American newspapers—the predominant news form until twenty-five years ago—have always been parochial in outlook: published, edited, and written by people who have made long-term commitments to the city they cover, and who have a stake in its viability. The modular, transient nature of American business in the last twenty years has cut into this parochial tradition, to be sure; newspaper people move from city to city, as do middle-management executives and professional engineers. And the enticing economics of collectivism, in the form of burgeoning wire-service use and the use of "packaged" features, has added to the standardization of the local daily.

Nevertheless, the American newspaper, augmented by the rise of the suburban press and even by "alternative" weeklies, remains a voice of its environment: idiosyncratic, steeped in the complex history of local controversies and concerns, familiar with the performances of civic leaders. Its faults are several and familiar. It is too ready to accept "official" versions of controversial events, slow to accept social change as its host community is slow to accept social change, boosterish, encrusted with its own anachronistic biases. But through it all, the daily paper often manages to be a benign intervener, a flawed but generally diligent chronicler of the ongoing processes of a city's life.

The television news department, by contrast, has seldom been able to escape a colonial persona. It is an emissary to a community, not an indigenous product of it. Its reference point is time present; unlike the newspapers, the TV station seldom bothers to accumulate a reference library in which reporters can check the past coverage of an ongoing issue. Often (as is the case with the fifteen network-owned stations and the dozens of other "group" stations) the TV news staff responds to the pure marketing priorities of absentee ownership. The on-air men and women look and sound less like their fellow citizens than like some idealized product of genetic breeding. This may be good for viewers' sexual fantasies; it does not do much for a station's credibility. The anchor-gods and -goddesses seldom remain long in a given "market"; they are nomads, their aspirations fixed on New York, whence their loyalty often derives.

Television stations reap enormous profits from the communities they are licensed to serve. Annual pretax profits of between $2 million and $10 million, depending on market size, are not uncommon. Average rates of return on sales are consistently between 30 and 50 percent—robust figures indeed in the American industrial community.

Until local television news ceases to exploit the entertainment bias that is conditioned by its host medium, and shares some of the profit with its "market" in the form of comprehensive, compact newscasts, it is engaging in a pollution of the worst sort: a pollution of ideas. Its options should be the same as those of any polluter: Clean up the mess or pay the consequences.

It seems like a hundred years ago when Newton Minow, then chairman of the Federal Communications Commission, called television "a vast wasteland." Actually, it was less than twenty. Minow's criticism undoubtedly caused some brief anxiety and petulant denials from the broadcasting and advertising industries, his twin targets. But Minow soon went back to his private law practice and the hubbub faded away.

Since then, although there have certainly been some thoughtful critiques of television's role in our contemporary society, most questions about the makeup and the level of entertainment have been shut off by referring to the audience measurements. There is one fallacy in that logic, however: Audience ratings are based entirely on the programs that are available. What about the wishes and interests of nonviewers of the programs being surveyed by the Nielsen ratings?

Ten years ago, Aubrey Singer, then head of feature and science programs of the BBC, questioned whether television was a window on our culture or merely a reflection in the glass. One of this country's most perceptive analysts of television is Robert Lewis Shayon, and in his book, *The Crowd-Catchers*, from which the following essay is excerpted, he deals directly with that question. Concerned about the passive nature of this all-encompassing medium, Shayon urges that the audience become more active by sending as well as receiving television messages—a subject further discussed in Section Four on the future.

Walt Whitman once wrote, "To have great poets, we must have great audiences, too." If he were alive in his native Brooklyn and part of our television-mediated society, Walt would probably write that line again and end it with an exclamation point.

Millennial Dreams and Nibblers— Will TV Be Different Tomorrow?

Robert Lewis Shayon

Television has been criticized on many grounds—mediocrity, overcommercialization, and a pervasive encouragement of acquisitive, materialistic values, which are often insensitively juxtaposed with profound human emotions generated by serious dramatic programs and solemn events in news broadcasts. Radio, when it was the dominant form of broadcast entertainment, was also criticized on the same grounds. The criticisms are important, and they have been and continue to be debated by those who criticize television and those who defend it; but television's impact on society can be confronted at the more serious level where passivity and participation collide in diagonal tension. The problem of television becomes at this level more than a matter of quality versus quantity of entertainment, or of good taste over bad, or of affronts to the intelligence of television viewers, or of achieving a proper balance between programs for the so-called highbrow viewers as well as for the alleged "lowbrows.". . .

The most important social questions about television's impact on the public concern the individual's relation to his culture and his feelings of strength, weakness, and insignificance as a member of that culture. To confront these questions you must look at the problem through the lens of the polarity, passivity versus participation. It is a commonplace of our technological, mass, urbanized society that the people who live in it often have doubts about their own identities. Who am I? How do people deal with my claims for individual recognition? These questions are not exclusively asked by existential authors or social philosophers. People generally have vague, unarticulated anxieties about the meaning of their lives. Television is responsible for a dramatic sharpening of these doubts and suspicions. Many thoughtful observers are convinced that the medium—by virtue of its omnipresence, glamour, and authority—has become the central hub around which revolves the wheel of all other aspects of our lives, political, economic, social, psychological. I believe that anyone who studies television seriously cannot escape the same conclusion. The reader may reject the notion as too grand and all-embracing, but at least he will understand how people who take the medium seriously regard it in its largest dimension as a force for good or evil. The reader will also have a useful vantage point from which to look ahead to television's future. He can focus his attention on things that really matter instead of fixing his gaze on developments that are of short-range interest but not significant in the long run in the struggle of passivity versus participation. . . .

The role of the media in recent years, particularly television, has come to be more and more influential in shaping people's identities, in strengthening or weakening their capacities for empathy, and in enhancing or restricting their right to action. We have felt the impact of television in all matters affecting social integration and consensus. Looking backward from television to radio and beyond radio to the earlier times before broadcasting, we note that people were not so passive in their consumption of entertainment and information. . . .

Television represents the apotheosis of the passivity principle.

We have obviously designated participation as the "good guy" and passivity as the "bad guy" in our metaphor of the tug of war between the two opposing forces. In our Western society, as distinguished from that of the oriental nations of the Far East, the cultural norms imposed upon us by tradition and heritage favor *doing* and *becoming* instead of just *being*. The United States is probably the most *action-oriented* of all the Western nations (the phrase represents an interesting juxtaposition of words, for the Orient . . . is the source of philosophies that are prejudiced in favor of passivity, and yet here we are using the word "oriented" as a partner of the word "action"). Action is important in our culture; it confers status upon those who take action. Television encourages passive watching and listening. Action taken as a result of a message received, however, is but a part of the problem of passivity versus participation. The fact that the receiver in a communication event does not originate any of the messages in that event is of much greater significance. We are receivers only, never senders, as television viewers; this is the fact that is all-important in considering television's power and impact upon our lives.

Television's relationship with its audiences may be usefully compared to the relationship between the players of Monopoly, the real estate game. Properties are acquired, lost, or exchanged in the game, and each player's objective is to win all of the properties or at least to acquire a major share of them. In the television-audience game, by contrast—which is a game of communication—symbols, perspectives, and viewpoints are the commodities exchanged, and the object of the game should be to distribute these symbolic experiences as widely as possible. The game is not being played properly if only a few of the players corner all the messages. The viewers, in the television-audience game, are passive receivers of messages rather than active participants in the shaping and the sending of the messages, and it is this characteristic of passivity on the part of the individual viewers in the audience that contributes to a weakening of their identities and their ability as individuals to empathize with other people. The consequences of such a weakening are dangerous to the health and ethical character of our society.

Television's images, in the opinion of many observers, have become more important to viewers than the realities that are represented by the images. Edmund Carpenter asserts, in *"Oh, What a Blow That Phantom Gave Me," an Anthropologist in the Electronic World*, that electricity has "angelized us." It has made us angels—"not angels in the Sunday school sense of being good or having wings, but spirit freed from flesh, capable of instant transportation anywhere." The telephone, radio, and television are forms of this angelizing electricity, Carpenter argues, and he goes on to say:

The moment we pick up a phone, we're nowhere in space, everywhere in spirit. Nixon on TV is everywhere at once. That is St. Augustine's definition of God; a Being whose center is everywhere, whose borders are nowhere.

This ability of television to free man's spirit from its physical confines, according to Carpenter, confers upon the medium its magical authority. It explains why viewers watch television for hours during one viewing experience. It illuminates the assertion that a person's prestige is enormously enhanced by even a single appearance on television. The television image has become more significant than the real world. The television image is all-sufficient.

The Listener, the BBC's weekly magazine about British television and radio, printed a short story some years ago about an African boy. I do not recall whether the story was true or fictitious, but I have never forgotten it because it illustrates vividly the authority of the television image. The boy, an orphan, had been adopted by the mayor of his village, who had not been kind to him. The mayor was the prestigious possessor of the only television set in the local area, and every evening he would permit the villagers to gather in the compound outside his home and watch the programs. The boy disappeared from the village one day and a search for him was begun. He was located in another village two hundred miles away, two weeks later. The authorities who found him asked him why he had run away from home. He explained that he was "going to the Cartwrights; they would look after him." "Bonanza," with its kindly image of the Cartwright family on their ranch, the Ponderosa, was a part of the boy's real world. He had no need to verify the reality of the television series by reference to the world around him. Television to him was the real world. . . .

Television's messages, then, tend to become more important than our own, except in the narrow corridors of our personal experience. Television's identity—including the identities of all the people that we see on television—consequently becomes more important than our own. Television's identities are perpetually strengthened; ours are weakened whenever we view the tube and expose our own limited experiences to the apparently omnipresent and omniscient presence and power of the medium. Events that happen all over the globe, the endless number of people that we meet in television's dramas, comedies, talk shows, commercials, etc., all packaged for us daily, tend to overwhelm us with their collective identity and to generate in us feelings of smallness, aloneness, and powerlessness. If we have passive feelings before we tune in television, we generally come away feeling even more passive after we tune out. It is impossible, we feel, for one viewer to have any personal impact on this mighty tide of experience that submerges our own identities in the ocean of television's magical, universal identity. . . .

A viewer's own claims have no way of being heard in television's onrushing mainstream of message communication. He is compelled by the sheer weight of numbers to recognize the claims of other people's identities, and this weakening of his own identity is accompanied by an undermining of his ability to empathize with other people. White, middle-class, Anglo-Americans almost exclusively organize and send television's entertainment, information, and commercial messages. They enjoy better education than other groups, have higher incomes, and generally possess a strong sense of status in our society. Blacks, Spanish-speaking Americans, American Indians, and other ethnic minority groups are not adequately represented among the organizers and senders of television's messages. Television's images—images of reality that are imbued with an aura of truthfulness, authority, and prestige—consequently present predominantly white, Anglo-American, middle-class life-styles. The majority of television viewers are also white, middle-class, and Anglo-American, and they use television's images to reinforce the vigor and value of those life-styles. They have little opportunity to empathize, via television, to identify with the life-styles of other ethnic groups. They are like the winners in the game of Monopoly: they hold all the images but their winnings are images only of themselves. If the essential condition of an ethically healthy society is that all perspectives and views be liberally exchanged,

"...this mighty tide of experience... submerges our own identities in the ocean of television's magical, universal identity."

it can readily be seen that television, by distributing only white, middle-class, Anglo-American images, contributes to a weakening of empathy in all of its viewers, to the social detriment of all.

Television's messages are also characterized by a severe lack of exchange of political perspectives to the right or left of the nation's political center. The right to send undisguised political messages, to seek recognition for obviously ideological positions is not equally distributed. Television indeed dramatizes only those life-styles and those political and social ideas that tend to perpetuate the inequalities in the sharing of perspectives. When people can only listen and not speak, when they feel that their claims to recognition in the marketplace of ideas are allowed no entry, then their frustration may deepen into apathy or explode into violence. In this view, we may see the black, urban riots of recent years, the student demonstrations for peace, and the violent behavior of political dissidents at judicial trials as desperate attempts by the blacks, students, and dissidents to capture the attention of America's white, middle-class majority, after television had failed to afford them reasonable opportunity to present their claims to recognition, to send messages rather than to merely receive them. (We note in passing that the word "riots" is really a white, middle-class label applied to the events involving the urban blacks; the blacks themselves no doubt viewed the same events as righteous struggles for recognition.) The young and the ethnic minorities are not the only groups that do not share equally in television's exchange of perspectives. We may add the elderly, the white American poor, the mentally ill, the physically handicapped, the imprisoned, and all other individuals whose life-styles depart from the cultural norms of our society, which tell us what is and what should be, what is right and what is not.

Broadcasters and advertisers generally decry all such criticisms of television as I have just described. A common theme in their replies to such criticisms is that the latter are made by "intellectuals," who have enjoyed control of the printed word for centuries, since the invention of the printing press. Intellectuals, say some broadcasters and advertisers, are now threatened by the greater reach and more significant impact of the electronic media, especially radio and television. They are the high priests of the old world in which perspectives were exchanged through literary symbols, and they do not relish being displaced by high priests of the new world that is dominated by the electronic forms of symbol exchange. The counter-critics who defend television often assert that intellectuals really despise the so-called common man and his pleasures. They are "elitists," it is charged, with special tastes, and they do not truly believe in democracy or have faith in the average man. Intellectuals should be discounted, say these broadcasters and advertisers. They have not the proper respect for the fruits of America's good life and for its high standard of living, which is the envy of nations less blessed with natural resources, technical aptitudes, and know-how. They are not worth listening to, because they are contemptuous of material abundance, of the gross national product, and of the ever-rising curve of progress.

"Nobody likes us," lament the broadcasters, "except the people." The people, in the broadcasters' view, are very happy with free television, and they verify this conclusion by the assertion that television audiences continue to grow in numbers and that the hours that audiences spend in viewing continue to increase. Ours is the best of all possible broadcasting systems, say the crowd-catchers; there is room for improvement, of course, there always is—but such changes as may be desirable and in the public interest can be brought about by trusting the broadcasters to make the changes themselves, in their own good time, without interference by consumer advocates or by government regulatory agencies. The replies that the broadcasters make to the "intellectual critics" of television may be true; it is also possible that they may be false. The critics maintain, however, that in judging the merits of the controversy, there are more risks to society in ignoring the criticisms than in taking them seriously and in trying to do something about them.

You who choose to take the criticisms seriously will want to know how the allegedly dangerous vision of the future . . . can be reversed. What needs to be done to enable television to contribute to a healthier consensus, to a wider sharing of perspectives, to stronger personal identities, and to greater capacities for empathy among viewers? The answer is that viewers must also have the experience of sending television messages as well as of receiving them. If it is true that people who organize and send messages over television have prestige, share more equally with one another their claims to recognition, and satisfy more adequately their need for action in the American tradition, then it would follow that the more people who organize and send messages over television, the healthier and more ethically acceptable our society would be.

Popular music is a collective term that describes a wide range of musical styles that appeal to various "taste cultures." It is perhaps the most diversified form of popular culture. Realizing this, record producers, in order to be successful, must find a way to cultivate a kind of "common appeal" in their offerings. Popular music is also probably the most unpredictable of the mass entertainment arts. Formulas are certainly utilized by popular musicians in the quest for a "hit record," but the guarantee of success by relying on familiar patterns is not as great as it is in other areas of popular culture.

R. Serge Denisoff, one of the most incisive sociologists of popular music, examined the recording industry in a book titled *Solid Gold* (1975). While the content of popular music constantly changes, according to Denisoff, the structure "remains the same with industry, promoters, cultural gatekeepers and distributors producing a 'continuous cycle of discontinuous hits.' " Like every other type of mass entertainment, popular music is a business and must be ever conscious of that overriding consideration: "Will it sell?" By demystifying a subject that has generated so much myth making, Denisoff brings a much needed clarity and perspective to our understanding of the nature of popular music.

What Is Popular Music? A Definition

R. Serge Denisoff

A frustrated moviegoer, after standing in line for nearly an hour, glared at the sign of the box-office window reading, "Popular Prices—Admission $5.00," cursed and muttered, "popular with who?" and left. The retort is fairly simple, of course: "popular with the management." So it is with music. Record sales, taste cultures and social differences in musical preferences suggest "popular" is a term which enjoys currency with those who produce and manufacture records and in the everyday vernacular, but is difficult to locate in the real world.

There are few definitions of popular music of any substance. Most writers join with Carl Belz in the sentiment that "any listener who wants rock [a segment of the pop of the sixties] defined specifically is probably unable to recognize it." There is, of course, truth in this statement, but experience alone does not help clarify the maze called "popular music." British writer Richard Mabey outlines popular music as being "concerned with participation, with parties, dances, outings, demonstrations and any other social gatherings where camaraderie and simple shared emotions are important. . . . The music, in fact, acts as a further binding force on the group, and the observed responses of the other members are a way of clarifying your own." Popular music, therefore, is a cultural artifact shared by specific subgroups in the social order. Music may represent the taste of a subculture within a culture or that of a "contraculture" which exists in opposition to the dominant one. Jazz is a subcultural genre, while so-called punk-rock is perhaps indicative of Theodore Roszak's "counterculture." Mabey distinguishes pop music as a "subdivision" of popular, in that it operates as a mode of communication to "satisfy teenage tastes." This refinement has considerable merit as popular music does contain a number of sounds and styles which do not appeal solely to teenagers. Still, persons under the demographic cut-off point of 24 comprise the major constituency for popular music. So popular music is not "pop" but many parts of "pop" are found in popular music. . . .

The producer of popular music must address a generally amorphous, fluid, heterogeneous and unpredictable collectivity of people. Popular music is in fact an idiom designed to cut across a number of taste cultures predicated upon age, education, class, geography and race. Loyalties here are fickle. Consumer demand is difficult to measure because of the varied interests of those comprising the audience. Yet popular music remains popular, even if its internal parts change, as they frequently do. . . . The popular music idiom, as a structure, remains the same with industry, promoters, cultural gatekeepers and distributors producing a "continuous cycle of discontinuous hits."

The discontinuity of popular music is an important element in its makeup vis-à-vis age. The songs and artists preferred by the so-called bubblegummers and teenyboppers change nearly every two years. Heroes of the pubescent set have ranged from Fabian, Frankie Avalon and Mark Lindsay to Donny Osmond. Chuck Laufer, editor of numerous teenage magazines and the proprietor of the Partridge Family Fan Club, observed, "There *has* to be teenage idols, but the girls outgrow them. When they're 11 to 14, they can have a nice, safe love affair with somebody like Davy Jones, Bobby Sherman or David Cas-

sidy. By the time they're 16 they're having dates and they don't need them anymore."

At this level musical tastes are generally established. People outgrow an idol, but not the style. The screaming girls who discovered Elvis Presley stuck with the rock-a-billy style through 1958 when their hero and his imitators disappeared from the scene. The abandoned fans did not flock to Dick Clark's army of pretty teenage vocalists. Consequently, a popular-music fan is generally wedded to a specific style current in the idiom in his adolescence. As time progresses, taste publics loyal to a specific popular-music form proliferate—to the point that within any two decades a vast number of rock fans can be identified. Yet there is a vast difference between them. Only a few years can separate musical style preferences. A nine-year-old may "like" her idol. A twelve-year-old detests the idol and prefers a punk-rock band. Collegiates have more esoteric musical preferences than secondary-school students. The success of many so-called easy-listening formula stations which feature stylized versions of current youth-market hits and "oldies but goodies" further suggests that some carryover from adolescent tastes occurs. Older people tend to prefer more traditional genres or none at all. People who were teenagers in the days of Glenn Miller still like crooners in the swing genre. Older blacks have been reported to have tastes different from their soul-oriented adolescents. Older country-music buffs attend fiddle conventions and mock the mod musicians from Nashville. Those people who do maintain a strong interest in any form of music after their courtship days are statistically unusual. If they do, the preference is usually more likely to be in an esoteric style than in an exoteric one. People in their sixties, seventies and older, for example, remain ardent country and western fans.

While age remains the crucial factor in popular music tastes, other social character-

istics also have an effect. Sex and marital status complement age. Social class may be important. Paul Hirsch observed that the sons and daughters of upper-class and lower-class parents exhibit more unique musical tastes than those in the middle. Geography further complicates the situation. Polka fans are more likely to reside in Minnesota and Wisconsin than in New York City or Tennessee. Race has a great deal to do with musical preferences and record-buying habits. A composite of black and Latin music tastes would find a strong commitment in soul and ethnic material. Even in their early twenties, blacks buy more singles than whites, who predominantly favor albums after 16. Age is certainly the most important factor determining a person's allegiance to music. Race and geography further complicate the identification of taste units. . . . Some taste units are totally divorced from the Top 40 sound. Others, to their peril, do contribute to the *Billboard* Hot 100. . . .

The success of a given taste or style ultimately is determined by its popular acceptance in other taste clusters. Success depends on either attracting support from a small number of large taste units or by eliciting support from a large portion of small groups. A single, such as "I Think I Love You" by the Partridge Family, by appealing to a significantly large portion of the "bubblegum" audience, [was] an immediate success. The Monkees, with a regular television series, commanded an equally large segment of the same group. The size of Elvis Presley's fan clubs and followers still guarantees that all of his records will near the million-seller figure. Lesser-known and more esoteric artists are not afforded this cushion. Joan Baez's version of "The Night They Drove Ole Dixie Down" relied upon a much larger number of groups such as underground, country and folk, to finally make the Top 40 play list. The problem for record-company executives is precisely how these combinations operate. The comments of an industry advertising executive sum up the dilemma:

To be in the rock 'n' roll record business today, you've got to be a "total-crap-shooter" with a good instinct for money management. You've got to have enormous faith in your A&R people and your own ear. . . . You'll have a better shot playing black jack in Las Vegas with a stake of $10,000 using the house rules and an arithmetical progression money system.

In 1972, Amos Heilicher, an important record retailer and rack jobber, commented that this chance factor was declining while picking a hit was becoming more complex. "At one time, 80 percent of our volume was done from 20 percent of our inventory. Now it's done from 35 to 40 percent of the product we carry." In the same year, the Warner/Reprise bulletin *Circular* ran a headline announcing "This Time the Big Trend Is No Trend." Passing years have not contradicted the announcement. Considering the ever-expanding pop music audience some observers feel that no one trend will take over the charts.

The music industry is not quite as subject to Adam Smith's "invisible hand" as they would have others believe; nonetheless the formula for a hit popular record remains elusive. Yet this element more than others distinguishes popular music from its nonentertainment sister conglomerates and also from the specialty labels who by and large know what their audiences want—at least most of the time. The very nature of popular music is dynamic change and all that it implies; however, it should be kept in mind that while parts of popular music are transformed, other properties remain relatively unchanged. The industry itself has not greatly changed over the years. Promoters, disk jockeys, critics and other functionaries are not as fluid as the music and the artists.

Popular music is a whole that is different from the sum of its many diverse, static and dynamic parts. Keeping this in mind, we can attempt a loose definition of popular music. *Popular music is the sum total of those taste units, social groups and musical genres which coalesce along certain taste and preference similarities in a given space and time.* These taste publics and genres are affected by a number of factors, predominantly age, accessibility, race, class and education. As such the designation of popular music is more a sociological than a musical definition. People select what they like from what they hear. The reasons for this selection are influenced by many factors some of which have little to do with the esthetic quality of a song or instrumental piece.

Record companies, much to their dismay, must orchestrate this demographic cacophony in order to earn a profit. Unlike the classics, country music or jazz, the record company must deal with a mosaic of dissimilar genres and taste and age groupings. Kal Rudman's statement, "it is easier to get a bill through Congress than a record on the *Billboard* chart," is a correct assessment.

At the 1965 Newport Folk Festival, Bob Dylan committed an act of heresy, in the opinion of the folk music purists in the audience. Dylan came out on stage and performed a song with an electric guitar. To make matters worse, he was accompanied by a band that sounded suspiciously similar to those who played that most dreaded of musical styles—"rock 'n' roll." Dylan's erstwhile fans booed him vehemently but he eventually attracted more than enough admirers to offset the loss of the defectors. Folk singer Tom Paxton referred to the new "folk rock" sound Dylan had inaugurated as "folk rot," but Dylan paid little attention to labels and declared, "It's all music, no more, no less."

The furor surrounding Dylan's decision to "go electric" highlighted the traditional animosity directed toward rock 'n' roll by the "folk music" aficionados. The "folkies," as they were sometimes called, derided rock for being a commercially produced art form that could not be considered a true expression of "the people." Carl Belz, in *The Story of Rock* (1969), explodes this facile assumption. He points out that "folk styles change," that advanced recording techniques and sophisticated electronic equipment do not necessarily invalidate a musician's credentials as a folk artist.

Despite the economic pressures of "making it" in the recording industry, Belz contends that the emergence of rock in the mid-fifties and its continued existence reflect the needs and desires of the audience. In this sense, Belz contradicts what Oscar Handlin declared earlier about the lack of rapport between the entertainer and the entertained in the mass-mediated society. Rock 'n' roll bands, in fact, epitomize the kind of popular culture Handlin perceived in the nineteenth century. Even when they become successful, most bands retain a sense of identity with the communities in which they first struggled to become "as big as the Beatles."

Rock as Folk Art
Carl Belz

Rock is a part of the long tradition of folk art in the United States and throughout the world. However simple or obvious this thesis may seem at first, it nevertheless involves a number of complicated issues concerning the history of art, the relationship between folk art and fine art, and our notions about the creative act in either domain of expression. The fact that rock first emerged, and has since developed, within the area of popular art only complicates its relationship to the folk and fine art traditions. . . .

Distinguishing between folk, fine, and popular art has become extremely difficult. . . . We live in a culture which is determined to question the validity of such distinctions and in which such questioning has provoked some of the best artistic statements since World War II. The complexity of this situation is partly due to the phenomenon of Pop Art, a fine art style which has been directly stimulated by popular or mass culture. Pop paintings and sculptures draw their inspiration from billboards, comic strips, advertising, and supermarkets, and sometimes look deceptively like the original objects in our predominantly man-made environment. Similarly, certain developments of theater—particularly the "living theater," "happenings," and "environments"—encourage the notion that the entire panorama of life can be viewed as a work of art. In the face of all this, drawing lines between art objects and non-art objects, or even distinguishing between different *classes* of art objects, might seem a less important task than describing a seemingly delightful situation in which anything can be art and maybe everything is. For the critic-historian, however, these distinctions are fundamental. Rock has been considered as popular art, folk art, fine art, and even non-art. Which, in fact, is it?

The vast and current interest in rock might be viewed as a feedback from such phenomena as Pop Art. Taking a hint from the fine arts, the adult public has begun to appreciate material which was previously alien and embarrassing to the critics of modern American civilization. Such appreciation, however, is a development of the 1960's. The development of rock, particularly during the first decade of its history, took place in the absence of such appreciation. The music emerged in response to a series of changing values and vital needs—not as the result of a sophistication gleaned from art galleries, museums, or periodicals. Its history, moreover, must be seen as a youth movement and as the reflection of a way of life radically different from the one which prevailed before the 1950's. When rock emerged, it spoke to these new values, to this youth, and to this changed way of life. But it did so in its capacity as a voice *of* the people rather than an art which talked *about*

them from a detached and self-determined vantage point. On an immediate level as well as in its ultimate significance, the music has been a confrontation with reality rather than a confrontation with art. This distinctiveness of function marks rock as folk art rather than fine art.

The difference between the functions of folk art and fine art cannot be regarded as absolute or necessarily clear-cut. All art, it can be argued, arises in response to vital needs and reflects a changing way of life from generation to generation. Further, all art is admittedly concerned with reality. At this level of generalization, folk art and fine art become alike. But folk art and fine art are not so similar when we consider which elements are more or less important in the creation and appeal of each.

In the modern period the most advanced media of the fine arts have become increas-

"Real" Art: Self Portrait. The artist, Duane Hanson, is at left, the sculpture at right in this photo taken at the University of California Art Museum in Berkeley. Pop art often looks very much like the original objects that inspired it. UPI Photo

ingly conscious of their respective and unique identities. Painting, for instance, has consistently involved itself with questions of the intrinsic nature of its expression: its flatness, its shape, its opticality, and so forth. Furthermore, these questions have evolved into an explicit *content*. In other words, the most successful expressions in the medium have tended to force the viewer to recognize that he is looking at a painting, a work of art. Moreover, by recognizing its particular medium in this way, the individual work compels its viewer to recognize that the object of his experience—in this case, the painting—is also distinct from other kinds of realities and from life in general. To put it another way, fine art declares itself as being different in kind from life. This is not to say that fine art ignores life or is irrelevant to the concerns of reality. Rather, any fine art expression confronts life, and has meaning in terms of it, only by engaging in an immediate confrontation with itself. In this sense, fine art is conscious of its own being, and, more generally, conscious of art.

In folk art, "art-consciousness" does not occupy the primary role that it does in fine art. A folk idiom's immediate concern is with issues of life and reality and with an overt expression of those issues. It is not aware of the identities of the separate media that it may employ. In the sense I am trying to define, a folk idiom employs different media unknowingly; it regards the identities of these media as being passive, like entities that need not be confronted in themselves. More simply, the difference between folk art

and fine art can be stated in the following way: The work of folk art says of itself, as it were, "this is reality," while the work of fine art says "this is a picture of reality." In no way, of course, does this distinction imply that one type of expression is of a higher quality than the other....

The ways in which rock relates to the fine art–folk art distinction are apparent in various aspects of the music itself, in the fabric of media which has surrounded it, and in the responses it elicits. In the early days of the *American Bandstand* television show, for instance, a panel of three or four teenagers periodically reviewed newly released records. The record was played, the audience danced, and a discussion of the song's merits followed. This discussion invariably contained remarks such as, "It's got a great beat.... I'll give it an 80," or, "You can really dance to it.... I'll give it an 85." The panelists never talked about the artistic properties of the record: the way the song was structured, the relation between its structure and meaning, its manipulations of the medium, the implications of its content, or any of the kinds of issues that are central to a meaningful statement about a work of fine art.

No one who appreciated or understood the music ever expected such questions to be discussed, for they are not part of the folk response. That response is spontaneous, and it is directed to the thing-as-reality. In other words, the connection between listener and song is an immediate one; no aesthetic distance separates the two, no gap that would provoke art-consciousness. With rock, as with any folk idiom, a consciousness of art is unnecessary for grasping the full impact of a particular work. This fact probably explains why the *Bandstand* panelists, however "uncritical" they may have appeared, were usually accurate in naming the best— that is, the most folk-like—of the new records.

The adult audiences and the popular press

159

who condemned rock in the 1950's did so because they did not understand the identity of the music they heard. They failed to grasp the essential difference between folk art and fine art, a difference teenagers unconsciously took for granted. Adverse critics of the music complained that it was crude and primitive, that it used poor grammar and improper enunciation, and that its lyrics were literary nonsense. Even in the 1960's, on his *Open End* show, David Susskind continued the effort to embarrass the music by reading the lyrics of some typical rock songs as if they were examples of fine art poetry. This sort of criticism was as futile and irrelevant as an art historian's criticism that a painting by Henri Rousseau had awkward perspective or that its human figures were out of scale with the landscape.

Folk art is neither aware of, nor concerned about, the kinds of manipulations that constitute "proper" effects in the fine arts. The rock artist's "crude" enunciation sprang naturally from his spontaneous effort to express something real. Yet, the grammar of "Doncha jus know it" or "I got a girl named Rama Lama Ding Dong" does not alone transform a song into folk material. Artists in the fine arts have used unconventional or slang expressions for centuries, from Shakespeare to the present day. What distinguishes the folk artist is that he uses such expressions unconsciously rather than for a desired artistic effect. Unaware of the option at his

King of Rock. An idol to his fans more than twenty years after reaching stardom, Elvis Presley tosses a scarf into the crowd at a Providence, R.I., Concert in May 1977. The audience reacted spontaneously to rock's blend of country and western, rhythm and blues.
UPI Photo

disposal—between art and reality—the folk artist plunges naturally, though unknowingly, into the latter.

Just as rock does not "become" folk music simply because it includes certain kinds of grammar or sentence structures, its folk character is not assured by the use of particular musical instruments or by a devotion to specific subject matters. A common misunderstanding concerning these questions arose during the latter 1950's and continued into the 1960's. Groups like the Kingston Trio and individual singers like Joan Baez inspired a popular movement which seemed to equate folk music with songs telling a story or conveying a moralistic point and accompanied by the acoustic or solo guitar. To its enthusiastic audience, this type of music was pure, eschewing the so-called falsifications of recording-room manipulations. As such, it appeared to offer an alternative to the crude and primitive style of rock. The artists and audiences of this new trend failed to realize, however, that folk styles change. The acoustic guitar may have been all that was available to the folk artist of the 1930's, but his counterpart in the 1950's and the 1960's could work with electronics, with echo chambers, and with complicated recording techniques. Folk music could change its cloak—just as folk art changed its materials between the stone carvings of Cycladic culture, the bark paintings of Australia, and the oils of Rousseau.

A dramatic reflection of rock's essentially folk character is apparent in the large number of one-shot successes in the history of the music. A group or individual produces a high quality record on its first effort but fails to repeat that success. Although the group or individual artist generally issues a second or a third record, these follow-ups rarely achieve the special blend of ingredients that gave the initial song its impact. The explanation for this phenomenon—for the fact that the follow-ups are so often artistic failures—is directly connected with folk art's lack of art-consciousness. When the rock group produces its first record, it is not concerned with style or structure, but, rather, with a sense of immediate impact, with what the *Bandstand* panelists call "the great beat." With the second or third record, however, the group seems to become aware of *art*—that is, with the artistic character of the first record. The group tries to duplicate the elements of the first record with only minor or barely perceptible variations. Yet, as they try for artistic consistency, their folk orientation generally betrays them: Not really understanding art, or the complex blend of aesthetic decisions which produced the original sound, they produce an object bearing only superficial resemblance to the first record. In this instance, the folk artist's lack of art-consciousness plays an ironic role in his creative life: At a time when he consciously believes he is making art, he is merely producing reproductions of his own original and unconsciously creative gesture. . . .

Perhaps the greatest difficulty in distinguishing rock as a folk idiom lies in the fact that the music is so closely linked to the enormous and complicated commercial music business, whereas generally works of art in the larger folk tradition are not at all closely related to popular art. This has caused the adverse critics of rock to say that the music has been forced upon a gullible public by some mercenary wholesalers of bad taste. In addition, these critics feel that the artists themselves are exclusively interested in financial rewards and are unconcerned about the quality of their music.

Suspicions like these are based on the fallacious assumption that the quality of art and the salability of art are mutually exclusive. Such a point, however, does not immediately dispel the suspicions themselves. Admittedly, many rock artists have earned fortunes through the sales of their records. My question, at the same time, is whether such evidence provides any meaningful explanation of why rock came into being in the first place, or why it has continued to exist. Rock artists have won and lost commercially, but the experience of the music itself has continued to possess vitality. I cannot imagine any artist who would not *enjoy* the benefits of commercial success, but both folk art and fine art can be originated and can survive without it. On the other hand, popular art does depend on commercial success in order to exist. That is, popular art *must* be popular, whereas folk art and fine art need not be, although they *may* be at any given moment. This demand for popularity is linked to the fact that popular art invariably has a product to sell: The product may be a bottle of shampoo or a new automobile, but it may also be non-material, such as diversion or escape, the "look" of reality or even of art. Popular art has many guises, but unlike either folk art or fine art, it is not self-sustaining. . . .

Popular art avoids an encounter with reality just as it avoids an encounter with art. It succeeds by selling the "look" of reality. So although rock emerged in the same domain as popular music, it cannot be classified simply as popular music. Admittedly, the task of separating the two types of music is occasionally problematic, particularly at those points in rock history where an artist's work, Elvis Presley's for instance, undergoes a transformation from folk art to popular art. But generally the distinction is clear.

Although few observers were aware of the revolutionary implications of rock 'n' roll until the late 1960s, the music carried an inherent message of rebellion. By blending black rhythm and blues and country and western into a new popular musical style, rock implicitly challenged mainstream American culture. White middle-class youths were hearing the sounds of people who, in the words of Nat Hentoff, "couldn't come to dinner or be elected to the school board." By initiating a kind of musical integration, rock broke down cultural barriers and caused many young people to wonder why they had been erected in the first place.

Rock 'n' roll also seemed to have the capacity to stimulate overt rebelliousness. As early as 1955, some people were observing what they believed to be an association between rock and youthful unrest. The use of Bill Haley's "Rock Around the Clock" in the juvenile delinquency film *Blackboard Jungle* (1955) suggested such a link; a "riot" at Princeton University in May 1955 appeared to many to confirm the relationship. *Billboard*, a trade journal of the music industry, reported that the pulsating strains of "Rock Around the Clock" were first heard in one of the student dormitories. "Other phonographs joined in," according to *Billboard*, "making a mad medley which led to chanting and stamping by the staid Princetonians. About midnight they gathered on the campus, set fire to a can of trash and paraded through the streets. In the sixties a very similar spirit of restlessness often found an outlet in political protest demonstrations.

Nat Hentoff perceived the intensified importance of rock music to the inchoate counterculture in 1966. Something was indeed "happening," but the "straight" society of the Mr. Joneses failed to comprehend it. A subculture had begun to emerge that appeared "so radically disaffiliated from the mainstream assumptions of our society," observed Theodore Roszak in *The Making of a Counter Culture* (1969), "that it scarcely looks to many as a culture at all, but takes on the alarming appearance of a barbaric intrusion."

Something's Happening and You Don't Know What It Is
Nat Hentoff

T he medium is the message," Marshall McLuhan keeps insisting. Grownups hear fragments of the pounding beat and the electronically raw sound making it in pop music and they don't get the message. The words, it's hard to hear the words. And when they do come through, what are they *saying*? The young talk of Bob Dylan. "What do *you* think of Bob Dylan?" a reporter asks Howard Nemerov, poet and professor to the young. "Mr. Dylan is not known to me. Regrets."

There's no one to tell the adults in the language of the adults what's happening. The only writer who comes close is Ralph Gleason in the *San Francisco Chronicle*. He's been in the territory long enough so that he never says "pop culture." You won't find any maps to that land in *The New York Review of Books* or *Kenyon Review* or *Partisan Review*. (Well, Leslie Fiedler has acted as a guide partway for the readers of PR—"The New Mutants," *Partisan Review*, Fall, 1965. But he's telling it from a distance. And so am I. Besides, nobody can go that route for you. You have to listen for yourself. Dig for yourself. Dig yourself.)

But from a distance, you can hear some of the language, musical and others. And while you won't get to think in it if you're the wrong age, you may absorb part of its outer texture. Remember, the printed language can only travel a little way inside. You might try reading this with a transistor radio on. Almost any disc jockey will do, except, of course, those on the "good music" stations.

"The sound," says Gleason, "is the sound of the electronic age, a dissent from older forms. The costumes are a dissent from The Ed Sullivan slick . . . These performers *never* have a nose-bob or cap their teeth. Instead of hiding a so-called bad feature, they accentuate it, like a living caricature." And what of the words, which have to be heard inside the sound, not in books? A songwriter, Malvina Reynolds, "Little Boxes," talks of the "flexible, new, lively, American language" in them. British too. It takes listening, she, an adult, adds. "I am a prisoner of logic myself, but logic, like a neat appearance, has been used against the world."

It also takes at least a temporary suspension of the delusion that age makes for knowing, that only an adult's way of seeing, hearing and feeling is where things and people and death are really at. Like Pablo Casals, who called rock-and-roll "poison put to sound," he isn't going to get there. But he doesn't want to go. And Sinatra, who, when rock began to break through, called it a "rancid smelling aphrodisiac." He stopped being able to go to new places a long time ago.

Even a younger, a little too consciously hip observer like Pete Hamill of the magazines and the *New York Post* looks out of too-old eyes: "There is something elegantly sinister about the Rolling Stones. They sit before you at a press conference like five unfolding switchblades, their faces set in rehearsed snarls, their hair studiously unkempt and matted, their clothes part of some private conceit, and the way they walk and they talk and the songs they sing all become part of some long mean reach for the jugular."

They don't want your jugular, man. Even if you offered it. And who's rehearsed, them or you?

But a look at the Stones as the Stones, not as five unfolding switchblades, may be of some aid on the journey. They started from a distance. Not in age, but in the music. Growing up in London, they found a sound on American records that made visceral sense to them. Records by Negro blues singers. Muddy Waters, Jimmy Reed, Howlin' Wolf. Names still unknown to nearly all the white, and many of the black, American teenagers who find the Stones' sound makes visceral sense to *them*. It also happened to the Beatles, the Animals, and the other British rock groups who invaded our young, bearing what our young already had but didn't know they had. The Animals picked up on records by Tampa Red and John Lee Hooker. And they were ahead of the white American teen-agers in plunging into the rhythm-and-blues-based pop music of city Negroes their own age—Martha and the Vandellas, and that scene. And gospel singers.

"The real artists," Ringo Starr of the Beatles says like he oughtn't have to say it, it's so clear to him, "are mainly colored artists. I never did like the Perry Comos or the Sinatras. I don't buy that kind of art. If whites sang like the coloreds did, I'd buy their records." Simultaneously the British groups and Bob Dylan and the Lovin' Spoonful here were growing up, absorbing, so far as they could, black ways of reacting against and into the world. Being young, they were on the outside. Being bright and untied, they could see the naked lunch on the end of the white grownups' forks. Sure, it wasn't the same as living black, but the sound and the feeling in the sound were real, palpable. Not like Sinatra or Como and what they sang about and how they sang it.

It wasn't only black. Since the Second World War and since the end of the ASCAP [American Society of Composers, Authors and Publishers] monopoly (ASCAP writers had the melody, the white, big-city-with-

a-doorman melody), other outsiders were coming into the across-the-board pop music scene. Country and western singers. Bluegrass banjo pickers. And more recently, a Johnny Cash, part Cherokee. Out of Memphis into big hits and big money, swapping songs with Bob Dylan as both were making it, and recording an album, *Bitter Tears*, about how few have ever said anything about the civil rights bill applying to Indians. And going to the state of Washington for a march on the state Capitol by the Puyallup Indians who were bugged at a broken agreement by the state concerning their reservation. And

the chief, in his speech, using some of the words from Cash's songs.

So for a long time now, the pop charts have been democratized, miscegenated, deregionalized, unclassed. For the first time, without having to search, without having to be a "collector," a buff, all kinds of kids—including the white, middle-class kids in their little boxes—were hearing black and country. They were hearing all kinds of people who couldn't come to dinner or be elected to the school board where they were at physically. Where they were at inside their heads and with each other was their own business.

The Beatles: Mop-Topped Britons. The most influential popular music group of the sixties, the Beatles made their first American tour in 1964. Left to right: Paul McCartney, John Lennon, Ringo Starr, and George Harrison.
UPI Photo

Their parents didn't know anything about that, as *their* parents in turn hadn't. But these kids had different kinds of allies in their music than their parents ever had.

A shame, some of the parents said, and nearly all the old ASCAP songwriters said. A shame, middle-aged hacks in the Brill Building manufacturing this noise and bribing disc jockeys and force-feeding it into our young. But it wasn't like that. The parents didn't even know *that*. The songwriters making it now are young and often are themselves performers in one of the bags we're talking about. The a&r men are getting younger and younger. Sure, bread was passed in different ways, and still is, but no radio station makes it by trying to manipulate today's listeners. The bribery bit is a cultural lag. Old shortcuts die hardest even when they don't lead anywhere any more. You want to connect into what's happening these days, says Dylan, you turn on the radio. You don't go to plays or concerts. That's all dead, or for somebody else who uses old-time language, who didn't grow up with a transistor in his ear. And if the radio station isn't with it, you know that instantly. The radio station can't tell you what to want. You tell them. Except you don't bother. If one station switches to "good music," there are plenty of others that have learned where you are.

But what are they *saying?* "Do you plan to record any antiwar songs?" a reporter asks the Beatles. "All our songs," John Lennon looks at this museumed man, "are antiwar." But do those kids really understand

that jumble of surrealism (isn't it surrealism?) in Dylan's *Subterranean Homesick Blues?* "Don't follow leaders," a line in the song says. They understand that.

And Joan Baez, no longer lost back in her vibrato with those distantly tragic British ballads, announces the next number for an audience of the young. "This one is dedicated to President Johnson and his marvelous foreign policy," she smiles. And she sings part of a rock-and-roll hit by the Supremes, "Stop! In the Name of Love."

No, they're not all pacifists. Maybe none is. No, they don't read Martin Buber. And only a very few of them read I. F. Stone or *Studies on the Left*. The thing is, they are, to begin with. And they want to stay that way. You'll get them in the army, but more and more have had it with the abstractions and the abstract emotions. Free World? Christ, they've seen their parents up close. So far as the young know, existentially know, who could be less free? Let me not con you. Most of them will go that way too, later or sooner. And they know it. And the ones who haven't yet been entirely society-broken by school are putting that off for a while. But when they do go that way, they won't be as surprised later as their parents were by how bad it really is. In the decades ahead, look for sales of pills to go UP.

They know where the quicksand is. Beatle Paul McCartney, aren't you at least a little disturbed at the heroes who sent back their Orders of the British Empire because the Queen gave you an M.B.E.? "We think," says new statesman McCartney (party affiliation vague), "it's much better to entertain people and get medals than to kill them and get medals for that." But respect, respect. Where is respect? What of Hector Dupuis, a former Liberal member of the Canadian Parliament, who returned his M.B.E.? "I don't care if Mr. Dupuis eats his medal," says Ringo Starr in self-respect. "For once, young people get an award. What's wrong with that?"

The singers and their listeners still have

an illusion of mobility, not having yet been locked in place in the rationalized, the Great Society. We gotta get out of this place, say the Animals. "See my daddy in bed a-dyin', see his hair turnin' gray, he's been workin' and slavin' his life away. He's been workin', workin', work–work."...

What if Bob Dylan ran for office in five years? He won't. He's cut out from politics and protest. He doesn't think anything out there can be really changed. But what if he did? And others with charisma who know the way to put an end to war? Bring the vote down to sixteen. Or to fourteen. But that's an old-time fantasy.

And what is Dylan saying now? In his liner notes for *Highway 61 Revisited*, he's tlling about how "when the Cream met Savage Rose & Fixable, he was introduced to them by none other than Lifelessness—Lifelessness is the Great Enemy & always wears a hip guard—he is very hipguard... Lifelessness said when introducing everybody 'go save the world' & 'involvement! that's the issue' & things like that & Savage Rose winked at Fixable & the Cream went off with his arm in a sling singing 'summertime & the Livin is easy.' "

And inside the album, in "Ballad of a Thin Man," he's talking to you: "You hand in your ticket and you go watch the geek who immediately walks up to you when he hears you speak and says, 'How does it feel to be such a freak?' and you say, 'Impossible!' as he hands you a bone. Something is happening, but you don't know what it is, do you, Mr. Jones?"

But what is he *saying?* What are all of them *saying?* Ask a psychiatrist, of course. Like Dr. James F. Masterson, head of the Adolescent Out-Patient Clinic at the Payne-Whitney Psychiatric Clinic: "These songs reflect the mood of depression many teen-agers experience, the feeling of loss of old things, of childhood. Children mind losing their childhood."

Why is that, Dr. Jones? What are *you* saying, Dr. Jones?

Try just listening, Dr. Jones. Forget the words. Just move. Come into the beat, like it says in *Time*, the weekly newspeak: "... where the sound is so loud that conversation is impossible, the hypnotic beat works a strange magic. Many dancers become literally transported. They drift away from their partners; inhibitions flake away, eyes glaze over, until suddenly they are seemingly swimming alone in a sea of sound. Says Sheila Wilson, eighteen, a student at Vassar: 'I give everything that is in me. And when I get going, I'm gone. It's the only time I feel whole.' "

Is that what they're saying? Something about being whole?

"Oh, my God," says Mr. Jones in "Ballad of a Thin Man," "am I here all alone?"

Is it only your childhood you've lost, Mr. Jones?

"We don't smoke marijuana in Muskogee," sang Merle Haggard, and millions of Americans, bewildered by the rise of the counterculture, responded with genuine gratitude. Finally a song about old-fashioned values and life-styles, they thought, a song that praises rather than attacks America. The widespread chorus of applause that greeted Haggard's musical declaration indicated that being an "Okie from Muskogee" had more to do with a particular philosophical persuasion than with one's geographical location.

The popularity of country and western singers such as Merle Haggard with a broad cross-section of the American public mirrored the cultural "backlash" that first became evident in the late sixties. To the beleaguered "silent majority," country and western represented a repository of such traditional American virtues as patriotism, morality, and respect for law and order. Actually, as the following essay by three sociologists of music points out, the lyrics of country and western songs are not as conservative as most people believe. But in a time of political unrest and social turmoil, country and western offered many a welcome contrast to the perceived rebelliousness of rock.

During the past ten years, country and western has climbed to a position of prominence in popular culture. Johnny Cash's television variety series, which debuted in 1969, provided a powerful impetus to the rising tide of interest in the music. Since then, the trend has accelerated. Buck Owens and Roy Clark have become major celebrities as hosts of "Hee Haw," a kind of country version of "Laugh-In." And singers such as Loretta Lynn, Donna Fargo, Charley Pride, and Mel Tillis are regular guests on television shows and premier attractions on the nightclub circuit.

Singing Along with the Silent Majority

John D. McCarthy
Richard A. Peterson
William L. Yancey

While the Kennedy Administration patronized the fine arts, and the Johnson Administration was more likely to support well-known popular entertainers, the Nixon Administration, like none of its predecessors, . . . embraced "country-western music."

The president not only invited Johnny Cash and Merle Haggard, widely known country-western recording artists, to the White House for performances, but he followed by proclaiming October, 1970, as "Country Music Month." Thus the first president in history to claim roots in middle class suburbia has identified himself with the nasal twang sound of the songs of poor southern whites—a sound scoffingly referred to as "hillbilly music." It remained

for Burl Ives, however, to explicitly link country-western music with true Americanism. He proclaimed from the stage, at the ... 44th birthday celebration of the Grand Ol' Opry, "Country music is *the* music of this great land of ours."

President Nixon's embrace of country-western music raises a number of significant questions about this music and its devotees. What are the important themes in this music? Who are its devotees? Do these devotees exhibit a coherent ideological position which would put them solidly in the Nixon camp?

The country songs which have received the most notoriety ... express patriotism, regionalism, self-reliance, and displeasure with indolent youth—presumably views held by members of that fabled constituency, the Silent Majority. The wide popularity of two ... Merle Haggard record-

ings—"Okie from Muskogee," which castigates hippie life styles while extolling the small town virtues of football, liquor and sex, and "The Fightin' Side of Me," an affirmation of two-fisted patriotism—has led many casual observers to class the entire range of country-western music as ideologically conservative.

President Nixon ... apparently [drew] such a conclusion, as his invitation to Johnny Cash to perform at the White House included a request for Cash to sing, "Welfare Cadillac," a song explicitly denigrating welfare recipients by rehearsing all of the old saws about welfare chiselers. The fact that Cash balked at singing this song in the face of presidential pressure and did not perform it at the White House illustrates very dramatically the point we will argue below: country-western performers, their music,

Songs for the Silent Majority. Country-western stars Johnny Cash and wife, June Carter, and Dolly Parton, named Female Vocalist of the Year (1976) by the Country Music Association.
UPI Photos

and their audience cannot be neatly fitted into the conventional left-right ideological categories. . . .

Country and western music, while simple in melody and rhythm, has always featured complex and varied lyrics. Since the beginning of commercial country-western music in the 1920's, the dominant lyrical themes have most often stressed individual troubles. A number of different themes are treated, but as with other forms of popular music, most country-western songs deal with love. The matter-of-fact treatment of the love problems of mature men and women are most often portrayed as a war between the sexes, as, for example, "I Cried All the Way to the Bank," and "Thank God and Greyhoud You Are Gone."

Unlike the temperance songs of an earlier generation, liquor is now most often viewed in the context of an omnipresent view of love, economic, and family troubles and is normally seen as dissolving personal responsibility if not felt guilt. And while over-the-road truckers have replaced cowpunchers and railroad men as folk heroes, work songs continue to celebrate the victory of the strong, self-reliant, long-suffering working man over all obstacles of nature, the limitations of his body, and technology. A typical song depicts an overworked driver on pep pills highballing an overheated rig through an ice storm, in defiance of company orders, in order to get home to his wife. . . .

Unlike the labor union organizing songs of the 1930's, the many troubles which are chronicled in country-western music are rarely set in larger political perspective. More often fate, luck, the power of love, and liquor are the explanations for trouble. What is more, solutions to such problems are most likely to be stated in individual terms—self-reliance is the key here, a self-reliance which presumes a sort of frontier-like communalism. Thus, while political themes are rarely stated in overt terms, the values most often expressed in country music do have political connotations. . . .

During the summer of 1969 we interviewed 700 adult heads of households in Nashville, Tennessee concerning, among other things, their music preferences. These data taken in the context of the wide variety of other information gathered from these respondents afford us the opportunity to learn something more about the country music devotee. Our sample is not representative of the Nashville population because we purposefully oversampled lower and working class families. This sampling design, as we will show, is particularly appropriate for the analysis of country-western music fans,

> "The recent emphasis on politicized themes in country-western music . . . [is] symptomatic of the emergence of an explanation of troubles for those who have been apparently left behind."

beyond the obvious utility of using respondents from Nashville, the home of country-western music. . . .

Singing Along with the Silent Majority

At first glance, there are obvious connections between ideological conservatism and the situation of country-western music fans. They are predominantly southern and white, and are commonly thought to be one of the more conservative groups in America—especially in the matter of civil rights. As working and lower class whites, they have been left behind by the civil rights and poverty movements of the 1960's. William Brink and Louis Harris demonstrate that approximately 70 percent of a national sample of poor whites disapproved of the "War on Poverty" in 1968, and the most important reason for such disapproval was a belief that the program was designed for blacks. Perhaps reflecting in part their experience with these attempts at relatively radical social change, more than 60 percent of our working and lower class respondents agreed with the statement, "if you start trying to change things very much, you usually make them worse." The country-western fans among this group were substantially more likely to agree with this statement (where about 71 percent of the respondents agreed). We know that this group was more likely than any other in the South to prefer the candidacy of George Wallace in 1968, we might be led to believe that politically this group prefers a status quo, anti-black political platform.

On the other hand, . . . this group is con-fronted with a wide range of personal troubles. Do their prejudices get the better of their realization of their own disadvantaged economic position? The answer must be negative, based upon our survey evidence. When asked whether the federal government should provide health insurance, somewhat over 60 percent of the working and lower class respondents agreed, making them far more likely to agree than middle class respondents. When asked whether the government should have more power to deal with the problems of the poor, the majority of these respondents agreed, and country-western fans were quite a bit more likely to agree, where approximately 74 percent agreed with this statement. So we see that the country-western fans surveyed, even though white southerners, fit the characterization of economic liberalism and civil libertarian conservatism which has been applied to this class nationally.

Unlike the black American, lower and working class whites have no clear and obvious barrier or corresponding ideology which can be used to explain their failure to achieve success in the American system. The recent emphasis on politicized themes in country-western music, as seen especially in such songs as "Welfare Cadillac," "The Fightin' Side of Me," "Okie from Muskogee," and "Bus Them Children," are symptomatic of the emergence of an explanation of troubles for those who have been apparently left behind by the systemic changes which have taken place over the last decade. Yet in this case, the blame for failure is not placed upon the system—this would not fit in with the strong belief in the American dream—but rather on the agents of social change. The songs identify these agents: The Department of Health, Education and Welfare is the force behind school integration and busing; the poverty program and the welfare system are blamed for the presence of Cadillacs among the very poor, hippies and peace-niks are identified as causing crime in the streets, disruption, and the lack of support of our fighting men in Viet Nam; and weak national leadership is blamed for having allowed the country to drift. All of this is summed up by the anguished song, "Where Have All Our Heroes Gone?"

Yet the strong belief in the viability and sanctity of the American way of life does not solve the troubles experienced by this group of Americans, and we have some indication that they also favor change which would serve to confront some of their economic problems—changes that would be characterized as liberal in common parlance. This is so, even though they are suspicious of change as an abstract notion. . . .

Our evidence suggests that in spite of the recent popularity of presumably "conservative" songs in country-western music which reflect the strong beliefs in patriotism, individualism, and self-reliance among country-western fans, there is a large reservoir of liberal economic sentiment among these Americans. A politician who is conservative on both economic and social issues and who mistakes the strong feelings of primitive patriotism and support for the frontier virtues among the fans of country-western music as support for a conservative economic program may be making a serious error.

In many respects, the predicament of rock music in the late sixties recalled the dilemma of jazz in the fifties. In a manner similar to the numerous queries about what was happening to jazz, some observers began wondering "what is rock?" The basic "big beat" sound of rock and its distinct lineage back to black rhythm and blues had become obscured by the musical and social developments of the 1960s.

Musically, rock seemed to be moving toward greater complexity and improvisation, two elements that contradicted the simple, predictable patterns of "original" rock 'n' roll. Albums and concerts were, for many groups, merely showcases for their specialized talents, particularly those of the revered lead guitarists such as Mike Bloomfield and Eric Clapton.

Socially, rock had emerged as a powerful medium of protest for many of its creators and adherents. The Rolling Stones encouraged young people to join "the revolution" in their song "Streetfighting Man" (1968), while groups such as The Doors and Jefferson Airplane assumed positions of prominence as political commentators. Rock became such a serious business that the dance beat of the music—traditionally *the* most important feature—was considered insignificant, perhaps even undesirable, by those who saw visions of the glorious counterculture.

The so-called backlash against the radical aspects of rock music and the counterculture it helped to spawn was not restricted to the "silent majority." The youth culture itself began to show signs of dissatisfaction with the growing violence of the counterculture and the increasingly esoteric nature of rock. The Beatles articulated the revulsion toward violent protest in their song "Revolution" (1969) and groups such as Creedence Clearwater Revival became tremendously popular simply by playing old time rock 'n' roll. The pioneers of rock, notably Elvis Presley and Chuck Berry, experienced a musical renaissance in the late sixties as the "back to the roots" movement accelerated.

In the seventies, the preponderance of "easy listening" records indicated that "rock" had clearly become a misnomer. Robert Hilburn, of the *Los Angeles Times*, analyzes the trends that have brought about the merger of rock and "pop" music. One of his most noteworthy observations is that "prettiness" figures so prominently in the success of artists such as Peter Frampton and Olivia Newton-John. This contrasts sharply with the tendency of rock stars in the late sixties to "accentuate" a "bad feature," in the words of Ralph Gleason, "like a living caricature." As Bob Dylan sang in 1963, "the times they are a-changin'." Again.

Age of Pretty Pop
Robert Hilburn

This is the age of prettiness in pop. Peter Frampton and Olivia Newton-John, the reigning king and queen, are as comely as their music. Whatever you think of the pair's sounds, their albums have one advantage for fans: the covers are suitable for framing.

With the decade three quarters gone, most observers have given up on finding the bold, flamboyant Next Big Thing in pop music. Or maybe they've just realized the *next* sound already is here and it's not what they had in mind.

The face of pop has changed drastically in the '70s but not in a way that has demanded the sociocultural attention of Presley's rebellion in the '50s or Dylan and Hendrix's antihero stance in the '60s. The shift has been to a soothing, easy-listening sound that offers comfort and escape, not confrontation.

Though provocative rock surfaces occasionally, its commercial impact is slight when measured against an easy-listening alliance that includes such diverse talents as Elton John, the Eagles, Stevie Wonder, John Denver, Paul McCartney, Fleetwood Mac, Barry Manilow and Linda Ronstadt.

But no one symbolizes the easy-listening takeover as fully as Frampton, pop's hottest act. His "Frampton Comes Alive" LP—past the 13 million mark worldwide—is believed to be the biggest-selling pop album ever in the U.S., and his new "I'm in You" entered the charts [in June 1977] at No. 5.

Frampton, who represents the final break in rock's long-standing discomfort with easy-listening ties, completes a complex evolutionary swing that can be traced back through Elton John and Carole King to the Carpenters' arrival in '70.

Who ever thought a gentle, unassuming song like "We've Only Just Begun" was really a battle cry?

Though Richard and Karen Carpenter hardly seemed revolutionary at the time, they were a key step in the emergence of easy-listening music. Their "Close to You" wasn't the only ballad to make No. 1 in 1970, but the others either had a rock underpinning (the Beatles' "Let It Be") or a slight novelty tinge (B. J. Thomas' "Raindrops Keep Fallin' on My Head").

The Carpenters' music, by contrast, was an unabashed celebration of what had been dismissed throughout the '60s as old-fashioned, overly sentimental pop. No one took the Carpenters seriously at the beginning. They were just that well-scrubbed brother and sister act from Downey or wherever. Their records were so innocent and syrupy that they were like short pants in a tough, leather-jacketed world.

Surely, they'd pass from the scene the way so many other *novelty* acts had. Or so critics thought. But the Carpenters followed "Close to You" with 11 more Top 10 singles and their new "All You Get from Love Is a Love Song" may return them to the Top 10 shortly.

The Carpenters' success was a sign to record companies and radio station program directors that traditional pop could be a viable commercial force. Further proof: "Close to You" was followed in the No. 1 spot by Bread's soft, equally innocuous "Make It with You."

Just as important was the success of James Taylor's "Fire and Rain" in 1970. Where

The Versatile Elton John. Elton John's ability to perform different styles of music, from rock to easy-listenin' pop, made him one of the highest paid recording artists in history. UPI Photo

many in rock and folk dismissed the Carpenters' music as pap, Taylor's caressing ballad legitimized the move toward an easier-listening sound. Rock no longer had to be loud or explosive.

Taylor's record, with its supportive, understanding lyrics about having passed through troubled times, hit an emotional chord for those seeking a rest from the turbulence of the hectic '60s. Lines like "I've seen fire and I've seen rain" summarized for many their bad experiences with drugs and other forms of '60s experimentation.

The cushioned, sympathetic tone of "Fire and Rain" and the "Sweet Baby James" album made Taylor an immensely influential pop figure. He even made the cover of *Time* magazine. But the shy, soft-spoken singer-songwriter rejected the role of spokesman. His work has continued to be popular, but has shown little sociological impact.

Taylor, however, did make one other contribution to the easy-listening harvest. He helped reintroduce Carole King to pop audiences.

Until "Frampton Comes Alive," King's "Tapestry" was the biggest-selling U.S. pop album. But she was a cold property in 1970 when she opened for Taylor at the Troubadour in West Hollywood.

After writing such hits as "Will You Love Me Tomorrow" (for the Shirelles) and "Up on the Roof" (for the Drifters) in the '60s, she was driven from the pop scene by the Beatles-led English rock invasion.

Not only was pop reshaped by the Beatles, but most of the new groups wrote their own tunes. Record acts no longer turned to New York publishing houses and writers like King for material. She resurfaced in 1970 with an album of her own songs. The live show at the Troubadour went so well she went on tour with Taylor.

Besides responding to the old songs, audiences enjoyed her new ones. Like Taylor, King's music focused on simple, classic values of friendship, loved ones and the home. "You've Got a Friend" was typical.

Whereas Taylor had approached easy-listening music from a folk background, King's critically acclaimed style was rooted in more traditional pop sources. Pop—as opposed to rock—was no longer a dirty word. Possibilities began emerging.

Elton John also arrived in 1970. Appealing to both rock and pop audiences with his delicate "Your Song," he was soon crossing back and forth between the two styles in his albums, making the old distinctions unimportant. His tunes were well designed and engagingly performed. He became the most popular record-maker since the Beatles.

John's stage shows, too, worked against the serious tone of rock in the '60s. The only message from Elton was: have a good time. Pop or rock or whatever could be fun. Barriers had been broken.

While dozens of lesser artists leaped on the easy-listening bandwagon, several figures of stature gave the music some substance. From soul, Stevie Wonder and Al Green. From folk, Gordon Lightfoot and Joni Mitchell. From rock, Cat Stevens and, eventually, the Eagles.

Despite the variance in style and creative ability, the dozens of artists who enjoyed easy-listening acceptance made records with smooth, highly accessible features.

Considering the provocative themes of such artists as Mitchell and the Eagles, it's tempting to speculate much of their AM radio success was because people just listened to the soft textures and not the words.

But no one misunderstood Olivia Newton-John. She was the first step in the Pretty Pop twist on the easy-listening theme.

Though Carly Simon's, Linda Ronstadt's and Emmylou Harris' commercial successes have been aided by their looks, Newton-John is the most striking case of pretty face/pretty voice/pretty sales.

The 28-year-old English-born singer's first U.S. success was with a soft, willowy version of Dylan's "If Not for You" in 1972. The record's innocent, breathless tone was gently affecting, but hardly memorable.

Coupled with her alluring good looks, the disc's success seemed like a modern Cinderella tale in which a gorgeous but not particularly talented young woman got a chance to fulfill her dreams of stardom.

Even when she had hits two years later with "Let Me Be There" and "If You Love Me, Let Me Know," few took her seriously. There was such sparkle in her personality and music when she opened for the Smothers Brothers at the Greek Theater in 1974, I remember thinking how she must go through two tubes of Pepsodent a day.

But Newton-John's success in 1975 proved she was no fairy tale. Not only was she the year's biggest female album seller, but she won a Grammy for the year's best vocal. Her "I Honestly Love You" was named the top single.

Newton-John's voice has more range and character live than on record. She also has a warmly unpretentious stage manner. But she is hardly one of today's best vocalists. The awards show you just how off base the Grammy voting can be. . . .

It's no wonder Frampton is such a hit. He combines the good looks of Newton-John with the innocence of Cat Stevens and the gee whiz enthusiasm of John Denver. Who else would dedicate his new album to his fans, include a song he wrote for his dog and offer this gleeful message to his band in the liner notes: "Thank you fellas. You really knock me out."

The irony of Frampton's success is that he first came to attention in America as part of the hard-rocking Humble Pie group. After leaving that band, his early solo albums sold only modestly. But he built a following through endless touring.

Like Elton John, he was a wholly accessible, outgoing, unpretentious figure on stage. The spirit of his live shows was captured in the "Frampton Comes Alive" album. Whatever limitations his music may have, his hard-working, eager-to-please manner in concert is charming. . . .

The fact that the live LP could have ever made Frampton—whose music is little above Newton-John's in sophistication or challenge—rock's hottest property confirms what has happened to pop in the '70s.

Until the late 1860s, the United States had virtually no organized sports as we know them today. Even before the Civil War, the urbanization of the country saw the decline of informal sports, such as those found in country festivals and frontier frolics, or such diversions as barn raisings and husking bees. This diminution of physical activity on the part of the American people alarmed several noted observers, including Ralph Waldo Emerson and Edward Everett. Dr. Oliver Wendell Holmes, the "Autocrat of the Breakfast Table," lamented that "such a set of black-coated, stiff-jointed, soft-muscled, paste-complexioned youth as we can boast in our Atlantic cities never before sprang from the loins of Anglo-Saxon lineage."

The pioneer of SportsWorld, baseball, had evolved from the bat-and-ball games the early settlers brought with them from England. By 1858, about 2,000 people paid 50 cents each to see a baseball game at the Fashion Race Course.

Although the Civil War slowed down the growth of spectator sports, by 1869 the Cincinnati Red Stockings fielded a team of professional, salaried players. Even Mark Twain was a devotee, writing, "Baseball is the very symbol, the outward and visible expression of the drive and push and struggle of the raging, tearing, booming nineteenth century."

It took the colleges to introduce football in 1869, when Rutgers played Princeton for the first intercollegiate contest.

During the past century, sports have become a dominant part of our popular culture. Most American boys would rather win the Heisman Trophy or play center for the Boston Celtics than be President of the United States. But the SportsWorld of today is an amalgam of such diverse elements that Robert Lipsyte views it with an excited but critical eye.

SportsWorld
Robert Lipsyte

For the past one hundred years most Americans have believed that playing and watching competitive games are not only healthful activities, but represent a positive force on our national psyche. In sports, they believe, children will learn courage and self-control, old people will find blissful nostalgia, and families will discover new ways to communicate among themselves. Immigrants will find shortcuts to recognition as Americans. Rich and poor, black and white, educated and unskilled, we will all find a unifying language. The melting pot may be a myth, but we will all come together in the ballpark.

This faith in sports has been vigorously promoted by industry, the military, government, the media. The values of the arena and the locker room have been imposed upon our national life. Coaches and sportswriters are speaking for generals and businessmen, too, when they tell us that a man must be physically and psychologically "tough" to succeed, that he must be clean and punctual and honest, that he must bear pain, bad luck, and defeat without whimpering or making excuses. A man must prove his faith in sports and the American Way by whipping himself into shape, playing by the rules, being part of the team, and putting out all the way. If his faith is strong enough, he will triumph. It's his own fault if he loses, fails, remains poor.

Even for ballgames, these values, with their implicit definitions of manhood, courage, and success, are not necessarily in the individual's best interests. But for daily life they tend to create a dangerous and grotesque web of ethics and attitudes, an amorphous infrastructure that acts to contain our energies, divert our passions, and socialize us for work or war or depression.

I call this infrastructure SportsWorld. For most of my adult life, as a professional observer, I've explored SportsWorld and marveled at its incredible power and pervasiveness. SportsWorld touches everyone and everything. We elect our politicians, judge our children, fight our wars, plan our vacations, oppress our minorities by SportsWorld standards that somehow justify our foulest and freakiest deeds, or at least camouflage them with jargon. We get stoned on such SportsWorld spectaculars as the Super Bowl, the space shots, the Kentucky Derby, the presidential conventions, the Indianapolis 500, all of whose absurd excesses reassure us that we're okay.

SportsWorld is a sweaty Oz you'll never find in a geography book, but since the end of the Civil War it has been promoted and sold to us like Rancho real estate, an ultimate sanctuary, a university for the body, a community for the spirit, a place to hide that glows with that time of innocence when we believed that rules and boundaries were honored, that good triumphed over evil, and that the loose ends of experience could be caught and bound and delivered in an expla-

"We elect our politicians, judge our children, fight our wars, plan our vacations, oppress our minorities by SportsWorld standards that somehow justify our foulest and freakiest deeds..."

nation as final and as comforting as a good-night kiss.

Sometime in the last fifty years the sports experience was perverted into a SportsWorld state of mind in which the winner was good because he won; the loser, if not actually bad, was at least reduced, and had to prove himself over again, through competition. As each new immigrant crop was milled through the American system, a pick of the harvest was displayed in the SportsWorld showcase, a male preserve of national athletic entertainment traditionally enacted by the working class for the middle class, much as the performing arts are played by the middle class for the amusement of the upper class.

By the 1950s, when SportsWorld was dominated by what are now called "white ethnics," the black American was perceived as a challenging force and was encouraged to find outlets in the national sports arena. Although most specific laws against black participation had already been erased, it took cautious, humiliating experiments with such superstars as Jackie Robinson and Larry Doby to prove that spectator prejudice could be deconditioned by a winning team. Within a few years, pools of cheap, eager black and dark Latin labor were channeled into mainstream clubs.

So pervasive are the myths of SportsWorld that the recruitment of blacks has been regarded as a gift of true citizenship bestowed upon the Negro when he was ready. It has been conventional wisdom for twenty years that the black exposure in sports has speeded the integration of American society, that white Americans, having seen that

blacks are beautiful and strong, became "liberalized."

This is one of the crueler hoaxes of SportsWorld. Sports success probably has been detrimental to black progress. By publicizing the material success of a few hundred athletes, thousands, perhaps millions, of bright young blacks have been swept toward sports when they should have been guided toward careers in medicine or engineering or business. For every black star celebrated in SportsWorld, a thousand of his little brothers were neutralized, kept busy shooting baskets until it was too late for them to qualify beyond marginal work.

The white male spectator who knew few ordinary black men to measure himself against may have had his awareness raised by watching such superior human beings as Frank Robinson, Jim Brown, Bill Russell, O. J. Simpson, and other highly merchandised SportsWorld heroes, but it also doubled his worst fears about blacks: added to the black junkie who would rip out his throat was the black superstud who could replace him as a man—in bed, on the job, as a model for his children.

By the middle of the 1970s it seemed as though the black experience in SportsWorld might be recapitulated by women. SportsWorld seemed on the verge of becoming the arena in which women would discover and exploit their new "equality." It would be a complex test of adaptability for SportsWorld. The major sports were created by men for the superior muscles, size, and endurance of the male body. Those sports in which balance, flexibility, and dexterity are the crucial elements have never been mass-promoted in America. When a woman beats a man at a man's game, she has to play like a man.

There were signs, however, that women may not embrace SportsWorld as eagerly as did the blacks, profiting from that sorry lesson as well as from their own greater leverage in American society. It is no accident that Billie Jean King, while still an active player, became an entrepreneur and an important voice in American cultural consciousness while Jackie Robinson was a Rockefeller courtier almost to the end of his life.

A great deal of the angry energy generated in America through the coming apart of the 1960s was absorbed by SportsWorld in its various roles as socializer, pacifier, safety valve; as a concentration camp for adolescents and an emotional Disneyland for their parents; as a laboratory for human engineering and a reflector of current moral postures; and as a running commercial for Our Way of Life. SportsWorld is a buffer, a DMZ, between people and the economic and political systems that direct their lives; women, so long denied this particular playland, may just avoid this trap altogether.

But SportsWorld's greatest power has always been its flexibility. Even as we are told of SportsWorld's proud traditions, immutable laws, ultimate security from the capriciousness of "real life," SportsWorld is busy changing its rules, readjusting its alliances, checking the trends. SportsWorld is nothing if not responsive. Hockey interest lagging, how about a little more blood on the ice? Speed up baseball with a designated hitter. Move the football goal posts. A three-point shot in basketball. Women agitating at the college arena gates? Let 'em in. Give 'em athletic scholarships, "jock" dorms, and Minnie Mouse courses. How about a Professional Women's Power Volleyball League?

Stars, teams, leagues, even entire sports may rise or fall or never get off the ground, but SportsWorld as a force in American life orbits on.

Ah, baseball. Our National Pastime. An incredibly complex contrivance that seems to have been created by a chauvinistic mathematician intent upon giving America a game so idiosyncratic that it would be at least a century before any other country could beat us at it. And indeed it was. After a century in which baseball was celebrated as a unique product of the American character, Chinese boys began winning Little League championships, and young men from Latin America and the Caribbean began making a significant impact upon the major leagues. The highly organized Japanese, who had taken up the game during the postwar occupation of their country (perhaps as penance for yelling "To Hell with Babe Ruth" during banzai charges) were almost ready to attack again.

But SportsWorld had spun on. That other peculiarly American game, football, declared itself the New National Pastime. Baseball and God were announced dead at about the same time, but the decision against baseball apparently is taking longer to reverse, thanks in the main to pro football's colossal public relations machine. The National Football League played its scheduled games on Sunday, November 24, 1963, because its historic television deal was pending and Commissioner Pete Rozelle was determined to prove that nothing, *nothing*, could cancel the show. But that winter, NFL sportscasters infiltrated the banquet circuit with the engaging theory—quintessential SportsWorld—that America had been at the brink of a nervous breakdown after President Kennedy's assassination and that only The Sport of the Sixties' business-as-usual attitude had held the country together until Monday's National Day of Mourning unified us all in public grief.

Ten years later, though hopefully still grateful, America had grown bored with the cartoon brutality of pro football. America was boogieing to the magic moves and hip, sly rhythms of basketball, The Sport of the Seventies. We've had enough of pure violence, simulated or otherwise, went the SportsWorld wisdom, now we need something smooooooooth.

There is no end to SportsWorld theories— of the past, the present, the future—especially now that a new generation of commentators, athletes, coaches, and fans feels free to reform and recast sports, to knock it off the pedestal and slide it under the microscope, giving it more importance than ever. SportsWorld newspapermen dare to describe to us action that we have seen more clearly on television than they have from the press box, and SportsWorld telecasters, isolated from the world in their glass booths, dare to explain to us what the players are *really* thinking. SportsWorld analysts were once merely "pigskin prognosticators" predicting

the weekend football scores; now they may be as heavy as any RAND Corporation futurist. Is hockey an art form or is it a paradigm of anarchy, in which case are we obligated as concerned citizens to watch it? Is tennis more than just a convenient new market for clothes and building materials and nondurable goods? What will be The Sport of the Eighties? Will no sport ever again have its own decade? Will cable television and government-regulated sports gambling and the institutionalized fragmenting of society balkanize us into dozens of jealous Fandoms?

SportsWorld, once determinedly anti-intellectual, has become a hotbed of psychologists, physicians, and sociologists questioning premises as well as specific techniques. Should lacrosse players really be eating steak before games, or pancakes? Why are the lockers of defensive linemen neater than those of offensive linemen? Does athletic participation truly "build character" or does it merely reinforce otherwise unacceptable traits? Should communities rather than corporations own teams?

But very few people seem to be questioning SportsWorld itself, exploring the possibility that if sports could be separated from SportsWorld we could take a major step toward liberation from the false values, the stereotypes, the idols of the arena that have burdened us all since childhood.

SportsWorld is not a conspiracy in the classic sense, but rather an expression of a community of interest. In the Soviet Union, for example, where world-class athletes are the diplomat-soldiers of ideology, and where factory girls are forced to exercise to reduce fatigue and increase production, the entire athletic apparatus is part of government. Here in America, SportsWorld's insidious power is imposed upon athletics by the banks that decide which arenas and recreational facilities shall be built, by the television networks that decide which sports shall be sponsored and viewed, by the press that decides which individuals and teams shall be celebrated, by the municipal governments that decide which clubs shall be subsidized, and by the federal government, which has, through favorable tax rulings and exemptions from law, allowed sports entertainment to grow until it has become the most influential form of mass culture in America.

SportsWorld is a grotesque distortion of sports. It has limited the pleasures of play for most Americans while concentrating on turning our best athletes into clowns. It has made the finish more important than the race, and extolled the game as that William Jamesian absurdity, a moral equivalent to war, and the hero of the game as that Henry Jamesian absurdity, a "muscular Christian." It has surpassed patriotism and piety as a currency of communication, while exploiting them both. By the end of the 1960s, SportsWorld wisdom had it that religion was a spectator sport while professional and college athletic contests were the only events Americans held sacred.

SportsWorld is neither an American nor a modern phenomenon. Those glorified Olympics of ancient Greece were manipulated for political and commercial purposes; at the end, they held a cracked mirror to a decaying civilization. The modern Olympics were revived at the end of the nineteenth century in an attempt to whip French youth into shape for a battlefield rematch with Germany. Each country of Europe, then the United States, the Soviet Union, the "emerging" nations of Africa and Asia, used the Olympics as political display windows.

The 1972 Arab massacre of Israeli athletes was a hideously logical extension of SportsWorld philosophy.

SportsWorld begins in elementary school, where the boys are separated from the girls. In *Sixties Going on Seventies*, Nora Sayre recounts the poignant confrontation of a gay man and a gay woman at a meeting. She is banging the floor with a baseball bat, and he asks her to stop; the bat symbolizes to him the oppression of sports in his childhood. But to her the bat symbolizes liberation from the restraint that had kept her from aggression, from sports, in her childhood.

By puberty, most American children have been classified as failed athletes and assigned to watch and cheer for those who have survived the first of several major "cuts." Those who have been discarded to the grandstands and to the television sets are not necessarily worse off than those tapped for higher levels of competition. SportsWorld heroes exist at sufferance, and the path of glory is often an emotional minefield trapped with pressures to perform and fears of failure. There is no escape from SportsWorld, for player or spectator or even reporter, that watcher in the shadows who pretends to be in the arena but above the fray.

The American love for spectacles was a factor in our popular culture long before Cecil B. DeMille made *Ben Hur*, or even before "Buffalo Bill" Cody regaled the crowds for years with his Wild West Show. Television, with its mandate to attract the largest possible audience, quickly ascertained that spectator sports could not only attract but also hold vast audiences.

The Super Bowl has become the most lucrative annual spectacle in American mass culture. Why, in only eight years, did it overtake the Kentucky Derby and even baseball's World Series as the Numero Uno sports spectacle in this country? Why does it cost more to buy a minute of advertising during the Super Bowl telecast than during any other single program?

Michael Real's thesis in his book, *Mass-Mediated Culture*, from which this essay is taken, is that the Super Bowl combines electronic media and spectator sports in a unique way. As a cultural anthropologist, Real views this marriage between television and football as a "ritualized mass activity, which structurally reveals specific cultural values proper to American institutions and ideology." If, as he shows, the marriage was not made in heaven but somewhere between Wall Street and Madison Avenue, the 85 million who watched Super Bowl XI are not too concerned. For, as Real points out, although mass-mediated culture "tends to profane a civilization's most sacred and powerful words and images, in the process it also manages to elevate otherwise mundane events of no real consequence to the status of spectacles of a powerful, quasi-sacred myth and ritual nature." Ergo, the Super Bowl.

The Super Bowl: Mythic Spectacle
Michael Real

NBC Television Sports' "proud" presentation of Super Bowl XI to perhaps 85 million Americans from the Rose Bowl in Pasadena, January 9, 1977, ushered in a popular spectacle of intriguing cultural significance. Gilbert Seldes notes that the instant fame of Lord Byron upon the publication of "Childe Harold's Pilgrimage" reached some 2,000 people, while, in the era of mass culture, Lassie's first film meant for the dog "adoration on the part of ten million." A quarter century later, in 1969, when Joe Namath led the New York Jets to victory in Super Bowl III, announcing the coming of

age of the American Football Conference and the end of the Green Bay Packer dynasty, four or five times Lassie's original followers saw it all in their living rooms while it happened. And by 1974, when the Miami Dolphin line and Larry Csonka moved through the Minnesota Vikings for a 24 to 7 victory, more Americans watched than had seen the first man walk on the moon and only slightly fewer than the record 95 million who watched the funeral of President Kennedy.

What makes the Super Bowl the most lucrative annual spectacle in American mass

Super Bowl Spectacle. The Dallas Cowboys play the Miami Dolphins in the 1972 Super Bowl.
UPI Photo

culture? To answer that question this case study utilizes the 1974 Super Bowl VIII telecast on videotape as a data bank of cultural indicators . . . and then interprets that data to explain both the inner structure and the social function of the Super Bowl as a total mass-mediated cultural event. Methodologically it draws on a variety of communications-related disciplines to achieve a balance between Anglo-American emphasis on empirical data and Continental interest in philosophical implications. The thesis that emerges is this: The Super Bowl combines electronic media and spectator sports in a ritualized mass activity; it structurally reveals specific cultural values proper to American institutions and ideology; and it is best explained as a contemporary form of mythic spectacle. A cross-cultural mythic approach to Super Bowl VIII indicates why the annual Super Bowl may not be culture with a capital *C* but is popular with a capital *P* surrounded by dollar signs and American flags. . . .

Sports and Electronic Media: A Marriage Made in Heaven

By successfully blending electronic media and spectator sports, the Super Bowl has become the capstone of an empire. Even odds-makers agree it is the number-one game in what 1972 public opinion surveys found was the number-one sport in America. The president of the United States concocts plays and telephones them to coaches in the middle of the night; astronauts listen in orbit; cabinet members, top corporate executives, and celebrities vie for tickets to attend the game in person. In its first eight years, the Super Bowl surpassed the one-hundred-year-old Kentucky Derby and the seventy-year-old World Series as the number-one sports spectacle in the United States. Commercial time on the Super Bowl telecast is the most expensive of the television year, surpassing even the Academy Awards presentation. These are the figures on Super Bowl VIII:

Live attendance: 71,882
Television audience: 70 to 95 million
CBS payment to NFL for television rights: $2,750,000
CBS charge for advertising per minute: $200,000 to $240,000
Total CBS advertising income from game: over $4 million
Estimated expenditures in Houston by Super Bowl crowd: $12 million
Words of copy sent out from newsmen: over 3 million

Curiously, this mass cultural impact revolved around a telecast that was composed of a distribution of elements as illustrated in Figure 1. The excitement seemed to be about

a football game, but the total play-action time devoted in the telecast to live football was less than ten minutes. How has the combination of spectator sports and electronic media evolved into such curious and powerful expressions of mass-mediated culture?

Super Bowl VIII was only a recent climax in the sacred union of electronic media and spectator athletics. The courtship began with Edison's film of the Fitzsimmons-Corbett fight in 1897 and was consummated nationally in 1925 when the first radio network broadcast Graham McNamee's description of the World Series, and in 1927 when the first cross-country radio hook-up carried the Rose Bowl. . . .

The marriage, one is tempted to say, was made not in heaven but somewhere between Wall Street and Madison Avenue. The combination of television and sports has created substantial incomes for each, spilling into major corporate coffers. In addition, the viewing experience of the Super Bowl, taken in mythic perspective, has become peculiarly appropriate to life in the Wall Street–Madison Avenue dominated advanced industrial state. Of course, big-time football was not the only offspring of the wedding of electronic media and spectator sports. Over two and a half years in advance of the events, ABC had sold its television commercial time for the 1976 Summer and Winter Olympics for $62 million. . . .

Inside Super Bowl VIII:
A Structural Analysis of Football

Myths reflect and make sacred the dominant tendencies of a culture, thereby sustaining social institutions and life-styles. What are the common structural constituents that underlie both the parent American society and its game-ritual offspring, the Super Bowl?

Cummings takes a step toward a structural, semiotic analysis of American sports when he writes

The essential aspects of American sport are

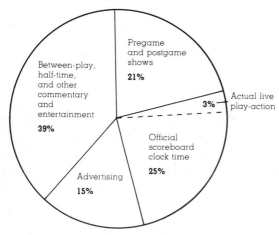

Figure 1 Distribution of elements in the Super Bowl telecast.

basic expressions of the American cultural pattern.... The very forms of our sports indicate dominant temporal and spatial national features. If the hunt was the central expression of sport in pre-industrial, state-of-nature America with its expansive landscape and assertion of a primal relationship between man and nature, then baseball, football, basketball and the like are the central expressions of an urban, technological, electronic America reflecting its concern with social structure and interpersonal relationships.... Since industrial America severed work from a sense of fulfillment, we have turned more and more to sport as an accessible means of self-contemplation. This is the reason for the cheer and sense of release when the batter sends the ball soaring out of the park; the pleasure of the stuff shot, the break-away; the satisfaction of the bomb, the punt return, the long gainer. Our modern sports are attempts to break out of an artificially imposed confinement [Ronald Cummings, "The Superbowl Society," in Browne, Fishwick, and Marsden, eds., *Heroes of Popular Culture* (Bowling Green, Ohio: Bowling Green University Popular Press, 1972), pp. 109–10].

But such surface observations do not touch the deep structure of any single sport. Football is not a mere parable or allegory of American life. It is not a story outside and about a separate referent. Rather, it is a story that is also an activity and a part of the larger society. Moreover, it relates organically to the larger whole. As such, the Super Bowl is a formal analog of the institutional and ideological structure of the American society and culture it is "about." *In the classical manner of mythical beliefs and ritual activities, the Super Bowl is a communal celebration of and indoctrination into specific socially dominant emotions, life-styles, and values....*

The nationalism of American sports is made explicit with the National Anthem at the beginning of virtually every competition from Little League baseball to the Super Bowl. Super Bowl VIII offered an ideal popular singer for middle America, Charley Pride, who is both black and country-western–working-class American, Archie Bunker and Fred Sanford, all rolled into one. The CBS announcer had the right country but the wrong song, when he proclaimed that Charley Pride would now sing "America, the Beautiful." (After Pride finished the "Star Spangled Banner," it was correctly identified.) Further appeal to middle America was evident when the six officials were introduced as "a high school teacher in Ohio ... a paint company official ... a medical supplies salesman ...."....

What is the relationship of this packaged experience to the concrete lives of viewers and the surrounding political-economic system? The Super Bowl, like the bulk of mass-mediated culture, is at once a celebration of dominant aspects of a society and a diversion from unmediated immersion in that society.

Despite all the Super Bowl's overt and latent cultural significance, it is popular as a *game*, that is, the formal competition itself has no overt functional utility. It is apart from the viewers' work, from bills, from family anxieties, from conflicts in the community, from national and international politics. Total psychic involvement becomes desirable because the game is enjoyed for its own sake, unlike most activities in the deferred-reward world of laboring for salaries, home, and self-improvement, or eternal salvation. In contrast to wars or family problems, the viewers are aware that they can enjoy or even opt out of the Super Bowl with the same free choice that they entered into it because "it's only a game." In this manner, the Super Bowl is typical of mass-mediated culture in arousing all the emotions of excitement, hope, anxiety, and so on, but as a displacement without any of the consequences of the real-world situations that arouse such feelings.

For the viewer, the Super Bowl, like much of television and mass culture, provides a feeling of a "separate reality." Despite its mass standardization, it has something of the magic and awesome appeal of the "non-ordinary states of consciousness.". . . The satisfaction that viewers seek in the Super Bowl is born in a hunger not unrelated to the search for ecstasy and comprehension around which mystic and esoteric traditions have been built. In the Super Bowl, however, the yearning is arrested at a low level, subject to what [William F.] Lynch calls the "magnificent imagination" that fixates rather than challenges the human capacity for creative imagery and symbolic formulations.

Historically, the Super Bowl parallels the spectacles of the Coliseum in Rome where the spoils of imperialism were grandiosely celebrated. As a game, the Super Bowl is not a simple, traditional diversion in the way that playing a hand of cards is. . . .

An understanding of contemporary media, the functions of mythic rituals, and the structural values of professional football in a cross-cultural framework takes one sufficiently inside the Super Bowl to explain why 85 million Americans watch it and, at the same time, provides the aesthetic distance to question the Super Bowl's global significance. The Super Bowl recapitulates in miniature and with striking clarity certain dominant strains in the society in which it was born and that takes such delight in it. As a mythic spectacle, the Super Bowl has developed as a perfect vehicle for reinforcing social roles and values in an advanced industrial state.

The structural values of the Super Bowl can be summarized succinctly: *American football is an aggressive, strictly regulated team game fought between males who use both violence and technology to win monopoly control of property for the economic gain of individuals within a nationalistic, entertainment context.* The Super Bowl propagates these values by elevating one football game to the level of a mythic spectacle that diverts consciousness from individual lives to collective feelings, and completes the circle by strengthening the very cultural values that gave birth to football. In other words, the Super Bowl serves as a mythic prototype of American ideology collectively celebrated. Rather than a mere diversionary entertainment, it can be seen to function as a "propaganda" vehicle strengthening and developing the larger social status quo.

While the critics may overstate their case, viewing the Super Bowl can be seen as a highly questionable symbolic ritual and an unflattering revelation of inner characteristics of mass-mediated culture in North America. Nevertheless, to be honest, for many of us it still may be a most enjoyable activity.

Whatever the judgment, the next time a network "proudly presents" a Super Bowl or its mass-spectacle successor, it may well be ushering in a communications event more culturally and symbolically significant than even the traditional American icons of apple pie, motherhood, and the flag.

The *dramatis personae* of SportsWorld come from all segments of American life. Bring two avid baseball fans to a crucial series between the Los Angeles Dodgers and the Cincinnati Reds and it makes not a whit of difference if one is a Ph.D. in nuclear physics from Cal Tech and the other a file clerk at an aircraft factory: They can soon be engaged in a heated discussion on whether the L.A. manager should walk Pete Rose in the eighth inning when the Reds have two men on base, two men out, and are trailing by a run.

Michael Novak is not only a brilliant essayist—he undoubtedly qualifies as the ultimate sports fan. In his recent book, *The Joy of Sports*, Novak compares sports to a religion, and not in a demeaning way. He would totally disagree with those who believe that "sports is the opiate of the masses." He believes, rather, that long after the Democratic or Republican parties have passed into history, maybe even long after the United States itself has disappeared, human beings will still find sports fundamental to their lives. In the following excerpt from his book, Novak explains why sports, in his view, transcend mere entertainment and may be America's true secular religion.

Sports:
The Natural Religion

Michael Novak

A sport is not a religion in the same way that Methodism, Presbyterianism, or Catholicism is a religion. But these are not the only kinds of religion. There are secular religions, civil religions. The United States of America has sacred documents to guide and to inspire it: the Constitution, the Declaration of Independence, Washington's Farewell Address, Lincoln's Gettysburg Address, and other solemn presidential documents. The President of the United States is spoken to with respect, is expected to exert "moral leadership"; and when he walks among crowds, hands reach out to touch his garments. Citizens are expected to die for the nation, and our flag symbolizes vivid memories, from Fort Sumter to Iwo Jima, from the Indian Wars to Normandy: memories that moved hardhats in New York to break up a march that was "desecrating" the flag. Citizens regard the American way of life as though it were somehow chosen by God, special, uniquely important to the history of the human race. "Love it or leave it," the guardians of orthodoxy say. Those on the left, who do not like the old-time patriotism, have a new kind: they evince unusual outrage when this nation is less than fully just, free, compassionate, or good—in short, when it is like all the other nations of human history. America should be *better*. Why?

The institutions of the state generate a civil religion; so do the institutions of sport. The ancient Olympic games used to be both festivals in honor of the gods and festivals in honor of the state—and that has been the classical position of sports ever since. The ceremonies of sports overlap those of the state on one side, and those of the churches on the other. . . . Going to a stadium is half like going to a political rally, half like going to church. Even today, the Olympics are constructed around high ceremonies, rituals, and symbols. The Olympics are not barebones athletic events, but religion and politics as well.

Most men and women don't separate the sections of their mind. They honor their country, go to church, and also enjoy sports. All parts of their lives meld together.

Nor am I indulging in metaphor when I say that nearly every writer about sports lapses into watery religious metaphor. So do writers on politics and sex. Larry Merchant says television treated the Super Bowl "as though it were a solemn high mass." Words like *sacred*, *devotion*, *faith*, *ritual*, *immortality*, and *love* figure often in the language of sports. Cries like "You gotta believe!" and "life and death" and "sacrifice" are frequently heard.

But that is not what I mean. I am arguing a considerably stronger point. I am saying that sports flow outward into action from a deep natural impulse that is radically religious: an impulse of freedom, respect for ritual limits, a zest for symbolic meaning, and a longing for perfection. The athlete may of course be pagan, but sports are, as it were, natural religions. There are many ways to express this radical impulse: by the asceticism and dedication of preparation; by a sense of respect for the mysteries of one's own body and soul, and for powers not in one's own control; by a sense of awe for the place and time of competition; by a sense of fate; by a felt sense of comradeship and destiny; by a sense of participation in the rhythms and tides of nature itself.

Sports, in the second place, are organized and dramatized in a religious way. Not only do the origins of sports, like the origins of

drama, lie in religious celebrations; not only are the rituals, vestments, and tremor of anticipation involved in sports events like those of religions. Even in our own secular age and for quite sophisticated and agnostic persons, the rituals of sports really work. They do serve a religious function: they feed a deep human hunger, place humans in touch with certain dimly perceived features of human life within this cosmos, and provide an experience of at least a pagan sense of godliness. . . .

Sports are religious in the sense that they are organized institutions, disciplines, and liturgies; and also in the sense that they teach religious qualities of heart and soul. In particular, they recreate symbols of cosmic struggle, in which human survival and moral courage are not assured. To this extent, they are not mere games, diversions, pastimes. Their power to exhilarate or depress is far greater than that. To say "It was only a game" is the psyche's best defense against the cosmic symbolic meaning of sports events. And it is partly true. For a game is a symbol; it is not precisely identified with what it symbolizes. To lose symbolizes death, and it certainly feels like dying; but it is not death. . . .

At a sports event, there may be spectators, just as some people come to church to hear the music. But a participant is not a spectator merely, even if he does not walk among the clergy. At a liturgy, elected representatives perform the formal acts, but all believers put their hearts into the ritual. It is considered inadequate, almost blasphe-

mous, to be a mere spectator. Fans are not mere spectators. If they wanted no more than to pass the time, to find diversion, there are cheaper and less internally exhausting ways. Believers in sport do not go to sports to be entertained; to plays and dramas, maybe, but not to sports. Sports are far more serious than the dramatic arts, much closer to primal symbols, metaphors, and acts, much more ancient and more frightening. Sports are mysteries of youth and aging, perfect action and decay, fortune and misfortune, strategy and contingency. Sports are rituals concerning human survival on this planet: liturgical enactments of animal perfection and the struggles of the human spirit to prevail. . . .

Cynicism, skepticism, and irreverence are not only compatible with sports; without them, sports would choke us with their cloying. They are preconditions for sports. Cynicism, skepticism, and irreverence with regard to the "serious things" in life give rise to sports. Athletes and fans know that entire industries are born and obsolesce, that governments come and go, that economic cycles ebb and flow, that empires rise and fall. The British Empire has not outlived cricket, after

> "Sports affect people, and their lives, far more deeply and for a longer time than mere diversion would."

all. Soccer will be played when China, Russia, and the United States no longer dominate the planet. A certain cynicism about the "real world" may be permitted those who live brief lives, enjoying the clear, cold taste of the combats of sports. The lessons here are eternal ones.

The news departments of our newspapers and television studios are constructed to attract consumers. Each day they give us headlines, tell of manufactured crises, and report on events created so they can report them. They pretend that in the last few hours something has happened in the world worth knowing. Like commercial sports, they are involved in selling. Buying a newspaper or a television station is a little like buying a franchise. The political myths and stories reported on the news may have less substance than the sports account of the local team's fifty-seventh loss this year. Who tells a more mythic story, the White House correspondent giving us sixty seconds on the president's day, or the local radio announcer calling the play-by-play, his sympathies clearly with the locals? The statistics of the business reporter may be less reliable than the seasonal statistics on the pitchers, hitters, fielders. Which world is more "real"? . . .

Those who think sports are merely entertainment have been bemused by an entertainment culture. Television did not make sports possible—not even great, highly organized sports. College football and major league baseball thrived for decades without benefit of television. Sports made television

commercially successful. No other motive is so frequently cited as a reason for shelling out money for a set. (Non-sports fans, it appears, are the least likely Americans to have sets.). . .

Television is peculiarly suited to football, and vice versa; the case is special. But football, whether in the fresh air of the stadium, in the foul air of a sawdust tavern, or in the private corner of one's home, is far more than *Mary Tyler Moore*. The animation on the faces of the fans, the groans, the yells will show you that while televised entertainment may leave its watchers passive, football doesn't. Wives can tell, rather quickly, whether their husbands' teams have won or lost. Sports affect people, and their lives, far more deeply and for a longer time than mere diversion would.

On Monday nights, when television carries football games, police officers around the nation know that crime rates will fall to low levels otherwise reached only on Mother's Day and Christmas.

We are, as I said, too close to sports to appreciate their power. Besides, our education is rigorously pragmatic and factual: those things are real which can be counted. It teaches us nothing about play, or myth, or spirit. So we are totally unprepared to speak about the things we love the most. Our novelists write poorly of women, of love, of tragedy. Our religious sensibilities, which in some are warm with fervor, in our major publicists are chill. Grown men among us are virtually inarticulate about anything that touches our souls. Grunts, groans, and silence. Being cool. Taciturn like Bogart, Grant, Fonda, Newman, Brando, Hoffman, the American male responds to beauty by seeing, by participating, by ritual acts, but not by speaking. Our women can get nothing important out of us. Women talk one language, men another. Our nation lacks cultural institutions, rituals, and art forms that would bridge the sexes. We have no truly popular operas, or suitably complex literature, or plays in which our entire population shares. The streets of America, unlike the streets of Europe, do not involve us in stories and anecdotes rich with a thousand years of human struggle. Sports are our chief civilizing agent. Sports are our most universal art form. Sports tutor us in the basic lived experiences of the humanist tradition. . . .

That is why the corruptions of sports in our day, by corporations and television and glib journalism and cheap public relations, are so hateful. If sports were entertainment, why should we care? They are far more than that. So when we see them abused, our natural response is the rise of vomit in the throat. . . .

Athletes are not merely entertainers. Their role is far more powerful than that. People identify with them in a much more priestly way. Athletes exemplify something of deep meaning—frightening meaning, even. Once they become superstars, they do not quite belong to themselves. Great passions are invested in them. They are no longer treated as ordinary humans or even as mere celebrities. Their exploits and their failures have great power to exult—or to depress. When people talk about athletes' performances, it is almost as though they are talking about a secret part of themselves. As if the stars had some secret bonding, some Siamese intertwining with their own psyches. . . .

Sports constitute the primary lived world of the vast majority of Americans. The holy trinity—baseball, basketball, and football—together with tennis, bowling, skiing, golf, hiking, swimming, climbing (not to mention gambling, Monopoly, cards, and other forms of play), are not simply interludes but the basic substratum of our intellectual and emotional lives. Play provides the fundamental metaphors and the paradigmatic experiences for understanding the other elements of life.

SportsWorld may be the edifice of the great American secular religion, as Michael Novak suggests. On the other hand, it may be nothing less than a chauvinistic tool used by politicians, the military establishment, and the super-patriots—a very useful tool during times of stress. The powers that be at the National Football League, for example, have boasted that sticking to their schedule the Sunday after John F. Kennedy was murdered enabled the country to make it through until his funeral on Monday.

Jerry Izenberg takes a cynical view of the attempt to use the sports arena to propagate "somebody else's idea of what our individual patriotism ought to be." He is dubious about the kind of halftime show held during the 1971 Super Bowl in Miami's Orange Bowl. At a time when militarism in America was under fire by some responsible congressional critics of the Vietnam war, a flight of U.S. Air Force planes buzzed the field, immediately followed by Miss Anita Bryant singing "The Battle Hymn of the Republic." Izenberg is rightfully indignant when popular culture, via sports or whatever other means, becomes so blatantly manipulative.

"Glory, Glory Hallelujah": The New Patriotism and Sports

Jerry Izenberg

From time to time I have wondered just how important sports are in this country—not how necessary or how much a part of our culture, but rather if at any time they could be translated into something else by someone or a group of someones who wanted to use them for his or their purpose.

I do not wonder anymore.

I went to Washington, D.C., in July, 1969, for baseball's annual All-Star Game. At least, I thought that's what I was attending when I got off the Metroliner at Union Station. What I walked into was something very different. . . .

We were, of course, smack in the middle of the most unpopular war in the history of this country. It was a war so unpopular that something like forty percent of the country was at various times reasonably alleged to have been opposed to it. This is not a majority, but it is a hell of a lot of people. Just to keep the record straight, I happen to be one of them. . . .

It is true . . . that sports are an accurate mirror of America. More than that, they are a barometer. Violence of all kinds began to show up on our ball fields just slightly ahead of the period when we first began to notice it in our streets. Sports expose us for what we are during any given social era, and for that very reason they can be used as an indicator of what we may be about to become if enough people will only use their eyes and ears instead of their throats.

The image that sports reflect is a true measure of their role as a mirror. But when someone tries to shape that image so that it will reflect what he wants, then we are into something which demeans sports, insults us all, and simply should not be allowed to happen without somebody yelling "Cop."

All right. So baseball was down in the nation's capital that week, and you can't knock baseball for riding a good tidal wave of publicity. Lord knows it could use one almost any month you care to name—in or out of season. The President of the United States, Richard M. Nixon, responded nobly to the moment. So did the cabal around him.

There was a reception scheduled for the East Room at the White House several hours before the ballgame. The game was a prime-time televised night event, ultimately rained out and rescheduled for the next afternoon. The reception went off on schedule. Mr. Nixon had invited most of the writers who were in town to cover the game, all the players, and many baseball officials to stop by for a drink.

An hour before the reception, Jack Murphy, the talented sports editor and featured columnist of the *San Diego Union*, and I were sitting in his room at the John Adams Hotel looking out the window, where dishwater-gray clouds were pressing down on the steaming city streets. The telephone rang. It was somebody on Herb Klein's staff.

Mr. Klein had been the editor of the *San Diego Union* between jobs as the roller-derby-type advance man for Mr. Nixon's varied jousts with the press. Now he was in the White House, and the purpose of his staff member's call seemed a little odd. He wanted to know if anything unusual had happened in the 1929 World Series. Jack couldn't think of anything, but then the two of us sat down, and we finally came up with the fact that Connie Mack, who managed the Athletics, had named Howard Ehmke, a sore-armed pitcher of very little ability that season, to open against the Cubs. Ehmke pitched and won.

Roughly an hour later we were standing in the East Room and Mr. Nixon was rubbing his hands together at the microphone, welcoming baseball to Washington. He then told an anecdote about his tenderest memories of baseball. They were all about the way as a teen-ager he had listened to the 1929 World Series on the radio and how he recalled that . . .

"He's going to tell our story," I said. You knew that four sentences ago, but I am a slow learner. So I laughed, and Murphy laughed, and what really was the difference, because everyone has speeches written for them anyway?

Well, the difference was this. Baseball writers are a strange breed, highly defensive about how they earn their living when there is no need to be. When Mr. Nixon finished to great applause, you couldn't have prevented what followed if you'd cut off their fingers at the knuckles. "Good for the game," they said. "A real fan," they said. They rushed out to write, and since the rain worked hand-in-hand with the Nixon press department when there was no game to write about, they zeroed in on America's spanking new Super Fan.

When Mr. Nixon finished to great applause, you couldn't have prevented what followed if you'd cut off their fingers at the knuckles. "Good for the game," they said. "A real fan," they said. They rushed out to write, and since the rain worked hand-in-hand with the Nixon press department when there was no game to write about, they zeroed in on America's spanking new Super Fan.

This made it a swell week for the President, because he had the Apollo II astronauts whizzing across the front page all week, and Richard Nixon, Super Fan, whizzing across the sports pages for a day or two, and a lot of people neglected to count the casualty lists from Vietnam that week.

In any event, a lot of interesting things began to happen that year. The President of the United States has gone through periods of his political life when all the favorable press he was receiving in any given month could have been engraved on the head of a pin with enough room left over for a band of angels to hold their own Harvest Moon Ball.

What happened next was that the President of the United States wound up in Fayetteville, Arkansas, that fall to watch the Texas-Arkansas football game. The game just happened to be on national television, and Mr. Nixon just happened to be interviewed. He also happened to do a little color commentary for the announcers, one of whom just happened to be the former Oklahoma coach, Bud Wilkinson, who just happened to be a former Republican candidate for the Senate, and who just happened to belong to Mr. Nixon's physical-fitness or some such committee.

Obviously the reaction around the country was extremely favorable. A new vista had been opened to the think-tank down at the White House. Richard M. Nixon, Super Fan, was again hurled full tilt at the sports pages.

The next step was reasonably obvious. If you could hurl Richard Nixon at the sports pages and bounce him off the fifty-yard line and into America's heart, why not dribble his policies along with him?

It began innocently enough. It began with the President of the United States and A.T.&T., and assorted golfers, quarterbacks, coaches, and pitchers. No matter where the President of the United States went, he was always in position to pick up the phone and get through to congratulate the man who had just won the Masters or the World Series or the Super Bowl. . . .

It went on and on and on. One day in the early spring, with the Super Bowl already history and the Masters, the NBA playoffs, and the opening of baseball season still in the future, I wrote a column conjecturing about the major crisis that gripped the White House. A check of the sports calendar showed there wasn't a single event of any consequence going on in the toy department that day. . . .

The 1970 football season was a beauty. Mr. Nixon's War, which had been Mr. Johnson's War before that and Mr. Kennedy's War before that, and General Eisenhower's War before that, was ripping the country apart. And still there was no solution in sight. It was about that time that hand-in-hand, professional football and the NCAA, which controls all the college football on network television, began to march into the horizon of their first full-fledged "God Bless America Season."

Nobody this side of Dave Meggyesy would seriously object to the playing of the national anthem at a football game, and nobody of any consequence did. The national anthem is hardly a slice of anybody's conspiracy—nor, for that matter, is the American flag. If it ever becomes such, then we can all forget about sports, because nobody will be playing any kind of game ever again around here anyway. . . .

But you may also recall that once upon a time, college bands put on half-time shows where the P.A. announcer said: "And now the band will form a locomotive and choo-choo across the fifty-yard line. Note the engine's steam emerging from the third sousaphone on the left." After that they might form a map of the United States in which the two clumsy clarinetists who were supposed to represent the Gulf Coast of Florida were generally ten yards too far in the direction of Caracas.

They would pull out streamers and simulate a county fair while three broads in gold tights twirled batons. There were variations on the theme as well.

But the 1970 season was something else. Now, before this thesis goes any further, you ought to be made aware of the fact that both professional football and the NCAA are in dire need of varied forms of help from the Congress and the government. The NCAA, you may remember, with enough friendly congressmen in its pocket, was able to get proper muscle exercised to keep the pros off television on Friday nights and Saturday afternoons in the fall when it would hurt the NCAA's members at the live gates of their games and in the battle of the Nielsen ratings. The pros, on the other hand, asked for and received congressional sanction for the merger between the American and National leagues, which some people considered an antitrust violation; for their player draft, which some people considered an antitrust violation; and for . . . etc., etc.

The NCAA, you may remember, with enough friendly congressmen in its pocket, was able to get proper muscle exercised to keep the pros off television on Friday nights and Saturday afternoons in the fall when it would hurt the NCAA's members at the live gates of their games and in the battle of the Nielsen ratings. The pros, on the other hand, asked for and received congressional sanction for the merger between the American and National leagues, which some people considered an antitrust violation; for their player draft, which some people considered an antitrust violation; and for . . . etc., etc.

It is also worth noting that Russell Long, the senator from Louisiana, and Hale Boggs, a congressman from Louisiana, were instrumental in obtaining that approval. Finally, the fourth and the sixth Super Bowls wound up being played in New Orleans, although the town was not reasonably equipped in restaurants and hotels to handle them. If you make one plus one equal two, then be advised that a lot of people add just the way you do.

So it is clear that the televised football proceedings—both professional and college—have a good deal of reason to keep the White House and the White House's Justice Department reasonably happy.

Never in the history of this country, with the exception of V-J Night, has "God Bless America" been played as many times as it has been played on televised football games beginning that fall. You may read "The Battle Hymn of the Republic" or "America the Beautiful" or "This Is My Country" in place of "God Bless America" if you prefer, because they threw them at us so fast and so often you couldn't tell the grace notes from the half-notes without a scorecard.

This came at a time when the President and his people were out hitting hard. If you opposed the war, you opposed America. Now, translate that to, if you opposed America (which you didn't in the first place), you opposed football, and if you opposed football, well, my God, where will it all lead?

It was, of course, impossible for anyone to come on out at half-time and chant "Burn the gooks," but, playing on the emotionalism of a divided country, inferring that all the "good people" were there on their feet singing their allegiance and chanting "We're number one," there was a far more subtle way to get it done. . . .

There were always prisoners of war.

And so it began. Nobody except that lunatic fringe of a segment of America's youth, which really doesn't understand the meaning of war and how horrible it can really be, can handle a loaded proposition like that. Of course, everyone wanted the prisoners home where they belong. But by injecting the minute of silence for them into the proceedings, football has been manipulated into dropping a continual emotional blockbuster during which nobody dared to ask why the hell they were sent there in the first place. It was a neat package.

Conversely, during the 1970 season ABC chose not to televise the University of Buffalo's half-time show, which reflected a different view of America. The show dealt with matters like ecology and pollution, and it did, indeed, deal with the Vietnam war. The decision not to carry the show was made by Roone Arledge, the American Broadcasting Company's vice-president in charge of sports programming. He dropped it on the theory that it was antiwar and, therefore, political. Critics wondered whether the Army-Navy game ceremonies weren't a bit political in the other direction. The ABC party line was that the Army-Navy game ceremonies did not *praise* the war, and therefore were no problem.

Perhaps.

Or perhaps the references to pollution might have been embarrassing to ABC, since its football telecasts were sponsored in part by an automobile company which is dedicated to the proposition that the only thing which can save America is two internal combustion engines in every garage. Perhaps.

Whatever the reason, the Buffalo half-time show was dropped out and hammered to death by Saturday and Sunday afternoons dedicated to reminding us of the Vietnam POWs. Well, we should be reminded about them. But then perhaps we should also be reminded, just once in a while, for the benefit of that forty percent which wonders, what the hell we were doing over there in the first place.

In any event, the beat rolled on. It rolled and it rolled, and it reached its absolute purple-tinted depths. It happened in Miami.

In January, 1971, the Baltimore Colts met the Dallas Cowboys in the Super Bowl. The game was lousy, the half-time spectacular. I have often wondered exactly how that half-time got put together. I called Jim Kensil, who is the administrative assistant to Pete Rozelle, who is the commissioner of football, and asked about it one day.

"We didn't do it," Kensil explained. "We naturally have total control over every half-time show at every professional game. But this was in the Orange Bowl, and they have a regular show director down there, and he is a good one. He put together the show. Naturally, we did have to approve it."

He didn't put together a show. He put together a recruiting poster. Bands, floats, drill teams, spear carriers, enough people to stock the original Exodus were scattered across the artificial turf. That's O.K., because it was a showcase event, and it required ex-

treme showmanship.

But there was something else.

With perhaps one out of every two Americans either at the park or sitting in front of their television sets, a flight of U.S. Air Force planes buzzed the field. It happened at a time when militarism in America was under fire in some reasonably responsible quarters. It happened at a time when there was no reason to suspect Fidel was going to kidnap the Orange Bowl, and in the unlikely circumstances he was, there were enough planes above to be guilty of overkill.

Into this stepped Miss Anita Bryant, the Orange Juice kid, to sing, *a cappella*, "The Battle Hymn of the Republic."

That's where we left pro football in 1970–71. When we picked it up again in the late summer of 1971, President Richard M. Nixon, Super Fan, was in Canton, Ohio, for the Football Hall of Fame ceremonies. Again, an Air Force honor guard soared overhead. This time it flew in a broken formation. The empty spaces were left to signify the missing prisoners of war.

Now, you simply do not call up your friendly neighborhood Air Force base and say, "Look, we're having this little bash over at our place, and we would like you to skywrite 'Happy Birthday, Herbie.' He's eleven you know."

So what happened? Well, Bob Cochran, who also works in the commissioner's office, was quoted as saying the Super Bowl planes were offered to the league. Apparently somebody called and said, "Anyone down there need a squadron?" and pro football said yes. It raises some interesting thoughts.

Moreover the military being what it is, no pilot in his right mind is going to say to the guy flying off his wing, "You move over and leave a hole, and we'll make a little symbolism." It had to be planned. The POW issue became a political smoke screen tied to political football, and the word "football" is used advisedly.

In between, of course, baseball made a fumbling gesture toward the same parity. After all, pro football had gotten all the good favor by shilling properly, even introducing the man who had led an abortive raid on a POW camp at a time when the prisoners were elsewhere, before a pro football game.

Baseball, unfortunately, is still baseball. Its big pitch for God, Country, and White House came just prior to the 1971 All-Star Game in Detroit, when it put 150 flag-bearers of the combined military services onto the infield at Tiger Stadium. Unfortunately, one of them, a marine, collapsed during the ceremonies (nobody will say what impact this had on marine recruiting in the Detroit area the following week), and a great debate transpired between a medic and a "baseball man" as to whether or not it was all right to stash the collapsee in one of the dugouts.

Certainly, there have been nationalistic overtones in our sporting events—even as there are in other countries. But no American government that has had highly controversial foreign and domestic policies has ever before been able to consistently propagandize through the athletic fields.

It is a dangerous thing. If you believe, as I do, that our playing fields reflect the mood and temper of our nation, it is dangerous to pervert that image to make people believe it is something other than it may actually be.

I think that kind of thing is bad for America. I think that you cannot attend a sporting event of any consequence in this country where the spectators are not made up of every shade of the American political spectrum, every ethnic background and racial group, and, in short, reflect every facet of what America is about. They do not have to be told how or what to think. . . .

I wonder about these blatant attempts to tie sports—which are a historic and important part of our culture—to an America which I can only hope does not exist, an America which says it will intrude on all our private beliefs to use the sports arena to propagate somebody else's idea of what our individual patriotism ought to be.

I wonder, for example, if just once during that long string of half-time shows someone had called for a minute of silence for all the cancer victims who did not benefit from research because the funds were spent on the space program, whether or not the management might not have judged that to be political, with no place in the sports arena. I wonder how many airplanes in what kind of formation the government would have agreed to send over for that one.

I wonder.

Sociologists and market researchers alike are invariably looking for the All-American city, that is, the aggregate collection of Americans who represent the average citizen of this country. Simple statistical theory verifies that more than two-thirds of us are clustered around the fullest part of the Great Bell Curve, so when Procter and Gamble wants to find if its latest soap will sell, it looks for the test city that encompasses Middle American values.

"Middletown" for sociologists Robert and Helen Lynd was Muncie, Indiana, which is not far from Indianapolis. This is *the* All-American city, according to Jeff Greenfield. Once a year the not-so-Silent Majority foregather some 300,000 strong for an extraordinary weekend of "revelry and release, fellowship and indulgence" unique in SportsWorld. Some come because they are indelibly hooked on the 500-mile International Sweepstakes, Indy's official title. Some come to see the violent denoument when a car crashes into a wall and the driver becomes a sheet of fire. But most come just to be there. Each year more Americans meet at the huge field off Georgetown Road than anywhere else in the country. This is the Mecca of Middle America, Greenfield believes. Why these hundreds of thousands make the annual pilgrimage gives us a picture of popular culture in America that probably would have made Alexis de Tocqueville smile and say to himself, "Ah, yes, I told you so."

Middle America Has Its Woodstock, Too

Jeff Greenfield

It is a warm night, and the sky overhead is lit up by searchlights. Cars, campers, trucks, buses, station wagons—thousands of vehicles with thousands of people in and milling around them—are parked in ragged rows that stretch back and forth across the huge field at 30th Street off Georgetown Road in the All-American city of Indianapolis, Indiana.

A cacophony of jazz, pop, rock and roll blasts into the night from speakers hooked to radios, tape decks, and stereos. Hundreds of barbecue grills broil steaks, hamburgers, hot dogs. Oceans of beer, surely more than 100,000 bottles and cans of it, are popped and twist-snapped open. The whine of motorcycles, their single lights cutting through the dark, speed up and down the fire lanes between the rows of cars. Grown men with wives and children shout their *macho* yearnings at young women.

"Hey sister, I'd sure like to get my dipstick into you!"

"Hey! Any of you girls wanna be liberated, you just come on over to this here camper, you hear? Sleeps six and lays twelve! Ha-ha-ha."

Almost as often, the men invoke another common denominator as well:

"Hey! Whattya drinkin'?"

"Coors! Great beer!"

"Aw, that's crap!"

"Goddamn, you don't know your beer!"

At the edge of the field, on a flat-bed truck,

a pleasant, balding man in his sixties, who could be the principal of a small-town junior high school, is trying to spread the good word of the Gospel.

"You boys and girls, you've got to please God by faith. How about you, young lady? Would you like to be called a child of God tonight? How 'bout you, young fella? Will you overcome the world?"

"Somebody get the preacher a beer!" shouts a crew-cut boy of fifteen, who well might be singing in the preacher's choir on another weekend. But not this weekend. This is the Friday midnight of Memorial Day weekend, and for these thousands, it is a time for furious revelry, release, and a strange blend of fellowship and indulgence, all part of one of the most extraordinary conglomerations I have ever attended anywhere: The Indianapolis 500 Mile International Sweepstakes.

Every year more than 300,000 people pack the fields and stands around the track of the Indianapolis Speedway, ostensibly to witness the running of the 500 Mile Race, with its million dollars in prize money, record-breaking speeds, and a constant promise of fiery death. It is the single biggest event held in America; in any given year more Americans meet in one place at one time here at the speedway than anywhere else in the country.

From May 1, when the speedway opens for practice runs, through the time trials to determine who qualifies for entry into the race, up through the neosacred Race Day, a fever begins to build all through Indianapolis. Indiana newspapers fill page upon page with history, legend, predictions, and interviews with everyone from the hot-dog concessionaires to John MacKenzie, the man who carries into Victory Lane the ponderous Borg-Warner trophy with which to honor the winner. More than 100,000 people attend the time trials on the weekends before Memorial Day. By the Friday night before the race, fans who drive here from as far away as California and Oregon are settled in their beer-swilling camping areas, ready for the gates to swing open at 5:00 a.m. on Race Day, so they can guide their cars into the enormous infield area of the track. From this vantage point, where not more than a tenth of the track can be seen, the fans set up platforms and chairs on the tops of vehicles. The resulting cluster of humanity is something like a tract of suburbia writ small, each family or group carving out a few square feet of land. And there, under an increasingly hot sky, inhaling the stench of gasoline, burning rubber and charcoal, the fans eat and drink away the dawn and the morning and finally the climactic afternoon during which thirty-three drivers in exotic-looking automobiles flash by them.

Why do the people come? Certainly, the city of Indianapolis is no part of the attraction. This is perhaps the worst metropolis in the entire United States—a city with endless miles of indifferent gray structures, Burger Chefs, and Kentucky Fried Chicken stands and a political climate that welcomed such spasms of paranoia as the Klan during the Twenties and the Birchers in the Sixties. Even if the Indy fans were drawn to such a city, none of them would leave their valued places at the speedway to journey downtown.

Still, it is not simply, or even primarily, the race that attracts the fans. It is the awesome, terrifying, hilarious spectacle surrounding the race, a spectacle that holds within itself a welter of contradictory yearnings tearing at what is left of our national spirit: glory, speed, wealth, fellowship, and death. After witnessing the Indy for a weekend, I came away with an overriding sense of sorrow at what we have done to each other and to ourselves.

The 500 itself is, in part, a celebration of technology, the continuation of an old American tradition, rooted in another age, when people traveled great distances from their isolated communities to hear Chautauqua speakers or witness the new marvels of the machine age: horseless carriages, dirigibles, airplanes, and the wonders of science that promised, at the turn of the twentieth century, to turn the United States into a streamlined technological paradise.

The first 500 Mile Race at Indianapolis was run in 1911. It was dreamed up by Carl Fisher, a local promoter-businessman and speed demon, who had originally built the track on which the races were run in order to test improvements for automobiles. Within a few years the race was attracting thousands of spectators from around the country, and it proved a powerful magnet as well for manufacturers, who saw a chance for free publicity by underwriting the cost of machines built with their parts. During the gasoline-scarce days of World War II, the speedway was abandoned. After the war it was brought back to life by Tony Hulman, its present owner and president, and since then the ties between the race and big business have become thoroughly entwined. Piston-ring makers, tire manufacturers, sparkplug producers, and the like help finance the machines, which cost up to $200,000, counting the maintenance costs. And the businessmen of Indianapolis have for fifteen years or so whipped up a promotional effort of Babbitt-sized proportions. Checkered flags, like those used to wave autos across the finish line, decorate the city. Throughout the month of May a series of events progressively builds up excitement: Festival queens are chosen, there are gin rummy and golf tournaments, a mayor's breakfast, and finally an eve-of-race parade down streets painted with the checkered flag pattern. So ingrained is the race that even the soul-saving evangelists working the camping area pass out tracts bearing the checkered-flag emblem and titled, "Souvenir Victory Edition."

Boosterism, however, cannot by itself attract tens of thousands of people to Indianapolis for a week of sleeping in open fields or in the back of campers. The race itself, of course, is a powerful magnet. Each year the cars are lower, sleeker, and more ingen-

The Indianapolis Speedway. Each year more than 300,000 people attend the Indy 500, the largest single event in America.
Norman Snyder

Camping in at the Indy 500. For some, the race is incidental to the gathering of a huge crowd for a good time.
Norman Snyder

iously designed. This year, for example, their surprisingly fragile fiber-glass bodies are equipped with a small wing in front and a wider wing in the rear; the air pressure against these wings pushes the car down, holding it to the road at speeds that, on the straightaways, approach 200 miles per hour.

The sheer power of thirty-three cars roaring around the speedway is unbelievable. From the turn, you hear a high-pitched, angry whine, like a brigade of enraged, giant hornets. Suddenly, the cars appear, hurtling around the banked track and seeming to fly straight at you. Then in a flash of energy, light, sound, dirt, and with an assault of rubber and gasoline smells, they zoom by. It seems odd, given supersonic airplanes and rockets to the moon, that automobiles can be so awesome in their speed. The reason they are, of course, is that the high-speed auto fits into a fantasy that is grafted onto everyday experience. Watching the race at Indy is like attending a Walter Mitty Me-

morial Convention. Every fan imagines himself behind the wheel of an Olsonite-Eagle or a Ford-McLaren thundering and skidding around the track.

"Boy," says Jennings, head of a family of a half-dozen that journeys here every year from eastern Pennsylvania. "I'd love to get in my Chevy and drive around that track just once. They got a little bus that'll give you a tour of the track for fifty cents, but, aw, I'd love to drive around it, just once. Or even get in one of those cars. I don't see why they don't have an old car they'd let you sit in and take a picture. You'd think they'd set it up for the fans."

Along with the specter of glory, fame, and speed, of course, is the specter of death. Driving a car at three times the maximum speed permissible on a superhighway is, to say the least, unsafe; running over a piece of metal on the track, making a slight miscalculation in braking or steering in a turn, can send the car smashing into a wall. And while no visitor will admit openly that it is the prospect of witnessing death that draws him to the race, the anticipation of danger is clearly present in many minds.

"Yeah," says Paul, a shipping clerk from Iowa. "I was here in '39 when Floyd Roberts got it, and I remember '64 when Eddie Sachs and MacDonald were burned up. Jeez, that was something. And in '68 I was right there when a guy got killed. Got a great picture of that wreck."

For Mike, a state trooper from Ohio who is half-Indian, witnessing the race in person cannot be equaled by television because "the thing that's wrong with TV, they try not to show the grisly part of it when it happens. Now you take this Jim Malloy, who got wrecked in the trials this year. Well, when it first happened, they didn't show the grisly stuff—you know, when he actually hit the wall, how bad it really was."

"You'd be surprised," says Cleek, a sun-reddened harvest hand in his sixties who drove in by himself from Oregon in a pickup. "Ninety-nine-and-nine-tenths of 'em come to see wrecks. You hear 'em say, 'Wasn't no good race, no wrecks.' Just like people watching a man on a ledge, most of 'em want him to jump. That's what a lot of people come here for, I believe. I dunno, I see it the other way. That just about ruins it for me. People gettin' pretty damned hard-hearted now. They don't give a damn about their fellow man."

The strange mixture of honor and bloodshed, sudden wealth and sudden death, courage and the mechanical skill involved in building a championship car and keeping it moving (a task assigned the "pit" crews who service the cars with the frantic speed and competence of a team of open-heart surgeons) can get a hold on a fan that lasts for a lifetime. It happened to Clyde de Botkin, who was stationed near the speedway during World War II, when it lay idle. "I said to myself, 'If they ever have a race here again, I want to see it.' I came back in '47, and that was it," he recalls.

Now in his late forties, Clyde is a round-faced, pleasant man who works as a handy man in Kaycee, Wyoming. For the last twenty-seven years the only vacation Clyde has taken has come between late April and early June. Every year, he has driven—most years by himself—to Indianapolis, taken a room in a boardinghouse, and stayed at the track from April 28 to June 5. He usually hangs out in Gasoline Alley, where the cars are stored and worked on; he has come to know the mechanics and pit crews by sight. The pride of his life is Special Pit Pass Number 777, which a speedway official gave Clyde a decade ago after he had noticed him at the 500 year after year; the pass permits him to watch the mechanics and drivers at work. The Indy is the only event outside of his daily routine that Clyde de Botkin has experienced in his adult life. He has never even seen another part of America.

"Why should I want to?" Clyde says. "This is the most exciting place in the world." Too exciting, in fact. Clyde has an enlarged heart, and he must lie down several times a day in the air-conditioned press room to safeguard his health. "I know it's dangerous," he says; "but if I couldn't be here on Race Day, I just wouldn't . . . " He shrugs.

Unlike Clyde de Botkin, who is caught up in the drama of the long, grueling challenge, a remarkable number of Indy fans are almost totally uninterested in the race. "I'd guess about one hundred thousand people here never see the cars in action, don't know who won, and couldn't care less," says a race reporter. For the fans who pack the infield, in fact, the race is almost impossible to watch. Even the more affluent spectators in the upper grandstand can see barely a fourth of the track—it's just too big to see in its entirety.

"We'll be watching the backstretch," says Sam, a shipping clerk. "We'll only see a tenth of the race. But when they go by, we'll see this one's first, this one's second, and so on. So if their positions change, we'll know somebody passed."

For a sports junkie like me, this was odd to contemplate; it was as if I could watch a hockey game only from a ten-foot-wide stretch of ice, or a baseball game from an obstructed view that revealed only a six-foot chunk of base path. What kind of sports fan would watch an event where he could not see who scored, how, and what outstanding achievements won or lost the game?

"See, that's the thing," explains Bill, who has been here since Monday to be first on line to drive through the gate to the infield. "You could just not run the race, and most people here wouldn't give a damn. The main thing is that people get together, and there's no fighting or anything. . . . I know these guys—they been coming here for years. They all park in the same spot at the gate, they mess around for three or four days with each other before the race starts, buying each other beer . . . they take care of each other. When we get inside the track, there'll be friends on both sides of us where we park, everybody sharing everything, and they all have a ball. No, we don't see each other the rest of the year. Just here. And we talk about the times we had and party it up."

What Bill says is echoed by many of the hard-core Indy spectators. They come because it is a "good time" and "the world's biggest party." For three or four days they live away from the home, the factory, or office. ("Why do I come here?" asks a Bendix-Westinghouse worker from Elyria, Ohio. "Four days away from the kids, with my buddies.") They move outside their existence. They see friends who are friends for a weekend each year. They drink endless cases of beer, grill their steaks together, and yell at the young girls in hot pants and T-shirts with no bras underneath.

"You know what this is like?" asks a dark-haired, muscular auto worker. "This is just like that Woodstock. Only those hippies had their music and their dope; we got beer and racing."

"Yeah," a buddy interrupts. "Only nobody around here is taking off their clothes and running around bare-ass. Goddamnit." He laughs.

There *is* a sense of Woodstock here, a sense of camaraderie. That sense is kindled by staying up all night together on Friday, waiting for the aerial bombs to explode at 5:00 a.m. Saturday signaling the opening of the track, and then the furious, Oklahoma-land-rush sprint to the best positions in the track. ("The real race is at 5:00 a.m.," says a security guard. "The car race, that's just an anticlimax.") But there is also a fierce sense of personal, material pride: in the outfitting of the campers ("We got four bunk beds here; paneling, a can, running water, air conditioning") and the food ("Now, most folks have cold fried chicken. Hell, we got eggs any style, bacon, ham, home fries, and then steak, baked potato and sour cream, salad with blue cheese dressing"). The dull glow

of television sets flickers in the late night air, that umbilical link with reality that cannot be turned off and left home.

I could not help thinking that we have at Indianapolis a metaphor for the way we live: Here before me are decent, hard-working people, seeking a sense of community and excitement beyond their individual lives, waiting patiently to be packed together with their small luxuries and large discontents, being told what is happening by electronic tote boards and a loudspeaker system, seeking what fun they can find from a spectacle whose drama they cannot very clearly see. Much of the pomp and majesty of the race—the start, the solemn intonation, "Gentlemen, start your engines," the pit stops, the salute to the victor—all of these important events go unwitnessed by those who have come the farthest and endured the most to be "where the action is."

An hour before the race ends, hundreds of spectators' cars are already streaming out of the speedway, under a cloud of gasoline fumes, dust, and heat, heading for home. They will not see the climax of the race, the victorious driver receiving his kiss on the cheek from the queen, the victor's slow, triumphal circuit of the track, nor the winning driver acknowledging the cheers from the grandstand. They have gotten what they came for in the revelry and release and camaraderie; and most of them will be back again next year.

"I been goin' to my sister's place for Memorial Day since 1938," says Cookie, a factory hand in his fifties who made his first visit to the Indianapolis 500 this year. "This is the first time I missed going to my sister's. And I think she's never going to see me no more."

"One thing about this," observed Cookie, speaking as one of the latest initiates to Middle America's perennial Woodstock, "I guess you either love it or you hate it. And I love it."

SECTION THREE: POPULAR CULTURE AND SOCIAL CHANGE

Popular culture has played a dualistic role in the process of social change in this country. On the one hand, popular culture has been guilty of perpetuating demeaning stereotypes of ethnic minorities and women and of maintaining the status quo in the areas of politics and life-styles. On the other hand, popular culture, especially within the last decade, has been utilized as a valuable tool in the struggles for racial and sexual equality and in the movements for political and cultural change.

Politicians and political life have always fascinated the creators of popular culture. Motion pictures, in fact, have nearly exhausted the repertoire of story lines and messages that relate to politics. Most of the "political" movies have tended to reaffirm basic democratic ideals and beliefs. Many of them have alluded to the need for social reform, but even the most radical generally exhibited some degree of faith in the democratic system. The films written and produced by Communists in the 1930s were no exception. As Granville Hicks noted, communism usually paraded as the highest form of "Americanism" and always at least paid lip service to democracy in the thirties.

The long tradition of political satire in popular culture also mirrored the widespread public acceptance of the democratic system. From Mark Twain to Mort Sahl, the satirists generally functioned as gadflies whose barbs were intended to prod politicians and the electorate into living up to the ideals of democracy. "If I criticize somebody," explained Mort Sahl in the late fifties, "it's only because I have higher hopes for the world, something good to replace the bad." Like that of the majority of political satirists, Sahl's commentary was rooted in what he termed a fundamental "democratic social philosophy."

Before the 1950s, the political protest element of American popular music was largely confined to the works of folk singers such as Woody Guthrie, who broke into the world of mass entertainment through radio and records but never commanded large audiences. Guthrie believed so strongly in the power of song to surmount political injustice that his guitar carried the inscription "this machine kills fascists."

Pete Seeger, who toured with Guthrie in the thirties and forties, became a moving force in the revival of the protest music tradition in the late fifties. With songs such as "Where Have All the Flowers Gone?" Seeger articulated the feelings of political dissent that were beginning to emanate from California, Wisconsin, and other American universities. Seeger and Guthrie also inspired young songwriters such as Phil Ochs and Bob Dylan and helped spawn the so-called topical-song boom of the early sixties. Following in the path of Seeger and Guthrie, this new breed of singer-songwriter tackled topical issues in a

style that could best be described as "musical journalism." The careers of Dylan and the other protest singers took on added social importance because they coincided with the civil rights movement, the peace crusade, and the rise of the small but intensely activist New Left.

Many of the articles on politics in this anthology deal with television. Although the medium has probably received too much credit for shaping public opinion, television can be a very

powerful influence in political life. Senator Joseph McCarthy, whom many Americans regarded as a hero because of his anti-Communist activities in the early fifties, learned how important television could be in the success or failure of a politician. McCarthy's popularity plummeted in 1954 when his investigation of Communist subversion in the army was given nationwide television coverage. The army-McCarthy hearings revealed the inconsistencies in the senator's accusations and highlighted his less-than-heroic characteristics. Two decades later, the Watergate hearings, which detailed the conspiracies of "the President's men," simply added another chapter to the history of television's impact on political life.

Television played a crucial role in the black civil rights movement, but even before the protests of the fifties and sixties, blacks had achieved a great deal of acceptance through their participation in popular culture. Sports has been one of the most important avenues to social equality for blacks, although even the superstars of black athletics have had to contend with racial prejudice.

Boxer Jack Johnson became the heavyweight champion in the early twentieth century, but the frantic search for a "great white hope" to dethrone him illustrated just how far blacks had to go to be accepted as equal. Jackie Robinson, who "broke the racial barrier" in professional baseball in 1947, had to keep a tight rein on his defiant spirit in order to make it in the previously all-white sport. Even in the supposedly enlightened 1970s, Henry Aaron's pursuit of Babe Ruth's home run record unleashed the latent racism of those who could not bear to see a black man surpass the legendary "sultan of swat."

Blacks have enjoyed prominence in popular music, but until the 1960s their success did not erase the stigma of racial inferiority. Bert Williams became a featured entertainer with the Ziegfeld

Follies in the early twentieth century, but he suffered humiliations such as having to take the service elevator to return to his hotel room after a performance. Louis Armstrong rose to national stature as a premier jazz musician, but it is doubtful the public adulation of "Satchmo" would have been so great if he had been a defiant agitator for equal rights.

Developments in popular music in the 1960s indicated the depth of the black rebellion. The new "soul" music style tended to reject the blues heritage of suffering. It was an assertive, forward-looking type of music that often contained very explicit statements of the "black is beautiful" or "black power" concepts that were in wide circulation. The Impressions sang, "We're a winner," while James Brown declared, "I'm black and I'm proud." Musicians such as Curtis Mayfield, James Brown, and Otis Redding often rivaled political leaders in their ability to inspire an audience with the spirit of self-respect.

Unlike popular music and sports, television and motion pictures have only recently reversed the trend toward fostering unrealistic and damaging ideas about blacks. Other minority groups, notably the Native Americans and Hispanic Americans, have also suffered from being stereotyped by the white creators of television and movies. Several articles in this section discuss this traditional tendency of popular culture and

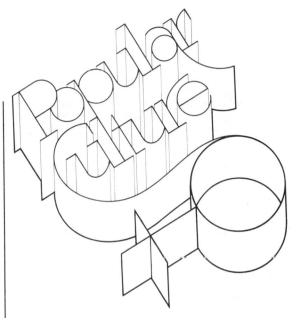

the recent developments that have challenged the history of discrimination.

Popular culture has both hindered and aided the struggle of women to liberate themselves from demeaning social stereotypes and to achieve political and economic equality with men. Betty Friedan's landmark book, *The Feminine Mystique* (1963), noted the power of the mass media in promulgating harmful images of women. Friedan examined the "women's magazines" and found that the overwhelming portrait of woman was that of the "happy homemaker." She attacked this stereotype and called the sacred institution of the family home nothing more than "a comfortable concentration camp" for many women.

The women's liberation movement that Friedan helped to inspire was mirrored in the popular culture. The mass media gave a great deal of coverage to the female protesters, due in large part to the

fact that they were "hot copy." Although the number of women actively involved in the movement remained fairly small, the dissenters managed to exert a great deal of influence in American society. The movement proved to be quite skillful in manipulating the media to its advantage. By dramatizing their protests, as they did whn they picketed the Miss America Pageant, the women's libbers at least caused Americans to think about their own conceptions of "woman's place" in society.

In the early 1970s, popular culture reflected an increasing awareness of the women's liberation movement. Numerous magazine and newspaper articles dealt with the protest of women, most of them from a fairly sympathetic point of view. In 1972, Gloria Steinem and others founded *Ms.* magazine, an important development in the "consciousness-raising" efforts of the female activists. By promoting their own ideas of what women should aspire to be, Steinem and her cohorts hoped to at least neutralize the "damaging" effects they believed magazines such as *Good Housekeeping* inflict upon the identity of women.

Several films of the seventies, such as *Alice Doesn't Live Here Anymore*, have attempted to portray women who are not dependent on men for their identity, but the motion picture industry, like every other facet of popular culture, is still overwhelmingly dominated by men and their views of the world. Television has lagged behind movies, but there have been some new portraits of women in such programs as "The Mary Tyler Moore Show," "One Day at a Time" and "Alice." Popular music has shown a similar trend toward the emergence of stronger, more independent women in recent years, but the specter of "male chauvinism" still exists in the recording industry. Women have probably taken greater strides toward equality in sports than in any other area of popular culture, due in large part to the success of tennis stars such as Billie Jean King and Chris Evert. The articles on women in this section provide interesting and in-depth discussions of female images and contributions in movies, television, popular music, and sports.

The specific protest movements of minorities and women are clearly mirrored in popular culture. Yet, as several of the articles in this section illustrate, we can also gain valuable insights into the ideas, attitudes, values, and life-style priorities of the millions of nonprotesting Americans by studying their taste in food and fashion and their choice of diversions and entertainment. The recreational habits of Americans can also serve as indicators of prevailing life-style patterns. An examination of the role of automobiles in popular culture is instructive in this regard.

The automobile rose to cultural prominence in the 1920s. During that decade cars, particularly the inexpensive Model T Ford, profoundly affected the landscape and the mind of America. Young people saw in the accessibility of automobiles a new age of personal freedom, whereas many older people were shocked to witness the effect these "bedrooms on wheels" had on the morality of the country. In spite of the concerns of some, the consensus feeling was one of excitement at the dawn of the automobile age. A 1926 Los Angeles Times editorial expressed the jubilance and optimism of the majority of Americans

by declaring that the automobile would allow a "swifter and surer" realization of our inalienable right of "the pursuit of happiness."

The automobile has continued to be a core element in the life-styles of millions of Americans. During the fifties and sixties, the "hot rod" subculture emerged, with large numbers of young people defining their styles of life by possessing a "mean machine" or "cherry set of wheels" and engaging in the ritualistic "cruising" of city streets. The counterculture's repudiation of materialism and the gasoline shortages of the seventies have tempered, but by no means ended, the American love affair with motor-driven vehicles.

Teen-agers still cruise in cars, motorcycling is both a popular activity and a big-time sport, and pickup trucks and vans are selling in greater numbers than ever. Twice as many vans, for instance, were sold in 1975 than in 1970. And "vanning" (or "trucking," a term many enthusiasts prefer) has become an elaborate hobby, with costly customizing of expensive vehicles serving as a means of self-expression. Food, fashion, and the all-American game of poker, the subjects of articles in this section, represent similar ways in which Americans define themselves.

The final article in this section concerns the so-called life-style rebellion that gave rise to the counterculture. The movement has had a strong impact on American society. Longer hair styles, more "expressive" clothing, the widespread use of marijuana and drugs such as cocaine, and the apparent liberalization of sexual relationships and attitudes have testified to this influence. In many respects, those "over thirty" were even more affected by the life-style rebellion than those under that mythical line of chronological and cultural demarcation. Louis Lundborg, president of the Bank of America, observed in his book *Future Without Shock* (1974) that the life-style rebellion had spawned a "new value system" in the country that could lead to more honest human relationships and, consequently, to a better society. Others in the "older generation" expressed similar feelings and even those who condemned the young lifestyle rebels had to reevaluate their own assumptions about "the good life" in order to defend them against their youthful assailants.

There are innumerable styles of life in American society and a multitude of ideas, themes, and types inherent in the popular cultural portrayal of politics, minorities, and women in American life. The student of popular culture should be wary of neat conceptualizations and all-inclusive categories. But by observing recurring patterns and similarities in content, we can arrive at some tentative judgments, some "educated generalizations" about the significance of popular culture in the process of social change.

The amount of "news" that appears in any daily issue of an American newspaper, a weekly news magazine like *Time* or *Newsweek*, or a newscast on radio or television depends on two discrete variables, space and time. With advertisements taking up at least 60 percent of available newspaper space, and another 20 percent filled with comic strips, recipes for Aunt Tilly's pickled popcorn fritters, and columns like Ann Landers' advice to the perplexed, only about 20 percent is left for the so-called newshole.

Profiles of the newspaper "gatekeepers," from David Manning White's initial study in 1950 to the most recent analyses, show that only about one-tenth of the news that pours into a typical newspaper from the wire associations (Associated Press, United Press International, Reuters, and so on) finally appears in the paper. The "gatekeeper" perforce has to reject nine-tenths of the incoming copy.

The perplexing question that Daniel Boorstin asked in his well-known book *The Image* was: How much of the newspaper's limited space that remains is truly news? Or is much of it, as he suggests, nothing more (or less) than *pseudo-events*, an aptly-phrased term he formulated.

In the following excerpt from *The Image*, Boorstin defines a pseudo-event and gives some explicit examples of how politicians use the mass media in calculated strategies to garner some of the media's limited space or time.

The Pseudo-Event

Daniel Boorstin

A pseudo-event . . . is a happening that possesses the following characteristics:

1. It is not spontaneous, but comes about because someone has planned, planted, or incited it. Typically, it is not a train wreck or an earthquake, but an interview.

2. It is planted primarily (not always exclusively) for the immediate purpose of being reported or reproduced. Therefore, its occurrence is arranged for the convenience of the reporting or reproducing media. Its success is measured by how widely it is reported. Time relations in it are commonly fictitious or factitious; the announcement is given out in advance "for future release" and written as if the event had occurred in the past. The question, "Is it real?" is less important than, "Is it newsworthy?"

3. Its relation to the underlying reality of the situation is ambiguous. Its interest arises largely from this very ambiguity. Concerning a pseudo-event the question, "What does it mean?" has a new dimension. While the news interest in a train wreck is in *what* happened and in the real consequences, the interest in an interview is always, in a sense, in *whether* it really happened and in what might have been the motives. Did the statement really mean what it said? Without some of this ambiguity a pseudo-event cannot be very interesting.

4. Usually it is intended to be a self-fulfilling prophecy. The hotel's thirtieth anniversary celebration, by saying that the hotel is a distinguished institution, actually makes it one. . . .

A trivial but prophetic example of the American penchant for pseudo-events has long been found in our *Congressional Record*. The British and French counterparts, surprisingly enough, give a faithful report of what is said on the floor of their deliberative bodies. But ever since the establishment of the *Congressional Record* under its present title in 1873, our only ostensibly complete report of what goes on in Congress has had no more than the faintest resemblance to what is actually said there. Despite occasional feeble protests, our *Record* has remained a gargantuan miscellany in which actual proceedings are buried beneath undelivered speeches, and mountains of the unread and the unreadable. Only a national humorlessness—or sense of humor—can account for our willingness to tolerate this. Perhaps it also explains why, as a frustrated reformer of the *Record* argued on the floor of the Senate in 1884, "the American public have generally come to regard the proceedings of Congress as a sort of variety performance, where nothing is supposed to be real except the pay."

The common "news releases" which every day issue by the ream from Congressmen's offices, from the President's press secretary, from the press relations offices of businesses, charitable organizations, and universities are a kind of *Congressional Record* covering all American life. And they are only a slightly less inaccurate record of spontaneous happenings. To secure "news coverage" for an event (especially if it has little news interest) one must issue, in proper form, a "release." The very expression "news release" (apparently an American invention; it was first recorded in 1907) did not come into common use until recently. There is an appropriate perversity in calling it a "release." It might more accurately be described as a "news holdback," since its purpose is to offer something that is to be held back from publication until a specified future date. The newspaperman's slightly derogatory slang term for the news release is "handout," from the phrase originally used for a bundle of stale food handed out from a house to a beggar. Though this meaning of the word is now in common use in the news-gathering professions, it is so recent that it has not yet made its way into our dictionaries.

The release is news pre-cooked, and supposed to keep till needed. In the well-recognized format (usually mimeographed) it bears a date, say February 1, and also indicates, "For release to PM's February 15." The account is written in the past tense but usually describes an event that has not yet happened when the release is given out. The use and interpretation of handouts have become an essential part of the newsman's job. The National Press Club in its Washington clubrooms has a large rack which is filled daily with the latest releases, so the reporter does not even have to visit the offices which give them out. In 1947 there were about twice as many government press agents engaged in preparing news releases as there were newsmen gathering them in.

The general public has become so accustomed to these procedures that a public official can sometimes "make news" merely by departing from the advance text given out in his release. When President Kennedy spoke in Chicago on the night of April 28, 1961, early editions of the next morning's newspapers (printed the night before for early-morning home delivery) merely reported his speech as it was given to newsmen in the advance text. When the President abandoned the advance text, later editions of the Chicago *Sun-Times* headlined: "Kennedy Speaks Off Cuff . . ." The article beneath emphasized that he had departed from his advance text and gave about

events. President Franklin Delano Roosevelt, whom Heywood Broun called "the best newspaperman who has ever been President of the United States," was the first modern master. While newspaper owners opposed him in editorials which few read, F.D.R. himself, with the collaboration of a friendly corps of Washington correspondents, was using front-page headlines to make news read by everybody. He was making "facts"—pseudo-events—while editorial writers were simply expressing opinions. It is a familiar story how he employed the trial balloon, how he exploited the ethic of off-the-record remarks, how he transformed the Presidential press conference from a boring ritual into a major national institution which no later President dared disrespect, and how he developed the fireside chat. Knowing that newspapermen lived on news, he helped them manufacture it. And he knew enough about news-making techniques to help shape their stories to his own purposes. . . .

F.D.R. was a man of great warmth, natural spontaneity, and simple eloquence, and his public utterances reached the citizen with a new intimacy. Yet, paradoxically, it was under his administrations that statements by the President attained a new subtlety and a new calculatedness. On his production team, in addition to newspapermen, there were poets, playwrights, and a regular corps of speech writers. Far from detracting from his effectiveness, this collaborative system for producing the impression of personal frankness and spontaneity provided an additional subject of newsworthy interest. Was

equal space to his off-the-cuff speech and to the speech he never gave. Apparently the most newsworthy fact was that the President had not stuck to his prepared text.

We begin to be puzzled about what is really the "original" of an event. The authentic news record of what "happens" or is said comes increasingly to seem to be what is given out in advance. More and more news events become dramatic performances in which "men in the news" simply act out more or less well their prepared script. The story prepared "for future release" acquires an authenticity that competes with that of the actual occurrences on the scheduled date.

In recent years our successful politicians have been those most adept at using the press and other means to create pseudo-it Robert Sherwood or Judge Samuel Rosenman who contributed this or that phrase? How much had the President revised the draft given him by his speech-writing team? Citizens became nearly as much interested in how a particular speech was put together as in what it said. And when the President spoke, almost everyone knew it was a long-planned group production in which F.D.R. was only the star performer.

Of course President Roosevelt made many great decisions and lived in times which he only helped make stirring. But it is possible to build a political career almost entirely on pseudo-events. Such was that of the late Joseph R. McCarthy, Senator from Wisconsin from 1947 to 1957. His career might have been impossible without the elaborate, perpetually grinding machinery of "information" which I have already described. And he was a natural genius at creating reportable happenings that had an interestingly ambiguous relation to underlying reality. . . .

He had a diabolical fascination and an almost hypnotic power over news-hungry reporters. They were somehow reluctantly grateful to him for turning out their product. They stood astonished that he could make so much news from such meager raw material. Many hated him; all helped him. They were victims of what one of them called their "indiscriminate objectivity." In other words, McCarthy and the newsmen both thrived on the same synthetic commodity.

Senator McCarthy's political fortunes were promoted almost as much by newsmen who considered themselves his enemies as by those few who were his friends. Without the active help of all of them he could never have created the pseudo-events which brought him notoriety and power. Newspaper editors, who self-righteously attacked the Senator's "collaborators," themselves proved worse than powerless to cut him down to size. Even while they attacked him on the editorial page inside, they were building him up in the front-page headlines.

Newspapermen were his most potent allies, for they were his co-manufacturers of pseudo-events. They were caught in their own web. Honest newsmen and the unscrupulous Senator McCarthy were in separate branches of the same business.

In the traditional vocabulary of newspapermen, there is a well-recognized distinction between "hard" and "soft" news. Hard news is supposed to be the solid report of significant matters: politics, economics, international relations, social welfare, science. Soft news reports popular interests, curiosities, and diversions: it includes sensational local reporting, scandalmongering, gossip columns, comic strips, the sexual lives of movie stars, and the latest murder. Journalist-critics attack American newspapers today for not being "serious" enough, for giving a larger and larger proportion of their space to soft rather than hard news.

But the rising tide of pseudo-events washes away the distinction. Here is one example. On June 21, 1960, President Eisenhower was in Honolulu, en route to the Far East for a trip to meet the heads of government in Korea, the Philippines, and elsewhere. A seven-column headline in the Chicago *Daily News* brought readers the following information: "What Are Ike's Feelings About Trip? Aides Mum" "Doesn't Show Any Worry" "Members of Official Party Resent Queries by Newsmen." And the two-column story led off:

HONOLULU—President Eisenhower's reaction to his Far Eastern trip remains as closely guarded a secret as his golf score. While the President rests at Kaneohe Marine air station on the windward side of the Pali hills, hard by the blue Pacific and an 18-hole golf course, he might be toting up the pluses and minuses of his Asian sojourn. But there is no evidence of it. Members of his official party resent any inquiry into how the White House feels about the whole experience, especially the blowup of the Japanese visit which produced a critical storm.

The story concludes: "But sooner or later

the realities will intrude. The likelihood is that it will be sooner than later."

Nowadays a successful reporter must be the midwife—or more often the conceiver—of his news. By the interview technique he incites a public figure to make statements which will sound like news. During the twentieth century this technique has grown into a devious apparatus which, in skillful hands, can shape national policy.

The pressure of time, and the need to produce a uniform news stream to fill the issuing media, induce Washington correspondents and others to use the interview and other techniques for making pseudo-events in novel, ever more ingenious and aggressive ways. One of the main facts of life for the wire service reporter in Washington is that there are many more afternoon than morning papers in the United States. The early afternoon paper on the East Coast goes to press about 10 A.M. before the spontaneous news of the day has had an opportunity to develop. "It means," one conscientious capital correspondent confides, in Douglass Cater's admirable *Fourth Branch of Government* (1959), "the wire service reporter must engage in the basically phony operation of writing the 'overnight'—a story composed the previous evening but giving the impression when it appears the next afternoon that it covers that day's events."

What this can mean in a particular case is illustrated by the tribulations of a certain hard-working reporter who was trying to do his job and earn his keep at the time when the Austrian Treaty of 1955 came up for debate in the Senate. Although it was a matter of some national and international importance, the adoption of the Treaty was a foregone conclusion; there would be little news in it. So, in order to make a story, this reporter went to Senator Walter George, Chairman of the Senate Foreign Relations Committee, and extracted a statement to the effect that under the Treaty Austria would receive no money or military aid,

only long-term credits. "That became my lead," the reporter recalled. "I had fulfilled the necessary function of having a story that seemed to be part of the next day's news."

The next day, the Treaty came up for debate. The debate was dull, and it was hard to squeeze out a story. Luckily, however, Senator Jenner made a nasty crack about President Eisenhower, which the reporter (after considering what other wire service reporters covering the story might be doing) sent off as an "insert." The Treaty was adopted by the Senate a little after 3:30 P.M. That automatically made a bulletin and required a new lead for the story on the debate. But by that time the hard-pressed reporter was faced with writing a completely new story for the next day's morning papers.

But my job had not finished. The Treaty adoption bulletin had gone out too late to get into most of the East Coast afternoon papers except the big city ones like the Philadelphia *Evening Bulletin*, which has seven editions. I had to find a new angle for an overnight to be carried next day by those P.M.'s which failed to carry the Treaty story.

They don't want to carry simply a day-old account of the debate. They want a "top" to the news. So, to put it quite bluntly, I went and got Senator Thye to say that Jenner by his actions was weakening the President's authority. Actually, the Thye charge was more lively news than the passage of the Austrian Treaty itself. It revealed conflict among the Senate Republicans. But the story had developed out of my need for a new peg for the news. It was not spontaneous on Thye's part. I had called seven other Senators before I could get someone to make a statement on Jenner. There is a fair criticism, I recognize, to be made of this practice. These Senators didn't call me. I called them. I, in a sense, generated the news. The reporter's imagination brought the Senator's thinking to bear on alternatives that he might not have thought of by himself.

This can be a very pervasive practice. One wire service reporter hounded Senator George daily on the foreign trade question until he finally got George to make the suggestion that Japan should trade with Red China as an alternative to dumping textiles on the American market. Then the reporter went straightway to Senator Knowland to get him to knock down the suggestion. It made a good story, and it also stimulated a minor policy debate that might not have got started otherwise. The "overnight" is the greatest single field for exploratory reporting for the wire services. It is what might be called "milking the news."

The reporter shrewdly adds that the task of his profession today is seldom to compose accounts of the latest events at lightning speed. Rather, it is shaped by "the problem of packaging." He says: "Our job is to report the news but it is also to keep a steady flow of news coming forward. Every Saturday morning, for example, we visit the Congressional leaders. We could write all the stories that we get out of these conferences for the Sunday A.M.'s but we don't. We learn to schedule them in order to space them out over Sunday's and Monday's papers."

An innocent observer might have expected that the rise of television and on-the-spot telecasting of the news would produce a pressure to report authentic spontaneous events exactly as they occur. But, ironically, these, like earlier improvements in the techniques of precise representation, have simply created more and better pseudo-events.

During the presidential campaign of Jimmy Carter, adviser Jody Powell convinced the former Georgia governor that he needed a "media expert" to help him win the highest office in the land. The job went to Barry Jagoda, a young CBS news producer. Jagoda has continued as Carter's "TV man" and has served as the prototype of Garry Trudeau's character Duane Delacourt, head of "White House Symbols," in the cartoon strip "Doonesbury."

"It is not my function to have TV enhance Jimmy Carter or to improve his image or to provide him with any additional charisma," Jagoda remarked in an interview. "My job is to mold TV so that it leaves him alone, so that it doesn't change him from the naturally credible and down-to-earth man he is." In other words, Carter is not presented as a "packaged" personality, in contrast to the manner in which Richard Nixon, according to Joe McGinnis' *The Selling of the President, 1968*, was peddled like a commodity in the marketplace.

Tony Schwartz, one of the leading media advisers in the world of politics, gives an insider's appraisal of the power of the "image makers." Schwartz dismisses the notion that voters "buy" candidates like they would products and argues that television is most valuable when it is used to "affect the inner feelings of a voter in relation to a political candidate."

The Inside of the Outside
Tony Schwartz

It has become popular to speak of political candidates as products that can be sold like soap, or formless creatures who need an *image* created for them by media specialists. Joe McGinnis, among others, has fostered a public interest in *image makers* and attributed almost magical powers to the tricks of their trade (*The Selling of the President, 1968*, Trident Press, 1969). Despite the critical tone of articles about them, image makers enjoy reading about the power they command, a power that has as much substance as the images they create.

Image makers concern themselves with makeup, lighting, camera angles, wardrobe, visual backgrounds, etc., or how a candidate *looks* to a viewer. His outside appearance constitutes his image. But this represents a serious misunderstanding of how television functions in relation to our senses.

The image makers follow a classic pattern of using an older medium (film) as the content of a new medium (TV). We have all witnessed this process many times. Telephone communication was filled with "telegrams." Print was filled with talk. Movies were based on books, plays, and scripts. Television was filled with movies. Records were filled with performances, and radio was filled with records. Even today, many of these media are used in the old way. However, the physical and structural characteristics of media exert greater control over our ideas and institutions than the content we receive from them. Media extend our senses into the world about us and structure our ways of learning, understanding, and communicating. Also, the introduction of a new medium may upset our sensory balance, thereby creating a new awareness of the world and new codes through which communication is structured. It is futile to employ television and radio in a political campaign as an extension of print or film. Television and radio are received differently from film or print. Our senses expect electronically mediated information to be organized in a particular way, and our brain applies different patterns in making sense of these data.

The "image people" work with concepts like *charismatic, handsome, youthful*, etc. And they strive to keep their candidate *moving*—through shopping centers, old-age homes, schools, etc. They utilize visual information on television to communicate this image. Television is thus conceptualized as a vehicle for bringing the voters to the candidate, where they can see and experience his glorious image.

I believe it is far more important to understand and affect the inner feelings of a voter in relation to a political candidate than to package an image that voters tend not to believe anyway. It would be more correct to say that the goal of a media adviser is to tie up the voter and deliver him to the candidate. So it is really the *voter* who is packaged by media, not the candidate. The voter is surrounded by media and dependent on it in his everyday functioning. The stimuli a candidate uses on the media thus surround the voter. They are part of his environment, his packaging.

In assessing the reactions of voters to candidates on television, it becomes very clear that a person sitting in his home watching a political figure on his TV set four or five feet away wants to feel that the candidate is talking to him. A politician who typically speaks to large audiences, in a grandiose style, must adjust his speech scale for tele-

vision or radio. Though he may be part of an audience totaling ten or twenty million people, a TV viewer experiences the candidate as someone speaking in his home to one, two, or maybe five people gathered around the set.

Any situation in which a politician is filmed may potentially find its way to the television viewer or the radio listener. Thus a politician on the street, shouting over the volume of traffic to fifty or a hundred people, must understand that a home audience of two or three million listening to him that evening will be put off by his shouting. The home viewer's ear is, in effect, only four or five feet away from the politician's mouth. And there are no diesel trucks or air hammers in his living room.

When I work with a candidate, I encourage him to speak to small groups or single individuals on the street, so the personal quality of his voice will fulfill the expectations

DOONESBURY   by Garry Trudeau

©1977 G. B. Trudeau/Distributed by Universal Press Syndicate.

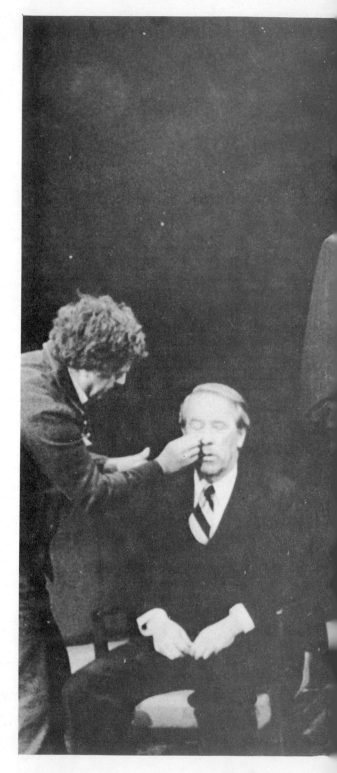

of a single person or small group listening to him on TV news programs. And when I record a candidate for radio or TV spots, I sit next to him and ask him to talk to me, not the microphone. If he sounds like he is reading from a script or begins talking to the mike, I interrupt and say, "You know, I don't feel you're talking to me." Many politicians in a recording situation will talk either to an imaginary vast audience spread across a wide geographic area, or *on behalf of themselves*, i.e., as if their position had been challenged by a reporter and they were defending it. A home listener is not interested in a politician who formally expresses a position. To the average voter, expressing-a-position-talk is what government officials do when they want to cover up something. A voter wants the candidate to talk *to* him, not *at* him; to use the medium not as a large public *address* system, but rather as a private *undress* system. Furthermore, many politicians tend to organize their thoughts for a home listener the way they might for a group of lawyers. But the logic of the positions they try to develop fails to impress the typical voter, who has one thought in the back of his mind whenever he listens to a politician: "How do I *feel* about him?"

Traditionally, successful politicians are usually quite effective in tuning their speech for a face-to-face audience. They learn to interpret very subtle feedback from a crowd and adjust their style to maximize the impact. However, when they have to speak to a radio or TV home audience (non-face-to-face), they often give a mechanical rendering

of their feelings. Rather than adjust for a more intimate relation to the listener, they project for a larger audience.

When a politician is both speaking to a large face-to-face audience and being broadcast on radio, it would be wise to insure that his talk is properly framed for the home listeners, who may number in the millions. Simultaneously, he must affect the large public audience and the private home listener.

There are two possible solutions to this problem. The first solution is not yet possible in the United States, but it is used by Russian politicians. The largest convention hall in Moscow has several thousand seats. Each seat is equipped with its own speaker. Thus, a politician addressing a large public audience in the convention hall, while simultaneously speaking on radio or TV, can speak as if he were in the personal space zone of each listener. The convention hall listener and the home listener have approximately the same distance relation to the speaker. Any comparable American convention hall utilizes several large speakers to amplify a voice, not individual speakers at each seat. Thus, someone sitting in the audience may be twenty, thirty, or one hundred feet from a source of amplified sound, while the home listener is only three or four feet from the speaker's mouth.

A practical solution to this problem for an American politician is to address the large public audience the way he normally would, and use an announcer to *frame* his speech for the home listener. At the beginning and end, and at appropriate times during the speech, an announcer can remind the home listener, "We are listening to Senator Jones address the United Auto Workers Convention." In this way, the home listener changes his expectations of the candidate. Senator Jones is no longer talking to him. Rather, he is overhearing Senator Jones speak to the convention. Proper framing of the candidate is absolutely essential when a small piece of a public address is to be extracted for use in a political spot. Unless the home listener is told that the candidate was speaking to a large crowd when the segment was recorded, he will think the candidate is shouting at him. One example of misframing I remember, occurred in a spot for the late Adlai Stevenson. The commercial opened with the announcer's voice, "Adlai Stevenson will now speak to you about his views on foreign aid." This was followed by a recorded segment of Stevenson speaking to a huge crowd.

To some degree, a candidate frames his own speech. He tells us that he regards the listener as a member of a large audience in a phrase such as, "My fellow Americans across this great land of ours . . . " And he frames a personal, one-to-one relation in a phrase such as, "Good evening, I appreciate the opportunity to come into your home tonight." Of course, tone of voice can support or contradict either of these frames.

It is much more important for a voter to feel a candidate than to see him. Despite all the myths to the contrary, a candidate's physical appearance alone does not win him many votes. But looks can lose votes. Generally, candidates tend to *look* dishonest, but *sound* honest. This visual handicap is magnified by the fact that most situations where a voter is likely to see the candidate are detrimental to his visual presentation of self. Television in particular is very difficult to structure for effective visual communication of a candidate. The candidate typically has no feeling of who is looking at him; he does not know which camera is on; and the lighting often puts him in a spotlight situation, not an interpersonal encounter. For these and other reasons, I tend to use the candidate much more on radio than on television.

The phenomenon of the "eyewitless news" teams analyzed by Ron Powers is not the only problem with television journalism. Even the programs anchored by the respected Cronkites, Chancellors, and Reasoners fail to provide much substantive information on key social issues or contemporary developments. Television apparently has an incurable infatuation with *action*, with presenting events and personalities that *move*. The line between information and entertainment is finely drawn in the world of television journalism.

Thomas E. Patterson and Robert D. McClure, two young political science professors at Syracuse University, have thoroughly documented the tendency of television to concentrate on the carnival and parade-like qualities of political campaigning. Their study of the impact of television on the 1972 presidential contest revealed a plenitude of prevalent myths about the power of the networks.

Since the time of John Kennedy's stunning "mastery" of the media in 1960 during his televised debates with Richard Nixon, we have become accustomed to thinking that "image" was the crucial ingredient in the success or failure of a candidate. Patterson and McClure discount this facile assumption and argue instead that the voters are not as easily duped as the media "manipulators" would have us believe.

Other observers might take issue with the authors' apparent faith in the wisdom of the electorate. They could even point to Patterson's and McClure's own findings about the influence of the five-minute political "commercials," designed as forums from which the candidates can discuss "the issues." Perhaps these are no more than slick pseudo-events in themselves, reinforcing the view that the media are more effective in shaping our ideas than we had ever imagined.

Political Campaigns: TV Power Is a Myth

Thomas E. Patterson
Robert D. McClure

A presidential election has all the pageantry, color, glamour, and hoopla of the Kentucky Derby. And network television reporting treats a general election exactly like a horse race.

The camera follows the entries around the country trying to capture the drama, excitement and adventure of a grueling run for the November finish line. Polls are constantly cited in breathless bulletins on the candidate's latest surge or falter. The feverish activity that accompanies the campaign provides the back-barn setting that lends color and "inside dope" to the coverage.

Crowds are essential. The crowds are rooting sections for the candidates; the die-hard railbirds are certain proof of the big prize at stake as the runners near the finish line.

On network television, all presidential campaigns are covered like horse races. The election in 1972 provided a clear test of this determination because it demanded no such coverage—it was never much of a contest at all. Nonetheless, it was made into a sports event with overtones of a soap-opera series.

The candidates offered the American people one of the clearest policy choices of this century. And although the election's outcome was never in doubt, the campaign had meaning precisely because the candidates did have distinct policy differences. Yet, on network television news, that meaning and those differences went unreported.

By popular myth, television presents a quite authentic picture of politics, and most voters get their knowledge of election issues from network TV news. Neither myth stands the test of fact.

During the 1972 Nixon-McGovern campaign, we audited and analyzed the content of every televised political commercial and every week-night evening newscast of ABC, CBS and NBC. Further, we held 2,000 interviews, each an hour long, talking with the same voters—at the start, in the middle, and at the end of the campaign. Thus we could discover how their thinking about the candidates and the issues changed, and what influence television played in these changes.

What emerges from this study is that the nightly network newscasts present a picture of politics that is thoroughly lacking in substance. They ignore major issues. They ignore the candidates' personal qualifications for the presidency.

In fact, during the 1972 general election, voters got more knowledge of candidate issue positions out of paid political commercials than they did from TV newscasts.

Another popular myth is equally askew from actuality. The myth is that "images," more than either issues or parties, win votes. As onetime Nixon assistant Raymond Price has put it, "It's not what's there that counts, it's what's projected." As onetime Humphrey aide Joseph Napolitan put it, "It's not what you say, it's how you say it." In McLuhan's phrase, the medium *is* the message. None of this is so. And most emphatically the medium is not the message.

Network news executives insist upon action and movement above all. From inception, the networks have had a policy of action pictures at the expense of informative reporting, harking back to the breathless, shouting days of radio news.

In place of serious matters, ABC, CBS and NBC substitute the trivia of political campaigning that makes for flashy pictures—hecklers, crowds, motorcades, balloons, rallies, and pompom girls.

Media consultants encourage their candidate clients to exploit this network bias. And the candidates, in their desire to create "positive" televised images, accede to, and even encourage, network coverage of campaign hoopla. Almost all campaign rallies and almost everything about them—timing, setting, even their function—are geared to create pictures for network news of candidates running, running, running.

As a result of all this subordination of substance to horse-race trivia and hoopla, our research shows, *steady viewers of the nightly network newscasts learn almost nothing of importance about a presidential election.*

From September 18 to November 6, 1972, the evening newscasts of ABC, CBS and NBC were examined for any reference to Nixon's or McGovern's qualifications in 12 important personal and leadership areas, ranging from their political experience and compassion for the less fortunate to the strength of their political convictions and their personal trustworthiness.

Any network news reference to either candidate in these 12 areas was recorded, including the number of news seconds given to the reference. Although all references, no matter how fleeting, were recorded, network news had no time to provide information that voters could use to judge candidates. ABC spent less than 20 minutes reporting on these 12 personal and leadership qualifications of the candidates: CBS only 16 minutes, NBC just eight minutes. As a network average these minutes represent only one percent of available news time during this period when the campaign was receiving its most intense, continuous coverage.

Nixon was the incumbent and had been subject to public scrutiny for more than 20 years, but McGovern was a newcomer and the public had little information about him, only fragmentary knowledge at best about his personal and leadership qualifications, or his lack of them. Yet, during the last two months of the campaign the networks on the average gave about five minutes of news time to facts about McGovern's personal and leadership experience, good or bad. The three networks averaged about 30 seconds each on the 12 qualities as they applied to McGovern.

Major issues of the campaign were equally ignored, and sacrificed to the horse-race drama.

A classic example: one noon during October in New York City, in ample time for evening newscast coverage, McGovern stated important policy positions on crime, prison reform, gun control, and the courts. Two networks completely ignored the address, covering instead a McGovern motorcade in Boston later that day. He was pictured in crowd scenes. Indeed, 60 percent of all campaign stories showed one candidate or the other hustling through crowds.

Political Pap

As a result of this emphasis, television's only effect on the American voter is to cheapen his conception of the campaign process and to stuff his head full of nonsense. Network news serves up pure political pap, and the candidates obligingly provide it. Their belief in the myths about TV's power and their false conception of the capacities and expectations of the American voter are both based upon a low regard for the citizen's good sense. From September 18 to

November 6, we tabulated every television reference to any of 26 positions the candidates had taken on basic issues, ranging from inflation, welfare, busing, crime, and drugs to withdrawal from Vietnam and amnesty for deserters. The results define a wasteland.

As a network average, only three percent of available news minutes were given to reporting the candidates' stands on the issues. The coverage given any single candidate's stand on an issue was so minimal—only a minute or two for the typical position—as to be meaningless.

Issue stories require "talking heads," which by network standards are dull. Like the McGovern speech mentioned above, many of the candidates' major statements of substance were ignored. When not ignored altogether, their audio discussion was woven into Derby Day action, and the story thus suffused with enough hoopla to obscure its content.

Issue coverage is so fleeting and so superficial it is little wonder the voter learns almost nothing from it. At the campaign's beginning and end, we asked the sample of voters where they thought the candidates stood on the 26 key issues. Because the same people were questioned at start and finish, it was possible to determine exactly how much their issue information improved during the campaign. Regular viewing of network news had no influence on how much these people learned.

By contrast, newspapers were far more effective than television in making voters better informed on the issues. The minutes people spent reading their newspapers, unlike the minutes they gave to watching network news, clearly increased their issue awareness.

Network News Is No News

An accurate estimate of the impact of network news and the newspaper requires that people's viewing and reading habits be considered simultaneously. Some were neither regular television news viewers, *nor* regular newspaper readers; this group showed a 19 percent gain in information anyway. Their gain was as much as that of people who watched television news regularly without paying much attention to newspapers. In other words, people who depended on network news did not come to know more than people who ignored all the news media. If they depended entirely on the newspaper, however, they learned substantially more.

The three main factors of television's issue coverage—the infrequent mention, then only in fleeting references, plus films showing unrelated and distracting "action" while the audio gives a glancing blow to an issue—all create an impossible learning situation that adds nothing of substance to the voters' civic education.

By contrast, and quite surprisingly, *the candidates' own television commercials prove to be an important means of improving the voter's information of where candidates stand on issues.*

This learning takes place quite apart from whether the impression gained by the voter is what the candidate seeks to convey. It can be just the opposite. And it happens despite the fact that some campaign commercials, like those for products, aim at people's hearts more than their heads, and follow the same assumption that decisions (whether voting or buying) are made for emotional rather than cerebral reasons.

The elitist fear that some voters might pick a candidate in the same way they buy soap obscures one remarkable aspect of tele-

vised political advertising: political commercials carry substantial information about candidates' stands on issues.

Of the political commercials televised during the 1972 campaign, 42 percent were primarily on issues and another 28 percent contained substantial material on issues. McGovern's television ads appeared almost 100 times during the campaign's last six weeks, Nixon's nearly as often. Together, they gave impressive information on 12 basic policy issues.

Nor did these ads bear much resemblance to soap commercials. Where product commercials are nonsensical, issue advertising is substantive. Where the product ad ducks conflict, issue advertising heightens it. Where the product ad tends toward the soft sell, the issue ad favors a harder sell. Where one tugs at the emotions, the other may at times try to make the voters think. They are slanted and oversimplified, but nevertheless convey much hard-issue information.

There is still another difference. Product commercials are becoming shorter, since market research shows that 20-second and 30-second spots are about as effective as 60-second ones. Political commercials are moving toward the five-minute spot, which accounts for more than 75 percent of all television time used in 1972 campaign commercials.... These longer spots can have more issue substance, more fully argued positions. Several such commercials in 1972 rivaled almost any newspaper campaign story—and overshadowed virtually every television news story on the campaign—in

the quantity and quality of their issue material. People who were heavily exposed to issue spots became much better informed.

The Price of Hamburger

Advertising educates voters because of the powerful ways it transmits the issue content, stressing advertising's three basics of simplicity, repetition and sight-sound coordination. An effective ad is remembered, as an oft-repeated McGovern commercial illustrates. Quoting Nixon's promise of recovery from runaway prices, it drummed in the fact that since he became President, the price of hamburger rose from 58 cents to 89 cents and the cost of living rose 19 percent. . . .

Nevertheless, simply because five-minute political spots are demonstrably effective, it is fallacious to assume—as many political observers do assume—that much longer ones would be much more so. Some argue that even five-minute spots are so short they reduce complex issues to trivial and misleading nonsense, and that broadcasts at least 30 minutes long are necessary to inform the voters adequately.

What these critics overlook is crucial. People watch spots, but longer programs get turned off. Faced with choosing between ''All in the Family'' or a 30-minute prime-time political broadcast, American viewers would overwhelmingly choose Archie Bunker over Scoop Jackson.

Longer broadcasts attract mainly the ardent partisans, and hence are the TV equivalent of the old political rally. So they can be valuable for fund-raising. They are wasted on the less-committed. Only one in 20 adults bothered to watch the typical 30-minute candidate broadcast in the last race. Moreover, among infrequent newspaper readers—precisely those least-informed—only one in 35 viewers bothered to watch.

Longer broadcasts are simply not the means to communicate with a cross section of the American electorate. But *the shorter commercials—particularly the five-minute ones—contributed heavily to the political education of the least-informed, those who paid the least attention to newspapers.*

In fact, the greatest beneficiaries of political spots were those who needed the information most, those who, because they ignored the newspaper, were the least informed. At best, regular newspaper readers learned very little from political commercials: Regular readers with low advertising exposure had a 46 percent increase in information, while those with high advertising exposure gained little more (49 percent increase). Spots act as "information boosters," raising the level of information for the less informed considerably higher than it would otherwise be.

However, this effectiveness raises the specter of potential voter manipulation. After all, the political spots are full of small distortions. They fail to inform fully about any single issue, and fail to inform about the full range of election issues. A candidate examines only those issues he thinks will help him or hurt his opponent.

Nevertheless, our careful study of the question indicates that *the vast majority of Americans are immune to advertising propaganda. They are not manipulated....*

The Empty Image
The final myth exploded by our study is that "images" win more votes than either issues or mere party loyalty. The candidates, cheerfully going along with the networks' horse-race format, believe that their staged television appearances—every one very much like the others—relay a message to the viewer. They think the message is that the candidate's capacity for leadership is mirrored in the crowd's reaction, his character portrayed in the close-ups of his face, his abilities measured by the smiling confidence he projects.

Nevertheless, *voter images of the candidates are influenced only marginally by the style and appearance they exhibit in television-news appearances.* Nixon's 1972 victory may settle forever any doubts on this question. Neither those voters already committed to a candidate, nor those voters who were undecided, were appreciably affected by all the strenuous imagemaking efforts.

Among those who are committed to a candidate because of party or issues, television fails at imagemaking because it cannot overcome this commitment. Imagemaking is trying to persuade the already persuaded. These voters see what they want to see when a candidate appears on TV. "Their" candidate looks good, his opponent looks bad. What is actually televised matters little.

The phenomenon involved here, familiar to psychological researchers, is selective perception. Most people have a biased view of what they see, and their perceptual defenses automatically go up when obvious efforts are made to persuade them. One series of McGovern "image" commercials showed him chatting with several different groups of people. The reactions of voters suggest how the ads simply reinforced existing views.

A 37-year-old, pro-McGovern viewer: "He really cares what's happened to disabled vets. They told him how badly they've been treated and he listened. He will help them."

A 33-year-old, pro-Nixon viewer: "McGovern was talking with these disabled vets. He doesn't really care about them. He's just using them to get sympathy."

A 57-year-old, pro-McGovern viewer: "It was honest, down-to-earth. People were talking and he was listening."

A 45-year-old, pro-Nixon viewer: "Those commercials are so phony. He doesn't care."

A 31-year-old, pro-McGovern viewer: "McGovern had his coat off and his tie was hanging down. It was so relaxed, and he seemed to really be concerned with those workers."

A 49-year-old, pro-Nixon viewer: "He is trying hard to look like one of the boys. You know, roll up the shirt sleeves and loosen the tie. It's just too much for me to take."

A 22-year-old, pro-McGovern viewer: "I have seen many ads where McGovern is talking to common people. You know, like workers and the elderly. He means what he says. He'll help them."

A 41-year-old, pro-Nixon viewer: "He's with all these groups of people. Always making promises. He's promising more than can be done. Can't do everything for everyone."

McGovern's image spots were not creating a televised image; they mainly provided voters an opportunity to express their own political views.

To determine the pattern of change in people's images in 1972, we asked voters to judge both Nixon and McGovern on seven image dimensions, both at the start and at the end of the campaign. The results:

Among those who already favored Nixon, his image had a 35 percent improvement, McGovern's a 25 percent decline.

Among those who already favored McGovern, his image had a 20 percent improvement, Nixon's a 20 percent decline.

Among voters who did not favor either candidate at the outset, images of Nixon and McGovern changed very little before they made up their minds, and in no consistent direction regardless of their exposure to either candidate's televised images.

Once these voters picked their candidates,

their images changed substantially, and in much the same manner as for the committed group. For those who chose McGovern, his image underwent a 40 percent improvement, and Nixon's a 50 percent decline. For those who chose Nixon, his image improved 35 percent and McGovern's declined 25 percent. Such postdecision shifts have been widely studied by psychologists doing cognitive-dissonance research. Once a choice is made, people avoid inner conflict by rationalizing any views or feelings that contradict a decision.

McGovern and the Media

McGovern was probably the least well-known presidential nominee in the quarter-century of TV campaigning. Even though his image spots did not influence people during the campaign, today's media campaigners tend to believe that a McGovern, or a Jimmy Carter, can now build his image instantly on TV, before the general election.

Our research undercuts this new shibboleth. The extent to which voters used the media in 1972 did not affect their evaluation of McGovern. Those who relied mainly on TV, and those who relied mainly on newspapers, had nearly identical impressions of him. Whether for him or against him, they largely agreed on his strong and weak points. His strengths were perceived to be his compassion for the less fortunate, his sincerity, his interest in people's problems, and his search for political answers. Both pros and antis gave their highest marks for his humaneness.

But McGovern's series of campaign blunders, misdirections and reversals undermined confidence in his leadership and gave voters a feeling that he was not above political expediency. It was in those areas that people had their lowest regard for McGovern.

Clearly, images depend on what a candidate represents—his party, his actions, his policies—and just as clearly on how a voter feels about what the candidate represents—his party, past actions, future policies. For almost every voter, a candidate's image depends on these two realistic factors and not on whether he looks good or bad on television.

To sum up, television has failed in its promise to raise the quality of campaign debate. The networks say they give the public what it wants, and it wants a horse-race format. The result is shoddy journalism that wastes time for millions of viewers.

The truth is that viewers have no discoverable enthusiasm for the way presidential campaigns are presented. To the 60 percent of all news time devoted to rallies and crowds, the typical viewer reaction is "seen one seen 'em all." By six-to-one, viewers said they would prefer fewer crowd shots. By two-to-one, they would prefer fewer rally films. By three-to-one, they would prefer more stories showing "candidates being interviewed by reporters," and by two-to-one, more "talking about the candidates" by experts and voters.

It is of course true that people often say they want better things that they later ignore, but on network television they have not been offered much of a choice. The industry has succeeded in making itself irrelevant to the democratic society in which it operates.

A starry-eyed, passionately patriotic, political neophyte comes to Washington, D.C. as a newly appointed United States senator. His overriding objective is to secure passage of a bill that would establish a nationwide summer camp program for young boys. In his quest for this noble aim, he discovers that corrupt business interests in his home state already have plans to construct a dam on the property he has designated as the future site of his boys' camp. In a classic confrontation of good versus evil, the young senator stages a herculean filibuster to thwart the sinister forces and allow truth and justice to prevail. Just as it appears that the gallant efforts of the idealistic hero are about to be doomed to failure because of an effective "smear campaign" against him, the senior senator from his state breaks down and admits his complicity in the crooked business enterprises of the infamous "Taylor machine."

To Americans today, accustomed to thinking in terms of politics as hopelessly corrupt and of politicians as dishonest and ruthlessly self-seeking, this scenario from Frank Capra's *Mr. Smith Goes to Washington* (1939) must seem terribly unrealistic. Jimmy Stewart's portrayal of Jefferson Smith, the lanky, homespun knight-errant of the senate, might momentarily rekindle our idealistic fires, but the political world of Capra's films appears to have little relevance to contemporary American society. A motion picture such as *The Candidate* (1972), in which Robert Redford is transformed from a Ralph Nader-like crusading lawyer into a successful but disenchanted politician, is more attuned to the cynical spirit of the seventies.

In the following article, Gerald Mast contents that, despite a veneer of cynicism, Americans have still held fast to a kind of movie mentality in their views of political life. We still respond to the "swellest guy," according to Mast, and believe that virtue will be rewarded and wrongdoing eventually punished. The experience of Watergate may have provoked many "so what's new?" sneers, but it also seems to have reaffirmed the "morality play" image of politics. The film *All the President's Men* (1976) might even lead us to believe that the "impossible dreams" of Frank Capra's characters can indeed be realized.

Politics in the Movies
Gerald Mast

I have just seen *Mr. Deeds Goes to Town* once again, and once again this 1936 Frank Capra film reminded me that the kinship between American movies and American politics goes a lot deeper than the mere fact that one of the leading presidential contenders was once a movie star. The hero of this political film is a most apolitical guy who has only one political belief: some folks are "just swell" and other folks ain't. The same political philosophy characterizes Mr. Jefferson Smith (whom Frank Capra sent to Washington) and "Long John" Doe (whom Capra launched on a national populist campaign).

For Capra, politics was a matter of the

Mr. Smith (Jimmy Stewart) Goes to Washington (1939). Along with Gary Cooper, Henry Fonda, and Spencer Tracy, Stewart was a model of virtuous behavior in political films spanning more than two decades.

heart, not the brain, of morality, not ideology. Issues and ideas were politically irrelevant; only the swellness of the soul mattered. Capra's evil political figures were inevitably cynical, snobbish or selfish. The swell-hearted hero could convert the cynical ones (they were usually newspaper reporters), for their cynicism was merely protection against all the phonies they had uncovered. Beneath the cynicism they were just swell folks, like the hero himself. The snobbish were more difficult to convert (for the veneers of bankers, lawyers, the rich and the educated were thicker than those of reporters), and the selfish were irretrievably fallen, creatures not simply mistaken but malicious and vicious. Their Golden Rule was to thyself be all, and their goals were only two: power and money. Capra's political comedy became moral allegory, a Manichean battle between God and the Devil in which the strategy of the fable was to determine who would take his or her place in the Legions of the Swell.

The Capra films were not aberrations. The very first feature film made in America, D.W. Griffith's *The Birth of a Nation* (1915), was also our first political film. In this Civil War clash of abolitionists and slaveholders, Griffith depicts his Southern family as a model of gentleness, mildness, friendliness, sweetness and light. In contrast, there are two representatives of the abolitionist position. The first is Congressman Stoneman (a parody of Thaddeus Stevens) who supports abolition because 1) he is power hungry, 2) he is trying

to please his mulatto mistress, and 3) he is physically vain. He wears a wig to disguise his physical ugliness, which unfortunately reveals itself nonetheless in the grotesque boot which covers his club foot. Like Shakespeare in *Richard III*, Griffith uses physical deformity as an external emblem of internal corruption. The other political villain in the film is a pureblooded descendant of melodrama—the mulatto Silas Lynch. Unlike Stoneman who is complexly in error, Lynch is quite simply selfish, lustful and mean. The possibility that slavery might be an unjust political institution and that those who oppose it might care about eradicating what they consider unjust does not occur to the filmmaker.

Griffith's *Intolerance*, made one year later, reveals the identical pattern. Despite the film's political title, it might just as precisely have been called Inhumanity, Insensitivity or Insincerity. The political act of intolerance in all four historical eras that the film depicts inevitably springs from human selfishness, spite or envy, not from any political philosophy.

John Ford's films, which span the generations of Griffith, Capra and beyond, reveal an identical assumption. His *Stagecoach* (1939), though admired as one of the classic

Hollywood westerns, contains far more political-moral allegory than feudin', fussin' and fightin'. Ford shows that the external, social differences between his characters are merely superficial. Though on the surface they represent different classes (rich and poor, genteel and common, educated and not), different backgrounds (East and West), different vocations (doctor, salesman, cowboy, sheriff), and questionable moral worth in the eyes of the world (prostitute, gambler, outlaw, drunk), underneath they are all swell folks. Their internal moral sameness is greater than their external differences—which allows them to stick together and survive.

The only real crook in the film is not "The Kid" (John Wayne), whom society has defined as an outlaw but who gets along very well with the sheriff. It is the banker, whom society has defined as respectable but who has stolen $50,000 from his own bank. The banker is the only character in the film who ventures political opinions about what the government ought to be doing and for whom. (Not surprisingly, he expects that the government ought to do everything for him.)

The Man Who Shot Liberty Valance (1962) is Ford's most explicitly political film. Once again, the politically valuable positions are products of the moral swellness of characters who are opposites on the surface and identical underneath. John Wayne plays the Western "Man of Law," the Man with a Gun who uses it in support of inevitably just causes. James Stewart plays the Eastern "Man of Law," an educated lawyer whose tools are law books, not pistols. The civilizing of the West requires both of them, however, who work in concert against the vicious villain, Liberty Valance—his name, like his life, a burlesque of the notion of freedom. Liberty's liberty is actually license—the undiluted exercise of self. The plot (like the title) of the film revolves about the confusion over exactly which of the two men of law really did shoot Liberty, for in their uni-fied commitment to humane values outside themselves, both men of law demonstrate the true meaning of liberty for John Ford.

Four actors have consistently portrayed the models for virtuous political behavior in American movies since the invention of synchronized sound: Gary Cooper, James Stewart, Henry Fonda and Spencer Tracy. I can't think of a political movie between *Mr. Deeds* and *Guess Who's Coming to Dinner* that didn't use one of them. There are superficial differences among the four. Cooper and Stewart play vaguely conservative figures while Fonda and Tracy play vaguely liberal ones; Cooper and Tracy seem vaguely folksier than Stewart and Fonda, who seem vaguely more educated. But all four are archetypal projections of immensely charismatic human warmth, sincerity, spontaneity, naturalness and niceness. Unlike such stars as Cary Grant, Clark Gable, Herbert Marshall and William Powell, who play and project creatures of brain, intellect, wit and snap, Cooper, Stewart, Fonda and Tracy play and project creatures of the heart.

Even the new spate of "CIA movies" (*Three Days of the Condor, The Killer Elite*) reveals an identical apolitical attitude toward political issues. While these films not surprisingly reduce political questions to ordinary good guy–bad guy melodrama, the underlying political philosophy of Sam Peckinpah's *Killer Elite* is that all politics and ideology is a bloody mess (very bloody—given the fact that it's a Peckinpah movie). Ideology is simply a confusing camouflage (very confusing in this film) for the old self-interests of money-making and power-grabbing. The elite killer-hero ends the film by sailing away (quite literally) from politics, his life, his job and the CIA altogether. Well, Frank Capra's ultimate political solution was also to fly away to a wishful never-never land of utopian dreams called Shangri-la, and D.W. Griffith's ultimate political solution was to stage wishful allegorical pageants about the founding of the New

Jerusalem on Earth at the end of both *The Birth of a Nation* and *Intolerance*. . . .

When one turns from American movies to American politics, a remarkable correspondence emerges. Perhaps the most common American political cliché is: "I vote for the man, not the party." To believe otherwise is almost un-American. But what does this voting for the man mean? In the political discussions I have heard (and overheard), particularly among those labeled "middle Americans" (who constitute a vast majority of the electorate), it means the candidate who strikes them as most warm, most sincere, most honest. In short, the swellest guy—the candidate who seems most like Gary Cooper, James Stewart, Henry Fonda or Spencer Tracy.

One can object, of course, that almost everyone admits that Gerald Ford is a swell guy, but the polls indicate serious doubts about his stature, intelligence and leadership. Even these doubts, however, are matters of "character" (in an esthetic sense) not of ideology. The difficulty with Ford's political *persona*, his archetypal "swellness," is that unlike Cooper, Stewart, Fonda or Tracy he seems to lack the underlying shrewdness, perspicacity and savvy—the delightful ability to unmask a charlatan or deflate a windbag with one quick folksy sally. (That ability was the primary basis for the success of the Truman archetype.)

The Richard Nixon *persona* might also seem to break the movie-politics connection, but both his success and his demise can be understood in movie terms. The Nixon archetype was "the tough guy in a tough world." This archetype could only "play in Peoria" (and how many times did we hear that *Variety*-style phrase?) as long as it seemed to be supported by an underlying commitment to the moral values and American ideals of unselfishness that united all the swell guys like Cooper and Tracy. The Watergate tapes destroyed that Nixon *persona* entirely, indicating that behind the "tough guy in a tough world" mask lay pettiness, venality, power-hunger and spite—those great evils of the Griffith-Capra-Ford political movies. The public exposure of this private face was a terrible error in dramaturgical terms—a little like catching Babe Bennett in Mr. Deeds' dressing trailer with her clothes off. The cameras never recorded the private activities of movie archetypes. Once this private, tape-recorded Nixon had violated the public *persona* of "President Nixon," on which his strength and popularity rested, the result was (to paraphrase a famous *Variety* headline): "Stix Nix Dix Trix."

Perhaps the pervasive creation of these charismatic archetypal *personae* in both American movie politics and real politics is the sign of a very deep American distrust of anything that has to do with ideas rather than sentiments. Or perhaps the political image-makers have watched enough old movies to know that to sell a candidate to an American audience (particularly in the television age when politics itself has become more of a mass entertainment medium than the movies) requires selling his archetype, not his issues and ideas. Has the movie art held the mirror up to American political life? Or does political life (as Jean Genet has developed) really hold the mirror up to art?

"You can't be a revolutionary without a television set," Jerry Rubin assured us in his book *Do It!* (1970). Rubin, along with Abbie Hoffman and other members of the Youth International Party (or Yippies) were skillful manipulators of the media. They knew what types of demonstrations would bring the greatest coverage by the press and the network news programs.

Perhaps their shining moment of triumph (or so they have concluded) came during the 1968 Democratic Convention in Chicago. The youthful demonstrators who assembled in Grant Park to protest the Vietnam war and assorted political issues were given extensive media coverage. And when the police began clubbing and arresting the dissenters, Rubin, Hoffman, and their cohorts assumed the "police riot" would help to "radicalize" sympathetic but uncommitted young people. Whether or not it actually produced this result has never been completely resolved. Some studies have shown, in fact, that the Chicago riot served to solidify the animosity most Americans had for radical youth.

In the case of the black civil rights movement, the argument for the radicalizing capabilities of the media seems to be valid. Most Americans had very little awareness of the plight of blacks until they were confronted with the fact by newspapers, magazines, and especially television. Scenes of National Guard troops escorting black children to school in Little Rock, Arkansas in 1957 and of black college students sitting at a lunch counter in Greensboro, North Carolina in 1960 asking to be served may have transformed very few individuals into social activists, but they definitely focused attention on the civil rights problem. William Small's essay analyzes the significance of this "revolution with television."

Television and the Black Revolution
William Small

The Black Revolution may be no different than other revolutions, in the general nature of what social revolution is and how it comes to be. It is considerably different in its impact, the speed in which its ideas are transmitted within and without the Black culture, and the manner in which those ideas are transmitted. It is, in short, a revolution with television. It is a "first."

To associate the Negro drive of the 60's with television may seem parochial. It reminds one of the story that received currency at the turn of the century when outsiders would tour the areas of the South still smarting from the Civil War. There was a melancholy tendency to date every event with the War.

"How beautiful the moon is tonight," the visitor would observe.

"Yes," the native would reply, "But you should have seen it before the War."

Before television, Black may have been beautiful but it was a quiet beauty. Though there were fifty years or more of Negro protest, the only real victory and the most important spark of public attention came in 1954 when nine white men, dressed in black, ruled that school segregation was unconstitutional. In those fifty years, according to the U.S. Crime Commission, over 4,500 persons were lynched. How conscious of this was America? In contrast, the television coverage that grew in the 60's served as companion to demonstrations. Unlike those of other years, attention was now paid. With success, the demonstration grew, the coverage increased, and the Revolution spun on with frenzied momentum.

It was untidy. Revolutions are. There were "civil insurrections." We tend to call them riots but riots, "race" riots, are different. These were not whites against Blacks; they were Blacks against their environment.

Historian Theodore H. White noting the emergence of both the Blacks and the rebelling young, said early in 1969: "In 1960 we still lived in the old environment. . . . During the past eight years we've had the Black revolt and the student revolt, which could take place only on the stage that TV provided. We have become accustomed to the new rhetoric of confrontation which Martin Luther King first devised."

He first used it in 1955 in Montgomery, Alabama. Rosa Parks, a Negro seamstress, was fined ten dollars for refusing to give up a seat on a public bus. The Black community of Montgomery started a bus boycott and a young preacher named Martin Luther King took over its leadership. The boycott lasted 381 days, ending in November of 1956 when a Federal court injunction prohibited bus segregation. During that year, Dr. King was arrested, his home was bombed, and his name became nationally known. Television. There was plenty of coverage in the print media but television brought home the picture of quiet eloquence, of determined righteousness.

The following year was the year of Little Rock. President Eisenhower sends in 1,000 paratroopers to escort nine Negro students into Central High School. Plenty of print coverage but none to match the scenes on television: armed guards walking next to teen-age Blacks, angry white mothers shouting scurrilously into the cameras, white officialdom saying "never."

Then came the 60's. On February 1st, 1960 a small group of Negroes began a sit-in at the Woolworth dime store lunch counter in Greensboro, North Carolina. Before the year was out, it had spread across the South (and some in the North) with sit-ins at lunch counters, hotels, movie theatres, libraries, supermarkets, amusement parks, bus depots.

On television, with its rapidly growing audience and rapidly increased news coverage, there was a collage of vivid scenes: young Negroes dragged out of buildings, grim-jawed sit-ins surrounded by angry whites, hoodlums pouring mustard on the heads of Blacks at a lunch counter, police moving in with brutal swiftness.

The chief Washington representative of the National Association for the Advancement of Colored People, Clarence Mitchell, wrote this author that: "People who did not bother to read newspaper stories of civil rights violations saw such violations dramatically produced on the screens in their homes . . . this had a profoundly constructive effect on many persons. In addition, some of those who perpetrated violence against persons exercising their civil rights seemed to have second thoughts when they viewed themselves on television. For example, I heard one restaurant proprietor on a program almost pitifully reproaching himself after he had seen a tape of his attack on some Negroes. I believe he put a messy mixture of flour, eggs or some other gooey combination on the heads of the demonstrators. His act came through on the screen as malevolently childish."

It is doubtful that many such acts of contrition or repentance resulted from viewing one's own actions on television. But millions of less committed viewers share the viewings. What impact there? Abe Lincoln, exactly one hundred years earlier said that public discussion is helping doom slavery: "What kills a skunk is the publicity it gives itself." . . .

Television had another effect. Newspapers which had treated the stories lightly (some did so even when it was in their own city) began to give the civil rights movement more attention. Local radio and television, in some places as protective of The Establishment as the local newspaper, were shamed into coverage because it was there, on the network newscasts.

Spring of 1963 saw one of the most dramatic displays of local, white authority in confrontation with demonstrators—the fire hoses and police dogs of Birmingham Police Commissioner "Bull" Connor. The 16 mm. film record of marchers, including school children buffeted to the curb under tremendous water pressure was seen across the country, across the world.

Then, in rapid order, came the flood of new impressions: Birmingham Negroes rioting after Dr. King's motel room and his younger brother's home are bombed; George Wallace at the University's "schoolhouse door" in Alabama reading his long statement on "oppression of State's Rights" as Katzenbach stands by ready to deliver a Presidential proclamation calling for the registration of two Negroes (all of this on the television); Mississippi NAACP State Chairman Medgar Evars murdered as he entered his home in Jackson; demonstrations and riots in Cambridge, Maryland and finally—the March on Washington.

August 28, 1963: the culmination of non-violence in the civil rights movement. A quarter of a million people, over one out of five are white, fill the Mall from the Lincoln Memorial to the Washington Monument. Live, network television carries much of the day; the networks coming in and out of live coverage of the program. It is the largest, most dramatic and most peaceful of all civil rights demonstrations and culminates with Dr. King's magnificent "I have a dream . . ." speech.

And less than three weeks later, a Birmingham church is bombed during Bible class and four little girls are killed, many other Negro children injured. President Kennedy expresses the "deep sense of outrage and grief" of the nation; Negroes express anger and frustration and the calls of "Freedom now" are louder. Many young Negroes begin to reject the non-violent rhetoric that has prevailed. Especially vocal are members of the Student Nonviolent Coordinating Committee (SNCC). They were the creation of a call to Raleigh, North Carolina by Dr. Martin Luther King in 1960 but already had moved away from his more cautious approach.

The pattern of protest changes in the mid- and late 60's. There is much more violence— riots in the cities begin, in Harlem, Rochester, Jersey City, Philadelphia; Malcolm X is murdered in the Audubon Ballroom in New York and Black Muslim headquarters are burned in that and other cities; Mrs. Viola Liuzzo is murdered on an Alabama highway and four Klan members are arrested for the shooting of this white civil rights worker from Detroit; James Meredith is shot as he begins his "March Against Fear" from Memphis to Jackson. . . .

There is a great deal more to television than these moments of confrontation. The newscasts and, increasingly, the entertainment programs (and most significantly, the

"The 16 mm. film record of marchers, including school children buffeted to the curb under tremendous water pressure, was seen across the country, across the world."

commercials) show more and more Negroes in the stream of American life. Once fearful that a Black face would hurt sales, many advertisers now seemed eager to show Black. It established credentials, it could open new markets, it might help protect against the embarrassment of boycott or picketing or worse.

The "tactile promptings" of television, as McLuhan put it so well, are touching Americans almost every hour as they watch. It is touching low-income Americans most of all. This includes most Blacks and many low-income whites who, with their lower middle-class brothers, are the heart of "white backlash." Adults in middle-class America watch television a few hours a day. Low-income adults watch it five hours a day. Low-income Blacks watch six hours a day. Their children watch more.

Think of eight hours as a typical workday and you are stunned to learn that one-fourth of low-income adults spend eight hours a day watching television (according to testimony before the President's Violence Commission). While 7% of middle-class teenagers might spend eight hours a day watching television on Sunday, twice that number of lower class whites and five times as many low-income Black teenagers do. It is said that 40% of the general public gets most of its news from television but 70%

of low-income Americans say TV is their main source. The majority of Americans say they believe television more than newspapers; an even larger majority of the lower class does. . . .

Many social observers are concerned that while television may titillate the aspirations of the Black community (for good or bad) and television may report momentous conflict, it tends to ignore the daily life of the ghetto. The Kerner Commission which investigated the riots of the summer of '67 said its major concern with the media was "not in riot reporting as such, but in the failure to report adequately on race relations and ghetto problems." . . .

The major network newscasts have been focusing on racial stories but there is a limitation; it is imposed by the restrictions of the time available and the need to present other material as well. "Shad" Northshield, then producer of the "Huntley-Brinkley Report," said, "I agree with [David] Ginsburg [a staff director of the Kerner Commission] that the Negro Revolution, or whatever you want to call it, is the most important story of our time, more important than Viet Nam, and we're trying to cover it. But what does Ginsburg want? After the commercials are lopped off, I've got only twenty-two minutes of news time, and within that time, I've got to put on the significant national and international news of the day."

Northshield's Washington bureau chief, Bill Monroe, complemented the argument about space limitation with the moral question: "There's a limit to how far the media can go in agreeing with the Riots Commission or anyone else that a certain kind of information ought to be emphasized on newscasts. If you assume, because the commission says it's so, that certain material ought to be seen by the country for the country's good, well it would be like brainwashing the country, and it would be a little frightening."

There is always a basic conflict of interest between do-gooders and journalists. As anywhere else where such a conflict exists, there was first a great attraction. Most journalists do have a sense of social purpose but the best realize that this is best fulfilled hewing to a sense of journalistic purpose, of covering the news at they see it.

Seeing it objectively presented the varied images that enhanced the Negro Revolution and those that might embarrass it. They ranged from the dignity of the little colored girl escorted to school by soldiers while a white housewife spat at her to the vulgarism of a Black militant shouting "Burn, baby, burn." Showing both was and is important.

Racial minorities were stereotyped, demeaned, and vilified long before the days of our mass-mediated culture. Shakespeare catered to his audience's prevailing prejudice in *The Merchant of Venice*. Antisemitism was a box-office draw in Elizabethan England.

From the nineteenth-century minstrel shows to Al Jolson singing "Mammy," white men blacked their faces to entertain audiences throughout the country. Blacks, on the other hand, had an extremely difficult time in just being themselves as entertainers. Eddie "Rochester" Anderson was one who made it, as Jack Benny's faithful factotum; others were to follow.

J. K. Obatala is not unduly pessimistic about the image of blacks in our popular media. Recognizing that there is truth in the charges that programs like "That's My Mama" demean blacks by their cavalier portrayal of the family, Obatala points out that the same can be said of television's picture of American society in general. He offers some positive suggestions that might be undertaken to actualize a positive picture of blacks and their experience in America.

Blacks on TV:
A Replay of Amos 'n' Andy?
J. K. Obatala

Before television and the civil rights movement, before "Black Is Beautiful" and "Good Times" and "That's My Mama" arrived on the American social horizon, radio was a main source of entertainment for the people of the rural black America in which I spent my childhood. It is still unusual for me to think about those evenings by the fireplace in the South of the late 1940s without also recalling Gabriel Heatter, Gang Busters or Fibber McGee and Molly.

But in those days the blacks I knew in Tift County, Ga., reserved their greatest loyalty for the "Amos 'n' Andy" and "Jack Benny" shows. Sapphire, Kingfish and Rochester were among the few people who could really compete for our attention against Rev. Armstrong's sermons or "quartet singing" at the little white-boarded church we all attended.

Even the rumors—which I subsequently found to be true—that Amos and Andy were really two white men didn't shake our loyalty. Sundays still found me sitting by the fireplace, chewing sugar cane as I waited for the shows to begin, or on my way to the home of Miss Nell (a friend's mother) to listen to the radio there.

Nowadays, television has supplanted radio as the dominant entertainment medium. Rochester, Kingfish and Sapphire have given way to Fred Sanford, the junk dealer, and to Archie Bunker's black neighbors, the Jeffersons. . . . More significant, the rustic innocence in which black culture of the "Amos 'n' Andy" era had its roots has long since dissolved in the heat of more than two decades of social and racial friction.

A notable consequence of this continuing conflict is that many blacks now judge media performance more on ideological than cultural grounds. For them, it is no longer enough just to be entertained or simply to have their existence as human beings reaffirmed through ridicule (which was, of course, the real appeal of "Amos 'n' Andy"). Guided by their heightened political awareness and ethnic pride, blacks are now demanding that the broadcast media provide a positive perception of blacks and their experience in America. Moreover, they insist that employment be extended not only to performers and writers, but to producers and other executives.

Nothing illustrates this new ideological mood better than the increasing criticism of some of the leading black-oriented television shows by blacks and certain would-be white "sympathizers."

Such critics often contend that the new shows—especially NBC's "Sanford and Son"—are actually throwbacks to the Amos 'n' Andy era. According to their detractors, programs like ABC's "That's My Mama" and CBS' "Good Times" degrade black women and fail to portray stable family units. Another frequent objection is that the new shows fail to depict black characters of intellectual or professional accomplishment.

Unfortunately, there is some truth in all these charges. Black-oriented television has a long way to go before it accurately reflects the current status and future aspirations of most black Americans.

The same, however, could be said of television's portrayal of American society in general. Do NBC's "Chico and the Man" and ABC's "Nakia" reflect the realities of life for Chicanos or American Indians? Of course not. But neither does "The Waltons" realistically portray life in white Applachia as it was—or is.

Some members of the black-consciousness movement, though, along with its white "sympathizers," choose to ignore all this. When Benjamin Stein, a white critic, tackled the subject in the *Wall Street Journal*, he likened "Sanford and Son" to "Amos 'n' Andy"—because Fred Sanford is "about the most shuffling, sly, stupid, cunning, dishonest, ridiculous buffoon to play a continuing character on television."

If this assessment of Fred is accurate—and it is not—what makes "Sanford and Son" a throwback to "Amos 'n' Andy"? Why not to "Our Miss Brooks," "I Love Lucy" or the "Beverly Hillbillies"? Surely, Lucy or Miss Brooks were dumb, outlandish characters, no more complimentary to white, middle-class American women than Fred Sanford is to the average low-income, first-generation migrant black American who lives in or around a junk yard.

Blacks who tend to agree with critics like Benjamin Stein ought to consider two simple questions: Do we really want white people to believe there are no blacks who live and act like the characters on "Sanford and Son"? If so, what is going to happen when real integration arrives and the cat is out of the bag?

Sandra Haggerty, the black columnist who appears in the *Los Angeles Times*, has been especially critical of "That's My Mama" and "Good Times" because the mothers are portrayed on both series as "large, robust and well over 30." She—and some black feminists—contend that Theresa Merritt, who plays the title role in "That's My Mama," is a "reincarnation of the old black mama, Beulah," because she is "big, loud, overbearing, unmarried . . . and emasculates her son."

Nonsense. "That's My Mama"—except for Junior, the superhip, soul-shaking character who has no business in the script—is one of the most positive series about black life to be offered on television since National Education Television's "Black Journal."

From a sociological standpoint, one can certainly criticize the lack of a strong father figure in the home—but television has always had a notorious inclination toward single-parent families. On "That's My Mama," the father's absence (he is deceased)

is largely compensated for by stable family conditions, a healthy attitude toward work and achievement, and a close relationship between the mother and her son, Clifton, whose attitude is more respectful than emasculated. It is his respect—not her dominance—that gives the mother leverage over her son. Similarly, the father is always spoken of with respect, though he is not idealized; in one episode he even had a community school named after him.

As for the sheer physical weight of the over-30 mothers in "That's My Mama" and "Good Times," it should only be noted that many black women are indeed "hefty" and over 30. Some are even fat. Whites need not watch these shows to discover this. They can see it on their way to work or, if they really choose to put themselves out, by driving through a shopping center in South-Central Los Angeles.

(It might also be pointed out to those who wince at fat black women on television that Americans of all races and sexes have weight problems. But that's another story.)

In fact, the negative impressions of the "black mama, Beulah," as played in old films by people like Hattie McDaniel (*Gone With the Wind*) and Louise Beavers (*Imitation of Life*), have little to do with the actual obesity of either actress. (Black film historian Donald Bogle has noted that directors made Louise Beavers pad her breasts to maintain the illusion—Hollywood required it.) Surely the distaste that developed among blacks for these "mammy"-like roles cannot be justified by assertions that they had no basis in fact. Actually, characters of this kind were fairly accurate depictions of black maids in a certain part of the country at a certain time in history.

Indeed, I have known more headrag-wearing black women than I care to recall who rode in the back seat (or, for that matter, in front), spanked white children, sang beautifully while working and submitted to white power. Although my own grandmother (who reared me) wasn't very fat, she embodied many aspects of the "mama Beulah" character. I remember too well the many occasions I went with her to do housework or pick up ironing and had whites hand me food out the back door—while their white kids inside the house were taking food off my grandmother's plate, as though she were their mother.

The problem, then, is not the "mama Beulah" role itself, but the fact that it became a stereotype; it came to appear that *all* black women acted in this manner. Yet it goes without saying that not *all* black women have looked or acted this way—nor do they now. Thus, the film industry has failed black people not by casting fat black women as fat black women but by failing to create a wide variety of roles reflecting the diversity and complexity of the black experience in America.

Like actresses of any color, Hattie McDaniel and Louise Beavers made a living by taking the roles the industry was willing to offer them. More important, they kept black artists visible in some of the best films of their era. In fact, these women, along with Tim Moore (Kingfish on TV), Eddie Anderson (Rochester) and others, served the cause of equality more by performing on the screen and on the radio than they would have by not doing so.

For it must be kept in mind that it was those of us who grew up watching the likes of Hattie McDaniel, Tim Moore and the great character actor Mantan Moreland (Charlie Chan's chauffeur, "Birmingham Brown") who nevertheless later instigated the social upheavals of the 1950s and '60s—events that changed the course of American history.

Abolishing those actors' roles, as the NAACP once advocated, might well have proved more destructive in the long run than any stereotypes enhanced by characters they portrayed. Likewise, even if the antics of Redd Foxx resemble those of "Amos 'n' Andy" to some people, they are still insufficient cause for dropping "Sanford and Son"—or even altering its format, Black-oriented shows that achieve top ratings should be left alone. If Redd Foxx, Demond Wilson and Whitman Mayo feel they have to act like Amos, Andy and Kingfish to keep "Sanford and Son" riding high, I see no reason for them not to.

At the present stage of the black struggle for equality in the public media, it is much more important that we have top-rated black shows than that we have shows that meet the ideological requirements of the black-consciousness movement—or its "white sympathizers."

Rather than damning "Sanford and Son," "That's My Mama" and "Good Times," blacks should use the high ratings and advertising revenues generated by these shows as a means of gaining leverage to increase the number of blacks employed off screen.

In my view, the fact that black actors are making money for the networks imposes a moral, political and economic obligation on television broadcasters to give qualified blacks the same opportunity to write, produce, direct and edit that whites now enjoy—on white shows as well as black. That's what the capitalist ethic is all about, or so we have been taught.

For what is really wrong with television's portrayal of blacks has far more to do with the lack of black writers, producers and directors than the size, weight and mannerisms of the people appearing on camera. In fact, when blacks are given the same opportunity as whites to write for television, many of the present casting and script problems—and there are some—will resolve themselves.

Allowing blacks to have greater creative involvement behind the scenes is one way for television to correct its portrayal of black people and acknowledge our continuing gains and achievements. We are not all comedians, mothers, cops and entertainers; neither are we all poor and jobless. Black Americans today fill jobs ranging from positions on the Federal Communications Commission to those on the factory assembly line. (By the way, most blacks live in homes with fathers, who have at least some education and hold steady jobs.)

The images on the television screen are devised and controlled by producers, writers, directors and editors. They create what we see on the screen—and are thus responsible for the images that television projects. So the critics of black-oriented television, if they mean what they say, should redirect their attack on what is happening on screen to the reality behind it.

People can be influenced by demeaning stereotypes, although the victims often retain fond memories of these stereotypes if they make them laugh.

Even now I fondly recall the calm summer afternoons when I set out to visit Miss Nell's house. As the sun set, I would make my way around tobacco fields and up the dirt road to her house.

Sometimes I ran barefoot, pulling a "packer" behind me for amusement (that's a syrup can filled with dirt). Sometimes I simply drifted from one side of the road to the other, looking for blackberries, picking plums, kicking a can or just daydreaming.

I liked going to Miss Nell's—she always cooked up fresh meat and sweet-potato pies. But most of all, I liked going, because when I got there, she always had the radio on, tuned to "Amos 'n' Andy."

In the world of popular culture, which, after all, reflects the power structure of the larger world, there is a disproportionate percentage of "heroes" and protagonists in general who are White Anglo-Saxon Protestants. Usually that means that the socially undesirable counterparts to the WASPs are seen as blacks, Puerto Ricans, Chicanos, Orientals, and, of course, American Indians.

The next selections deal with the manner in which Hollywood, the Great American Dream factory, usually treats blacks, Puerto Ricans, and Indians.

There has been black cinema in the United States for more than sixty years. In 1917 an outfit called the Ebony Corporation made a movie called *Spyin' the Spy*. There were black leading performers, Paul Robeson, for example, decades before Sidney Poitier became respectable enough to invite to dinner. But for the main part, blacks were stereotyped in a detrimental way. For the rare film like *Sounder, End as a Man*, or *Lilies of the Field* (which received critical acclaim but did poorly at the box office), we have had a plethora of films like *Shaft, Superfly*, and lesser blaxploitation releases, whose common theme is that a black man can achieve success in this society only by being more violent than those who surround him.

To Find an Image
James P. Murray

In the United States, cinema has gone a long way in projecting a kind of beautiful sterility. It has presented images to people who wanted desperately to believe in the American dream of unbridled opportunity and in the possibility of wealth, splendor, and freedom from unhappiness. The early Hollywood offerings were particularly successful, because the films usually depicted situations wherein the success or failure of the hero was determined, not by his force of character, but by the role. Thus, the tall cowboy in the white hat always outdrew the one in the black hat, no good girl ever lost to a bad girl, and we all knew that after the fadeout, sexual activity culminated in simultaneous and ecstatic orgasms.

A more subtle but equally potent projection was the stereotype of successful (therefore worthwhile) people. The man was tall, white, handsome, and self-assured. The woman was small, white, lovely, and self-assured, although often a bit naive. Almost everyone was wealthy. No woman went to the bathroom except to change her makeup.

Hollywood became the creator of folk heroes. The United States, a country too young to have traditional folk heroes, created instant celluloid giants. And most Americans believed in these images. They worried about which "star" was doing what, what so-and-so was wearing, or whom so-and-so was being seen with. This is what America was all about: the ideal. It is necessary to examine the effect of this kind of propaganda rather than its objective merit. For although we may say that Hollywood was producing "un-reality," the effect on the country in terms of image and life style was, and still is, very real. Little girls grew up wanting to be Shirley Temple, and those who did look like Shirley Temple were valued more than their plain sisters. Similarly, little boys who were handsome, tough, self-assured were valued more than little boys who were not. When Veronica Lake wore her hair in a certain style, women all over the country did the same and felt more a part of the culture.

Films reflect not only the aspirations of individuals, but also those of society as a whole. The concept of manliness was more important to the "serious" business of life than that of womanliness. Whites were the good guys; Indians, the bad guys; Orientals, the cooks and valets. During the Second World War, most stewards serving on ships in the U.S. Navy were either blacks or Orientals. Not necessarily because these people made better stewards, but because they fulfilled the proper image.

What was the movie industry doing for black people in this country? It was telling them the same things it was telling whites during the thirties and forties: that whites were the important people, the more valued people, and the people on whose side were such notables as God and Cecil B. DeMille. It told black children that white skin was beautiful. And that blue eyes and straight blond hair were beautiful. It was clear that a black-skinned, kinky-haired girl with dark eyes could not be beautiful. And so blacks went to drugstores and beauty parlors and straightened their hair and bleached their skin and accepted, in frighteningly large measure, the value of a white physical appearance. But a more devastating element of what Hollywood was producing was the custom of excluding blacks from the majority of films. The fact that blacks did not exist in the film world contributed more toward their denigration than anything else. It was whites, not blacks, who were significant.

There were some films, however, depicting blacks in a detrimental way. Blacks were shown as cowardly, subservient, obsequious, lazy. These pictures did more to reinforce the attitudes of whites than they did to injure the self-image of blacks. For blacks could no more identify with the shallow creatures on the screen than could whites with badly drawn white characters. The picture of Tarzan beating off fifty Africans prompted black children to identify with the white hero rather than the Africans.

Undoubtedly, movies will continue to exert a strong influence on the way people think of themselves. As techniques evolve, more and more people will be drawn into visual media, if for no other reason than its facility in reaching audiences. The chances are great that visual media will play an increasingly important role in direct education as well. Since the media exert such influence, and because they have historically excluded blacks to the detriment of the black image, blacks, if they are to rectify this omission, should use the media to create their own versions of society. And, to some degree, this is what is happening today.

In discussing black-oriented cinema, it would be more accurate to define cinema as "black" when all aspects, including financing, distribution, and advertising, are black-controlled. However, I choose to call "black" any cinema in which blacks exert significant influence, either by direct input (such as writing the screenplay, starring in, producing, or directing the film) or by indirect participation (such as accepting roles in which no creative involvement is permitted, but in which a black theme has a decided effect).

The three goals of black cinema are: correction of white distortions, the reflection of black reality, and (as a propagandizing tool) the creation of a positive black image. The majority of black pictures will probably be primarily reactive until blacks can gain full control of their productions. This is because so far it remains easier to get funding for a picture that sharply delineates whites and blacks than for one that minimizes their differences or ignores whites altogether. A picture featuring a black–white clash in which the blacks defeat a very mediocre corps of whites does not offend whites because of the mediocrity of the white actors (or their roles) and because the film points out that blacks and whites are, essentially, at odds. If, at the same time, blacks can be made to look somehow despicable, so much the better. Thus, certain movies will continue to show the "good" black guy as a pimp or involved in drug trafficking and the like. The reactive film, responding to the oppression that blacks feel in the everyday world, does little to alter the black image but is still superior to a Tarzan singlehandedly chasing hundreds of Africans away from Jane.

The concept of black reality divorced from the American dream, which had never been real to either black or white Americans, is the most promising aspect of black cinema. But black reality in cinema will still depend for some time on what white backers see as that reality.

The use of film as a medium for propaganda should not be overlooked. Directed toward both blacks and whites, it holds a promise of understanding that books have not delivered. The visual images of blacks, brought into white living rooms on the six o'clock news, first informed the white public of black anger and resentment. These same images may one day alert whites to the fact that the struggle for existence in the United States is a broader, more profound experience than they imagine.

* * *

The first problem of black cinema is survival. When a new black women's magazine appeared several years ago, it was very distinctive due to the picture of a lovely black girl on the cover. The following month there were two other magazines on the stands with cover portraits of black women. By the

"...black reality in cinema will still depend for some time on what white backers see as that reality."

time of its second issue the new magazine was being challenged.

Black filmmakers are being challenged by white producers and studios who see in the black film a source of easy revenue. The films that the studios employ blacks to produce and direct are no different from exploitation films made by whites. To say that the answer lies with black investors would be to oversimplify. People with enough money to produce a film must be found. These people must choose film investments rather than securities or futures or other proven financial ventures. After a film is produced it must be profitably distributed. Mishandling at any point can completely wipe out profits.

Film producers support distributors who support theater owners, and the process also works in reverse. Each element of the industry supports the others. Independent film producers are forced to buck the whole system. Books from independent black publishers have been refused by bookstores and ignored by critics. Black film producers face the same problem. The future of independent black film companies is therefore uncertain despite the success of Van Peebles or some of the early black filmmakers. Even now, as major black talents emerge, they are largely absorbed into white production companies. It is probable, then, that black films will be an influence and a force within the American cinema rather than a separate entity.

That is not to say there will be no independent black filmmakers. There have been black companies for over fifty years, and some undoubtedly will continue to flourish. But there are already indications that independent companies will not play the largest part in bringing black images to the screen. The companies springing up on both coasts have not yet shown the capacity for sustained productivity. Much of the impetus for these companies comes from the increased amount of trained black personnel.

Thanks to occasional help from the government and opportunities won for them by Belafonte, Poitier, Greaves, Van Peebles, Davis, and others, hundreds of young blacks have been trained in the scores of jobs required to make a feature film. Some are now working for the major studios. Others are supplying the needs of black producers and black production companies.

In other creative areas, there has been progress. John O. Killins, Ossie Davis, Lorraine Hansberry, William Branch, and Lonne Elder are among the blacks who have written feature films.

Blacks have also begun composing music for films. Three-time Academy Award nominee Quincy Jones scored forty films between 1966 and 1971. The music from *Shaft*, by Isaac Hayes, was a spectacular success and earned a gold record within weeks of its release. It sold as a single and as an album. The recorded sound track eventually earned platinum status, signifying two million dollars in sales. Hayes won several awards, including a Grammy and an Academy Award, for his first effort.

Film editor Hugh A. Robertson has made olympic strides. After winning an Academy Award nomination for his work with *Midnight Cowboy*, he moved on to *Shaft*, became a consultant on *Georgia, Georgia*, and then directed his first feature, *Hang Tough!* for M-G-M.

Greaves and Van Peebles are examples of the growing number of black filmmakers who have proved their cinematic ability and won prestigious film honors.

The black film itself has become the subject of serious study. Black film festivals were held at Knoxville College in 1970, at Spelman and Rutgers in 1971, and at the University of Pennsylvania in 1973. They offered the chance to study the old, compare the present, and talk about the future. With intellectual interest in black films, research and writing on the topic is increasing.

Organizations like the Hollywood chapter of the NAACP, and *Soul* are now giving film awards.

The creation of an image is one of the primary objectives of black filmmakers.

It may take five years. It may take longer, but there will come a day when a black man—any black man in the world—will walk into a theater, see himself in a movie, and learn something while being entertained. Something that will stimulate his emotions and increase his pride and self-respect. Something that will generate his concern for his fellow man. Something that will transform that concern into involvement. Something that will identify and communicate blackness, like an Aretha Franklin concert, a Malcolm X speech, a store-front church service, a Don Lee poem, or a young brother with billowing afro.

An image, a symbol, a style, a heritage. Something any black man will look at and about which he will say, "That's me . . . and it's good."

Black Cinema.

Minority groups in the United States in recent years have begun to strike back at the negative, demeaning images of themselves promulgated by the mass media. Latin Americans, especially Mexican Americans, were constantly humiliated by television commercials. The message from the omniscient tube was that Mexicans stink ("If it [Arrid] works for him, it will work for you"), are funny little bandits ("Frito Bandito"), or are too indolent to improve themselves (L and M's "Paco" never "feenishes" anything, "not even the revolution"), and so on. After many futile protests by the Mexican-American Anti-Defamation Committee to the Frito-Lay Corporation and Liggett and Myers about the racist stereotypes used in their advertising campaigns, the committee sought legal remedies. Frito-Lay, their advertising agency, Foote, Cone and Belding, and the CBS and NBC networks were collectively sued for $610 million in damages on behalf of the 6.1 million Americans of Mexican descent because of their failure to discontinue advertising corn chips at the expense of Chicanos, after having promised to stop. The message finally sank in: The Frito Bandito disappeared.

Stereotypes of Latin Americans still abound in Hollywood's films, however, as Professor Edward Mapp shows in his article on the portrayal of Puerto Ricans in the movies.

Puerto Ricans in American Films
Edward Mapp

The Puerto Rican in American films is mostly shadow and little substance. He might be a boy in Central Park in *The Out of Towners*, a prisoner in *Fuzz*, or a soldier in *The Dirty Dozen*, rarely emerging from the background of films in which others are major characters.

Early in 1951, the eminent Puerto Rican actor, José Ferrer, received Hollywood's highest accolade, the Academy of Motion Picture Arts and Sciences award for the best performance by an actor in a leading role. Although the official announcement of the award occurred at a presentation ceremony in California, Señor Ferrer actually received his "Oscar" from Luis Muñoz Marin, then Governor of Puerto Rico, in a triumphant one-day visit to the Island. Only hours after accepting the coveted statuette, Ferrer presented it to the University of Puerto Rico as a permanent trophy. Acknowledging his ethnic heritage, Ferrer said, "I want to express my pride as a Puerto Rican and as a man for the effort that the Puerto Ricans are making in the face of the most adverse circumstances, determined not to be defeated either by scarcity or illness nor to be dominated by hatred or envy." The actor's eloquent remarks would have carried even greater significance had he won the award for portraying a heroic Puerto Rican figure instead of the flamboyant fictional Frenchman, Cyrano de Bergerac. Borrowing a phrase from Cyrano, Ferrer referred to holding high and unsullied "my plume," perhaps not fully realizing, himself, how difficult that task would be. In the years since Ferrer's signal achievement, the incidence of positive Hispanic characterizations in films has been rare, and those often portrayed by "gringos." The casting of Peter O'Toole as the *Man of La Mancha* is a conspicuous example of this trend.

When Puerto Ricans do appear in American motion pictures, they are frequently portrayed in a demeaning manner. Witness the stereotypical presentation of Puerto Ricans in a film such as *Popi*, which starred Alan Arkin in the title role. *Popi*, a Puerto Rican widower in New York, is determined to remove his two young sons from the unwholesome environment of the ghetto slum in which they reside. One can accept the notion of a desperate man terrified by the junkies, muggers, thieves and street gangs of Spanish Harlem, but try to find a "Boricua padre" who would even contemplate casting his beloved "hijos" adrift in a rowboat on the treacherous Atlantic Ocean with some fantastic scheme to have them rescued and adopted as Cuban refugees. Seeing this apparently religious Puerto Rican parent attempt suicide by drowning was as difficult to swallow as it was for Popi to down the Miami surf. This is not to suggest that the film was bereft of truth about some facets of Puerto Rican life in the tenements of New York. The life-sized mannequin propped up by the window, the pre-recorded barking dog, the multiple door locks have the ring of truth about inner city survival. There is the foraging at a hotel banquet for remnants and morsels which can be brought home as a treat for the "niños." There are the unsuccessful efforts to conceal his sexual relationship with a mistress (Rita Moreno) in the next apartment from the eyes of two very "hip" little fellows. Regretfully, Arkin's accent as Popi is part Spanish, part Yiddish— a further challenge to credulity. *Popi* is no one's reality, least of all the Puerto Rican's.

Films which deal with school themes tend to be less reluctant to recognize the presence of Puerto Ricans. An unfortunate corollary of such recognition is that most youngsters in such films are characterized as problem Puerto Ricans. As early as 1955, Rafael Campos appeared as the Puerto Rican class clown of a vocational high school English class in the movie *Blackboard Jungle*. At that time Campos was the "token" for roles involving young Chicanos, Puerto Ricans and Apaches. Hollywood recognized no ethnic or cultural distinctions among these groups. It is common knowledge that Puerto Ricans imbue in their youngsters a respect and reverence for authority, education and educators. Yet, in *Blackboard Jungle*, Campos, as Pete Morales, a Puerto Rican boy, helps disrupt the classroom discipline of a sympathetic and patient teacher. Not content with this negative image, Morales is held up for derision by his classmates because of his thick accent and his excessive and indiscriminate use of a single expletive. The film would have us believe that Morales is not intelligent enough to know when he is being mocked. Oddly enough, with a non-stereotype portrayal by Sidney Poitier as a student with leadership capability, blacks fared better than Puerto Ricans in *Blackboard Jungle*.

The Puerto Rican is again seen as student in *Up the Down Staircase* (aren't there any Puerto Rican teachers?) but this time he is portrayed with dignity by José Rodriguez. José had been reticent in Miss Barrett's English class until she decided to simulate a courtroom trial as enrichment of a literature selection. José was assigned the role of judge and emerged from his cocoon with an unexpected fervor. The class and the teacher were overwhelmed not only by the costume José managed to acquire for the occasion but by his surprisingly authoritative manner. "I'm the judge and you gotta listen," he announces.

In stark contrast is the role of Aníbal, the young Puerto Rican in Frank and Eleanor

> "When Puerto Ricans do appear in American motion pictures, they are frequently portrayed in a demeaning manner."

Perry's film, *Last Summer*. Aníbal, portrayed by Ernest Gonzalez, experiences complete humiliation at the hands of some corrupt post-pubescent WASPs who are out for a season of fun on Fire Island. Aníbal comes out from New York City to keep a computer-arranged blind date with Rhoda. He does not complain when Rhoda brings her three friends along on the date. Slowly and insidiously, the cruel quartet begin to ridicula Aníbal, deliberately calling him Annabelle, getting him drunk, sticking him with the check and finally abandoning him to a gang of hoodlums who beat him unmercifully. His pathetic cry, "Ayúdeme, por Dios," goes unanswered by those whom he guilelessly assumed were "amigos." Movie script-writers seem to attribute innocence to Puerto Ricans as eagerly as they once attributed indolence to blacks.

Almost as vulnerable as Aníbal is Jesus Ortiz as played by Jaime Sanchez in *The Pawnbroker*. Although the Jewish pawnbroker rejects the proffered friendship and admiration of Ortiz, the Puerto Rican youth's warmth and spirit remain intact. He promises his "madre," no more stealing, peddling or numbers. Ortiz is resolved to make something of himself. He beseeches the pawnbroker to teach him the secrets of the trade. As apprentice to the pawnbroker, he will learn a business and therein gain security and respectability. Despite his ambition and goals, the film stresses the Puerto Rican's inability to be punctual. Twenty minutes late for work one day, he tells his employer, "I'm gonna be here practically early on Monday." Score one for another stereotype. In his eagerness to assimilate, Ortiz admonishes his mother to speak English, not Spanish. Misguided by the embittered pawnbroker to believe that money is everything, Ortiz flirts with crime in a moment of disillusionment. During a robbery which he made possible, Ortiz is slain in a courageous attempt to protect the pawnbroker. American films have a proclivity for offering up third world people as sacrifices for the salvation of whites. Another discordant note in this film involves the girl friend of Ortiz, a black prostitute who happens to be unselfishly devoted to him. An aspiring young Puerto Rican who lives with his mother and wears a crucifix might use the services of a prostitute but is highly unlikely to acknowledge her as his girl friend.

Juano Hernandez, the distinguished Puerto Rican actor who forged a screen career in Hollywood portraying black Americans, contributes a small but memorable characterization to *The Pawnbroker*. He is seen as a pathetic and lonely customer of the pawn shop.

An Elvis Presley movie is an unlikely place to find realism and his *Change of Habit* proved no exception. The film is about a guitar-playing physician (Elvis) and some female medical assistants (would you believe nuns on loan from a convent?) who try to solve the problems of an urban ghetto population. One of their problems is Julio Hernandez, a stuttering, emotionally ill Puerto Rican teenager. When Julio isn't stealing an icon from the local church or attempting the rape of a nun (Mary Tyler Moore, no less), he is uttering pseudo "macho" lines such as "My knife make me big man." Implicit in the film's conclusion is that Julio will receive psychiatric care, speech therapy and possibly a jail sentence, not necessarily in that order.

Further linking Puerto Ricans with crime

and imprisonment, a producer had the insensitivity to film *The Honeymoon Killers*, based upon the actual criminal alliance of Raymond Fernandez and Martha Beck in the lonely hearts murders for which they were executed in 1951. The real tragedy of such a film which depicts a Puerto Rican as criminal lies in its imbalance. *Bonnie and Clyde* is counterbalanced by numerous positive film images of whites but no such redress exists for negative film images of Puerto Ricans.

Puerto Rico is sometimes evident in American films even when Puerto Ricans are not. The action-filled conclusion of a Mafia melodrama entitled *Stiletto* was shot on the Island of Puerto Rico with historic El Morro used as the setting of an exciting chase sequence. Twentieth Century Fox shot locations for its film *Che!* in Puerto Rico because of the similarity to Cuban landscapes. Many of the guerilla warfare scenes in *Che!* were photographed in a Puerto Rican rain forest.

West Side Story, winner of no less than ten academy awards including an "Oscar" as best film of 1961, represents the summit of Puerto Rican prominence in motion pictures. Told in Romeo and Juliet fashion, *West Side Story* is essentially the drama of a Puerto Rican girl who falls in love with a Polish boy, despite the open hostility of their respective ethnic groups. Ever faithful to fantasy, Hollywood engaged Natalie Wood, an actress of Russian descent, to play Maria, the Puerto Rican heroine. Perhaps as a

concession to reality, it cast Rita Moreno, a Puerto Rican actress, in the lesser role of Anita, spitfire-confidante of Maria. Miss Moreno played the role with zest and perception, earning an "Oscar" as best actress in a supporting role. Previously Miss Moreno had enacted minor roles in Hollywood films in which she merely had to flare her nostrils, gnash her teeth and look spirited. *West Side Story* came not a moment too soon for this talented Puerto Rican actress, who was losing patience with stereotypical dialogue of the "Yankee pig, you stole my people's gold" variety. *West Side Story* must be applauded for its fine musical score, brilliant photography, imaginative choreography and overdue recognition of the presence of Puerto Ricans in New York City. The film also takes cognizance of the strong familial bonds which exist even within uprooted Puerto Rican families. Unhappy about a Polish boy's interest in Maria, Bernardo warns him, "You keep away from my sister. Don't you know we are a family people!" The film's positive aspects end there!

Some of the song lyrics denigrate Puerto Rico, alluding to it as an island of tropic diseases, bullets, over-population, inadequate roads, no electricity and hundreds of people in one room. One line actually asks, "what have they got there to keep clean?" The Puerto Rican gang members and their girl friends are costumed in gaudy attire in keeping with still another myth. As a rather sheltered and parochial Puerto Rican girl, Maria seems almost too eager for intercultural romance. With names like Leonard Bernstein, Robert Wise, Ernest Lehman, Arthur Laurents and Leonard Robbins heading up the venture, there should be little surprise at the lack of an authentic Puerto Rican perspective. Yet even the casting of Rita Moreno as the Puerto Rican Anita represents progress of a kind. Her performance and its subsequent recognition tells motion picture audiences that Puerto Ricans do exist and that they too have value.

"*West Side Story*, winner of no less than ten academy awards..., represents the summit of Puerto Rican prominence in motion pictures."

No one knows with certainty what the future holds but it does not look too bright, if *Badge 373* is a prognosticator. Independence for Puerto Rico is one theme of this film, recently shot on location in New York City. In the story, Felipe Luciano plays a young Puerto Rican, who is helping to send arms to a revolutionary faction in Puerto Rico. The film depicts the Puerto Rican as prostitute, racketeer, crooked policeman and junkie. While it is true that other ethnic groups are portrayed negatively in *Badge 373*, a greater frequency of appearances for them permits a balance of more positive screen images. The Puerto Rican is seen so seldom in motion pictures that each and every characterization counts a great deal.

José Torres makes the valid point that talented Puerto Rican script writers and well-to-do Puerto Rican investors can do much to provide movie audiences with satisfactory films about Puerto Ricans.

The portrayal of Puerto Ricans in films of the past surely entitles them to a brighter future. It is time for humane and honest films about Puerto Ricans. The potential and possibility are there. It only remains to be realized.

The near genocide of the American Indian is not one of this country's prouder sagas. While we remember Andrew Jackson as a colorful frontiersman who made it to the White House, we tend to forget that one of the cruelest orders against the American Indian occurred during his administration and that of his favored successor, Martin Van Buren. One hundred twenty-five thousand Indians were dragged from their homes and deported west of the Mississippi by military force under the guise of treaties. Every trick of intimidation, bribery, fraud, threat, and force was used. So inhumane were the conditions of their deportation that nearly 40,000 died on the journey.

Our popular culture, from dime novels of the nineteenth century to Hollywood's depiction of the red man, has focused on the Indian as a savage fighter. The many contributions of the Indian to our everyday life—cigars, hammocks, canoes, and the names of such cities as Chicago, Seattle, Milwaukee, and Omaha, to name a few—are seldom considered.

In the following selection, the noted film historians George N. Fenin and William K. Everson describe the way in which the Indian has been portrayed by Hollywood. If, in such films as John Ford's *Cheyenne Autumn* or Arthur Penn's *Little Big Man*, the tide seems to be changing in recent years toward a less chauvinistic view, it is about time.

Another Red Man Bit the Dust

George N. Fenin
William K. Everson

Except for the first phase in the history of the Western, and the contemporary phase, the Indian's existence in the United States has been dealt with by the movies in a stereotyped manner. The tragedy of the Indian tribes, pushed backwards and backwards again in violation of treaties and agreements, their confinement on reservations where unscrupulous Indian agents exploited them shamelessly, the disintegration of their fighting spirit and their traditional desire to live in peace with the white man—all these were aspects of Indian life which American audiences were seldom able to witness, evaluate, and reflect upon on the screen.

"The only good Indian is a dead Indian." This belief, which was strictly held and put into practice in many parts of the West, represented an inviolate pillar of thought for the creators of screen formulae. The most that the Indian could expect in Hollywood's hands was a presentation as the white man's equal; but this only so that he could be killed, coldbloodedly, under the same "justice" that dispatched badmen who were white. But the Indian was usually not even granted those human failings and influences which motivated the crimes of whites. Despite the writings of James Fenimore Cooper and German's Karl Mai, whose many books had as much success in Germany as did the works of Zane Grey in America, the Indian proved to be a far less useful character to film-makers than the cowboy, the Texas Ranger, or even the infrequently seen Canadian mountie. Initially, at least, the Indian was seen as a hero almost as frequently as the white man, but already there was a difference. He seemed more of a symbol, less of an individual, than the cowboy, and he was presented in a more poetic, and often more tragic, light. But after 1910 he was not really presented as an individual at all, not until the racial cycle of the late Forties. In the interim, he was an unmotivated enemy; villains might be presented as individuals, but the Indians were always shown *en masse*. There were very few Westerns with Indians as the only heavies, for the simple reason that without motive there could be no plot. Maynard's *Red Raiders* of 1927 is one of the few exceptions in that it has no white villains, and depends on Indian aggression for its sole action. While admitting that Indians can be human enough to want peace, it still dealt with them as warlike children, and never as believable human beings. Few Westerns have emulated *Red Raiders'* example of eliminating white villains entirely. Ford's *Stagecoach*, in which the menace is provided by the pursuit of Geronimo's Apaches, found it necessary to tack on a climactic (or *anti*-climactic) duel between the hero (John Wayne) and an outlaw (Tom Tyler).

This is not to say that the Indians have always been depicted as villainous savages; but in the bulk of the "B" Westerns their function was primarily to provide formula action by taking to the warpath in opposition to the heroes. In films like *Prairie Thunder* (1937) they were spurred on by white renegades; in *The Law Rides Again* (1943) and countless others, they took to the warpath because of fancied grievances against the whites (a crooked white Indian agent had been stealing supplies promised them by the government); and in *Fort Osage* (1952) their

warlike actions were deliberately provoked by white renegades who hoped that an Indian war would cover their own depredations. In such Westerns, the Indian was alternately villainous and misunderstood, but he rarely emerged as a human being.

This changed to a very great degree after the advent of *Broken Arrow* (1950). Once Hollywood made up its mind to make up to the Indian for past misrepresentation, the pendulum swung completely to the other side. From now on it was to be the Indian who sought peace, and the white man who was the agitating aggressor. But the pendulum was not to swing so far as to dehumanize the white man as had once been done to the Indian. There were always to be individual motives attributed to the white villain which made him atypical of his race, e.g. the villainous trader who knows that peace with the Indians will mean an end to his illicit traffic (Grant Withers in Ford's *Rio Grande*), and most common of all, the martinet military commander who hates Indians with a blind passion (Jeff Chandler in *Two Flags West*, Henry Fonda in *Fort Apache*) and is opposed to any means which will bring about a cessation of hostilities short of total defeat of the Indians. Since such men are almost always presented as complete or near-complete neurotics, they stand midway between guilt and innocence, and they are made to appear very much the exception rather than the rule. The Indian is presented in this case in a more realistic fashion; he is the victim rather than the aggressor, but the question of blame, which should rightly be placed on the governmental policies of that time, is neatly side-stepped.

The authentic motives for Indian hostility were seldom, if ever, explained; the main function of these Americans consisted in providing a convenient mass enemy, and a series of spectacular moving targets. Once the cliché was accepted, explanations of motivation were in any case no longer necessary. The very word *Indian* became synonymous with savagery and villainy, just as the words *German, Japanese, Nazi* or *Communist* in themselves later became not merely descriptive nouns, but adjectives of automatic infamy in many areas of world and cinematic affairs. . . .

The rehabilitation of the Indian was a must, but Delmer Daves' *Broken Arrow* (1950) tended to go too far in the opposite direction, and several later films have had whites in the villain's roles. Although failures from a serious historical and sociological point of view, films like *Sitting Bull* (1954) and *Broken Arrow* nevertheless displayed an attitude in the desire to approach the real frontier from a radically different point of view. The Indian is finally achieving his important place in the Western saga just as the Negro in Southern literature is becoming, in the words of Callenbach, "a moral problem and a symbol."

Definite progress can be noted in the sympathetic and realistic depiction of the American Indian when one compares *Broken Arrow* with the similar *Run of the Arrow* (1957), directed by Samuel Fuller some seven years later. Although *Run of the Arrow* is a lesser film, far too sensational and unnecessarily brutal, far too little given to the gentle poetry that so distinguished Delmer Daves' earlier film, it is nevertheless a basically honest picture. Both deal with a white man who comes to the Indians as a sympathetic stranger, learns their ways, and lives as one of them. In *Broken Arrow*, the hero's first meeting with the Apaches comes just after he has seen the mutilated bodies of two whites, tortured to death by the Indians. Thus the cliché image of Indians as brutal savages is initially sustained, although there will be no more such brutality in the film. Once the hero and the Apache chief, Cochise, have gradually formed a firm friendship, the worthwhile point is made that the Indians are also human beings, with a code of behavior worth respecting. But that code is made to resemble the white man's code; it

is a "civilized" code because it is a reasoning one, devoid of barbarity. The earlier episode of callous torture is ignored, and it is hoped that the audience will not recall it. *Run of the Arrow* likewise introduces its hero to the Indians—in this case the Sioux—in a savage episode of torture emphasizing the barbaric nature of the Indians. By the time white man and Indian finally make friends, the film has established that grounds exist for compromise, a mutual respect for bravery and basically similar religious beliefs. The climax comes in a shocking scene in which the Sioux, in accordance with their tribal laws, put to death a captured white man, slowly skinning him alive. It is this act which finally forces the hero to the conclusion that he can no longer live as a Sioux; he acknowledges that the Sioux have a perfect right to live, unmolested, by their codes, but he is also forced to the reluctant admission that their codes can never be his. He then returns to his people, taking with him his Indian wife and adopted Indian child. The solution is more mature than the one presented in *Broken Arrow*. . . .

Tell Them Willie Boy Is Here (1969) and *A Man Called Horse* (1970) were also disappointing in their portrayals of the Indian, updated but still intrinsically similar to the old Western stereotypes. A more distinctive film was Ralph Nelson's *Soldier Blue*, adapted from a novel by Theodore V. Olsen describing the massacre of Sand Creek on November 29, 1864. In retaliation for an attack on a stagecoach, the soldiers of the U.S. Cavalry, led by Colonel Chivington, mas-

sacred about 500 Cheyenne men, women, and children. With this episode Nelson wanted to depict on the screen the real story of the relationship between the whites and the Indians. Present-day events have made many Americans re-examine their past and discover that they, not the Indians, were the real villains of the West. As director Nelson is quoted in the catalogue of the "International Cinema Meetings," Sorrento, Italy, in September, 1970: "Our official position is that we are in Vietnam to honor a commitment. But let us not forget that we have signed 400 treaties with the Indians, violating them all, one after the other."

Soldier Blue is the story of Honus Gant, a "blue soldier" (as the members of the U.S. Cavalry were then called), and a white woman, kidnapped by the Cheyenne, married to a chief, and later given back to the whites. They both witness the massacre of Sand Creek. Honus refuses to take part in it, is chained to a wagon, and will face a court-martial, while the woman, horrified by the carnage, repudiates her people and decides to share the squalid destiny of the surviving Cheyenne.

The massacre is the climax of the picture and its *raison d'être*. In its brutality and callous violence the film was clearly influenced, as was *The Wild Bunch*, by the Italian school. It must be considered one of the most impressive efforts towards a true historical perspective on the Western past. It is unfortunate, however, that Nelson did not complete his excellent essay on historical truth with a deeper, more realistic portrayal of the Indians themselves as well as the events in which they were involved.

This re-evaluation in depth was left to be done by Arthur Penn in his *Little Big Man* (1970), the best Western of the decade, based on the novel by Thomas Berger and adapted by Calder Willingham. The adventures of Jack Crabb, a one-hundred-twenty-year-old man who claims to be the sole white survivor of Custer's Last Stand, are an extraor-

dinary testament to the American Dream of the West. At first, the witness is a ten-year-old boy, raised by the Cheyenne after his pioneer parents are killed by another Indian tribe. He is rescued by the whites five years later and forced into a multitude of new roles, including two marriages, bankruptcy, patent-medicine selling, and tar and feathers as a result, alcoholism, risking death at the hands of both whites and Indians, and finally facing Custer in his last hour against the braves of Red Cloud and Crazy Horse. It is a magnificent fresco, moving, funny, and bitter. As in *Soldier Blue*, one of the finest sequences in this film is also a massacre: the massacre of the Cheyennes on the Washita River in Oklahoma on November 27, 1868, by seven hundred men of the U.S. Cavalry led by George Armstrong Custer, then a colonel. In that horrible event, according to Custer's biographer Frederick van de Water, all one hundred-fifty-three Cheyenne males were killed, and the fury of the whites consumed women and children as well—only fifty-three of them were taken prisoners to Fort Hays after the carnage. Moreover, upon specific orders from Custer, even the eight hundred seventy-five Indian ponies were shot down. . . .

The real force in this film is not the star, Dustin Hoffman, although he is excellent. Rather it is Dan George, a Canadian Indian playing the Cheyenne chief Old Lodge Skins, who is the center of attention, embodying the dignity, pride, and resilience of a race that is still waiting for the redressing of uncounted wrongs. Penn uses the film to express his personal philosophy with vigor, saving his most passionate feeling for describing past horrors reminiscent of present ones. His excoriation of George Armstrong Custer is one of the most pitiless indictments of a pompous fool ever witnessed on the screen.

Several critics found *Little Big Man* too much a mixture of tragedy and comedy, a jarring juxtaposition of passion and amusing superficiality. It must be realized that Penn was obliged to telescope a large number of multifaceted historical events into 157 minutes, quite a feat considering that he did not spare any of the classical myths of the Western in the sweep of his iconoclastic vision. The deaths of Wild Bill Hickok and General Custer, for example, show how far the Western has progressed since the days of *The Plainsman* and *They Died with Their Boots On:* from romanticism to deliberate and didactic realism. *Little Big Man* is a milestone in the history of the Western, beyond any doubt the most advanced document in the process of re-evaluating its sacred myths, a work of art in the cause of peace and understanding.

Two other notable films have also dealt with the tragedy of the Indian in very different ways. *The Long Walk* (1970) by Phillip Greene is a documentary rather than an adventure story like *Little Big Man.* This excellent sixty-minute work describes the devastation of the Navajo nation between 1864 and 1865, two years in which they were subjected to every possible brutality by the whites in the notorious "concentration camp" of Bosque Redondo. A series of interviews with elder tribesmen provides detailed insight into the history and tradition of the Navajo and the current efforts to improve the lot of the descendants of these proud people, including the activity at the Indian-run Rough Rock School. It is a little gem, a sincere appeal for understanding the complex problems of the Indian within the white man's society, and it must not be missed in any honest evaluation of the Indian past and present.

Carol Reed's *Flap* (1970) is quite a different treatment of the modern Indians' plight, on both the tragic and the comic level. Clair Huffaker's excellent adaptation of his novel *Nobody Loves a Drunken Indian* is the story of Flapping Eagle, an Indian who fights desperately against the intolerance and indifference of the whites, finally paying for the awakening of his fellow citizens with his life. Anthony Quinn, himself of Mexican Indian descent, gives a magnificent portrayal of a decent tribesman who believes in human dignity and who wishes to find a "place in the sun" for his unhappy, dejected, castaway people. The film was shot in New Mexico; among the most splendid views are those of the plains and the city of Acoma, the oldest continuously inhabited town in the United States, in existence long before Columbus' discovery of the New World. Against this background *Flap* presents the contemporary second-class status of the Indian, in moving and often funny terms. The combination of Huffaker's taut and meaty story and Sir Carol Reed's sympathetic, profoundly human direction makes a powerful film. . . .

The American Indian is finally being taken out of his stereotyped villainous role, and the historical realities of the Indian in the old West are being re-examined.

In 1972 a subcommittee of the House of Representatives held lengthy hearings regarding the negative image of ethnics in American mass media. This pressure on the Interstate and Foreign Commerce Subcommittee came about because some of the nonnatives were getting restless. Italian Americans, for example, were furious at the producers of the then current hit, *The Godfather*, for suggesting that the terms "Mafia" and "Cosa Nostra" were an integral part of Italian life. Polish Americans were livid about the frequency of "Polish" jokes on television, while Mexican Americans were upset about many of the ads and TV commercials epitomized by the Frito Bandito.

If nothing else, these congressional hearings alerted the nation to the casual way discrimination and bigotry had become part of our mass-mediated messages. Deleterious stereotypes were not limited to Chicanos, blacks, Indians, Jews, and Orientals; America's largest minority, the first and second generation of Poles, Greeks, Italians, and Rumanians, also had to be included.

Csanad Toth is one of those "minority Americans" who are concerned about their image in our popular culture. Toth, of Hungarian descent, calls for a media portrayal of ethnics that acknowledges their diverse cultural contributions instead of merely laughing at their accents.

The Media and the Ethnics
Csanad Toth

The Silent Majority's odd man out is the Middle American ethnic. He is silent not because he has nothing to say but because he is voiceless. He is silent because he can't get a word in edgewise among the flag waving declamations supposedly on his behalf. He is silent because in America's self-gratuitous celebration of cultural pluralism, he is considered quaint at best, awkward and a bigot most of the time. He is silent because the media creates the impression that he is not worth listening to, and what the media does not pick up, does not blow out of proportion, does not analyze to death, or in short, does not communicate, ceases to exist or exists only in an imperfect manner below the level of national consciousness.

Were it not for Archie Bunker's ethnic slurs, who would know about him? He is un-black, un-young, unpoor and unrich, a bore, and thus if you follow the current Nielsen yardsticks, unexisting and non-news worthy.

If the communications media is one of the keys to man's understanding of himself and his society, I have yet to receive a clue from the television, the radio and the newspapers to understand who and what I am and who my fellow ethnics are. If there is a growing ethnic consciousness, a rich ethnic cultural heritage and a political message in all this, the media's messages do not yet convey it. . . .

With some forty million Americans, I find myself on the road to discovering that I am more (or less?) than just an American and, following a process of elimination I decided that since I am neither Black, Chicano, Indian nor Anglo-Saxon, I must be an ethnic. With that recognition in mind, I embarked upon a search for some commonality with Czechs, Poles, Rumanians, Greeks, Armenians, Russians, Italians and all the other first and second generation Americans, together with whom, I am told, I am a member of America's largest minority. Not being overly fond of number games, this fact does not seem significant on face value. . . .

The commonality with ethnics and the shared experience with middle America goes much deeper than a country of origin and the wasteland of the media. Ethnic, or native, we share a feeling of powerlessness, of being left out, forgotten and silenced by a faceless, incomprehensible and inaccessible power that shapes our destinies. We feel battered by the impact of a highly technological and immensely complicated world with its myriad conflicting interests and values. Our lives have become overorganized and victimized by societal frustration and disorientation. This leaves us progressively less able to discern who we are and who we seek to become.

All these feelings are magnified by the impact of a daily mass communications bombardment which renders each of us less able to deal with the problem of identity and self-image, to distinguish lies from the truth, the packaged advertising from the managed news on the screen and in print. In this age of instant communications, everything is "now." The present assumes inordinate importance, the future some and the past none. Our life is measured out between the Walter Cronkite's daily "and that's the way it is today." There is little time to absorb that which is presented into one's cultural patterns or to integrate it with familiar references. This attachment to the "now" as served up for immediate consumption by the media transforms our lives into a shallow experience of transiency, rootless, thoughtless and without hope.

In a frantic search to make some sense from it all, the most outlandish propositions become plausible as long as they purport to explain and place the blame somewhere. We are often tempted to attack the media unconsciously imitating ancient oriental rulers who chopped off the heads of any messenger daring to bring ill tidings. There is a temptation to yield to prevailing paranoia about the role of the mass media in our society. Though it is the mirror image of ourselves that we ought not like, we prefer to break the mirror for telling us that we are not the fairest of them all. Some want to pry behind the mirror, like Vice President Agnew, to find as the culprits "a tiny, enclosed fraternity of privileged men elected by no one" or, depending upon one's political predilections, the corruptors of our young or the lackeys of "corporate Amerika" who determine what message the media will bring into our homes.

This is a temptation which should be resisted. It is the message and not the media which we should find repugnant. One function of the media is to serve as a window on the world. It is not the fault of the window, if we find the world view repugnant.

When it comes to ethnics, however, this window is boarded over. Aside from a handful of documentaries, television truly fails more by omission than commission. The blue collar middle American ethnic is never shown as he actually exists: squeezed beyond endurance by house payments, car payments, medical expenses, college for the kids and approaching retirement on an oatmeal and peanut butter budget. This man is also troubled about the war, violence in the streets, rising taxes, property values and all the other social concerns of our time that cut across race, religion or national origin. He is also concerned because he feels ignored by the government except on April 15. He is a human being with all the fears and fleeting delights felt by his fellow Americans in higher income brackets. But television never shows anything but the surface dimensions of his existence. At best he provides a milieu or inanimate background for daring detectives and debonair dames, dashing doctors and wise lawyers having a good time in Chinatown (or Germantown, Polish town, Armenian town). Like a revolving stage, the settings change but the people who inhabit them never really come alive. . . .

The middle American ethnic and the rest of us are victims of lowest common denominator in television programming. Television functions as a mind-numbing tranquilizer rather than stimulating a quest for personal or national identity. Few questions are raised about personal or national priorities. The function of television's great wasteland is one of pacification and not stimulation.

Combined with this diet of unrelieved blandness which numbs the mind, is an insidious element which serves to destroy ethnicity. This is not done through smear campaigns or vicious attacks which have the potential for creative backlash. It is done through pervasive neglect. In our society, what is not communicated ceases to exist and ethnicity is not communicated.

Black children can, after many years of nonbenign neglect, find something on television which reinforces their identity. The Electric Company, Sesame Street, Bill Cosby's specials, Flip Wilson and scores of Black entertainers provide hero images worthy of emulation and also provide cultural reinforcement. But for the children of middle American ethnics no similar service is

"Television functions as a mind-numbing tranquilizer rather than stimulating a quest for personal or national identity."

provided by television.

Even when shown in a sympathetic light, the ethnic is no hero but one paternalized as a pathetic refugee who epitomizes the "poor and huddled masses" welcomed at Ellis Island. His cultural heritage is ignored or reduced to the banal level of folk dances. The great writers, artists, composers, and inventors who left their indelible mark on the world's culture suffer benign neglect and all that survives are dancing peasants.

Television has become a great divider between ethnic parents and their children. My folksy tales, the legends of my forefathers who are my children's forefathers too, cannot compete with the lavishness and lure of the programs of the electronic media. The sad point is not only that my children's ethnic heritage has little chance of flourishing. More depressing is that in order to narrow this gap between my and their emotional and experiential background, I am forced, bit by bit, to surrender to my five and ten year old's cultural tastes and choices to the degree that my own ethnic heritage is eroding.

Of course, it cannot be said that commercial television is the sole culprit. The so-called "educational" channels, with the prestige implicit in their designation, commit a degree of "ethnocide" with much greater effectiveness. Their programs have perhaps the most selective memory, choosing to depict only those aspects of history and culture that reinforce domestication into the prevailing system. A pathetic example of this was the presentation of Kenneth Clark's "Civilisation" series. It was a biased and flagrant affront against the history of civilizations outside Western Europe. Being somewhat of a culture snob parent, my daughters sat through intently absorbing the whole show. In the end, they had to conclude that since Hungary, Poland and Bohemia were not even mentioned, the region where I came from had contributed nothing but have only been consumers of the civilization of others. Of course, I knew better,

Clark knew better and the educational T.V. knew better. But will my children ever know?

It must, however, be also admitted that much of the melting pot myth that is now being so vehemently attacked as a WASP plot to recycle immigrants into the WASP's image of themselves, happened with many of the ethnics' wholehearted cooperation.

Michael Novak, in his work, *The Rise of the Unmeltable Ethnics*, aptly describes the message of the media as "inevitably WASP, modern, homogenizing" and as a proselytizer of the superculture. But again, if the media omitted to transmit other cultures and denied and neglected the ethnics, they did so with the tacit approval and connivance of the ethnic intellectuals and artists. They constantly hoped to appear in America's eyes more Western (or Western European) than the French, and more unflappable than a British Lord. . . .

But in particular it is with regard to the image, conveyed, perpetuated and impressed upon the masses of Americans through the communications media where ethnic intellectuals were grossly negligent. To write, produce, and stage programs of quality on the ethnics, their history, their culture, would have made the ethnic intellectuals "look" ethnic and admit their own ethnicity. This would mean public identification not with the cosmopolitan set but with the smoggy neighborhoods of working class districts.

With every word they wrote, with every ounce of their creative energy, they strained to transcend what they considered their parochial origins and speak about the universality of things through American symbols and slang to American audiences. It may have been the WASPs who looked down upon the ethnics at first, but it was the ethnic intellectuals who falsely attested to their own inferiority by denying their own culture, their origin and their own people. . . .

Courtesy of the entertainment and news media, the ethnic perception gets duller every day. It is ridiculed, falsified and ignored. Things we are attached to, the heritage we try to cling to and the beliefs we hold get little airing, understanding or acknowledgement. The window on the world through communications, from the ethnic view, remains boarded over. . . .

If the existence of the ethnic media is a result of a long neglect of the middle American ethnics by the established media, it should not remain a convenient excuse for continued neglect.

There is great resistance within the media to the criticism that U.S. mass communications does not adequately serve the ethnic community. Their response is that the ethnic community has its own press to serve its needs. Their secondary response is that U.S. mass communications serves a pluralistic society and must aim for a broad base rather than using a shotgun approach which offers program diversity rather than broadly based market. They stress pragmatics and explain that advertising is based on circulation which requires a lowest common denominator approach at the expense of specialization.

But a television industry that has the imagination and technological know-how to put color television cameras on the moon, can find the way, I trust, to focus more sharply on the ethnics. This is a challenge they cannot, however, accept and implement using past performance as a yardstick of evaluation. However, an entertainment media which has been unable or perhaps even unwilling to portray the unvarnished reality of U.S. culture, to progress beyond "Bonanza," to appreciate the contribution of the American Indians to the building of this nation, can hardly be expected to do more for late arrivals with foreign habits and accents. . . .

No, the challenge is more direct and more honest. The television, radio and the press should sincerely attempt to overcome what, in the mind of those deeply concerned about cultural reinforcement and ethnic identity, is their most serious failing. They should try to depict both the contemporary evolving culture and history in America's ethnic communities and the culture and history of the "old countries" as they actually are. That means, to present the value structure of the middle American ethnic as it truly exists; to present the music, art and multidimensional culture of the countries of origin as they impress the world today. Such programs need not be uncritical nor lacking in praise. America's culture will not diminish in comparison. Appreciation of alien cultures is not a zero sum game but a contribution to a healthy pluralistic society. Cultural exchanges could be immensely improved notwithstanding political differences. . . .

Maybe the media is not the best babysitter or parent surrogate to teach young generations of Americans their heritage, if parents themselves don't care. But it can be a helpful partner in telling them who we were and who we have become. Then and only then will ethnics cease appearing as foreigners who act in strange ways and who "talk funny" to their children and fellow Americans. Then and only then will they be seen as people with both a past and a present, and in dignity which is their share in the American Dream.

Shortly after Betty Friedan's book, *The Feminine Mystique*, became a best-selling manifesto of the modern women's movement, she was asked by *TV Guide* to analyze the image of women on television. What she saw on TV in 1964 was that millions of dollars were being spent developing commercials whose primary message was that women were too repulsive to be endured unless they bought the various advertised powders, deodorants, and detergents. And the soap operas and weekly series sponsored by these products reeked of guilt with their tales of unspeakable sexual shame.

In the fourteen years since her piece appeared, the women's movement has worked assiduously to overcome that image of women as it was being presented not only on television but in all of the mass media. Many scholarly studies have demonstrated the damage to women's self-confidence from growing up with that denigrating image bombarding them day after day.

The television image of women has begun to change dramatically, although the commercials still have a long way to go. A number of popular television series, and even some family sit-coms and soap operas, now offer heroines who are bright and gutsy and have good jobs, heroines who are no longer passive sex objects but individuals who act adventurously in their own lives, heroines like Maude, Rhoda, Mary Tyler Moore, Police Woman, and even the Bionic Woman.

Even though many of the false and demeaning images of women that television presented in 1964 are beginning to change, Ms. Friedan's essay is still relevant in showing how the most pervasive popular culture medium was dominated by Madison Avenue's version of the feminine mystique.

Television and the Feminine Mystique
Betty Friedan

If the image of women on television [in 1964] reflects—or affects—reality, then American women must be writhing in agonies of self-contempt and unappeasable sexual hunger. For television's image of the American woman is a stupid, unattractive, insecure little household drudge who spends her martyred, mindless, boring days dreaming of love—and plotting nasty revenge against her husband. If that image affects men—or at least reflects the men who created it—then American men, in their contempt, loathing and fear of that miserable obsessed woman, must be turning in revulsion against love itself.

This is the rather horrifying feeling I had after sitting for several weeks in front of my television set, trying to reconcile the image of women projected by television commercials, family situation comedies, soap operas and game shows, with the strangely missing, indeed virtually nonexistent image of woman in all the rest of television: the major dramatic shows; the witty commentary, seri-

> "Put the two images together—the woman on the screen and the one watching it—and you see how television has trapped itself in the feminine mystique."

ous documentary and ordinary reportage of the issues and news of our world.

In fact, the most puzzling thing about the image of woman on television today is an eerie *Twilight Zone* sense that it is fading before one's eyes. In the bulk of television programs today, and even, increasingly, in commercials, one literally sees no image of woman at all. She isn't there. Even when the face and body of a woman are there, one feels a strange vagueness and emptiness, an absence of human identity, a missing sexual aliveness—is it a woman if it doesn't think or act or talk or move or love like a person?

Behind that fading image, the nonwoman on the television screen, I found, talking to producers, network decision-makers, agency executives, an even more unpleasant image: their image of those millions of American women "out there" watching that television, controlling that dial, determining those ratings—the American housewife who, they say, "has taken over television" as she is supposed to have taken over control of her husband, children, home, the U.S. economy and the nation in general. Put the two images together—the woman on the screen and the one watching it—and you see how television has trapped itself in the feminine mystique.

This whole process of the feminine mystique is projected on television to such an extreme that the question is not only what the mystique and its stunted, dehumanized, sick image of woman is doing to real women, and their respect for themselves, or men's love and respect for women—but what it is doing to television.

Consider first that drab, repulsive little housewife one sees on the television screen. She is so stupid that she is barely capable of doing the most menial household tasks. Her biggest problem is to get the kitchen sink or floor really clean, and she can't even do that without a kind, wise man to tell her how. ("To think that just a few months ago I was in college and now I'm a wife and mother," she weeps on the television commercial. "I want to be everything Jim wants in a wife and mother. But he says I'm inefficient, I can't cook and clean. I've tried and tried and I just can't get that sink clean.") Her biggest *thrill* is when, with that old man's magic help (which comes in a can), she gets that sink *clean*.

Her other biggest problem is how to keep doing all that cleaning and still keep her hands *"feminine."* She is so unattractive and feels so insecure that she needs all the help and mechanical contrivances modern science and industry can supply to keep her man from leaving her. ("How long has it been since your husband took you dancing . . . brought you flowers . . . really listened to what you said? Could it be that gray in your hair?" Bad breath? Irregular bowels?)

She isn't even adequate as a mother to her children. ("Even the most careful mother can't completely protect her family from household germs," the kind, wise man reassures her. "Is there really more than one vitamin?" she asks him, having never finished fifth grade herself.) In fact, she is barely capable of feeding the dog. (That wise old man has to tell her how to get the mutt out of his "mealtime rut.")

Less than a fifth-grader, more like that simple animal in her capacity to understand or take part in modern human society, this television-commercial woman has no interest, purpose or goal beyond cleaning the sink, feeding her kids, and going to bed.

The whole world beyond her home—its politics, art, science, issues, ideas and problems—is evidently beyond her comprehension. For not only is there no television image of a woman acting in the world, but the programming of daytime television and, increasingly, even prime time, assumes she has no interest in it or ability to understand it. She lives only for love.

But beneath the sacred exaltation of marriage, motherhood and home in the soap operas and the religious tones of the commercials, there is a crude assumption on the part of television decision-makers that all those women out there are panting through their boring days of mindless drudgery in a state of permanent unappeased sexual hunger. From a little after eight in the morning until the late, late hours after midnight, they evidently want from that television screen only the image of a virile male. At least this is the superficial reason given for that disappearing image of woman on the television screen, and the preponderance of male cheesecake ("beefcake," is it called?). "It's women who control the dial, and what a woman wants to look at is a man—a man with sex appeal, a man who's available to her," I was told over and over again up through the ranks of television decision-makers.

Several years ago, when the networks were under attack from the Federal Communications Commission, CBS put on a daytime news program. The producer, new to daytime, suggested a woman commentator. The network brass said he was out of his mind. In simple four-letter words, they explained to him that of all things the dames didn't want to see at 10 A.M., it was a woman. They wanted a man they could jump right back into bed with. But CBS did put a news-oriented show, *Calendar*, into that 10 A.M. time period, and hired actress Mary Fickett to act as Jill-of-all-trades. She did the household commercials and acted as pretty little straight man to commentator Harry Reasoner. The condescension with which he talked to the women out there may have marred his sexual charm. *Calendar* died. . . .

In the daytime soap operas, the martyred superiority of the wives doesn't even have to be demonstrated; it's just mysteriously, axiomatically *there*. Since the housewives in *As the World Turns* and all the rest must conduct their warfare with men day after day during the day, the major dramatic problem seems to be to get the men home to be manipulated. It is amazing how often those busy lawyers and doctors and businessmen on television soap operas come home for lunch! But the neatest trick—which simultaneously accomplishes revenge and keeps the man home permanently to be controlled, or perhaps just to provide the soap-opera housewife with someone to talk at—is to paralyze the husband and put him in a wheelchair.

However it is accomplished, the real emotion played to by this image of woman who supposedly lives for love is hate. As a former network vice-president in charge of program development put it: "They [those housewives out there] don't want to look at husbands who are nice or strong. They only want to look at attractive younger men or old codgers out of the battle between the sexes. In the average dame's life the husband is the enemy, the guy you have to manipulate, push around, be happy in spite of. When the daytime serial features a strong husband, and the wife is not the controlling one, the rating is invariably low. The husband becomes acceptable only if he is manipulated by the good, kind, loving, all-wise wife.". . .

Could the very absence of any image of women active or triumphant in the world explain the dream of revenge and domination over the male, the sexual insecurity and self-contempt and even that supposedly unappeasable sexual hunger which television plays to, in its nasty image of the American housewife? . . .

It's not strange that the unwritten law which permits only the drab "average housewife" image of women on television is causing this fade-out of any image of women at all. For the daily tedium of a life whose biggest challenge is to clean the sink is simply too devoid of human action, involvement with other human beings, or human triumph to provide the basis for drama—or even the basis for a sense of human identity. That's why real housewives who live within that empty image have so little sense of themselves that they need a man to make them feel alive—even a man who talks down to them on television—and why they also are choking with resentment against men, whose lives at least provide enough action to dramatize. Beneath the clichés of the feminine mystique, television plays consciously to this tedium, and to the resentment it engenders—narcotizing woman's very capacity to act and think into a passive, sullen, vengeful impotence.

After all, if it weren't for the real tedium of the so-called average housewife's day, would she ever willingly endure the tedium of daytime television, or the sneering contempt for women explicit in the game shows? *The Price Is Right* assumes an average IQ of 50 (submoron) in the American woman; surely, if my psychology doesn't fail me, *most* women are not feeble-minded, though years of bombardment by television in that isolated house could make them so. Why else would middle-aged women dress up in children's dresses and hair bows to lumber through an obscene reincarnation of themselves as high-school cheerleaders? The suave man at the mike can hardly veil his own contempt at those fat grown-up women making such a public spectacle of themselves ("a siss and a siss and a siss boom bah!").

What does such a denigrating image of real women do to young mothers watching, who are no longer sure who they are, or to girls who don't even know who they can be? What does it do to women or girls—or the boys and men whose love they want—to see no image at all of a self-respecting woman who thinks or does or aims or dreams large dreams or is capable of taking even small actions to shape her own life or her future or her society?

One hesitates to accuse television of a conspiracy to keep women confined within the limits of that demeaning housewife image, their minds anesthetized by the tedium and lack of challenge of those empty hours, their very confidence in their own abilities to act or think for themselves destroyed so that they meekly buy whatever the kind, wise, authoritative man tells them to. Undoubtedly there are such mindless, passive housewife robots among American women, but why is television doing its best to create more in their image?

Why is there no image at all on television of the millions and millions of self-respecting American women who are not only capable of cleaning the sink without help, but of *acting* to solve more complex problems of their own lives and their society? That moronic-housewife image denies the 24,000,000 women who work today outside the home in every industry and skilled profession, most of them wives who take care of homes and children too. That image also insults the millions of real American housewives, with more and more education, who shape U.S. culture, politics, art and education by their actions in the P.T.A., the League of Women Voters and local political parties, and who help to build libraries, art galleries and theaters from Detroit to Seattle, and even strike for peace. . . .

". . . television's image of women is *creating* millions of unnecessarily mindless, martyred housewives. . ."

Is it a coincidence that millions of real girls who have grown up watching television—and seeing only that emptily "glamorous" housewife image of women—do not, in high school, have any goal in their own future except being such a passive housewife? Is it partly from lack of any self-respecting image of a woman as a person herself that so many stop their own growth in junior high to start that frantic race to "trap" a man, get pregnant in high school, or quit college to take a "housework" job in industry to put their husbands through medical or engineering school. By seducing real girls into evading the choices, efforts and goals which would enable them to grow to maturity and full human identity in our society, television's image of women is *creating* millions of unnecessarily mindless, martyred housewives, for whom there may never be a thrill or challenge greater than that dirty kitchen sink.

Thus television's little housewife monster becomes a self-fulfilling prophecy. You can see it happening in the increasingly drab looks, whining voices and general stupidity of the new young housewives in the commercials. Not very many years ago, the average American woman could supposedly identify with a pretty, bright, self-confident dame, eager to grow and educate herself and seize any challenge that came along. For instance, Betty Furness. That was *her* image—and it certainly sold refrigerators and stoves to millions of American women, who evidently shared her eager, life-loving self-confidence.

All of a sudden it was decided that Betty Furness's image was making "the average little housewife" uncomfortable. She looked too intelligent or independent or individual, or maybe just too eager and alive. Couldn't she dim herself down somehow, put on a housedress, give off a smell of dirty diapers and unwashed dishes and burned chops in the background to make that "average housewife" feel less inferior? Betty Furness

looked "smart" as well as "feminine," and she was proud of it. She had the assured professional air of authority, which is necessary to sell anyone anything: "I try not to open my mouth unless I know what I'm talking about," she said. "I know who I am and I like it. I can't look dumb. I can't dim myself down to that so-called average housewife." [*TV Guide* here added, "An agency spokesman said there was no attempt to temper the Furness 'image.' "]

So she moved on, from commercials to daytime television. And then it was decided her image was too "intelligent" for daytime television; she went to radio, like Arlene Francis and the few other intelligent women on TV with whom evidently the new "average" housewives could not identify.

But these new teen-age housewives—the growth-stunted young mothers who quit school to marry and become mothers before they grew out of bobby socks themselves—are the female Frankenstein monsters television helped create. And they may writhe forever in that tedious limbo between the kitchen sink and the television game show, living out their century-long life ahead, in a complex world which requires human purposes, commitment and efforts they never even glimpsed. How long can even television channel their pent-up energies into vicarious love affairs . . . , vicarious death by leukemia, even vicarious revenge against that husband who is surely not their real enemy?

How long will boys and men love women if this nasty, vengeful martyr is their only public image of woman, and becomes an increasingly vengeful private image? The female Frankenstein monsters, after all, are created by the minds of men. Does the new plethora of widowers, bachelor fathers and unmarried mature men on television, who pay a maid or houseboy or soon perhaps a robot to get the household drudgery done, signify unconscious rebellion against that "housewife" altogether? Do they really want her for a wife? One suddenly realizes that there are no real love stories on the television screen—in the sense of the love stories that one can still see in the old movies, with Ingrid Bergman, Joan Crawford, Norma Shearer, Claudette Colbert and all the rest. No love stories, no heroines—only those housewife drudges, the comic ogres who man the war between the sexes.

Television badly needs some heroines. It needs more images of real women to help girls and women take themselves seriously and grow and love and be loved by men again. And television decision-makers need to take real women more seriously—not for women's sake but for their own. Must women only be used as weather girls or "straight men" diaper-and-pot-holders for the male news commentators? Must they be shown only as paid or underpaid dishwashers for fear of making real housewives uncomfortable?

I've had letters from thousands of these real women, and whatever the reasons why they tried to settle too soon for this narrow, humiliating image, a lot of them want a second chance to grow. Television could help them get it, not keep cutting them down. Is it a coincidence that daytime network television, which has banished real women with minds like Arlene Francis and Betty Furness to radio, is having less success with that "average housewife" than radio, which feeds their minds with intelligent talk, much of it from women—not only Betty and Arlene but also the Martha Deanes, Ruth Jacobs, and all the bright women on local radio and television?

The men who decide the image of women on television could take a tip from a blonde who interviewed me on a local TV show in Los Angeles last summer. She called me at my hotel the day before to ask me some questions, explaining she'd stayed up all night finishing my book. It was refreshing for someone to take the trouble to read my book before interviewing me, and it was a good interview. Over breakfast later she said she liked reading such "tough" books; she hadn't been to college herself. She also said she was taking a pay cut from $750 a week as a night-club singer to accept this job as television commentator at $250 a week.

"It's the mental challenge of it," she said. "It makes me feel alive. I'm sick of just being a body. I want a chance to be someone myself—and give something of myself—in this world."

Hollywood's image of American women invariably mirrored the prevalent notion that they were the "weaker sex," that their dominant goal in life was to marry and become mothers, and in fact they were not "real women" unless they did so. The number of movies in which the woman is given the option to sacrifice love for a career might be counted on two hands. Even when Katherine Hepburn played the role of a "career woman," as in *Woman of the Year*, the script had her as an overweeningly ambitious person, with so few of the traditional qualities a woman was supposed to have that she neglected the child she and her husband Spencer Tracy had adopted. Tracy, in contrast, was the doting father, even though he continued to be a damned good newspaperman. Ergo, both love and ambition could not exist in a woman.

Molly Haskell's book, *From Reverence to Rape*, is the definitive study of the treatment of women in the movies. In this excerpt from her book, she substantiates her charge that Hollywood, the propaganda arm of the American Dream machine, has reinforced "The Big Lie."

The Big Lie
Molly Haskell

The big lie perpetrated on Western society is the idea of women's inferiority, a lie so deeply ingrained in our social behavior that merely to recognize it is to risk unraveling the entire fabric of civilization. Alfred Adler, unique among his professional colleagues as well as among his sex in acknowledging that occasionally women had ambitions similar to men's, called attention to this "mistake"—the notion of women's inferiority and men's superiority—fifty years ago. At about the same time, Virginia Woolf wrote, "Women have served all these centuries as looking glasses possessing the magic and delicious power of reflecting the figure of man at twice its natural size." How ironic that it was in the security of this enlarged image of himself, an image provided by wives or, more often, mothers, that man went forth to fight, conquer, legislate, create. And woman stayed home without so much as "a room of her own," her only "fulfillment" the hope of bearing a son to whom she could pass on the notion of male superiority.

The prejudice against women is no less pernicious because it is based on a fallacy. Indeed, to have sanctioned by law and custom a judgment that goes against our instincts is the cornerstone of bad faith on which monuments of misunderstanding have been erected. We can see that women live longer than men, give birth, and endure pain bravely; yet they are the "weaker sex." They can read and write as well as men—are actually *more* verbal according to aptitude tests. And they are encouraged to pursue advanced education as long as they don't forget their paramount destiny to marry and become mothers, an injunction that effectively dilutes intellectual concentration and discourages ambition. Women are not "real women" unless they marry and bear children, and even those without the inclination are often pressured into motherhood and just as often make a mess of it. The inequity is perpetuated as women transmit their sense of incompleteness to their daughters. But men, too, are victimized by the lie. Secretly they must wonder how they came to be entitled to their sense of superiority if it is to these "inferior" creatures they owe the debt of their existence. And defensively, they may feel "emasculated" by any show of strength or word of criticism from their nominal dependents.

In the movie business we have had an industry dedicated for the most part to reinforcing the lie. As the propaganda arm of the American Dream machine, Hollywood promoted a romantic fantasy of marital roles and conjugal euphoria and chronically ignored the facts and fears arising from an awareness of The End—the winding down of love, change, divorce, depression, mutation, death itself. But like the latent content of any good dream, unconscious elements, often elaborately disguised, came to trouble our sleep and stick pins in our technicolored balloons. The very unwillingness of the narrative to pursue love into marriage (except in the "woman's film," where the degree of rationalization needed to justify the disappointments of marriage made its own subversive comment) betrayed a certain skepticism. Not only did unconscious elements obtrude in the films, but they were part of the very nature of the industry itself.

The anomaly that women are the majority of the human race, half of its brains, half of its procreative power, most of its nurturing power, and yet are its servants and romantic slaves was brought home with peculiar force in the Hollywood film. Through the myths of subjection and sacrifice that were its fictional currency and the machinations of its moguls in the front offices, the film industry

maneuvered to keep women in their place; and yet these very myths and this machinery catapulted women into spheres of power beyond the wildest dreams of most of their sex. . . .

Audiences for the most part were not interested in seeing, and Hollywood was not interested in sponsoring, a smart, ambitious woman as a popular heroine. A woman who could compete and conceivably win in a man's world would defy emotional gravity, would go against the grain of prevailing notions about the female sex. A woman's intelligence was the equivalent of a man's penis: something to be kept out of sight. Ambition in a woman had either to be deflected into the vicarious drives of her loved ones or to be mocked and belittled. A movie heroine could act on the same power and career drives as a man only if, at the climax, they took second place to the sacred love of a man. Otherwise she forfeited her right to that love. . . .

According to society's accepted role definitions, which films have always reflected in microcosm, the interests of men and women are not only different, but actually opposed. A man is supposedly most himself when he is driving to achieve, to create, to conquer; he is least himself when reflecting or making love. A woman is supposedly most herself in the throes of emotion (the love of man or of children), and least herself, that is, least "womanly," in the pursuit of knowledge or success. The stigma becomes a self-fulfilling prophecy. By defying cultural expectations, by insisting on pro-

fessional relationships with men who want only to flatter and flirt with her, a woman becomes "unfeminine" and undesirable, she becomes, in short, a monster. This may explain why there is something monstrous in all the great women stars and why we often like the "best friends" better than the heroines, or the actresses who never quite got to the top (Ann Dvorak, Geraldine Fitzgerald, Mary Astor) better than the ones who did (Joan Crawford, Bette Davis, Elizabeth Taylor). The arrogance, the toughness were not merely make-believe. In a woman's "unnatural" climb to success, she *did* have to step on toes, jangle nerves,

antagonize men, and run the risk of not being loved.

In no more than one out of a thousand movies was a woman allowed to sacrifice love for career rather than the other way around. Yet, in real life, the stars did it all the time, either by choice or by default—the result of devoting so much time and energy to a career and of achieving such fame that marriage suffered and the home fell apart. Even with allowances made for the general instability of Hollywood, the nature and the number of these breakups suggest that no man could stand being overshadowed by a successful wife. The male ego was sacred;

the woman's was presumed to be non-existent. And yet, what was the "star" but a woman supremely driven to survive, a barely clothed ego on display for all the world to see. . . .

And yet, in nefarious old Hollywood, where the feminine ideal could be, and often was, seen and stated in its crudest form, such stars as Davis and Crawford, Katharine Hepburn and Marie Dressler, Dietrich and Mae West, and so many others who were nothing if not unconventional and often troublemakers to boot, managed to survive. Sure, they had to be punished every so often, particularly as women's real-life power in society and in the job market increased. In the forties, once they had filled men's positions left vacant by the war, they were not so easy to dislodge. As women represented real threats to male economic supremacy, movie heroines had to be brought down to fictional size, domesticated or defanged. But even so, and in the midst of mediocre material, they rose to the surface and projected, through sheer will and talent and charisma, images of emotional and intellectual power.

Women have figured more prominently in film than in any other art, industry, or profession (and film is all three) dominated by men. Although few have made it to the seignorial ranks of director and producer, women have succeeded in every other area where size or physical strength was not a factor: as screenwriters, particularly in the twenties and thirties; as editors; as production and costume designers; as critics; and of course, and most especially, as actresses—as the stars who not only invaded our dream lives but began shaping the way we thought about ourselves before we knew enough to close the door. In the roles of love goddesses, mothers, martyrs, spinsters, broads, virgins, vamps, prudes, adventuresses, she-devils, and sex kittens, they embodied stereotypes and, occasionally, transcended them.

Some, like Mae West, Greta Garbo, Katharine Hepburn, and Joan Crawford, were institutions: stars powerful, eccentric, or intimidating enough to choose their projects and determine their own images, for at least some of their careers. Others, like Lillian Gish, Marlene Dietrich, and Monica Vitti were Galateas, molded and magnificently served by their Pygmalions; or, like Marion Davies and Jean Simmons, ruined by their patrons. . . .

But whatever their roles, whether they inspired or intimidated, the women in the movies had a mystical, quasi-religious connection with the public. Theirs was a potency made irresistible by the twin authority of cinematic illusion and flesh-and-blood reality, of fable and photography, of art and sociology. Until the disintegration of the studio system in the fifties and sixties, they were real gods and goddesses, and we were the slumbering, intransigent clay, yearning for formal perfection.

And women, in the early and middle ages of film, dominated. It is only recently that men have come to monopolize the popularity polls, the credits, and the romantic spotlight by allocating to themselves not just the traditional male warrior and adventurer roles, but those of the sex object and glamour queen as well. Back in the twenties and thirties, and to a lesser extent the forties, women were at the center. This was amply reflected in the billings, which revealed the shifts in star dynamics from decade to decade. Women were often billed ahead of men, either singly, as in the silents, or as the pivotal member of a team, the dominant form of the thirties. In the forties, because of the shortage of male stars during the war, available leading men were treated as spear-carriers and made to follow women on the marquee.

Far more than men, women were the vessels of men's and women's fantasies and the barometers of changing fashion. Like two-way mirrors linking the immediate past with the immediate future, women in the movies reflected, perpetuated, and in some respects offered innovations on the roles of women in society. Shopgirls copied them, housewives escaped through them. Through the documentary authenticity (new hair styles, fashions in dress, and even fads in physical beauty) that actresses brought to their roles and the familiar, simplified tales in which they played, movie heroines were viscerally immediate and accountable to audiences in a way that the heroines of literature, highbrow or popular, were not. Movie stars, as well as the women they played—Stella Dallas, Mrs. Miniver, Mildred Pierce, Jezebel— were not like the women in print or on canvas. They belonged to us and spoke to each of us personally from what, until the sixties and seventies, was the heart and emotional center of film itself. . . .

If the American woman of the movies is anything like the American woman of fiction—the Hester Prynne that Lawrence saw as a quintessentially American she-devil— it is because her intelligence has been too long insulted and her hunger for life too long unsatisfied. If men had not insisted quite so vehemently on their supremacy, perhaps women would not have felt the need to counterattack so violently. Much of the totalitarian stridency of women's current demands for power stems not just from the image of their own dependency, reiterated in novel and film, but from man's insistence, in film after "macho" film, on his independence of women.

Women have grounds for protest, and film is a rich field for the mining of female stereotypes. At the same time, there is a danger in going too far the other way, of grafting a modern sensibility onto the past so that all film history becomes grist in the mills of outraged feminism. If we see stereotypes in film, it is because stereotypes existed in society. Too often we interpret the roles of the past in the light of liberated positions that have only recently become thinkable. We can, for example, deplore the fact that in every movie where a woman excelled as a professional she had to be brought to heel at the end, but only as long as we acknowledge the corollary: that at least women *worked* in the films of the thirties and forties, and moreover, that early film heroines were not only proportionately more active than the women who saw them, but more active than the heroines of today's films. Here we are today, with an unparalleled freedom of expression and a record number of women performing, achieving, choosing to fulfill themselves, and we are insulted with the worst—the most abused, neglected, and dehumanized—screen heroines in film history. . . .

The fifties were, by unanimous consent, a bland period, but deceptively so, and by no means the wasteland that some of its survivors would have us believe. It is fashionable to claim to have misspent one's adolescence in a movie theater, in escape from the horrors of dating-and-mating rituals, studies, and other impositions of an insensitive society. And one director has reconstructed his autobiography as a kid who knew "even then" the difference between a dolly and a tracking shot. But this reclamation of the fifties is not entirely the work of specious rationalization or staircase wit. For it was under the cover of the fifties that the seeds of disillusionment were germinating. Many of the divisive forces whose consequences we are only now beginning to feel took hold behind that impassive facade: the break in the historical continuity of film as a mass medium, in the graduated pace of social change, and in woman's acceptance of her traditional role.

Going once or twice a week to the movies, we responded in the degree to which we identified with Elizabeth Taylor, Audrey Hepburn, Doris Day, Marilyn Monroe, Debbie Reynolds, and so on. But already movies were beginning to suffer a credibility gap, a gap between themselves and their mass audiences, between what the movie stars were and what we were. It was in the space of this gap that women began to take stock and stretch their wings, and the seeds of alienation that were sown in the fifties may account for the high preponderance of the fifties' veterans in women's lib generally. . . .

Whether in the European or the American film, whether seen as sociological artifact or artistic creation, women, by the logistics of film production and the laws of Western society, generally emerge as the projections of male values. Whether as the product of one *auteur* or of the system (and if I gravitate, critically, to the former, it is because I see history and cinema and art in terms of individuals rather than groups), women are the vehicle of men's fantasies, the "anima" of the collective male unconscious, and the scapegoat of men's fears. And in the principle of compensation that seems so fundamental a link between our conscious and unconscious, one is never far from the other.

Woman is idealized as the "feminine principle incarnate" by sexual Victorians like Griffith and Chaplin—sometimes out of a hostility that, like Norman Bates' matricide in *Psycho*, masquerades as its opposite. Eventually misogyny will out, as it does, with a vengeance, in the seventies' malevolence of *Straw Dogs* and *A Clockwork Orange*.

Or woman is worshipped as "mother"— by Ford, Fellini, and other Catholic and crypto-Catholic directors—and thereby kept in her place, inoculated with sanctity against the disease of ambition.

Or she is venerated by European directors like Bergman and Renoir, but as an "earth goddess," as an emblem of the natural order; or, for Jean-Luc Godard, as an "enigma" who would as easily betray as love and whose amoral cruelty inheres in the very quality, the innocence, for which he loves her.

Or she is celebrated and feared as separate-but-equal by American directors like Keaton and Hawks. Or perceived, in some remarkable "women's films" of Max Ophuls and Douglas Sirk, as both heroine, capable of radical decisions and intense feelings, and victim, at the mercy of a system that militates against the free play of such choices and feelings. The "noble sacrifice" by which the "woman's film" traditionally rationalizes the housewife's life boomerangs in the films of Ophuls and Sirk, where children are not their mothers' pride and joys but their jailors, carriers of a disease called middle-class family life.

After all this, woman reaches, perhaps understandably, a dead end of emotional apathy: first, as the heroines of the films of Rossellini and Antonioni; then as the heroines of the "neo-woman's films"— *Klute, Diary of a Mad Housewife, Something Different, Wanda*. The women of these films, torn between the negative and positive of the feminist consciousness— rage at the old order, hope for the new— have arrived, anesthetized, at an emotional and cultural "stasis," a death. But it is out of this death, out of the ashes of her sacrifice, that the new woman will be born.

When in 1972 Congress passed Title IX, that highly controversial bill giving women the right to participate in all phases of athletics on an equal basis, it was hailed as a significant victory for the women's movement. If to some men it was only a locker-room joke, after six years the joke is wearing thin, for women in our colleges and universities are becoming increasingly involved in athletic activities.

Still, if Dr. Gallup were to poll a cross-section of Americans on what Title IX is, it is doubtful whether one out of ten could give the correct response. Perhaps the turning point for women's sports took place in 1973, when an audience of 40 million televiewers watched Billie Jean King trounce Bobby Riggs. Given the huckster antics of Riggs, whose exaggerated male chauvinist stance may have been part of the "hype" to augment the tennis match's coverage, what Billie Jean accomplished in an hour went far beyond any clever media pseudo-event.

In her 1974 autobiography, Billie Jean wrote, "Women's liberation means that every woman ought to be able to pursue whatever career or personal life-style she chooses as a full and equal member of society without fear of sexual discrimination. That's a pretty basic and simple statement, but, golly, it sure is hard sometimes to get people to accept it. And because of the way other people think, it's even harder to reach the point in your own life where you can live by it." Shelley Armitage reviews this struggle of "The Lady as Jock" in the following selection.

The Lady as Jock
Shelley Armitage

To be popular, the hero may embody the values of his worshipping public or he may be a product of the Madison-Avenue trickery of his fabulators. In either case, heroic stature is dependent on exposure or the media, whether this media be the consenting grunts of pre-historic tribesmen gathered at a watering hole around their chieftain or the family television that centers a nation of spectators on common people and events. Since a stigma to heroine-making in women's sports has been both its lack of media-coverage and the controversial image of woman as athlete, we may look with curious interest at one symbol of the athletic woman—Wonder Woman of Marvel Comic fame. Though this heroine may pale in the shadow of the likes of John Wayne, who is pictured in *Psychology Today* ascending into heaven replete with six-shooters, a posse of seraphim, and a sagging paunch, she accomplishes impossible heroic feats with a "feminine" body. Yet in all her story from the front of comics to the indignant tee-shirted chests of fem libbers, she has not sacrificed one dimpled curve for muscle tone. She is the *femme fatale par excellance*. She signifies the winning combination of "lady" and "jock"—the necessary combination for the popularity of women's sports and the changing image of women.

That women have always been on the losing end of status is a phenomenon not only of the body politic but of the body personal. Because of cultural and psychological conditioning, women long have been in touch with their bodies from without. Throughout history, with the possible exception of attitudes about childbirth, the female body has been regarded as a repository of evil, unfit to darken the door of important institutions such as churches or exclusively-male status organizations.

One of the most common explanations for recurrent negative attitudes is the belief, common to many cultures, that the female is a castrated male, indeed, half a person, or, at best, second best. Though her fertility has constituted some status, even so her menstruation is a sign of impurity, weakness, and even insanity. Yet her attempts to become a whole person and thus to operate exclusive of roles that reaffirm her femaleness, which is said to be passive, weak, and inept, have resulted in rebukes from her peers ranging from scathing looks of disapproval at her dress in a supermarket to more obvious ramifications like a single life of loneliness without man and marriage. . . .

When modern women do act physically to "come out on top," it is in the very sporting arena where they may profit from being the inert, passive and helpless creatures we know them to be and where body contact, application of force to a heavy object, and face-to-face competition may be guised by the dark. For, as we are told by articles like "How to Become Sexually Active Over 35," the bedroom is the one field where pros like happy hookers and amateurs alike may secure a place in the world by conforming to those physical attributes that supposedly attract men. So, winning for women has become a coquettish game of losing to men. And the only game in town is the femininity game.

Given such cultural conditioning and im-age-making, how then have women's competitive athletics ever attracted females? Bascially, the means of popularization has come in three areas: educational necessity, feminist efforts, and advertising.

The need for physical proficiency first was necessitated by the stress of attending college. Believed to lack the physical stamina necessary to withstand the rugged schedules at college, women were conditioned through physical education programs instituted by Vassar, for example, in 1862 and at Wellesley in 1875. After the addition of facilities for tennis, skating and swimming at Wellesley, and regular exercise classes directed by a woman physician at Smith College, the U.S. Commissioner of Education in 1884 gave a favorable report on women's health in the schools and attributed the improvements to physical education programs. As a result, by 1890, most schools had gyms for women and special sports programs.

Perhaps as significant as these educational inroads is the fact that, once allowed to condition their bodies, women began to prefer competitive sports. With the introduction of basketball in 1891, volleyball in 1893, and field hockey in 1897, there was a qualitative change in women's physical education. What had been education for health and beauty became sports for competition. . . .

Freeing the mind must entail freeing the body. What physical education programs had done for educational opportunities of younger women, feminists' efforts would do for older women. The first vehicle of such change was a piece of technology: the bicycle. Though early publicity went to women like Lillian Russell, friend of Diamond Jim Brady, who rode a fancy machine (handlebars of diamonds and rubies) on the side-streets of New York, Frances Willard and Gladys, as she called her plain, black bike, were the dynamic duo. As head of the Women's Christian Temperance Union, Willard wrote *How I Learned to Ride the Bicycle—A Wheel Within a Wheel*. No doubt Willard's text made an interesting companion piece with other "how-to" manuals of the times which were almost exclusively concerned with the "perfect home." For health, Willard advocated getting out of the home. Reportedly, one young lady took her seriously enough to mount her newly-bought bike and ride away, forever leaving husband and perfect home behind.

According to Willard, the bike gave incredible freedom to women. As a cure-all for societal ills and lack of co-ordination, it was also a salve for nerve wear for the 53-year-old Willard who said, "I found a whole new philosophy of life in the wooing and the winning of my bicycle, through the learning of every screw and spring. . . ."

Willard's modern successor, at least in the area of cycling, Sheila Young, proved the point most dramatically last year in the World Cycling Championships in San Sebastian, Spain. Fouled by her Czech rival in the last race, at a speed of about forty miles an hour she crashed into the track. After opting for doctors to staple the wound rather than have numbing stitches taken, bandaged and bloody, Sheila captured the gold medal. It was a stoic performance worthy of an Olympic medal and a world-wide audience, except that Olympic cycling remains a men-only event. Obvious in this isolated example, which is like so many others (that no doubt we have not heard of due to lack of coverage), is that popularity of women's sports hinges not only on brave performances or on dreams of women like Frances Willard, but on media exposure.

Historically, advertising media cleverly has lent this kind of buoyancy to women's sports in times of stress. For example, in the thirties, the influence of Mrs. Herbert Hoover, who headed up the Women's Division of the NAAF and the committee on Women's Athletics, found that girls were performing on the basketball courts with men rather than remaining in their expected roles as spectators. Apparently, what bloomers had done

for cycling, women's gym clothes were doing for competitive athletics—exposing the female body. So, even though Mrs. Hoover's harangues led to a drop in the number of colleges sponsoring varsity competition for women from 22 percent to 12 percent in 1930, the image of women athletes in revealing clothes was seized as a selling point by advertisers. At the same time that bloomers were criticized for prompting more than passing looks from males, the Pan Handle Scrap tobacco company included with its product a series of cards picturing women athletes in bathing suits along with body specifications and records. Bike posters of the same period displayed attractive young women in bloomers at the side of the company's bikes.

In retrospect, we can recognize the unwritten rule of these advertisements is that the buyer will be enticed by attractive displays of the female body, athlete or not, and not by the likes of a Frances Willard (described by one newsman as "a fat boy who was blessed with neat ankles") or the bloodied Sheila Young. A recent example of this necessary selling point is the situation of jockey Mary Bacon who has done several advertisements for Revlon cosmetics. Despite the fact that the pretty blonde has made her name as one of the first successful female jockeys, Revlon rejected an early take for an advertisement of Mary in the stables and at the side of a thoroughbred. In fact, the final ad shows Mary, in a close-up that could be of any good-looking model in habit and make-up, away from the barn and the horses. Advertising will sell the idea of physical astuteness only inadvertently when it is a means of capitalizing on what the public accepts as traditionally "beautiful" and "feminine."

Behind the effort to cover stable odors with perfume is the underlying major obstacle in the popularization of women's sports: the contradictory role expectations of women and athletes. Physical education coach Peggy

Billie Jean King and Bobby Riggs. King laughs on September 19, 1973, as Riggs tells how he will win their $100,000 winner-take-all match. King's deafeat of Riggs the next day, before a viewing audience of 40 million, is regarded as a turning point in women's sports.
UPI Photo

Burke admits that this conflict and resulting fear of being tagged "masculine," has influenced her recruitment: "I encouraged attractive girls to become physical education majors regardless of their skill levels and discouraged the highly skilled, motivated girls from being majors because they did not meet any standards for appearance and behavior." Though there are inconsistencies in attitudes expressed by women athletes about the effect that sports has on their feminine image, generally there exists a dichotomy between behavior that is traditionally feminine and behavior that is traditionally regarded as athletic. . . .

Swimming against the mainstream is undoubtedly as difficult as violating the historical precedent of rhythmic dancing being the sport offered for early sportswomen. In lieu of this difficulty is the traditional alternative which reinforces traditional role expectations of women and rewards them as well—the femininity game, so called in the book of the same name by Dr. Thomas Boslooper and Marcia Hayes. The prime goal of the game is the woman's interest in getting a man and in getting married. The sporting equipment includes charm, guile, social shrewdness, cosmetics, clothes, and hopefully a sufficiently enticing physical apparatus. Since the victory pay-off is love and security, all of a women's competitive and aggressive skills are rechanneled into this game. The major rule of this game is that a woman must be ready to lose at all other

games. Because men don't love women who win, girls learn early to lose rather than to be rejected.

Of course, as a result, girls at puberty are conditioned socially to pursue what attracts boys rather than their own special interests. Any contrary activity, though it may bring success, often results in anxiety. . . .

Sociologists John Roberts and Brian Sutton-Smith explore the conditioning that dictates such attitudes in a recent study that establishes a correlation between choice of games and the roles expected of boys and girls. Competitive team sports involving the display of power and physical skill were game

on 7,000 adults that business executives, politicians, and other men in positions of power overwhelmingly favored games that combined strategy and physical skill. Men having blue-collar jobs enjoyed games of pure skill, whereas women (and members of ghettoized minority groups) showed a preference for games of pure chance, or for those providing strategy, like bridge.

Obviously both strategy and chance are needed to play the femininity game and these, in turn, are tools of every second class citizen who sees his chance for success as determined by his fortunate or shrewd connection with those first-class citizens who attain success. Women have learned in their auxiliary roles to use this same guile and chance to approach success indirectly, through marrying a man who himself has the drive, ambition, and assertiveness to directly attain success. However, strategy is less and less effective as one's chances fade with age and women whose identity is based on the rewards of good looks become correspondingly unhappy with age. Boslooper believes that these women are happiest who "are physically active and feel feminine, no matter what they do." He adds that "all mature, intellectually creative women were tomboys when they were young," and he concludes that "what's important for women is to have a positive and realistic attitude about their strength and physical abilities, about aggressiveness, about competition."

A most positive and lasting identity, then, seems to be related to the degree to which one may control his fate through honing the bodies and pitting oneself competitively against others via set rules and regulations. Thus, learning to be in touch with oneself has increased the popularity of women's sports for participants. A most vociferous proponent of this popularity, Billie Jean King, indicates in her magazine *WomenSports*: "I know from experience that athletes, or athletically-minded people, tend to be independent, sure of themselves, and their bodies,

models mostly for boys whose parents encouraged achievement and success. Games of strategy—chess and backgammon—were found to mirror childhood training in responsibility. As models for social responsibility and for power, games, like football, which combine physical skill and strategy, were chosen. However, games of chance and fortune—bingo and fish—were the choice of two groups, children who had been strictly disciplined in obedience, and girls. Because they were discouraged from initiative and achievement, these children dreamed their desires could become real through chance alone. Follow-up research revealed in polls and tend to think for themselves." In this editorial King supports this personal view with data collected from her own readers. . . .

Future popularity of women's sports depends on the projection of positive and respected images of participants by the media as encouragement for more women to get hooked on the rewards of the flesh. To date, small, yet subliminal, tributes have been made through such ads as Peggy Fleming's endorsement of ballpoint pens, Billie Jean King's winning Colgate smile, and more television spots on sporting events that involve women such as the Super Stars competition and women's pro football. However, it is doubtful that any sportswoman can match the Joe Namath breakthrough. What Broadway Joe is to pantyhose, it is doubtful that even Billie Jean King will become to jockey underwear. Yet, that Namath flair for "show-biz" is another necessity for the popularization of women's sports. A major turning point for women's sports was the recent King-Bobby Riggs' match, gimmicks and all. Beneath the huckster techniques of Bobby's Sugar Daddy image was a seriousness that King drove home in front of a television audience of 40 million, 6-4, 6-3, 6-3.

This publicity should start young, and one manner in which young women can be influenced to pursue athletics is to have before them, on television, on cereal boxes, on bubblegum cards, the image of a sportswoman. Many new books, both fiction and non-fiction, are beginning to fill this area. Works include *Delilah* by Carole Hart (about a liberated ten-year-old who plays drums and basketball), *Zanballer* by R. R. Knudson (about a 13-year-old who persuades her friends to leave a dance class for the football field), and *Not Bad for a Girl* (which is about a girl's attempt to play Little League Baseball and has been adapted for television) and non-fiction like *Karate for Young People* by Russell Kozuki and *Swimming the Shane Gould Way*.

Legislated opportunities may include Ti-tle IX, the controversial bill which affirms the right of women to participate equally in all phases of athletics. . . . Though the final draft of the regulations of Title IX by the HEW is especially vague in the area of what constitutes a "basic equality" of funding, the law has made possible publicity for the negligible attitudes of schools toward women's sports. Since 1972, when it was passed by Congress, Title IX is credited with improvements in budgets, scholarships, and audiences for women's sports. One example of this change is at Michigan State University where the women's budget jumped from $34,000 to $84,000 between the '72–'73 and '73–'74 academic years. The new budget included services men have always received such as tutoring, medical treatment, a modern dressing room, and the movement of women administrators to the traditionally all-male field house. Of course, huge discrepancies still exist nation-wide as exemplified by the budget at Ohio State where women receive $43,000 compared to the men's $6 million a year. There women swimmers are allowed to use the pool from 6:30 a.m. to 9 a.m. and at dinnertime when the men are not using it. Other laws which have been newly discovered by coaches and participants alike in their fight for equality include the Title VII of the 1964 Civil Rights Act, the Equal Pay Act, the Equal Protection Clause of the Fourteenth Amendment to the Constitution (used by high school basketball player Rachel Lavin to win the right to play on a boys' team), and the Equal Rights Amendment.

While these battles ensue in the trenches for amateurs, the desirability (and profitable nature) of being a woman athlete are enhanced by emerging real life heroines, the pros. Women like Billie Jean King offer an alternate lifestyle to that which girls have been reared to anticipate. As a symbol of the "lady jock," King offers a healthy alternative to the cultural prototype of femininity. Spectacled and muscular, she is as robust physically as she is aggressive athletically. Yet she, like Mary Joe Peppler, the winner of the 1975 Women's Super Stars, appears comfortable in her long gown in an interview on the *Tonight Show*. In fact, King may seem enigmatic to those who still view the expression of femininity through fluttering false eyelashes and prescribed morality. Though in her extravaganza with Bobby Riggs, King was carried high in her Queen's chair, she still embodies the values of the old hero type. She disciplines herself. While Riggs was popping an undetermined number of vitamins a day for the match, King was lifting weights and working on her serve. She disdains the partying and pampering so many athletes demand. But even as she says that discipline "is the secret of champions," and "means giving things up," so her abortion, her feminist sympathies, and her magazine, *WomenSports*, represent a liberal self-indulgence which characterizes the modern heroine.

King, and other fem stars (like Carol Mann in golf, Olga Korbut in gymnastics, Mickey King in coaching) have in hand what seems to be the ultimate proof of success (and, therefore, "right reason") in America: they have been what they are, women athletes, and have made money doing it. But, hopefully, the ultimate result of this popularity will not be in measurable materialism but in attitudes. The ultimate influence of women's sports is as a vehicle of cultural change. As Judith Bardwick says in *Psychology of Women*, "Those women who have developed an independent sense of self and positive self-esteem will be able to elect their roles and enjoy their freedom of choice." Boslooper indicates another advantage in this new-found liberation: "One of the reasons men put women down professionally is that they are accustomed to putting them down physically. Men can keep women in a secondary position by keeping them weak and the best way to keep them weak is to keep them physically inactive." So, as the "firsts" include women reporters covering locker rooms, women trainers being admitted to Professional Trainers Association, and Super Stars getting Sunday prime time coverage, new advances are being made to broaden the concept of femininity. By being successful in sports, traditionally a high-status occupation, women may up their status, which historically has been auxiliary and low compared to men. . . .

The resulting blurring of sex roles would free not only women but men as well. "Woman winning" would not mean "men losing" but rather the de-stereotyping of roles for each. . . .

So with all the whoopla about women's sports, we can hope that women athletes will accomplish more than just create new markets for clothes, cosmetics, and exercise salons. After all, it is a little insulting that *Vogue* magazine in its May, 1975 issue can capitalize on the new vogue of sports by putting its same models in sports clothes and calling them sportswomen. Ideally, women's invasion of the masculine territory of sport will help erase its modern cosmetic quality and return to it some of the patience, perseverance, and sacrifice that are traditionally called feminine qualities. Actually, whether sports are seen in their original etymological context, as "diversion," or in their post-World War I transformation as a masculinity rite, somewhere there is an aesthetic aspect of sport that has been lost in all the poop sheets on individual scoring, total yardage, r.b.i.'s, and other so-called measurements of skill. It would be encouraging if the popularization of the woman athlete could be the popularization of "feminine" attributes in sport which have been forgotten by the male majority of athletes and spectators.

Percy Bysshe Shelley once said, "Poets are the unacknowledged legislators of the world." In the domain of popular music (as in politics, business, and the professions) the "legislators" have been, almost exclusively, men.

A quarter of a century ago, when he was just a professor of semantics instead of a United States senator, Dr. Sam Hayakawa studied the lyrics of Tin Pan Alley songs and showed that they gave listeners an idealized fantasy of love and marriage. These lyrics were the same as the stereotypes of women in advertising, full of "wishful thinking, dreamy and ineffectual nostalgia, self-pity and sentimental clichés."

Although this unrealistic, innocuous view of women's role in American life was demeaning, at least it wasn't blatantly sexist. Then the macho music of rock emerged in the 1950s and the sub-servient image of women issued from every jukebox throughout the land.

Marion Meade argues persuasively that rock degrades women, a position that would have been hard to refute in 1971. Since the time of Meade's article, the situation has changed considerably. Men may still write unrealistic or damaging lyrics about women, but the success of female artists such as Carly Simon and Helen Reddy has helped to turn the tide toward a more enlightened view of women in American society. Helen Reddy's song "I Am Woman" captured the spirit of the "consciousness-raising" movement among women. The fact that 70 percent of those who purchased the record were women indicated that popular music could be a potent force in the struggle for social equality of the sexes.

Does Rock Degrade Women?
Marion Meade

In the spring [of 1970] I sat through three hours of the film *Woodstock* alternating between feelings of enchantment and repulsion. Sure, there was all that magnificent music, along with the generous helpings of peace and love and grass. And yet I found something persistently disturbing about the idyllic spectacle on the screen.

For one thing, with the exception of a pregnant Joan Baez who couldn't seem to stop talking about her husband, all the musicians were men. Sweaty, bearded men were busy building the stage, directing traffic, shooting the film, and running the festival. *Brother*hood was repeatedly proclaimed, both on stage and off. Woodstock Nation was beginning to look ominously like a fantasyland which only welcomed men. How about the women? Barefooted and sometimes barebreasted, they sprawled erotically in the grass, looked after their babies, or dished up hot meals. If this was supposed to be the Aquarian Utopia, it reminded me more of a Shriners' picnic at which the wife and kiddies are invited to participate once a year.

Looking back, I think the movie confirmed an uneasiness I'd felt for some time but had refused to admit: Rock music, in fact the entire rock "culture," is tremendously degrading to women. I reached this conclusion reluctantly and with a good deal of sadness because rock has been important to me. And while I still dig the vitality of the sound, I find myself increasingly turned off in nearly every other respect.

Stokely Carmichael recalls that as a child he loved Westerns and always cheered wildly for the cowboys to triumph over the Indians until one day he realized *he* was an Indian. All along he'd been rooting for the wrong side. More and more, women rock fans are discovering themselves in the same curiously surprised position. For those who have taken the trouble to listen carefully, rock's message couldn't be clearer. It's a man's world, baby, and women have only one place in it. Between the sheets or, if they're talented like Arlo Guthrie's Alice, in the kitchen.

The paradox is that rock would appear to be an unlikely supporter of such old-fashioned sex-role stereotypes. In fact, its rebellion against middle-class values, its championing of the unisex fashions and long hair styles for men seem to suggest a blurring of the distinctions between male and female. But for all the hip camouflage sexism flourishes.

The clearest indication of how rock music views womankind is in its lyrics. Women certainly can't complain that the image presented there is one-dimensional. On the contrary, the put-downs are remarkably multifaceted, ranging from open contempt to sugar-coated condescension. Above all, however, women are always-available sexual objects whose chief function is to happily accommodate any man who comes along. This wasn't always the case. Elvis's pelvis notwithstanding, the popular songs of the 'fifties and early 'sixties explored such innocuous adolescent pastimes as dancing around the clock, the beach, going steady, and blue suede shoes. In those days before the so-called sexual revolution, the typical woman portrayed in rock was the nice girl next door with whom the Beatles only wanted to hold hands. Then suddenly came the nice girl's metamorphosis into "groovy chick," the difference being that a groovy chick is expected to perform sexually. In rock songs, she never fails.

The worst picture of women appears in the music of the Rolling Stones, where sexual exploitation reaches unique heights. A woman is a "Stupid Girl" who should be kept "Under My Thumb," a "Honky Tonk Woman" who gives a man "Satisfaction." In "Yesterday's Papers," where women are equated with newspapers, the dehumanization is carried to an extreme. Who wants yesterday's papers, the song arrogantly demands, who wants yesterday's girl? The answer: Nobody. Once used, a woman is as valuable as an old newspaper, presumably good only for wrapping garbage.

But the Stone's album *Let It Bleed* is surely unrivaled when it comes to contempt for women, as well as lewdness in general. One cut in particular, "Live With Me," is explicit about woman's proper place:

Doncha' think there's a place for you
  in-between the sheets?

And only an extraordinarily masochistic woman could listen to the album's title song with any sense of pleasure whatsoever. There a woman is represented as a drive-in bordello, a one-stop sexual shopping center offering all the standard services plus a few extras casually thrown in as a kind of shopper's Special of the Day.

The Stone's next album has been tentatively titled "Bitch." It figures.

Misogyny is only slightly more disguised in the music of Bob Dylan who, in his early work at least, tended to regard nearly every female as a bitch. For example, in "Like a Rolling Stone," Dylan apparently feels so threatened by Miss Lonely (whose only sin as far as I can tell is that she has a rather shallow life style) that he feels compelled to destroy her. First he takes away her identity, then he puts her out on the street without shelter or food, and in the end—obliteration, as he makes her invisible. "How does it feel?" he asks.

There's no more complete catalogue of sexist slurs than Dylan's "Just Like a Woman," in which he defines woman's natural traits as greed, hypocrisy, whining, and hysteria. But isn't that cute, he concludes, because it's "just like a woman." For a finale, he throws in the patronizing observation that adult women have a way of breaking "just like a little girl."

These days a seemingly mellowed Dylan has been writing about women with less hatred, but the results still aren't especially flattering. Now he calls his females ladies and invites them to lay across his big brass bed. In short, he has more or less caught up with Jim Morrison's request to "Light my fire" and with John Lennon's suggestion, "Why don't we do it in the road?"

Again and again throughout rock lyrics women emerge either as insatiable, sex-crazed animals or all-American emasculators. Although one might think these images indicate a certain degree of aggressiveness in women, oddly enough they still wind up in a servile position where they exist only to enhance the lives of men.

As for romance, rock hasn't rejected it entirely. Rock love songs exhibit a regular gallery of passive, spiritless women, sad-eyed ladies propped on velvet thrones as the private property of a Sunshine Superman. From the Beatles we get motherly madonnas whispering words of wisdom ("Let it be, let it be") or pathetic spinsters like Eleanor Rigby who hang around churches after weddings to collect the rice. Leonard Cohen's romantic ideal is the mystical Suzanne who wears rags from the Salvation Army and acts, the composer asserts, "half crazy." Seldom does one run across a mature, intelligent woman or, for that matter, a woman who is capable enough to hold a job (one exception is the Beatles' meter maid, Rita). Only the Stones' Ruby Tuesday insists on an independent life of her own.

Since rock is written almost entirely by men, it's hardly surprising to find this frenzied celebration of masculine supremacy. But it's also understandable in terms of the roots from which rock evolved. In both blues and country music, attitudes toward women reflected a rabid machismo: men always dominated and women were fickle bitches who ran off with other men. Often they were seen in relationship to the wandering superstud who recounts his conquests in every town along the road, a fantasy which remains fashionable in rock today.

Apart from the myths of female inferiority proclaimed by rock lyricists, the exploitation and dehumanization of women also extends into the off-stage rock scene. How else can one account for a phenomenon like the groupies? That these aggressive teenage camp followers could possibly be regarded as healthy examples of sexual liberation is certainly a cruel joke. In fact, groupies service the needs of the male musicians and further symbolize rock's impersonal view of women as cheap commodities which can be conveniently disposed of after use. The Stones said it: nobody in the world wants yesterday's papers.

Finally, rock is a field from which women have been virtually excluded as musicians. Not only is it rare to find an integrated band, but the few all-female groups have been notably unsuccessful. The very idea of a women's rock band is looked upon as weird, in the same category as Phil Spitalny's all-girl orchestra, a freak show good for a few giggles.

The problem is that women have been intimidated from even attempting a career in rock. Women, the myth says, aren't smart enough to understand the complexities of electronics or tough enough to compose music of sufficient intensity or physically strong enough to play drums. The guitar is acceptable but the electric guitar is unfeminine.

As for female rock singers, you can count them on a few fingers. We did have Janis Joplin, a blueswoman in the finest tradition of Bessie Smith and Billie Holiday. When Janis wailed about love as a ball and chain and women being losers, now there were ideas with which women could identify. At least we knew what she meant. The soul sounds of Tina Turner and Laura Nyro also radiate the feeling that they know what it's like to be a woman. Otherwise, just about the only rock queen left is Grace Slick. Although some may regard her private life as liberated in that she decided to have an illegitimate child and generally appears to care little for society's conventions, even her work with the Jefferson Airplane is hardly oriented toward women.

Which leaves us with Joan Baez, Judy Collins and Joni Mitchell, who specialize in the bland folk-rock deemed appropriate for a delicate sex.

At this point, what does rock offer women? Mighty little.

Recently, however, rock bands have reported strange happenings at concerts. Instead of the usual adoring screams from the women, every so often they've been hearing boos and unladylike shouts of "male chauvinist pigs." Because the bands tend to regard these disturbances as a puzzling but passing phenomenon, they've made little effort so far to understand the changes taking place in their audience. What they fail to recognize is that the condescending swaggering which worked for Elvis in the 'fifties and the sadistic, anti-woman sneers of Mick Jagger in the 'sixties are no longer going to make it in the 'seventies.

There's no question that rock is already in trouble. The current spiritual and economic malaise has been variously attributed to the Hendrix-Joplin deaths, the general tightness of money, as well as lackluster albums and tired performances from the popular stars. Whatever the reasons, rock listeners today are plainly bored. Does anyone really care if John, Paul, Ringo, and George ever get together again? Not me.

On the other hand, isn't it about time for women to band together and invade the chauvinistic rock scene? Only then will the vicious stereotypes be eliminated and, one hopes, some fresh energy generated as well. For too long we've sat wistfully on the sidelines, acting out our expected roles as worshipful groupies.

Women have always constituted an important segment of the rock audience. Unless the industry is willing to alienate us completely, they'd better remember what Bob Dylan said about not needing a weatherman to know which way the wind blows. For the times they are a-changin', eh, fellas?

Games can be more than idle diversions. The youthful passion for pinball machines, which has been immortalized in the song "Pinball Wizard" (original by The Who and reprise by Elton John), has developed into a true cult. There are no doubt a host of psychological explanations why people enjoy keeping the little silver ball ricocheting off the bumpers, lighting the "special" targets, and winning "replays."

For one thing, the pinball machine represents a controlled environment. There are no unknown forces to impinge on one's pursuit of success, except possibly a power shortage. Unlike "real life," the pinball machine offers an unlimited supply of second chances (as long as the coins last, that is). The closest equivalent to death in the world of pinball is the old nemesis "tilt," but even that is not permanent and can be avoided by skillful playing. The element of skill, in fact, along with a bit of luck, is paramount in games such as pinball. While Americans may suffer countless misfortunes in their lives, they can at least gain some vicarious satisfaction by mastering a pinball machine.

Rex Jones interprets the appeal of poker in similar terms. He sees the pastime as "a pure expression of the American dream," a game that fosters the "ever-present notion that anyone with skill, individual initiative, patience, foresight, and a little luck can easily make the leap from rags to riches." The fact that some 47 million people attest to the joys of playing poker indicates the magnitude of this diversion in the popular culture panorama.

The significance of poker in popular culture has also been exhibited by the innumerable times the poker game has been utilized in television programs, movies, and other areas of entertainment. The situation comedies of television tell us that a "night out with the boys" for dear old dad usually means one of two things—going bowling or playing poker. A television or movie Western would seem incomplete without the obligatory card-table scene, which often ends in gunplay over an accusation of cheating. Needless to say, cowboys took their poker (and their money) very seriously. To many people today, poker is tantamount to a religion, and even the less devout are fascinated by the ritualistic qualities of the game. Leonard Cohen managed to capture the essence of the popular reverence for poker in a song from the movie *McCabe and Mrs. Miller*, which refers to the all-American diversion as "the holy game of poker."

Poker and the American Dream
Rex L. Jones

Poker is an American game. Its origins, style of play, and language are all American. The draw poker clubs of Gardena in southern California recognize this fact. An advertising brochure of one of the clubs states:

Poker is America's favorite card game. Seventy million adults play cards and some 47 million prefer poker. Poker is as American as baseball and hotdogs. Many of our most famous Presidents were poker enthusiasts.

Poker is a pure expression of the American dream. Embodied in the action of the game is the ever-present notion that anyone with skill, individual initiative, patience, foresight, and a little luck can easily make the leap from rags to riches. In a recent article entitled, "Who Dealt This Mess?" Barry Golson says that poker "is as perfect a microcosm as we have of the way a free-enterprise system is *supposed* to work, except that the rich don't necessarily get richer." He goes on to say that "in a limit game . . . a grocery clerk can humiliate an oil tycoon through sheer bravado—the object being, without exception, to bankrupt the bastard across the table."

Poker is an expression of the American dream in many other ways. We recognize the person who has achieved the American dream by conspicuous consumption. A house, a car, a color TV, a pocket full of credit cards, and a politician in the closet are some of the indications of success. In poker, the "winner" is easily recognized by diamonds, stickpins, car, clothes, bankroll, and the hangers on who flank him. He exudes rugged individualism—the winner at poker is his own man.

In the realization of the American dream, the arena is the system of free enterprise, where everyone has an equal chance; in the poker game, the arena is a system of free play, where all begin on equal footing. In the American dream, society is classless, anyone can play; it is the same with poker. In the American dream, the way to the top is up to you and you alone; in poker, too, winning is solely an individual effort. In the American dream, the winner takes all; in poker, there is no such thing as sharing the spoils.

The American dream and the game of poker thus have much in common. The latter is the microcosm of the former. In Gardena, this melodrama is reenacted every day from 9 A.M. until 5 A.M. the next day. Most of the people who participate are the senior citizens of America—the retired, and the widowed, or that element of our society for whom the American dream has indeed become a living nightmare, because old age and retirement have made its realization next to impossible.

Daily, elderly men, living on their pensions and savings, and elderly women, living on inheritances and insurance premiums of their deceased husbands, frequent the poker clubs, often in shared taxis or cars, to pursue their vision of the American dream. They meet their friends, share stories of winning and losing, compare notes on racing forms, watch TV, eat, drink, and participate in the "action" with people from all walks of life. Small businessmen, bartenders, teachers, construction workers, doctors, students, hustlers, prostitutes, the unemployed, and tourists intermingle with the senior citizens, who all too often in our society are

Poker Parlors, Gardena, California. Poker is the major industry of this Los Angeles suburb, but more than that, it gives meaning to the lives of the senior citizens who frequent the clubs.
Courtesy of The Horseshoe Club and The Gardena Club.

The spacious Card Room of The GARDENA CLUB is set in a colorful, relaxing mood.

The GARDENA Club
The HORSESHOE Club

The HORSESHOE CLUB Card Room is tastefully designed for the enjoyment of its customers.

confined to the sterility of old-age homes or the loneliness of their rooms.

In Gardena, the poker clubs may be many things to many people, but to the aged they are—as expressed to me by an 83-year-old woman—a "godsend." In the clubs their lives attain new meaning. In Gardena, few discuss their aches and pains or their imminent and inevitable deaths. The talk centers around poker and especially winning, which few if any are able to do consistently. No matter, there is always hope, and such hope is justified every day, when a few hit a big win. Winnings are remembered for years; losses are forgotten the next day. In the process, however, the American dream is perpetuated through poker play, and even the old can participate in the myth.

Poker Playing in Southern California

In California there are over 400 licensed and legalized draw-poker clubs. In Gardena, a sprawling suburb of about 50,000 people, located 10 miles south of downtown Los Angeles, poker is the major industry. The poker club payrolls amount to around $5 million annually. Thousands of southern Californians are attracted to its six poker parlors every year, most of them regular players. The Gardena clubs are the largest and best equipped of any of the California draw-poker clubs.

Each club is limited, by city law, to thirty-five tables; each table seats a maximum of eight players. In addition to the card tables, each club features a restaurant, lounge, and one or more color TV rooms. The restaurants serve decent food with diversified menus, at relatively low prices. Many serve weekly specials and buffets that attract hundreds of people who never sit at the poker tables. The clubs are tastefully decorated, by California standards, well lit, and provide free parking. They are located near major freeway systems and are therefore easily accessible to motor-crazed southern Californians.

Draw poker is still the number one attraction. In Gardena's clubs, as in most poker parlors in California, the house has no interest in the stakes of the games. The house provides the tables, cards, chips, game supervision, and other services, but the deal rotates among the players. Each player pays a "collection" to the house at the end of each half-hour of play, the amount being determined by the stakes of the table. The lower the stakes, the less the collection. The house then, essentially rents its services to those who wish to play poker. The collection, however, is no minor variable in terms of winning and losing.

Because of the collection at the end of each half-hour, a low-stakes game is a death wish. It took me some 1000 hours of poker playing to figure out this mathematical formula. In a game of, let's say, $1.00/$2.00 draw, the collection is $1.25 each half-hour. The "buy in," or the stakes that you are required to place in front of you on the table is $10.00. If all eight players at the table are of equal skill, and if at the end of 4 hours of play no player has won or lost at the card play, there will be no money on the table. Each and every player will be broke. Collectively, it costs $80.00 for 4 hours of play. The rent is not cheap.

As one moves to a higher-stakes game, the collection increases, but it increases disproportionately to the stakes of the game. For example, at a $10/$20 low draw game, the collection is $3.00 per half-hour. Collectively, at the end of 4 hours of play, it costs $192.00 per table to play. But the buy-in at $10/$20 low draw is $100.00. It would take from 16 to 17 hours, everything being equal, for the players at the table to go broke.

What this means for the regular players at Gardena is quite simple. Those who regularly play the low-stakes game, *even if they win at cards consistently*, will find it next to impossible to "beat the collection." They will lose money, not to the other players, but to the house. In 1970, I played regularly for 6 months in low-stakes games at Gardena, usually 1/2 high draw or 2/4 low draw. I played on the average of 50 hours a week, or a total of 1500 hours. It cost me in collection fees an average of $3.00 per hour, or a total for 6 months of some $4,500. In tabulating the amount of money I spent at Gardena during that 6-month period, I estimate expenses of $2000. Out of that $2000 also came my food, transportation, and such other things as cigarettes and drinks. Any way I calculated it, I had won at cards. I estimate my winnings at close to $3000, yet my bank account was some $2000 short. What happened to the money? It went to the house.

I am convinced that this happens to every regular player at Gardena in low stakes games. This is substantiated by hundreds of interviews with people who play poker at Gardena and are aware that the house wins in the end. How else could the clubs meet a $5 million annual payroll, pay Gardena taxes, and also make a profit?

As indicated, the majority of the regular players are senior citizens. Surveys of five clubs at different intervals of the day and week during the summer of 1974 revealed some of the following statistics: Out of a total sample of 1473 people at the tables, 789 (53 percent) were over 60 years of age. Of the total sample, 1089 (74 percent) were men and 384 (26 percent) were women. Of the men, 503 (46 percent) were over 60, and of the women, 286 (74 percent) were over 60. These figures indicate that the majority of players are of retirement age. Three-fourths of all women who play are at the retirement age and probably either widowed or playing their pensions or inheritances.

The surveys were backed up by some 3000 hours of participant observation at the tables over a period of 5 years. During that time, I have informally interviewed hundreds of regular players, most of whom indicated to me they were retired or living on pensions, inheritances, or savings.

Furthermore, the majority of the aged and

Poker Champ. Doyle (Dolly) Brunson sips a soft drink after winning the World Series of Poker and $340,000 (on table) at Jack Binion's Horseshoe in Las Vegas. Thirty-four gamblers ventured $10,000 each in the event, held in May 1977.
UPI Photo

retired play low-stakes games. I estimate roughly three-fourths or more. The reasons are simple. They are generally unable to afford the potential losses of high-stakes games, which at any given period of play can run into several hundred dollars or more.

In both formal and informal interview situations and during the course of hours of play, I found that consistent winners are few, probably less than 2 percent, and are of a certain type. They are invariably young (between 21 and 35 years of age), male, and single. These data correspond roughly to another study of poker playing in northern California by Martinez and LaFranchi, who claim that the consistent winners were single or divorced, male, and younger than most of the other players. In that study, they also indicated that less than 10 percent of the players were consistent winners. They described the remainder as "break-evens," "losers," or "action players." I feel that a similar situation exists in Gardena, with one exception. In the Martinez-LaFranchi study there is no mention or analysis of the variable of the house collection. The majority of Gardena players probably fall into the area of "break-evens" or "losers" in terms of the card play, but I am convinced that well over 90 percent of all people who play poker regularly in the Gardena clubs lose money, regardless of their card play. I would add only one variable to Martinez and LaFranchi's description of the consistent winner, and that is that he will probably be found in the high-stakes games, especially $10/$20 draw.

The conclusion to my study is that the

senior citizens who regularly play poker at Gardena lose money in one way or another. They spend their pensions or savings in order to frequent the clubs. The amount they lose is consistent with their income. The club owners recognize this, implicitly if not explicitly. As an example, last summer I played frequently at a $5/$10 low-draw game with a woman who was 76 years old and consistently lost money. In such a game, the losses can be heavy. An average win at a period of play in that game will range from $150 to $300. An average loss will amount to the same or more depending on the player. This woman knew this, because she had played the game in Gardena, in the same club, for over 20 years. She first began playing in the 1950s after moving to California from New York with her husband. Her husband, a successful businessman, died shortly after the move, leaving her with a fairly large income. After a period of boredom and loneliness, the woman soon discovered poker at Gardena, through a friend. Because she had the money, she rapidly moved to the high-stakes games, where the action was faster and more to her liking. During her play, she talked constantly, and frequently claimed that she had paid for the entire west wing of the club through collections over the years. She said that last year she had cashed $20,000 in checks at the cashier's window. At the end of the year, the owner of the club invited her into his office for a personal conference, and begged her to play at a lower-stakes game where she would not lose so much money. She refused, and said, "What else have I got to do with my money? Go on a goddamned world cruise with a bunch of old ladies? I'd rather lose it at poker!"

To the club owner, it matters little whether such people play low- or high-stakes games. The difference in the collection is not so great. What matters is keeping his customers happy and playing, regardless of their losses or winnings. He feared that the woman might go broke, or anger the other players by creating disturbances over her losses, none of which were to his advantage. Thus, the conference was held to "help her out." The important thing was to keep her playing, and playing happily.

Why Poker Playing at Gardena?

As I have maintained, the people who play poker at Gardena are mostly senior citizens, and most of them lose money on a regular basis. The "diamond-studded woman" of Gardena who coldly calculates her cards and shrewdly takes in her winnings, as described by Jack Richardson in a recent Playboy article, is a rarity, if not a myth. The player you are most likely to find across the table from you is an elderly male in wrinkled slacks and a $5.00 sport shirt, losing his pension, or an elderly female with a wig and make-up, losing her inheritance or savings.

It is my contention that the aged and retired play poker in Gardena for social and recreational reasons. They are reliving the American dream, which gives meaning to their lives. Poker functions to make them young again.

The Gardena clubs take the place of home life for the aged. They function quite simply as old-age homes, but offer a more exciting and stimulating environment than do regular institutions for the aged in our society. The clubs, unlike old-age homes, are not places to go and die but places to go and live. Here the aged, the retired, and the widowed are able to interact on a one-to-one basis with thousands of young people, who frequent the clubs simply to play cards. Here the regulars meet tourists from all over the United States and Canada. They meet and interact with people from all walks of life. The clubs offer something more to the regulars than the loneliness and passivity of old-age homes, where people spend most of their time thinking about illness, misfortune, and death. Such discussions are out of place in Gardena. . . .

As one 83-year-old woman put it at the end of an interview in which she systematically pointed out the evils and absurdities of playing poker at Gardena, "Son, if they closed Gardena tomorrow, I would die."

If the old chestnut, "you are what you eat," has any degree of validity, millions of Americans may be in serious trouble. The McDonald's jingle tells us "we do it all for you," but do we really *want* them to? And what exactly *are* they doing for (or, more likely, to) us? Everyone would probably agree that all of us "deserve a break today" or any day for that matter. But are we willing to settle for Big Macs and the latest gimmick drink (what could top those lime-green Shamrock Shakes?) as our "break"?

The so-called fast-food trend, which continues to spread like the blob of science fiction fame, reveals more than the sad state of nutritional consciousness in the United States. It also mirrors the frenetic life-styles that seem to dictate that Americans frequent eating establishments featuring instant preparation and immediate dissemination of meals that can be quickly consumed. A great deal of criticism has been leveled at the low nutritional and gastronomical quality of "junk food," but millions of Americans apparently love it, or at least have become, in the words of the song, pathetic "junk food junkies."

Elaine Kendall examines the cultural significance of the American acquiescence to "consensus food." Like most other aspects of the popular culture, the business of eating in America tends to foster an oppressive standardization. Travelers on the nation's interstate highways and turnpikes are especially victimized, having no choice but to eat at the Holiday Inns and Howard Johnsons if they want to continue making "good time" on the road. There may be nothing wrong with the food at such establishments, but where does that leave those who believe "variety is the spice of life"? Probably off the freeway taking their chances at the local Bert's Beanery. According to Kendall, the malcontents are few, however. Since Americans eat standardized food at home, it is not really surprising that they would prefer "the same sort of reassurance and the same monotony in the food they consumed elsewhere."

What does it say about our culture that the visage of Colonel Sanders on the giant bucket and the symbol of the golden arches are more recognizable to Americans than a Picasso painting or a piece of sculpture by Michelangelo? Should we worry about our overcommercialized society or take comfort in the fact that we will always have something to look forward to, wondering when McDonald's will proudly announce, "Over one trillion served."

The Happy Mediocrity
Elaine Kendall

The idea that we are what we eat has always been a tantalizing hypothesis, too obvious to deny, but rather tedious to prove. At its most intriguing, it implies an intimate connection between a society's diet and its character.... Food, surely one of the great basics of life, is universally bypassed in favor of far more trivial or ephemeral aspects of our culture. Few people, after all, ever go to the theater, many never vote, millions have never bought a book, but everybody eats. . . .

America is in a privileged class by itself. This country is, in fact, the perfect case for the old hypothesis. . . . We're the first—and perhaps the only—country to be able to eat exactly what we like, and what we like is essentially the same from sea to shining sea. The whole polarized nation files docilely in and out of Howard Johnson's and Mc-Donald's. Publicly at least, we agree about cornflakes, hamburgers, and frozen pizza. Privately, we may sometimes opt for hot pastrami, barbecued ribs, or mama's spicy meat sauce. There's a growing trend to stone-ground flour, natural rice, and organically grown, spiritually satisfying nut cutlets, but most of the time Americans cheerfully and willingly eat consensus food. Grosse Point and the East Village are served by the same supermarket chain; standard brands appear on the tables of flower children and corporation executives alike. The hard hats, the student radicals, and the girls in the steno pool all break for doughnuts and coffee. There has to be a lesson in there somewhere, an enlightening and perhaps surprising guide to what we really are and how we got that way. . . .

The recent boom in the food franchising business amounts to a rare and almost perfect example of American historical inevitability at work. The public companies . . . formed . . . to purvey hamburger, fried chicken, and hot dogs to America [were] the glamor stocks of the 1960's, and their track records [made] old champions like AT&T, General Motors, and electronics look lame by comparison. In a single year some of the food franchisers have shown price increases so huge as to be incredible—McDonald's up 346 percent from 1967 to 1968; Kentucky Fried Chicken up 700 percent; Lum's, essentially a frankfurter operation, up 1,280 percent. Nineteen seventy was a letdown. Lum's earnings rose only 165 percent, Kentucky Fried a mere 26 percent; McDonald's was up 30 percent. . . . Every one of these companies is built on certain basic American attitudes toward food, attitudes that have been plain enough all along, but have suddenly become considerably plainer and almost certainly irreversible. The wonder is only that it took so long to happen.

As befits a prototype, the McDonald's Hamburger Empire illustrates these attitudes beautifully. Although Ray Kroc, the president of McDonald's, doesn't attribute his success to anything as vague or chancy as historical inevitability, he certainly hasn't sold more than [twenty-two] billion hamburgers without a profound understanding of his market and the forces that shaped it.

Fifty seconds is regarded as the optimum

length of time to prepare a McDonald's meal, which typically consists of a hamburger, a milk shake, and an order of french fries. McDonald's stores have an eerily exaggerated resemblance to seventeenth-century New England dining rooms. Most contain no chairs, though a few experimental units with seating have been tested. "Things change," says Mr. Kroc, "and so do we." When and if America ever becomes a nation of two- or three-minute epicures, Mr. Kroc will be ready, but for the time being, the Puritan code is strictly enforced. Adults as well as children stand to feed, and there's no lolling around a McDonald's. . . . When Mr. Kroc looks for a site, he counts "church steeples, signs of substantial family neighborhoods." This policy was widely publicized toward the end of 1968, just as Mr. Kroc was embarking on his second thousand set of stands.

The ideal location for a McDonald's is the "above-average residential area." "We want young families," say the McDonald's scouts, and unlike the older highway drive-ins, which relied heavily on a snack trade, McDonald's attracts and gets a family dinner business. If they don't choose to lean against the bare walls inside for the time it takes to swallow the food, Mom, Dad, Sis, and Junior can sit in their car, depreciating their own upholstery, running their own heater, and listening to the radio. . . . McDonald's . . . serves an important side dish of security with each order. Every burger is guaranteed to be just like every other. The possibility of variation has been finally routed, thereby averting invidious comparisons with burgers past, as well as eliminating squabbling among the children for the biggest, the rarest, or the best. A McDonald's burger puts a moratorium on that kind of table (or back-seat) talk forever. The last one and the one before that, all the way back to 1955, were identical in every respect. The roast beef sandwich has been discontinued completely. It had an unfortunate tendency to deviate from a single standard.

Each stand must be managed by a certified graduate of McDonald's "Hamburger University" where the curriculum consists of courses in Q.S.C.—Quality, Service, and Cleanliness. "We at McDonald's," says Mr. Kroc, "believe in these fundamentals and really live by them." Although Hamburger University has a limited catalogue, it maintains an active research and development program. For instance, by the end of 1970, the company had adopted a scoop that delivers the same number of french-fried potato pieces every time, regardless of who is running the machine or where. The company laboratories, of course, have long since arrived at the perfect meat-fat ratio, the perfect size (3½ inches by 3/16 inch B.C.—Before Cooking), and the perfect roll measurement (3¾ inches), thus assuring a bun surround of no less than ¼ inch. The university seems to have a strong science and math department.

There is still another, subtler factor that contributes to the success of these plans. Franchise shops are not dependent on that rare and mercurial personage, the chef. The chef's place in this country has always been awkward and ambiguous—a man doing woman's work, a kind of super-servant who has to be treated like an artist or, at least, a craftsman. Few people have ever been attracted to so dubious a profession, but lots of Americans are available and willing to press buttons and work levers. There is nothing effeminate about that. Franchised food is manufactured, rather than "cooked" in any true sense. Its components are delivered to the shop already blended, assembled and portioned. The store only heats it. The methods have been scientifically developed, and the serving is done according to the assembly-line principles that we approve. The new food is simply bought and consumed, out of stock. The identical recipe serves everyone. . . .

If these places existed only to cater to people caught on the road at mealtime, they'd be readily explainable, but that's not the case. The fact that they often serve that purpose is really quite incidental to the whole idea. They are on the road because America is mostly road, but as Mr. Kroc says, and the others agree, residential and business neighborhoods make the most desirable locations. The idea is for someone in the office to bring back a bag of hamburgers for the steno pool or for Dad to pick up dinner while the family waits in the car or in front of the TV. . . .

The food that Americans eat at home has been thoroughly branded, standardized, and nationalized for more than fifty years, and it should have been obvious that the public would welcome—would eventually *demand*—the same sort of reassurance and the same monotony in the food they consumed elsewhere. . . .

In many medium-sized American cities and in most suburbs, hamburger, hot dog, pizza and chicken stands are the only restaurants. An entire generation of children has already grown up thinking that McDonald's is the word for hamburger the way Kleenex is the word for tissue and that "fried" always modifies "chicken.". . .

It seems clear that the American people yearn to be told what to eat, long to have that particular decision made for them. Only half a dozen options are available from these places, out of all the thousands of edibles that can be raised, grown, processed, and marketed in this huge, temperate, rich, and fertile country. We have narrowed the choices down to a nearly irreducible minimum. We, the most various collection of people ever assembled into a single nation, have agreed that we will be satisfied with these rigid limitations and that we all will stay satisfied from the time we can first be propped into a car seat until long after we're eligible for Medicare. If we have a widening generation gap, irreconcilable racial discord, or a new sense of individuality, no one would ever know it from the menu at the franchise shop. There the whole experience of eating has been completely drained of every last personal, social, and sensual aspect. You never have to give it a second thought.

Social commentator Michael Harrington, writing in the late 1960s, observed that the mass media seemed to cater to the insatiable thirst of Americans for novelty. "Yesterday's avant-garde is today's cliché and tomorrow's vaudeville," Harrington remarked tersely. His assessment of American society focused on the ability of popular culture to undermine political dissent by sensationalizing it one day and discarding it the next. The same sad commentary, however, could be applied to almost every feature of American life, from our short-lived fads to the "new-and-improved" mentality of our advertising.

The fanatical desire for a constant stream of newness in one's life was anything but new in American society in the 1960s. The perceptive French writer Alexis de Tocqueville reported in the 1830s that Americans sought novelty in their lives because they lived in such a dreary materialistic society. They also, according to Tocqueville, lacked reverence for tradition and thus thought only in terms of the "here and now" in their quest for the new and the exciting.

Truman Moore examines the "nouveaumania" of Americans, as reflected through fashion trends. He sees the 1960s as a crucial decade in the history of fashion. During the sixties, large numbers of Americans turned their backs on the standards set by the professional designers and, according to Moore, "began to dress out their beliefs" in an effort to achieve "instant communication" with one another. Many rebellious young people, for instance, considered their bizarre clothing, as well as their long hair, as symbols of defiance. In many respects, their appearance represented a kind of statement of their values and priorities.

As radical as some of the features of the "counterculture" were, the movement followed a typically American line in its infatuation with "style." And the youthful rebels seemed to share the conventional American propensity for changing styles simply for the sake of change. The counterculture also reinforced the American fetish of trying to remain forever young. Counterculture personality Jerry Rubin articulated this popular prejudice when he stated that "growing up means giving up your dreams." Truman Moore argues that this zeal for youthfulness is a key contributory factor in the perpetuation of nouveaumania. "Being in style is always being new, hence young," Moore observes.

Fashion as New Self

Truman E. Moore

Apparel," said Shakespeare, "oft proclaims the man." In America, we have developed the notion that frequent changes in apparel and grooming proclaim as many new personalities, all released from the soul of a single individual. This idea became quite popular during the nineteen-sixties and early seventies when clothing styles underwent a series of radical changes that distorted the relationship between clothes and the man—or the woman—and created an illusion of eternal youth and constant rebirth through the packaging of the self. Fashion, in other words, got mixed up with inner being.

Prior to this time, clothing styles were largely indicators of status. Their dissemination followed a familiar and predictable course. Diana Vreeland, former editor of *Vogue* magazine, called fashion a social contract, "a group agreement as to what the new ideal should be." The agreement was made between the designers, who continually proposed something new, and the acceptance of those ideas by "the society that counts."

Once this select group had adopted a new style, it filtered down to the masses, usually in a diluted form, until it became a cliché of dress, ready to be displaced by the next arrival. By this aristocratic but orderly system, the personal appearance of men and women all over America was constantly altered by styles adopted in the halls of the mighty and salons of the wealthy.

The fashions accepted by the trend setters were not arbitrary and random offerings of remote designers, but were, Ms. Vreeland tells us, reflections of the age, or in the words of designer Calvin Klein, "very today."

When the development of twentieth-century technology opened the vistas of mankind, the designers freed women from their corsets and bustles and gave them looser garments of brilliant color. And as the war approached in 1939, styles changed to "hard chic"—masculine suits with squared-off and padded shoulders.

In the last fifteen years, the increased tendency to discover new ages and generations brought confusion to fashion trends just as the events of those years brought confusion to our social and political life. The decade of the sixties was filled with tumultuous events and much shouting. Placards, chants, and slogans reduced discussion and debate to the size of a bumper sticker. People, as if attempting to achieve the same kind of instant communication, began to dress out their beliefs. Abbie Hoffman's American-flag shirt and his long, frizzy, uncombed hair were supposed to be an extension of his political views, a sign of his consciousness. He meant his attire to be a visible social comment, and as observers of the scene reported, "a costume is an idea, not a look—it's part of the person wearing it, not just a mere body wrapping."

Young Americans came to equate fashion and personal style not only with their opinions but with their egos. Dress was an extension of self, but it did not simply proclaim *the* man, *the* self, in the Shakespearean sense, but *a* man, *a* self among many. Personal identity was not fixed, but changed with the times. A young writer about to turn thirty was able to reflect on four past selves in her precocious memoirs—headlined in a magazine article as "A last burp from the Pepsi Generation"—and view their obsolescence with the detachment of a historian reviewing ancient civilizations. First, she described her beatnik self of the fifties with

"black turtleneck, beads, wraparound olive green skirt, sandals." She and her friends were constantly engaged in "deep talk," dividing the people of the world into two great categories, deep and shallow. Shallow included people who cared about clothes.

The second self came with Raga Rock, circa 1964. "The Beatles were in Kutra shirts and everybody knew how to say Maharishi Mahesh Yogi." Third, there was the organic period. "I wore long skirts and cooked grains." The fourth self developed in 1969, when she "entered the Women's Liberation Movement as a spy. I was going to write something snide. I came out a convert."

This four-stage metamorphosis was roughly paralleled by the lives of many other young people, and in fact marks national epochs. Each phase, with its distinct costume, look, and concept of self, was as different from the preceding one as the butterfly from the caterpillar. American fashion trends were influenced by the individual's attempt to display an unlimited number of new selves;

new editions of himself. Being in style is always being new, hence young, not just in appearance but—we are encouraged to believe—in essence.

As life style and clothes were seen as inextricably bound together, mass-produced garments were presented as expressions of the wearer's individuality. For example, *Mademoiselle* featured six young women who lived in different parts of New York City and who therefore each had a different life style. The article included photographs of each young lady in the clothes that matched her personality and her particular mode of living. The article made no attempt to explicate the relationship between the clothes, the life styles, and the young women, but the implication was that a relationship did exist, that it was not just a matter of taste that was reflected in the clothes, but some profound intuition.

The perception of new identities, personalities, and life styles expressed in the passing fashion carried the fable of the emperor's new clothes into another dimension. It was the emperor himself who was perceived to be new, and he acquired a new (imaginary) personality to go with his new (imaginary) clothes.

The style-as-self concept became a standard theme in the fashion magazines in the fifties. As a *Glamour* editor, my wife was an early writer on this theme. Later, as copy editor of *Simplicity* and *Modern Miss*, she set what may be a record in prescribing personal transformations, going from "Be a New

The Jeans Scene. Caroline Kennedy, daughter of the late President, going to work at the *New York Daily News*, where she was a copy person in the summer of 1977. Beginning in the mid-sixties, young people set the pace in fashion.
UPI Photo

You by Monday" (1960) to "A New You in Nine Hours" (1962).

Time has not dulled the editorial taste for transformation. The August 1975 issue of *Glamour* was headlined: "Make Me Over for My New Life."

No magazine has celebrated the link between fashion and self more lyrically than *Vogue*. It got particularly carried away in announcing the arrival of the "new prettiness," which it defined as a "whole new take on prettiness. Modern, upbeat, with a zing and style to it—the way we all want to feel in our clothes today, moving with ease through our lives, knowing we look well and not worrying about it—enjoying ourselves in fashion." The *Vogue* editors never lingered over their definitions and seemed confident that their readers would be able to fill in the logical blanks, of which there were many.

Vogue is unrivaled in its ability to combine mental states, physical characteristics, and editorial omniscience. It saw clothes as being willed into existence by the woman wearing them. The clothes then transformed her as if they acted upon her physical and mental being in a manner perfectly divined, so to speak, by the editors.

Clothes, make-up, and fashion accessories were not promoted as simple objects but as humanized accomplishment of the self, ever new, ever up to date. This tendency to see people as coming in styles, with annual or seasonal model changes, is production-line American thinking.

The fashion magazines did not invent the renewable self, of course, but picked it up and amplified it. They played it back to their readers loud and clear, but with no hint of the problem of personal obsolescence which eventually plagues everyone in the land of the young.

The fashion system upon which the public depended for its supply of new "looks" has been under pressure in the last fifteen years. Prior to the early sixties, there were few extreme differences in the style of dress between age groups. Zoot suits and bobby-socks came and went, but in general, when young and old dressed up, they dressed alike. Even generational differences were minimized. In 1960 Bennett Berger said that the term "younger generation" was being stretched to include increasingly younger and older people. American children began dating, dancing, and drinking at a younger and younger age, while men in their late thirties still belonged to the "junior" chamber of commerce.

When the generational war broke out in the mid-sixties, the stretching of the generation was abruptly halted and young people

303

seized control of dress and style. A break occurred between age groups in fashion.

The admonition not to trust anyone over thirty also meant not to dress like anyone over thirty. With the advent of the hippies and yippies, campus styles changed radically. Young people let their hair grow and began to affect strange dress. The older end of the generational stretch found it difficult to dress, look, and act like the younger end. They were threatened with the social death of being outdated and of becoming one of life's discontinued models. Fashions ceased to filter down from the upper levels of society in quite so orderly a manner. They were now in the process of being forced up from below.

The English designers translated the generational split into mod fashions, and the American male, like Berenger in Ionesco's *Rhinoceros*, vacillated between standing his ground and joining the new herd, or as management consultant and business philosopher Peter Drucker called it, the Peacock Revolution. The blatant pretentiousness of some of the new fashions trapped many men between their desire to keep up with the times and a revulsion to dressing the part of a dandy. It was an interesting spectacle. Insurance salesmen, optometrists, agency account men, doctors, corporate executives, and accountants one had known for years as sober and conservative dressers suddenly appeared in flared pants, safari jackets, aviator glasses, square-toed shoes (later high heels), and wide ties that glowed in sunlight. Barbers reported business off 30 percent as men hot-combed their lengthening hair over their ears.

The disorder in the fashion system culminated in 1970 when the American woman rejected the midi skirt being touted by the establishment. The manufacturers, following the Paris showings, had invested heavily in the below-knee dress. The department stores in New York were loaded with the new midi look, but it didn't sell. The mass of women on whom manufacturers depended for sales and profits refused to ratify the social contract. Conditioned by the fashion anarchy of the previous decade, they refused to be pressured.

Having rejected the main line of the new fashion trend, they bought all the minor variations and novelties, causing Gloria Emerson of the *New York Times* to cry out in 1973 against the jumble of scarfs, pendants, bracelets, rings, over-sized sunglasses, big-brimmed hats, platform shoes, wide pants, streaked hair, and shopping bags that made the New York woman a "mess." The "fashion industry cannot keep the trends coming fast enough. It is, after all, the very place where the bullet belt and the fun-fun dogtag were launched. . . . If the idea is new, it must have merit. This is the reasoning and the results are often sad. . . . A wide range of synthetic materials makes us look wrinkled and limp. . . . Perhaps this is the natural punishment for caring so much about keeping up with fashion. It is this eagerness, perhaps, that makes so many women look so mindless and confused.

"Not trusting ourselves, we want to look alike. Someone must tell us what to wear, what we should be pretending to be." Three years after the midi revolt, the field was in disarray.

The impetus for these fashions did not originate with the established designers, but came from the streets and campuses where the young congregated in protest and celebration. Their radical clothes were refined by the retail trade with more conservative taste.

Clothes and hair styles were made to carry a heavy burden of meaning. The older Americans who were somewhat reluctantly influenced by the new styles found that they at least had the virtue of being more changeable. If one's outward style was accepted as a reflection of one's inner being, one could display an unlimited number of new selves quite easily.

Since we believe that the transition from one style to another is progress, the individual reviewing his past may be chagrined to see his obsolete selves but is gratified that his or her present self is the best, most improved self. The new you is better than the old you. The "new prettiness" or the "new beauty confidence" (another *Vogue* discovery) is better than the old.

By way of contrast, the dilemma of the trapped housewife, about which so much has been written, is that she has been largely excluded from the game of changing self. The suburban housewife experienced no metamorphosis, but only got a little older each year and more resentful of what she was missing. There were no new life styles available to her.

One of the great traumas of American life is the sense of being trapped in a style and shut off from the opportunity to try on and exhibit a succession of selves. Maturity implies a settling of character, coming to terms with and accepting oneself. Nothing of the sort occurs in the evolution of American character, and the conformity demanded in the suburban-corporate world stands in conflict with our need for constant rebirth. The great feminist uprising generated its heat and power from the friction of this conflict and was ignited by stifled housewives trapped in their worn-out selves.

Widespread discontent in American society arises partly from the fact that growing old is equated with wearing out. It is difficult to see how any degree of well-being can be attained when people feel the constant need to feign eternal youth with a series of transparent selves which binds them to the destructive illusion that constant changes in style will buy them immortality on the installment plan.

Many people are currently asking, "What happened to the counterculture?" The virtual absence of any overt signs of youthful dissent has led many to assume that the counterculture has completely disappeared. But even a cursory examination would reveal that many of the life-style changes of the past decade have remained and have, in fact, influenced the thought and behavior of most people. The "consciousness revolution," expressed in the popularity of such cults as Transcendental Meditation, clearly has roots in the counterculture of the sixties.

There are, however, some definite distinctions between the styles of life of the seventies and those of the sixties. Many rock groups, for example, still promote, at least implicitly, the use of drugs and the enjoyment of other sensual pleasures. But the specter of materialism has returned. The rock group Aerosmith may look like the Rolling Stones of the sixties, but one of the members admitted, "What I dig is money. It pays for things. I'd like to buy myself a Porsche." And even the Rolling Stones of today, along with Bob Dylan and the former members of the Beatles, have realized the dream of economic success on a grand scale.

In the following selection, from the introduction to his book on "the life-style rebellion," John Pendleton examines the origins and development of the counterculture as a movement of protest against the values and priorities of the "American Way of Life."

The Life-Style Rebellion
John Pendleton

More than 400,000 persons gathered in August 1969 to take part in a major "happening," a term that seems trite and passé today but one that conjured up visions of great cultural significance in the sixties. The multitude that congregated on the rolling hills of Max Yasgur's dairy farm near Bethel, New York had come to enjoy the pleasures and appreciate the importance of the so-called Woodstock Music and Art Fair. From the beginning, most of the audience and the performers sensed that Woodstock would be more than a showcase for popular musicians and groups such as Jimi Hendrix, Joan Baez, Janis Joplin, Jefferson Airplane, and the Who. The name itself carried enormous cultural symbolism, mainly because Bob Dylan lived in the small upstate New York community of Woodstock, some forty miles from the festival. Despite the rainstorms and crowded conditions, most of those who went to Woodstock were not disappointed. Many of them, in fact, felt the festival illustrated that large numbers of people could coexist peacefully in a culture devoted to the pursuit of happiness and pleasure.

The success of the Woodstock festival offered convincing evidence that the numerous "hippie" subcultures throughout the country were not isolated social aberrations. Abbie Hoffman, a leading organizer and public relations man for the radical youth movements, argued that a "Woodstock Nation" had emerged; others simply called it a "counterculture." Although the term has a rather vague connotation and has been applied to a variety of cultural and political dissenters, the counterculture as a "culture of opposition" can be viewed as the culmination of a life-style rebellion that had been developing since at least the 1950s. This rebellion was simply the collective expression of many individual searches for ways to live that were somehow more satisfying and fulfilling than the conventional styles of life adopted by most Americans. The quest for alternative life-styles mirrored a deep sense of dissatisfaction with the values, priorities, and patterns of living of the overwhelming majority of Americans. For many, the spirit of rebellion began in a very visceral manner, as a vague feeling of uneasiness and discontent rather than a consciously articulated critique of American culture. The life-style rebellion, to the bewilderment of many, also originated in the more privileged social-economic classes, among white, primarily young, affluent Americans.

The late sixties abounded with reflections of the life-style rebellion. Appearance, behavior, and the values and priorities they expressed signified the growing challenge to the life-styles of mainstream America. Most of the rebellious young could have afforded nice, new, conventional apparel, but they preferred to wear old, often dirty, clothes or bizarre costumes drawn indiscriminately from such sources as Indian and American-Indian styles and military surplus garb. Long hair and adornments such as "love beads," feathers, and medallions added other dimensions to the unconventional images cultivated by life-style rebels. The way a person looked, of course, was not always a guarantee of his cultural affiliation. There were many so-called plastic hippies who donned the regalia of the counterculture for the weekend, but who adhered to the rules and,

at least implicitly, shared the mentality of the "straight society."

Behavior offered a more reliable index of the burgeoning life-style rebellion. The young rebels proclaimed, and did their best to demonstrate, their freedom from "hang ups" about sex or any other area of human relationships. Some of them lived in communes or participated in cooperative ventures such as the "free stores" that sprang up in nearly every hippie community. For the less industrious, the practice of panhandling became a common means of surviving and a popular way to exhibit scorn for the work ethic.

The use of drugs was perhaps the most striking example of dramatic behavioral changes among white, affluent youth. The American Medical Association committee on drug dependence estimated that the number of Americans, mostly young, who had smoked marijuana increased from a few thousand in 1960 to around eight million by 1970. The use of LSD, mescaline, and other hallucinogenic or "mind-expanding" substances also increased sharply. Like other facets of a person's behavior, ingesting drugs often constituted a statement of values. In 1967, *Look* magazine interviewed some "typical" student drug enthusiasts who acknowledged that taking LSD, for instance, symbolized a basic attitude toward life. One "acid head," as the LSD-eaters were called, admitted that the drug had profoundly altered his life-style priorities. "My goals have really been changing the last few months," he said. "I really held on to the nice car and the American-Way-of-Life bit. I wanted to make a lot of money and have a comfortable life. Now, more than anything else, I want happiness and peace."

Putting aside the fact that many who revel in materialistic pursuits may also seek "happiness and peace," the quote suggests the essential ingredient in the life-style rebellion: a disenchantment with the "American Way of Life." The distinguished historian

Arnold Toynbee, hardly a promoter of the counterculture or an observer given to hyperbole, noted the significance of this factor when he viewed the hippies as "a red warning light for the American way of life." The phrase may be even more ambiguous than "counterculture" but, in relation to the life-style rebellion, the "American Way of Life" had some very distinct connotations.

According to Will Herberg, who popularized the phrase, the American Way of Life had become, by the 1950s, a kind of "common religion," based on faith in such general and ill-defined ideas as democracy, God, and the American dream of success. This secular religion helped to unite people of diverse cultural and racial backgrounds and maintain a sense of cohesiveness in society. It is interesting to note that Congress, when confronted with the threat of internal political subversion in the 1940s, created the House Committee on Un-American Activities with the confidence that "American" thought and behavior could be readily distinguished from un-American ideas and activities.

The American Way of Life rested on a foundation of values such as work, achievement, winning, and discipline of mind and body. Norman Vincent Peale, an extremely popular religious figure and social spokesman of the 1950s, emphasized the need to "control yourself" in order to be successful at any endeavor. "That is the secret," Peale reiterated, "control, control, control."

Many young people recoiled at advice such as Peale's. Instead of keeping a tight rein on their emotions and a check on their enjoyment of sensual pleasure, the life-style rebels tended to "go with the mood" and "let it all hang out," to quote two popular phrases of the counterculture. Rather than deferring their gratification, they decided, in the words of a popular rock song of the sixties, to "live for today." Janis Joplin's "get it while you can" philosophy, rather than the mentality of "saving for a rainy day" that Perry Como sang about in "Catch a Falling Star," was more in tune with the intellectual temper of the life-style rebellion.

The American dream of success, with its emphasis on individual initiative, competition, and equal opportunity for all to improve their social and economic status, functioned as a kind of "sense of purpose" in the American Way of Life. The dream was not a uniquely American one, but the United States seemed to offer greater possibilities for success and upward social mobility. Many Americans, in fact, assumed the dream of success had been realized on a broad scale after World War II.

The country had not lapsed into another depression, as many feared might happen with the transfer to a peacetime economy. Veterans found abundant opportunity to make up for lost time and "be somebody." The GI Bill of Rights offered them financial assistance to go to college and to purchase a house. This reward from the government for "a job well done," combined with their own resourcefulness and hard work, enabled millions of former fighting men to achieve the cherished goals of the American dream: a sound education, a secure job, a comfortable home, and a happy family life. In the minds of most Americans, the United States had truly become the "Affluent Society," where "the good life" reigned supreme.

The life-style rebels saw nothing particularly good about the so-called good life, and the American dream appeared to them to be little more than a rationale for the pursuit of materialism. The youthful dissenters criticized the tendency of Americans to define the national dream in strictly economic terms. The American dream seemed to stifle the spiritual qualities of human beings and to perpetuate a grossly commercialistic culture that interpreted success as the acquisition of material goods and happiness as the consumption of those products. Herbert Marcuse, a social theorist whose ideas appealed to some of the more intellectually inclined cultural radicals, observed that Amer-

icans "recognize themselves in their commodities, they find their soul in their automobile, hi-fi set, split-level home, kitchen equipment."

For many discontented young people, the American dream and the life-style it helped to maintain simply did not offer enough spiritual satisfaction. Again, the word "spiritual," like so many of the words and phrases heard so often during the life-style rebellion, is rather vague. But it apparently had a definite meaning for the cultural radicals of the fifties and sixties who sought a life of spiritual or religious quality that somehow would transcend the material world. Even drug cultists such as Timothy Leary, who founded the League for Spiritual Discovery, promoted the use of hallucinogens as a means of achieving mystical states and spiritual tranquility.

While the American dream was a highly individualized concept, it also manifested itself in the social and political nature of the country. Belief in the American dream, for instance, generally translated into support for American involvement in the Vietnam war. Lawrence Chenoweth, in his study of the success ethic, observed that the Vietnam war "was thought of in terms of winning and losing just as the American dream spoke of success and failure. Just as the race for success was accepted as a self-evident good, so also was participation in a war for victory not to be questioned."

The American dream, by stressing the need for self-reliance and personal responsibility, also tended to condone social problems such as poverty and racial injustice. The fact that many Americans eagerly pursued material success, while allowing an economic system of unequal opportunity to exist, outraged many young people. They considered it hypocritical, another key word of the life-style rebellion vocabulary, to believe in a dream of equal opportunity for all and, at the same time, to support a status quo that negated that noble vision. The disparity between professed ideals and social reality was simply too glaring for sensitive, discontented, and perhaps guilt-ridden youth to ignore. Michael Harrington's comment that the political radicals of the sixties seemed to be doing "penance for the sins of affluence" could also be applied to many of the life-style rebels.

Like most concepts, the American Way of Life that came under such intense fire by alienated youth was more a potentiality than a reality. It was certainly grounded in tangible social situations, but it also contained a good deal of ideological content that did not always find systematic and consistent expression in everyday life. Americans, in other words, seldom concerned themselves with whether they were fulfilling the main tenets of the American Way of Life or whether some of their actions contradicted some of their values. Yet whenever they felt their value system was endangered, the guardians of the American Way of Life became extremely defensive. The public preoccupation with the "threat of communism" in the fifties highlighted this tendency.

Although Americans certainly worried about military aggression from the Soviet Union and China and grew anxious about the danger of political subversion, they also feared communism because it represented an alien and hostile value system. Those who railed against communism often used the word as a metaphor for a wide range of ideas and behavior they deemed "un-American." Most Americans perceived communism as being in direct opposition to the American Way of Life because it rejected God, democracy, and the dream of economic success.

Will Herberg presented some statistics in his book *Protestant, Catholic, Jew* (1955) that offered an insight into the defensiveness of Americans who feel their value system is being threatened. When asked whether they could show love for someone of a different religion, 90 percent of those polled said yes; of a different race, 80 percent replied in the affirmative; for a business competitor, 78 percent could show love. But when it came to a person they would consider an "enemy" of the nation, only 25 percent could muster any love for such an individual.

In the opinion of many, the life-style rebels, like the communists (a name occasionally used to label the cultural radicals),

"...the plentitude of social ills in the fifties and sixties made it quite natural for young people to become highly critical of American culture."

qualified as national enemies because of their assault on the American Way of Life. This extreme viewpoint only further entrenched the young rebels in their attitudes and styles of life, which in turn stimulated even stronger rebukes from mainstream society. By the late sixties, the adversaries had become so polarized that seemingly insignificant actions or events could spark major clashes between the two warring cultures.

Ironically, the life-style rebellion posed only a partial threat to mainstream society. Discontented youth criticized the work ethic, but not the notion that work could be meaningful. Individualism came under attack, not because the idea was inherently wrong but because there was too much stress in American society on individual competition at the expense of cooperation among human beings. The critique of rationalism stemmed not from a rejection of logical thinking, but from a concern that too much emphasis was being placed on the intellect at the sacrifice of feelings, emotions, and the senses.

In light of the historical circumstances of the postwar period, it is understandable that most Americans sought security and stability by clinging tightly to the social and intellectual moorings of the American Way of Life. The young life-style rebels, most of whom were born in the 1940s, failed to appreciate their parents' concern for security. They had not experienced a severe economic depression or a world war. They consequently viewed the Affluent Society as uninteresting and lacking in vitality. As literary historian John Aldridge noted, the older generation fashioned, in the postwar years, an environment that "resembled nothing so much as the military world we had just escaped." The sheer differences in historical experience between young and old, a situation that gave rise to the phrase "generation gap," helped to stimulate the conflict of values that launched the life-style rebellion.

The very nature of the Affluent Society contributed to the onset of the life-style rebellion. The unprecedented, and relatively uninterrupted prosperity of the fifties and sixties brought with it an expansion of leisure time for most Americans. Being raised in an atmosphere of affluence, young people were freed from the drudgery of having to work to help support the family. They had an abundance of leisure time, perhaps too much of it for many to handle. Having too much free time, and the boredom that often accompanied it, were important factors in the upsurge of middle-class juvenile delinquency, and the less harmful youthful "hell-raising," in the 1950s. For the more serious-minded, leisure time offered the opportunity to reflect upon such things as the "quality of life" and to analyze the dominant values and priorities of American society.

Freedom to think about life does not necessarily have to promote rebelliousness, but the plenitude of social ills in the fifties and sixties made it quite natural for young people to become highly critical of American culture. Youth had traditionally questioned the values of the older generation and, more often than not, found them unsatisfactory to some degree. But the life-style rebels attacked the American Way of Life much more vehemently because most of them felt such a deep disappointment with the failures of their society to confront its most pressing problems.

Aside from the fact that the life-style rebels were profoundly alienated from the American Way of Life, the value system upon which this nebulous concept rested was in disarray. The values of hard work, self-reliance, and the competitive spirit were increasingly being given only lip service. Sociologist David Riesman, in *The Lonely Crowd* (1950), and business analyst William H. Whyte, in *The Organization Man* (1956), argued that a new "ethic of consumption" and a trend toward conformity had replaced individualism and the work ethic as the defining features of American life. While the discontented youth challenged the individualistic competitive spirit as much as they did conformity and the zealous consumption of material goods, young people might have shown more respect for the authority of an older generation that illustrated some fidelity to their professed ideals.

Young people had no consistent, strong and, in the minds of many, no credible value system to follow. The internal contradictions of the American Way of Life made it an easy target for discontented youth. Once attacked, however, the guardians of the American Way of Life closed ranks and mounted massive campaigns to defend their cherished, if somewhat neglected, values and institutions. Yet the defensiveness and rigidity of these custodians of mainstream American culture often served as a shield to hide nagging doubts about the viability of their ideas and life-styles.

Playwright Arthur Miller offered a very perceptive analysis of this situation in the late sixties. He argued that the young effectively challenged their elders in three crucial areas: work, war, and sex. "It is infuriating" to Americans, observed Miller, "to confront young people who think it is stupid to waste a life doing hateful work." It is even more upsetting "to hear young men calling war the ultimate defeat." And it is frustrating to adults to witness young people living together "without shame," when their own generation has such "an investment in sexual shame." The life-style rebellion, according to Miller, was "psychologically and

spiritually" threatening to the adult American male, who "knows that if he really starts listening to what his son is saying to him, he will have to, in effect, vomit up a good part of his life."

In some respects, the life-style rebellion of the fifties and sixties seemed like a traditional expression of youthful unrest. The "revolution in manner and morals" of the 1920s had some definite similarities with the cultural revolt three decades later. The philosophical core of the life-style rebellion, with its emphasis on sensuality and its distrust of the intellect, seemed to be little more than another outbreak of the recurring romanticism found in advanced industrial societies. The subcultural life-styles adopted by discontented youth in the fifties and sixties also had precedents in the early twentieth century in the bohemian community of Greenwich Village. And the criticism of the American Way of Life was a long-standing component of artistic and intellectual life in America by the 1950s.

The historical circumstances of the post-World War II era, of course, gave the life-style rebellion its particular shape and tone. The dawn of the atomic age, the protracted period of foreign policy crises, the great increase in prosperity and leisure, and the rise of radical political movements gave the life-style rebellion its special contours. But, more than anything else, the pervasive influence of popular culture made the life-style rebellion rather unique.

The advent of commercial television in the late 1940s had an immense and varied impact on society. Some of the guardians of the American Way of Life considered television a positive force that could promote family togetherness by giving the individual members of a family a common pastime. Television did, in fact, further the "stay-at-home" trend that had already been indicated by the decline in motion picture attendance. Most of the television programs, especially the "family shows" such as "The Adventures of Ozzie and Harriet" and "Father Knows Best," helped to reaffirm the goodness of American values and minister to the public need for security.

Although it is difficult to document, television also appeared to serve as a radicalizing agent in the life-style rebellion. The bulk of those who joined the assault on the American Way of Life were members of the first "television generation." Growing up with the medium seemed to influence the mentality and behavior of many of the life-style rebels. Those used to instant and continual entertainment became bored very easily with the mundane world of reality, a factor that aggravated their feelings of discontent. Being used to switching channels or turning off the television set when they became restless, the young rebels also had little patience with the authority of adults, whose messages they learned to turn off mentally.

Television taught the young the art of instant communication by means of symbols, images, and catch phrases. How well they learned the lesson could be seen in the propensity of life-style rebels for slogans and in their infatuation with style. Rather than becoming involved in lengthy discourses on their ideas and attitudes, many young people apparently assumed their appearance and behavior expressed very clearly who they were and where their "head was at."

Television, by increasing the general public awareness of such problems as the lack of equal civil rights for blacks, undoubtedly reinforced the discontent of some young people. Constant exposure to scenes of white brutality against black political activists and of U.S. involvement in questionable foreign policy entanglements offered them a virtual confirmation of the "sickness" of American society. While most of those who criticized various aspects of the American Way of Life would probably have developed such attitudes without the aid of television, the medium certainly accelerated the process of "radicalization." When life-style rebel Jerry Rubin declared that "you can't be a revolutionary without a television set," he merely articulated a widespread belief that this vital area of popular culture could be an important ally in the movement for social change.

Despite the possible effects of television in promoting the life-style rebellion, the medium seldom mirrored the ideas, attitudes, values, and life-style patterns of the alienated youth. Motion pictures, popular literature, "underground" newspapers, styles in fashion, and especially popular music were much more significant in reflecting the assault on The American Way of Life. The study of popular culture is especially fruitful in examining the life-style rebellion because the majority of those who participated in the movement never articulated their ideas. Popular culture functioned as an important voice of these people, although the accuracy with which entertainment expressed the thinking of the entertained can never be completely determined.

Most of the ideas and attitudes of the life-style rebellion were far from novel, but their dissemination through the mass media of entertainment and information gave them the capacity to become highly influential. The creative and intellectual communities had been firing salvos at American culture since at least the early nineteenth century, with little effect on popular thought. While the life-style rebellion did not involve a majority of affluent youth, it nevertheless constituted a major social movement.

The impact of popular culture has to be considered a primary factor in expanding the scope of the life-style rebellion. Without the mass media of communication there would have been isolated pockets of dissent from the American Way of Life, but there would have been no sense of cultural cohesiveness, no idea of an emerging counterculture. Popular culture showed the alienated youth that others felt the same way, and it served to alert them to the new trends and events of the life-style rebellion.

The role of popular culture as a mirror of the life-style rebellion seems fairly obvious, although the mass media often distorted the nature and intentions of the young rebels. But even when such periodicals as *Time* and *Newsweek* promulgated sensationalized or blatantly erroneous images of groups such as the hippies, the magazines may have unwittingly furthered the life-style rebellion by publicizing their ideas and activities. There is evidence, in fact, that some young

people in the hinterlands of America learned about the "summer of love" in 1967 by reading magazines or watching television and decided to travel to San Francisco or New York's East Village to join the hippie communities.

The phrase "the media giveth and the media taketh away," of course, suggests that the popularity accorded the youth movements proved to be a double-edged sword. Whenever a particular brand of dissent no longer represented "good copy," due to its being overexposed or overcommercialized by popular culture, the mass media quickly abandoned it. And there are those who believe that popular culture is inherently harmful to social protest because it acts like a massive sponge, soaking up dissent and rendering it ineffective by making it simply another commodity of the marketplace.

Popular culture did more than merely reflect the life-style rebellion. It also helped initiate and shape the ideas, attitudes, and life-styles of many young people. Since most of the life-style rebels never articulated their feelings about the content of the movies and television they watched, the books, magazines, and newspapers they read, and the popular songs they listened to, the historian can make only tentative judgments about what effects popular culture had. But whenever historians journey into interpretations of cause and effect, they enter treacherous territory and can never return with a completely satisfying answer. In the case of the life-style rebellion, there are enough testimonials to the impact of popular culture to allow for some educated observations.

Most of those who gave allegiance to the life-style rebellion never read the "great minds" of the counterculture, social theorists such as Herbert Marcuse, Paul Goodman, and Norman O. Brown. They studied alienation by watching James Dean in the film *Rebel Without a Cause*; they acquired insights into the "rat race" of American society by reading Jack Kerouac's novels; they

"Without the mass media of communication there would have been isolated pockets of dissent from the American Way of Life, but there would have been...no idea of an emerging counterculture."

heard about the bankruptcy of American values by listening to the comedy routines of Lenny Bruce; and they learned that defiance could be a way of life by witnessing the career of Bob Dylan. These popular cultural celebrities functioned as major intellectual figures for many young people. Their ideas may not have been innovative, or even noteworthy, but they were expressed through the mass media and thus reached a large, and apparently receptive, audience.

Popular entertainers are often very perceptive individuals who mirror the frustrations and expectations of certain segments of the populace and who reflect upon and occasionally analyze major social concerns. The entertainer is not completely unique. When he expresses himself, he is bound to say what others have been thinking. But he also plays the role, however unwittingly, of a spokesman, "putting it all together" for people and articulating their unspoken thoughts and feelings. As Joan Baez proclaimed, "Bobby Dylan says what a lot of people my age feel but cannot say."

Popular entertainers such as Dylan also served as life-style models. The way they looked and acted and what they thought often set the standard for the less-than-famous participants of the life-style rebellion. This tendency of entertainers to become models of appearance and behavior represented perhaps the greatest contribution of popular culture to the life-style rebellion. It is one thing to speak in generalities about the assault on the American Way of Life; it is quite another to say here is James Dean or Lenny Bruce or Bob Dylan. By simply looking at these individuals, young people could see the end results of the quest for alternative life-styles.

Popular artists such as Dean, Kerouac, Bruce, and Dylan were, in essence, the vanguard of the life-style rebellion. Aside from their natural artistic inclinations, these four members of the avant-garde had much in common. They all had personal adjustment problems, and they all exhibited varying degrees of distaste for institutional religion, formal education, and other dominant features of the American Way of Life. As seekers of alternative life-styles, they also found inspiration in the subcultures of the "underground" and the outsider. The cultures of blacks, Jews, American Indians, poor Southern whites, drug addicts, juvenile delinquents, and political radicals all had important influences on the vanguard of the life-style rebellion, and on many of the others in the movement.

From the fifties to the late sixties, popular culture played a vital role in reflecting and shaping the life-style rebellion. The rise of rebel heroes such as James Dean; the emergence of rock 'n' roll and the youth consciousness it spawned; the critiques of the Affluent Society formulated by the Beat Generation writers, *Mad* magazine, and social satirists such as Mort Sahl and Lenny Bruce; and the statements of social protest and personal alienation articulated by Bob Dylan and the numerous rock groups of the sixties represented some of the major manifestations of the assault on the American Way of Life. By the late sixties, popular culture declined somewhat in its significance to the life-style rebellion, in part because the rapid pace and sheer magnitude of events seemed to surpass the capabilities of popular culture to keep up, but also because the major patterns of thought and behavior had already been expressed. As Beat Generation poet Gregory Corso observed in 1967, "the hippies are acting out what we wrote."

SECTION FOUR:
THE FUTURE
OF POPULAR
CULTURE

It is 1988. The United States, thank heavens, passed through 1984 without Big Brother's gimlet eyes peering into our living rooms. Actually, the technology of communication has advanced far beyond Orwell's fictional vision of telecommunications. Our 1988 homes are standardly built to accommodate the most sophisticated hardware of mass communications, devices that were in the research laboratories only ten years ago in the late 1970s. It's hard to remember the old days before we had MOTHER, political scientist Douglass Cater's ingenious acronym for "Multiple Output Telecommunication Home End Resources."

Wasn't it great when laser technology changed our television "screens" into three-dimensional facsimiles of reality? Will you ever forget that historic night in 1983 when we could watch Archie and Edith Bunker in holographic three dimension? In 1988 we take it for granted that we can give the powers that be in holocasting a direct feedback on what kinds of programs we like, simply by using the digital device on our sets.

And how about the nifty computer hookup the Federal Telecommunications Agency worked out a couple of years ago with the Library of Congress? Junior has never been so intrigued with learning new information. . . .

Perhaps this all sounds like a science-fiction scenario of the future of popular culture, but it need not be. In the laboratories of our leading communications firms, what may be the most important development in mass communications has been under vigorous research for years. The use of fiber optics is almost ready for a revolutionary application in telecommunications. Using light instead of electricity as the medium for transmitting voice, video, and computer data, it will replace copper wire with a strand of glass as slender as a human hair. Laser experts believe it will be possible in the next few years to send 4,000 simultaneous phone messages through a single strand. A bundle of optical fibers the diameter of a pencil will be able to carry hundreds of thousands of calls and at the same time transmit 100, 200, or more television programs.

To be sure, it is not quite that simple. Even though scientists and engineers are coming up with technological innovations at a surprising pace, the utilization of these breakthroughs will take time. We tend to underestimate the complexities of innovations. So, maybe MOTHER won't be in our living rooms until 1998 or 2008, instead of the optimistic speculation of 1988.

One of the main problem areas remains in the legal and political arena. The cable television people and the three big networks have been battling over marketing control for years. Still, if the

Laser Beam over Los Angeles. Laser technology will permit radical new developments in communciations.
UPI Photo

Federal Communications Commission, which up to now has banned the use of telephone outlets for cable television, were to change its position, the revolution of two-way video communication could quickly follow.

Actually, the two-way communications network that the prophets of the future predict has already started. We do have a worldwide telephone system that has been in place for the last ten years. Already, the world has been divided into nine numbering zones with a maximum of twelve digits for world telephone numbers. In the United States we already have four "gateway" cities to route worldwide messages—White Plains, New York; New York City; Miami; and Oakland, California.

Despite the glaring political and legal problems that must be solved before we have a true two-way communications system, there is some hope that it will develop before long. For example, passage of the new copyright laws of October 1976, which established fair prices to be paid by cable television operators to the Bell System, was one such positive step in this direction.

The Communications Satellite Act of 1962 was another important milestone, for it spurred the development of the Communications Satellite System. Within a year the International Telecommunications Satellite Organization, Intelsat, also had been developed. Intelsat is now in its fourth generation of communication satellites and the fifth generation is on the planning boards.

Already Intelsat has had a revolutionary effect on the poorer nations. With the use of satellites, a thirty-foot disc antenna, and membership in Intelsat, an emerging country can literally leap into the twentieth century. India started its first program a couple of years ago, linking 5,000 villages into an educational broadcasting system that stressed the subjects of birth control, agriculture, reading, and writing. Intelsat will soon provide domestic television systems, both educational and entertainment, for vast areas of Indonesia and Brazil. One satellite, one major transmitting station, and a large number of low-cost receiving stations can do much to transform a nation.

While the use of satellites will play an extremely important role in the emerging nations, we in the United States are one level higher in the communications revolution. We have the hardware available for cable television, and because we are a wired nation, we are approaching the first level for an SRS (Subscriber Response System).

In our wired nation, most futurologists envision two steps in our evolution into actual two-way communication systems. The first, as we have noted, will evolve around the touch-tone dial system and the telephone network. As fiber optics, using laser transmission, come into use, the channels available to the

home subscriber will increase a hundredfold. Then, using their home computers, home subscribers will code their individual interests into a computer console and receive only the entertainment and information that interests them. As Alvin Toffler has pointed out, this will in effect spell the end of the *mass media* as we know them today. We will be breaking away from the homogenized product of the three major networks into an era of individualized communications.

In this second level we will have complete information handling service. There will be two-way audio, video, and data capability. Our homes will be linked with schools, hospitals, libraries;

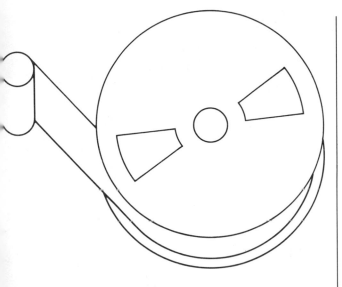

there will be home printers to print individualized newspapers or business information—whatever we as individuals desire. With optical fibers as the key, we will be able to browse through Macy's or Sears Roebuck from our homes, hear lectures and participate in a university class from Oxford or Berkeley, even bring the office to our home through a computer terminal and wall-sized video screen.

Maybe all of this sounds too utopian or like a wish-fulfilling fantasy of the future. But it truly is feasible, unless we allow the future to be stolen from us. There is no inexorable force pulling us into a future society that combines the worst aspects of Orwell's *1984* and Al-

dous Huxley's *Brave New World*.

Will we fully utilize the new communications vistas that technology can offer? If history repeats itself, we may indeed fail to make use of these new opportunities for the enrichment that the technological breakthroughs we've discussed can provide for us.

Along with Erik Barnouw, we must wonder who will be the "gatekeepers" of the evolving communications systems of the future. Will we have concentrated authority in government, or will individuals exercise their powerful democratic mandate? Will the many channels offered provide a diversity of choice, or will they only proliferate the present condition where the media are rivals in conformity? These are some of the imponderables we face in the inevitable telecommunications revolution and the computer network data banks that the next few decades will bring.

In the essays that follow, two writers who look at the future, Kas Kalba and Erik Barnouw, are quasi-optimistic, whereas R.A. Lafferty and Shepherd Mead have deep reservations about the future of popular culture in this country. As in many debates over the past, present or future effects of popular culture in our society, one is again reminded of Alfred North Whitehead's rational observation: "There are no whole truths; all truths are half-truths. It is trying to treat them as whole truths that plays the devil."

In only three decades since it began to be marketed widely, television has surpassed all previous forms of popular culture as a "time-filler" for the American people. Its social implications, almost from the beginning, became more wide reaching than any forecaster of the early 1950s could have prophesied. Quickly, it altered family communication, the way children are socialized, the urban environment, and many other facets of our daily lives. Whether its total effect has been for good or bad is the source of continuing debate.

However, we have only begun to utilize this electronic *wunderkind*, according to Professor Kas Kalba. It will soon be far more than a passive spectator device gluing us to the tube while the Minnesota Vikings make a desperation stand on the three yardline against the Dallas Cowboys or Archie Bunker berates the entire ethnic spectrum. The Electronic Community envisioned by Kalba will use television in a way in which we may all directly engage in the "act of learning, shopping, voting and working." In fact, he is optimistic that this kind of Electronic Community can enhance the quality of our lives, and in this essay he explains why.

The Electronic Community
Kas Kalba

There is more (and not less) to television than meets the eye. Television . . . affects not only our senses through its programming and our pocketbooks through its commercials, but also our entire social and cultural environment. The technology of television affects, and is affected by, the culture of television, which in turn has an impact on overall social change.

More specifically, [this] essay represents an attempt to speculate about the future of television. The future that will be considered is not that of television alone but of related emerging technologies as well, especially those associated with cable television. For if the recent projections of both equipment manufacturers and social visionaries are accurate, the TV household of today is soon to be transformed into a supermarket of electronic gadgetry, connected to the outside world by the electronic highway of cable communications.

According to these projections, tomorrow's household will contain a facsimile copier to capture the day's news; a remote learning and shopping terminal; a videotape recorder for delayed playback of entertainment and cultural programming; special terminals to give access to computational services, bank accounts and office files; a wall-size TV screen for viewing abstract art or baseball games; monitoring systems that will prevent burglaries and heart attacks; a television camera for two-way video conferences; and a variety of other communications services and devices. The role of electronics in American life, which has already adapted to the telegraph, the telephone, the record player, and the TV set, will have been extended *ad infinitum*, and, some would add, *ad absurdum*.

As one cartoonist has already depicted, the human anatomy may have to be considerably modified merely to cope with this new technological outpouring. The eyes and ears will expand in proportion to the increased sensory input at their disposal. The hands will grow additional fingers to be able to push all the buttons. Legs will shrink and atrophy while the rump quadruples in size, since there will be little need for walking or traveling. This cynical caricature of humanity adapting to technology's needs (rather than the converse) may hold considerable truth and serve as an appropriate epitaph to our captivation by technology's unbridled progress.

Yet there is another vision of the impact that the new electronic media will have on our social and community structure. After all, the services that will become available over the home communications consoles of tomorrow may merely supplement rather than replace those that are already available today. They may do away with the inconveniences of having to write a letter in order to make a reservation or of having to watch a television program at a pre-scheduled time. They may expand our choice with respect to shopping goods, jobs, political viewpoints, and cultural or educational amenities. They may increase our access to medical and social services. And they may diminish our reliance on the automobile for personal mobility, thereby decreasing traffic congestion, air pollution, and energy consumption in a single swoop.

It is difficult to choose between these two perspectives of our communications future. One appeals to our long-standing faith in technological betterment, the other to our growing disenchantment with this belief. However, the two perspectives converge in one respect—they both foresee the emergence of a new communications environment that will alter our lives as members of families, as consumers, as citizens, and as

cultural beings.... They both raise profound issues concerning the evolution of our "electronic community," issues that television critics and policy makers have hardly begun to contemplate....

Tomorrow's Electronic Community

The last area of social and economic activity that the local neighborhood continues to dominate is the provision of community services. For most households it remains the locus of the school, the police and the fire precinct, the access road, and the garbage pickup. In some instances it is still the place where commercial and professional services are provided—for instance, banking, newspaper delivery, shopping, and medical services. But it is also this area of community services that is being prospected by the proponents of the new communications technologies. As television matures into the home communications center of tomorrow, they argue, it will be able to deliver many of these same services directly to the home.

How will this extension of television's traditional powers occur? From a technological point of view, this question can be answered in a relatively straightforward manner. (The answer in terms of social impact is, as I will suggest further below, more complicated.) In essence, the new communications media will extend television's capabilities in the following ways:

1. *Channel Abundance*: Today's cable television systems are mandated by FCC regulation to carry 20 television channels. Some systems already have the capability to transmit over 30 channels, and more could be added in the future if needed. The point is that it is now possible to transmit more television to the home than simply by the over-the-air channels that are available in a given locality. Viewers can become more selective about when or what they watch.

2. *Audience Divisibility*: Programmers can also be more selective about who they reach. Through multiple head ends or special con-

verter and scrambler devices, and ultimately through computer addressing of programs, programmers will be able to pinpoint the specific audience (by income, ethnicity, neighborhood, special interests, etc.) that they are most interested in reaching. Early forms of this capability are currently in operation in pay television experiments, medical programming for physicians, and local-origin programs that are aimed at a specific community rather than an entire metropolitan area.

3. *Display Alternatives*: Programmers will not be limited to transmitting video messages alone. The augmented television terminals of tomorrow will be capable of receiving a variety of data, sound, and video messages, including stop-frame displays of print, facsimile, stereo sound, and large-screen television. Various hybrid communication forms will undoubtedly emerge, involving simultaneously or in sequence still pictures, moving images, captions, textual printouts, or supplementary sound tracks.

4. *Feedback Mechanisms*: Some of the home devices will allow for inputs as well as outputs. The consumer or a surrogate (e.g., his electricity meter or home burglar alarm) will be able to send messages back to the programming source, eliciting particular programs, registering opinions, or responding to questions regarding his banking transactions, shopping needs, or knowledge of early American history. Home response mechanisms are likely to be limited to data and possibly voice communication. However, full-scale two-way video conferences may also be feasible on a limited basis, for example, between businesses or institutions.

5. *Storage Capability*: Finally, both programmer and viewer will have access to increased storage capability. Data banks tied to the programmer will monitor and record various transactions between the viewer and the programmer, storing these for future reference. The viewer, on the other hand, will be able to record television programs on video cassettes (or to acquire them directly in that form) for playback at a convenient time. In fact, repeated and selective playback will be possible, as a result of which television will function more like the audio record or the book and less like a mass broadcasting system.

These are some of the capabilities that will be introduced by the new communications media, in particular by cable communications and a variety of ancillary technological developments. All of these capabilities are available in the laboratory today, and most of them are already being tested in selected areas. The questions that remain are how rapidly will these developments permeate our society and how desirable are they? What is no longer uncertain, however, is that in the future, whether five or ten or fifteen years from now, television will affect virtually all aspects of our daily lives.

The days of television as a spectator activity, during which we passively witness the unfolding of a Sunday afternoon football game, a light comedy serial, a Geritol psychodrama, or a national political convention, will be replaced by a television through which we directly engage in the act of learning, shopping, voting, and working. . . .

The Future of Television
Television has already passed through several phases of transformation and is likely to continue doing so. It has become a complex

"The days of television as a spectator activity... will be replaced by a television through which we directly engage in the act of learning, shopping, voting, and working."

social innovation, one that cannot be defined solely by its technical parameters, or by static concepts of economic demand. Both old and new technical properties of television interact with changes in business markets, government decisions, and social or cultural needs and preferences.

And the medium will continue to evolve in the future. But in what ways? How will the transition from today's mass medium to tomorrow's electronic community be accomplished?

One way in which television will evolve—and is, in fact, already evolving—is in the direction of more "selective" communications services. It should be noted in this regard that television viewing patterns have changed considerably over the past ten years. The typical household no longer has only one TV set. Various economic factors have encouraged this new multiple set household to come into being, including increased discretionary income, the reduction in the price of TV sets, and the availability of color television. At the same time the more individualistic viewing pattern that has resulted has been caused by, and has as well contributed to, several larger social transformations, including the disappearance of traditional local forms of recreation (e.g., bars, neighborhood theaters, social clubs) and the fragmentation of entertainment and information pursuits within the family. . . .

The advent of multi-channel cable television and of pay television will reinforce this trend, already apparent at the margins of broadcast television (i.e., UHF stations, morning and late-evening programs, etc.), toward a more selective utilization of the medium. The viewer of tomorrow will have greater choice about when a program can be viewed, what that program is, and the manner in which television can be responsive to his or her needs. Cultural, educational, and other forms of nonentertainment programming will begin to flourish.

At the same time, the fragmentation in television viewing resulting from this increased selectivity is likely to have social and cultural consequences. If viewers watch sports or local news instead of national news, this may affect our level of national integration, in which television as a mass medium has played a major role. If viewers are drawn more and more to programs that correspond to their minority tastes, whether cultural, ethnic, or life-style related, this may create social, economic and possibly political tensions. And if within a given household TV viewing becomes highly individualistic, the nuclear family will experience further strains, leading possibly to a transformation of its current functions. . . .

As the time approaches when television will not only affect our spare time but our everyday activities, its significance as a communications medium will also change. Television will no longer be solely a purveyor of consumer products and social relaxation. More and more it will become a total communications environment, as complex and variegated as the offices, schools, department stores and neighborhood parks, where our social and economic activities take place today. Increasingly important portions of our community life will occur on television, through television, or as a result of television and the other emerging electronic media.

The electronic community that will be created will at times enhance community life as we know it today and at times undermine it; more often than not it will compete with it for our attention, our response, our resources and values. As we have already seen, television today is capable of heightening our concern about safety in the streets; tomorrow it may substitute for much of our need to use these streets as community spaces. Television has already started to short-circuit our schools and political institutions by creating a more palatable and accessible electronic medium for the consumption of educational and political imagery. Tomorrow it may replace these institutions by interactive, multi-media linkages between central data banks and dispersed subscribers. And, as Martin Pawley has recently suggested, it may lead to the further privatization of both family life and national identity. The community of today may become a museum, a mere archaeological referent for new electronically-supported life-styles and social institutions.

The Luddites would, of course, prefer to shatter the electronic community before it is too late. The espousers of technological utopia see its arrival as a new level of human evolution. Both, however, recognize that the most phenomenal aspect of the electronic community is its developmental pace. In less than a quarter century its foundations have been ubiquitously laid throughout our society. In another quarter century it may become the predominant environment in which we live.

In short, the challenge of ensuring that the electronic community enhances the quality of life and encourages active and equitable involvement in this new community sphere cannot be underemphasized. Our recent experience with the physical and social environment in which we currently live has hopefully shattered our naiveté concerning how a convivial yet complex living environment is brought into being. The naiveté of the business firm that claims it is only adding a new product or technology to the marketplace; the naiveté of government that formulates its policies in response to short-term political pressures rather than long-range communications priorities; the naiveté of the systems planner or engineer who believes that a neatly-drawn blueprint can anticipate the needs of a dynamic, pluralistic society; and the naiveté of the citizen who leaves decision-making about the future up to others until that future impinges on his doorstep: these are not adequate postures for the building of a new communications environment.

A few years ago the noted American critic Michael Novak was watching television in a large hut in a Vietnam village. The room was full of Vietnamese adults and children looking at "Batman," "Matt Dillon," and other popular shows. He wanted to tell them that what they were viewing surely didn't represent *any* place in America. Knowing that not even the creators of such shows lived in such worlds, he wondered whose *real world* television actually represents.

Shepherd Mead, in this excerpt from his book, *How to Get to the Future Before It Gets to You*, probably has asked himself the same question, but with a little different twist. Unlike Professor Kalba, Mead is not so hopeful that television can or will change in the future. The technology, after all, already exists that could make television into far more than a purveyor of banal soap operas, game shows, old movies, a medium aiming at the largest common denominator most of the time.

But as long as the commercial media moguls can squelch the growth of cable TV, the future of Kalba's Electronic Community lies in doubt. The commercial television broadcasters may rightly be afraid that cable TV will make them lose money. But the real losers are the American people, Mead believes. His hope for the future: Elect people who will make the laws that enable TV to change.

The Untouchable Wonders
Shepherd Mead

We are all being walked over, bamboozled, and swindled out of a heritage. We have built an incredible playhouse and forum and fountain of knowledge as big as the whole earth, and we've filled it with spit and garbage.

And there *is* something we can do about it. We are going to have to make it a strong political issue. It is not enough to have a little committee sitting over at the Federal Communications Commission. We are going to have to elect representatives to give the air to us—the citizens—even if we have to pass amendments to the Constitution to do it.

We need the air, and the space above the air, and the ground under it, because now we can use them all. The wonders of our electronics are bound to increase and multiply, but at this moment we have the technical know-how to do almost anything we can imagine. The only thing stopping us is a monstrous tangle of political and corporate red tape and finagling, all of it ever so legal. Legal means laws, and in a democracy laws can be changed by the people, by us.

What can be done now, using today's technology, has been outlined by Peter Goldmark, the wide-ranging genius who invented the long-playing record, a color television system, and about 158 other things. He was for many years head of the CBS laboratories.

The main key to the wonders, says Gold-mark, is broad-band communication, which includes cable television. We're now using, in more than 5 million homes already wired for cable TV, the old coaxial cable, which can carry about a thousand times more information than a telephone line. And we already have wave guides, hollow tubes that can hold many times that, and in experimental form flexible glass-fiber channels, or "light pipes," through which lasers can haul an almost infinite amount of electronic bits, enough for thousands of television or phonavision channels.

But let's go back to the old Model-T coaxial cables. Here is what is technically possible today, has been possible for years, and is probably as politically and bureaucratically impossible now and for perhaps decades to come as would be a weekend on the dog star. You could have twelve or more television channels, even including local TV, which comes in only over the wire, and some that could be piped in from anywhere, say, the BBC, or television from satellites, piped directly from the system's ground antenna to you; also, a professional TV channel especially for you, if you're a doctor or a public official; educational channels to which you could react or respond; a printer which could give you the daily paper or sports or market results, or even print out personal letters to you; a "frame grabber" which will make an instant print of any image on the television; access to special programs, such as a championship fight or game or a Broadway first night.

The two-way facility would enable you to order things from a store, perhaps directly from a shopping program, which would show you the items; take part in public opinion polls, or give your opinion (thumbs up or down) on the program you're watching; be warned of fire or burglary; have meters read; or even be able to make sure (if you're away) that your lights or water are turned off, and if not, to turn them off. And, of course,

you'll have better-quality reception in all these than you now have from broadcasts.

The whole system would be connected to a computer, which any subscriber could query for information. It is technically possible for each of us to have a complete computer terminal, with the whole Telex-type keyboard, and display tube, but it would be expensive. Peter Goldmark suggests a simple and much cheaper substitute, a sort of "twenty questions" gadget, with just a few buttons, perhaps on the TV set. It would be, he says, like "choosing from a menu. With each incoming frame the user is asked to choose one of several alternatives (up to ten) to define more precisely the information he wants. For example, if he were seeking travel information, he would with the first frame indicate whether he wanted to go by airplane, train, bus, or taxicab. The second frame (if he chose, say, air travel) would enable him to specify what airport he would use. The process would continue until the user had before him on his television screen the schedule of all airline flights of interest." He could press his "frame-grabber" at any stage and have all the information printed, in his hand, within perhaps a minute or two after pushing the first button.

Dr. Goldmark goes further (still keeping well within our present technology) and suggests three kinds of cable (or other broad-band) networks, the first similar to the one just described, and organized into neighborhood subcenters of perhaps 3,000 to 15,000 homes, with local services and information.

The second would be another broad-band "pipe" carrying "the equivalent of 30 television channels in both directions. It would interconnect the major public institutions of the city, such as health, education, or emergency services."

As an example of what this could accomplish, the Massachusetts General Hospital in Boston is now connected by two-way television with a Veterans Administration Hospital in Bedford, seventeen miles away.

Consultation via Television. Doctors at Massachusetts General Hospital use television for consultation with doctors at another hospital.
Dan Bernstein/Massachusetts General Hospital

Specialists in Boston can examine patients in Bedford, read electrocardiograms, examine X rays, and so on, and give immediate advice. In the future, vast remote areas like parts of Alaska, northern Canada, Brazil, Africa, or the Australian outback could all be linked by broad-band communications and satellite with medical centers, giving advice to local doctors or even to nurses and partially qualified medical assistants. No new technology is needed, just money, work, and the cutting of miles of red tape.

The third network would represent what Dr. Goldmark calls the city's "sensory nerves," sending information to administrative centers on weather, pollution, traffic, the location of ambulances or fire engines or other emergency vehicles, and so on. Of course, most of this is now done to some extent by telephone, but the cable would expand the services greatly.

But possibly the most valuable use of the broad-band system, supplemented probably by domestic satellite, would be in education.

If all these wonders are possible now, why can't we have them? In a very good and often angry book Brenda Maddox explains why we can't, in convincing detail. Every legislator, and, in fact, every concerned citizen, should read it [*Beyond Belief: New Directions in Communications*, New York: Beacon, 1974].

Incredible as it sounds cable TV has been for all practical purposes excluded from almost every major city in the United States.

"There has been," says Mrs. Maddox, "a greater choice of television in northern Vermont or Montana than there is in Boston and Pittsburgh. . . . The tough restrictions of the FCC have kept cable television from selling its most desirable product—out of town television programs—in the 100 biggest television markets. . . . The great information medium of tomorrow, in other words, has been excluded from cities larger than Augusta, Maine."

The villain, of course, as Mrs. Maddox makes clear, is not just the FCC, but also all those people who are afraid that cable TV will make them lose money—especially the commercial television broadcasters. They're afraid it will reduce their audiences, and they've fought it bitterly.

In fact, the FCC became one of the villains by trying, earlier, to be a hero. When our UHF television was developed, it meant there could be more television channels than with the old longer wavelengths. The well-meaning but slightly addled FCC rushed in to encourage local people to set up their own UHF television stations, as an addition to the standard network fare.

Doesn't that sound reasonable, and idealistic, and totally good? But as any broadcaster could have told them, very few local groups can afford to do the kind of programming on a full-time basis that even their neighbors would want to watch. They could give local services and information, but the entertainment often rotted down to ancient movies. Many of the UHF stations went bankrupt, and the FCC, feeling guilty for encouraging them, tried to help. Part of that help was to fight cable TV, which they felt might be the final straw to break UHF's back.

The commercial networks were happy to join the FCC in jumping on cable TV, and the whole battle was almost like a gang war, with the cables coming out last. Their biggest stronghold is New York City, and that's largely because of all the tall buildings. In many parts of New York you can't get a decent picture without a cable. But even in New York programs produced in another city—even nearby Philadelphia or Boston—cannot be brought in by cable.

The other major possibility is the communications satellite, and it is being hogtied almost as efficiently as cable TV.

There are really two uses of a communications satellite, and at the moment we're concentrating on just one—as a substitute for ocean cables. . . .

The whole earth can now be reached by the Intelsat satellites. According to my information from Comsat Laboratories, four of the big new *Intelsat IV's*, weighing over six-

teen hundred pounds each, are in position over the Atlantic, Pacific, and Indian oceans, each capable of handling twelve television channels or more than three thousand telephone calls at once. There are also several of the smaller No. III's in orbit. All of them are used primarily for telephone service and occasional television relays. And there is no question that larger and more efficient ones will be developed.

However, it's the second use of satellites that should be far more important in the future, because it's something that perhaps *only* a satellite can do—to spread information to every remote corner of the world. Used together with local cable systems, they could do almost anything we can imagine.

At the moment, the Intelsats send only to the big-dish antennae at the Intelsat ground stations, but new transmitters already developed will enable them to send to much smaller installations and eventually to home antennae. For example, in the educational television system now being planned for India . . . villages will be able to build their own antennae out of chicken wire for as little as twenty-five dollars—and receive the signal coming from 22,300 miles away!

Satellites now orbit directly above oceans to connect continents, but the great satellites of the future will hover above continents to connect people.

Probably the first plan to do this was prepared by an American, Fred Friendly, for the Ford Foundation, back in 1966. He said there should be a domestic satellite, and it should be owned by the public. (In fact, it is amazing that *all* satellites are not at least 90 percent owned by the public, because it was the public, through taxes, who paid almost all the cost of development, as part of the multibillion-dollar space program. The greatest cost, of course, was the development of the rockets to put them up there.) This publicly owned satellite, Friendly suggested, could transmit the commercial television programs—could do it for less than they were

"...the great satellites of the future will hover above continents to connect people."

328

paying for wire transmission—and make enough money to pay for educational and other noncommercial programming, which it could then broadcast to local town antennae and rebroadcast to the whole country, free.

It was too good to be true, or to be allowed. One problem was that the FCC was already considering proposals by the American Broadcasting Company to put up its own satellite. Brenda Maddox, who does a superb documentation of the whole satellite-throttling tragedy, says, "The practical effect of the Ford plan, in fact, was to paralyze the FCC by making the issue seem even more complicated than it had originally."

The upshot of all this is that the United States has never had a domestic satellite, though at least two are now flying for other countries and broadcasting. On October 14, 1972, the Russians put up their *Molniya I*, a domestic satellite for their own people, which followed by about two weeks *Molniya II*, intended for world communications. And on November 9 NASA launched *ANIK-I* for Canada, capable of broadcasting ten channels of television, in both French and English, to all of Canada, including the vast and previously unreachable northern country. It will also make telephone communications possible from the U.S. border to the Arctic circle. . . .

We'll put them up for others, as we should, but our own people may be last. "After all, old boy, you can't step on all those toes, can you? Think what it would do to the ratings!"

American noncommercial television and educational channels will continue to limp along, begging for handouts, scrimping on programming, the ragged urchin of the world's richest country. There is no need to shackle commercial TV. The two can coexist, as they do peacefully in England or even as they do in most European countries where television is publicly run, but where paid commercial advertisements are inserted, usually in bunches, but never in the middle of a film, a play, or a concert. This is something that happens only to Americans.

Or, as a BBC viewer said to me after a visit to America, "Occasionally the advertising is interrupted by entertainment."

If we're going to get a future with really intelligent or informative television fare, and material for minority groups of all kinds, if we want something beyond the bland pudding we're getting now, then we're going to have to act like the citizens of a democracy and elect people who will make the laws to make it possible.

Our constitutional right of freedom of speech must, in the future, include the right of the free speech to reach us. At the moment we're like a man dropped to the bottom of a well and told that he may speak freely about anything.

Whatever new means of communication we develop—television, facsimile, holography, or anything else—must, like book publishing today, be open to all comers, to all intellectual ranges, and to all opinions. Because these media are expensive to use, it is going to take a lot of figuring, but it is going to have to be done. We cannot let new technologies be stopped because they may compete with some older system. Technically, we can now do almost anything—but we must be allowed to do it.

Our technology proliferates so fast that the "future shock" of today undoubtedly will be eclipsed by systems being prepared for tomorrow. As Alvin Toffler has pointed out, those who do not study the future will be forced to endure it, and merely being hopeful will be of small avail.

One relevant anxiety about the future concerns our constant bombardment by thousands of would-be persuasive messages each week. In a mass-mediated society, as we have seen throughout this book, we are the target of pitch-men of all persuasions. When truth stands in the way of their messages, they employ what George Orwell, in his classic *1984*, termed "new-speak." Thus, when held to a stalemate in a highly unpopular war in Vietnam, we decide to quit, President Nixon calls this action a "disengagement." When this doesn't jibe with previous statements, his press secretary newspeaks them away with the term "inoperative."

If the powerful force of the mass media continues to be used manipulatively and cynically, what does it portend for Americans in the year 1984 or 2004? R.A. Lafferty, a leading science-fiction writer, deals precisely with this question in the following short story. Whether or not his vision of the sterile society is exaggerated, the danger from future mind-managers using the media is surely real and not just a science-fiction fantasy.

About a Secret Crocodile
R.A. Lafferty

There is a secret society of seven men that controls the finances of the world. This is known to everyone but the details are not known. There are some who believe that it would be better if one of those seven men were a financier.

There is a secret society of three men and four women that controls all the fashions of the world. The details of this are known to all who are in the fashion. And I am not.

There is a secret society of nineteen men that is behind all the fascist organizations in the world. The secret name of this society is Glomerule.

There is a secret society of thirteen persons known as the Elders of Edom that controls all the secret sources of the world. That the sources have become muddy is of concern to them.

There is a secret society of only four persons that manufactures all the jokes of the world. One of these persons is unfunny and he is responsible for all the unfunny jokes.

There is a secret society of eleven persons that is behind all Bolshevik and Atheist societies of the world. The devil himself is a member of this society, and he works tirelessly to become a principal member. The secret name of this society is Ocean.

There are related secret societies known as The Path of the Serpent (all its members have the inner eyelid of snakes), The Darkbearers, the Seeing Eye, Imperium, The Golden Mask and the City.

Above most of these in a queer network there is a society that controls the attitudes and dispositions of the world—and the name of it is Crocodile. The Crocodile is insatiable: it eats persons and nations alive. And the Crocodile is very old, 8809 years old by one account, 7349 years old if you use the short chronology.

There are subsecret societies within the Crocodile: the Cocked Eye, the Cryptic Cootie and others. Powerful among these is a society of three hundred and ninety-nine persons that manufactures all the catchwords and slogans of the world. This subsociety is not completely secret since several of the members are mouthy: the code name of this apparatus is the Crocodile's Mouth.

Chesterton said that Mankind itself was a secret society. Whether it would be better or worse if the secret should ever come out he did not say.

And finally there was—for a short disruptive moment—a secret society of three persons that controlled all.

All what?

Bear with us. That is what this account is about.

John Candor had been called into the office of Mr. James Dandi at ABNC. (Whisper, whisper, for your own good, do not call him Jim Dandy; that is a familiarity he will not abide.)

"This is the problem, John," Mr. Dandi stated piercingly, "and we may as well put it into words. After all, putting things into words and pictures is our way of working at ABNC. Now then, what do we *do* at ABNC, John?"

(ABNC was one of the most powerful salivators of the Crocodile's Mouth.)

"We create images and attitudes, Mr. Dandi."

"That is correct, John," Mr. Dandi said. "Let us never forget it. Now something has gone wrong. There is a shadowy attack on us that may well be the most damaging thing since the old transgression of Spirochaete himself. Why has something gone wrong with our operation, John?"

"Sir, I don't know."

"Well then, *what* has gone wrong?"

"What has gone wrong, Mr. Dandi, is that it isn't working the way it should. We are caught on our own catchwords, we are slaughtered by our own slogans. There are boomerangs whizzing about our ears from every angle. None of it goes over the way it is supposed to. It all twists wrong for us."

"Well, what is causing this? Why are our effects being nullified?"

"Sir, I believe that somebody else is also busy creating images and attitudes. Our catechesis states that this is impossible since we are the only group permitted in the field. Nevertheless, I am sure that someone else is building these things against us. It even seems that they are more powerful than we are—and they are unknown."

"They cannot be more powerful than we are—and they must not remain unknown to us." Mr. Dandi stabbed. "Find out who they are, John."

"How?"

"If I knew how, John, I would be working for you, not you working for me. Your job is to do things. Mine is the much more difficult one of telling you to do them. Find out, John."

John Candor went to work on the problem. He considered whether it was a linear, a set or a group problem. If it were a linear problem he should have been able to solve it by himself—and he couldn't. If it were a set problem, then it couldn't be solved at all. Of necessity he classified it as a group problem and he assembled a group to solve it. This was easy at ABNC which had more group talent than anybody.

The group that John Candor assembled was made up of August Crayfish, Sterling Groshawk, Maurice Cree, Nancy Peters,

Tony Rover, Morgan Aye, and Betty Mc-Cracken. Tell the truth, would you be able to gather so talented a group in your own organization?

"My good people," John Candor said, "as we all know, something has gone wrong with our effects. It must be righted. Thoughts, please, thoughts!"

"We inflate a person or subject and he bursts on us," August gave his thought. "Are we using the wrong gas?"

"We launch a phrase and it turns into a joke," Sterling complained. "Yet we have not slighted the check-off: it has always been examined from every angle to be sure that it doesn't have a joker context. But something goes wrong."

"We build an attitude carefully from the ground up," Maurice stated. "Then our firm ground turns boggy and the thing tilts and begins to sink."

"Our 'Fruitful Misunderstandings,' the most subtle and effective of our current devices, are beginning to bear sour fruit," Nancy said.

"We set ourselves to cut a man down and our daggers turn to rubber," Tony Rover moaned. (Oh, were there ever sadder words? Our daggers have turned to rubber.)

"Things have become so shaky that we're not sure whether we are talking about free or closed variables," Morgan gave his thought.

"How can my own loving mother make such atrocious sandwiches?" Betty Mc-Cracken munched distastefully. Betty, who was underpaid, was a brown-sack girl who brought her own lunch. "This is worse than usual." She chewed on. "The only thing to do with it is feed it to the computer." She fed it to the computer which ate it with evident pleasure.

"Seven persons, seven thoughts," John Candor mused.

"Seven persons, six thoughts," Nancy Peters spat bitterly. "Betty as usual, has contributed nothing."

"Only the first stage of the answer," John Candor said. "She said 'The only thing to do with it is to feed it to the computer.' Feed the problem to the computer, folks."

They fed the problem to the computer by pieces and by wholes. The machine was familiar with their lingos and procedures. It was acquainted with the Non-Valid Context Problems of Morgan Aye and with the Hollow Shell Person Puzzles of Tony Rover. It knew the Pervading Environment Ploy of Maurice Cree. It knew what trick-work to operate within.

Again and again the machine asked for various kinds of supplementary exterior data.

"Leave me with it," the machine finally issued. "Assemble here again in sixty days, or hours, I always forget which is the longer period, and I will have answers."

"No, we want the answers right now," John Candor insisted, "within sixty seconds."

"The second is possibly the interval I was thinking of," the machine issued. "What's time to a tin can anyhow?" It ground its data trains for a full minute.

"Well?" John Candor asked.

"Somehow I get the number three," the machine issued.

"Three what, machine?"

"Three persons," the machine issued. "They are unknowingly linked together to manufacture attitudes. They are without program or purpose or organization or remuneration or basis or malice."

"Nobody is without malice," August Crayfish insisted in a startled way. "They must be totally alien forms then. How do

"The Disestablishment has been firmly established for these several hundred years and we hold it to be privileged. It must not be upset by these three randoms."

they manage their effects?"

"One with a gesture, one with a grimace, one with an intonation," the machine issued.

"Where are they?" John Candor demanded.

"All comparatively near," the machine issued, and it drew three circles on the city map. "Each is to be found in his own circle most of the time."

"Their names?" John Candor asked, and the machine wrote the name of each in the proper circle.

"Do you have anything on their appearances?" Sterling Groshawk inquired and the machine manufactured three kymograph pictures of the targets.

"Have you their addresses or identifying numbers?" Maurice Cree asked.

"No. I think it's remarkable of me that I was able to come up with this much," the machine issued.

"We can find them," Betty McCracken said. "We can most likely find them in the phone book."

"What worries me is that there's no malice in them," John Candor worried. "Without malice, there's no handle to get hold of a thing. The Disestablishment has been firmly established for these several hundred years and we hold it to be privileged. It must not be upset by these three randoms. We will do what we must do."

Mike Zhestovitch was a mighty man. One does not make the primordial gestures out of weak body and hands. He looked like a steel worker—or anyhow like a worker at one of the powerful trades. His torso was like a barrel but more notable than ordinary barrels. His arms and hands were hardly to be believed. His neck was for the bulls, his head was as big as a thirteen gallon firkin, his eyeballs were the size of ducks' eggs and the hair on his chest and throat was that heavy black wire-grass that defines steel plowshares. His voice—well he didn't have much of a voice—it wasn't as mighty as the rest of him.

And he didn't really work at one of the powerful trades. He was a zipper repairman at the Jiffy Nifty Dry Cleaners.

August Crayfish of ABNC located Mike Zhestovitch in the Blind Robbin Bar which (if you recall the way that block lies) is just across that short jog-alley from the Jiffy Nifty. And August recognized big Mike at once. But how did big Mike get his effects?

"The Cardinals should take the Colts today," a serious man there was saying.

"The Cardinals—" Mike Zhestovitch began in the voice that was less noble than the rest of him, but he didn't finish the sentence. As a matter of fact, big Mike had never finished a sentence in all his life. Instead he made the gesture with his mighty hands and body. Words cannot describe the gesture but it was something like balling up an idea or opinion in the giant hands and throwing it away, utterly away, over the very edge of contempt.

The Cardinals, of course, did not take the Colts that day. For a moment it was doubtful whether the Cardinals would survive at all. From the corner of the eye, red feathers could be seen drifting away in the air.

August Crayfish carefully waited a moment and watched. A man walked out of the Blind Robbin and talked to another man in that little jog-alley. From their seriousness it was certain that they were talking baseball.

"The Cardinals—" the first man said after a moment, and he also made the gesture. And seconds later a man playing eight-ball in the back of the Blind Robbin did the same thing.

August was sure then. Mike Zhestovitch not only could shrivel anything with the gesture, but the gesture as he used it was highly epidemic. It would spread, according to Schoeffler's Law of Dispersal, through the city in short minutes, through the world in short hours. And no opinion could stand against its disfavor. Mike Zhestovitch could wreck images and attitudes—and possibly he could also create them.

"Do you work alone?" August Crayfish asked.

"No. The rip-fix and the button-sew girls work in the same cubbyhole," Mike said with his curiously small voice.

"Do you know a Mary Smorfia?" August asked.

"I don't, no," Mike said, a certain comprehension coming into his ducks'-egg-sized eyes. "And you are glad that I don't? Then I will. I'll find out who she is. I see it now that you are a wrong guy and she is a right girl."

Then August Crayfish spoke the slogan that would be unveiled to the ears of the world that very night, a wonderfully slippery slogan that had cost a hundred thousand dollars to construct. It should have warned Mike Zhestovitch away from his mad resistance.

Mike Zhestovitch made the gesture, and the slogan was in ruins. And somewhere the Secret Crocodile lashed its tail in displeasure.

"Do you want to make a lot of money?" August Crayfish whispered after a long re-evaluation pause.

"Money—from such as you—" Big Mike didn't finish the sentence, he never did. But he made the gesture. The idea of a lot of money shriveled. And August Crayfish shriveled so small that he could not climb over the threshold of the Blind Robbin on the way out and had to be aided over it by the shod toe of a kind man. (This last statement is a literal exaggeration but it is the right direction.)

Nancy Peters of ABNC located Mary Smorfia in the King-Pin Bowling Alley, where she was a hamburger waitress and a beer buster. Mary was small, dark, unpretty (except for high-frequency eyes and the beautiful gash across her face that was her mouth), lively, smart, busy, a member of that aberrant variety of the human race that was called Italian.

"Snorting Summer should take the Academy Award," one nice guzzling lady at the counter was saying to another, "and Clover Elysée is the shoeless shoo-in for best actress of the year."

And Mary Smorfia made the grimace. Ah, it was mostly done with the beautifully large mouth and yet every part of her entered into it, from the blue lights in her hair to her crinkly toes. It was a devastating, all-destroying grimace. It gobbled up, it nullified and it made itself felt to a great distance. The nice guzzling lady had not even been looking toward Mary Smorfia but she felt the grimace like a soul shock, and she herself did the grimace with a wonderful distortion of the features that weren't made for it.

And the grimace swept everything like quick contagion or prairie fire. Snorting Summer—gah! Clover Elysée—guggling gah! Those things were finished forever, beyond laughter, below derision. And Nancy Peters of ABNC noted the powerful effect carefully, for the original words of the nice guzzling lady were the very words that ABNC had selected to be echoed a hundred million times whenever the awards were thought of.

"Do you work alone?" Nancy Peters asked Mary Smorfia.

"Kid, I am so fast they don't need anyone else on this shift. I'm like silly lightning."

"Did you ever think of becoming an actress, Mary?" Nancy asked in honey-tones.

"Oh, I made a commercial once," Mary said out of her curly gash-mouth (she had to be kidding: she couldn't really have a mouth that looked like that). "I don't know whether I sold much of my guy's soap but I bet I got a lot of people off that Brand X. Ashes it was, worse even, after I monkey-faced it. They say I'm a natural—but once is enough."

"Do you know a Mike Zhestovitch or a Clivendon Surrey?" Nancy asked.

"I don't think so," Mary said. "What league do they bowl in? I bet I will like them both, though, and I will remember their names and find them."

Nancy Peters was nervous. She felt that

"...somewhere the Secret Crocodile lashed his tail in displeasure and unease."

the annihilating grimace was about to strike again on Mary's lightning-gash mouth. But it was time for the test of strength. Nancy spoke the new slogan that had been selected for presentation to the world that very night, a wonderfully convincing and powerful slogan that should bring this random Mary Smorfia to heel if anything could. And she spoke it with all the absolute expertise of the Crocodile's Mouth behind her.

The Grimace! And the slogan was destroyed forever. And (grimacing horror turned inward) Nancy caught the contagion and was doing the grimace herself. She was quite unable to get the thing off her face.

This was sheer humiliation that overwhelmed the Nancy person, who had suddenly been made small. And somewhere the Secret Crocodile lashed its tail in displeasure and unease.

"Do you want to make twenty thousand dollars, Mary?" Nancy asked after she had returned from the jane where she had daubed her flushed face and cooled her flustered body.

"Twenty thousand dollars isn't very much," Mary Smorfia sounded out of her panoramic mouth. "I make eighty-eight fifty now after everything. I could make a lot more if I wanted to go along with the cruds."

"Twenty thousand dollars is very much more," Nancy Peters said enticingly.

"It is very much more cruddy, kid." Mary Smorfia grimaced. Grimaced! Not again! Nancy Peters fled in deflated panic. She felt herself dishonored forever.

Well, do you think it is all water-melon pickles and pepper relish, this unilaterally creating all the images and attitudes for the whole world? It isn't. It is a detailed and devious thing and the privileged Disestablishment had been building it for centuries. (The Establishment itself had been no more than a figure of speech for most of those centuries, a few clinging bits of bark: the heart of the tree had long been possessed by the privileged Disestablishment.) Three quick random persons could not be permitted to nullify words from the Mouth itself.

Morgan Aye of ABNC located Clivendon Surrey in Speedsters Café. Clivendon was a lank and fair-haired man with a sort of weariness about him, a worldiness that had to be generations old. He had the superior brow and the thoroughbred nose that isn't grown in short centuries. He had the voice, the intonation, the touch of Groton, the touch of Balliol, the strong touch of other institutions even more august. It was a marvelous voice, at least the intonation of it. Clivendon's employer once said that he didn't believe that Clivendon ever spoke in words, at least not in any words that he was ever able to understand. The intonation was really a snort, a sort of neigh, but it carried the cresting contempt of the ages in its tone. And it was contagious.

Clivendon was really of Swedish extraction and had come off a farm near Pottersville. He had developed that intonation for a role in a high-school play. He had liked it and he had kept it. Clivendon was a motorcycle mechanic at Downhillers' Garage.

"Do you work alone?" Morgan Aye asked Clivendon.

"Naeu. You work alone and you got to work. You work with a bunch and you can slip out from it," Clivendon intoned. Yes, he talked in words and the words could be mostly understood. But the towering intonation was the thing, the world-wilting contempt of the tone. This man was a natural and Morgan felt himself a foot shorter in the very presence of that tone.

"Do you know a Mike Zhestovitch or a Mary Smorfia?" Morgan asked fearfully.

"That's a funny thing." The tone cut through earwax and the soft spots of the spleen. "I had never heard of them but Mary Smorfia called me up not thirty minutes ago and said that she wanted both of us to meet Mike. So I'll meet them in about twenty minutes, as soon as the clock there says that I'm supposed to be off work at Downhillers' Garage."

"Don't meet them!" Morgan cried out violently. "That might be the closing of the link, the setting up of a league. It might be an affront to the Mouth itself."

The tone, the neigh, the snort, the sharp edge of a wordless intonation sent Morgan reeling back. And there were echoes of it throughout Speedsters' Café and in the streets outside. The tone was as contagious as it was cutting.

Morgan started to speak the newest selected slogan from the Mouth—and he stopped short. He was afraid of the test of strength. Two very expensive slogans had already been shattered today by these randoms. 'No malice in the three,' the computer had said and: 'without malice, there's no handle to get hold of a thing,' John Candor had stated. But somewhere, in that mountainous and contagious contempt of tone that belonged to Clivendon Surrey there had to be some malice. So Morgan Aye reached for what had always been the ultimate weapon of the Crocodile's Mouth. It always worked—it always worked if any malice at all existed in the object.

"How would you like to make five thousand dollars a week?" he whispered to Clivendon.

"What garage pays that much?" Clivendon asked in honest wonder. "I'm not that good a motorcycle mechanic."

"Five thousand dollars a week to work with us at ABNC," Morgan tempted. "We could use you in so many ways—that marvelous scorn to cut down any man we wished! You could lend the intonations of your voice to our—"

The neigh was like a thousand sea stallions breaking up from the depths. The snort was one that crumbles cliffs at the ends of the earth. Morgan Aye had gone ghastly white and his ears were bleeding from the transgression of that cutting sound. There were even some words in Clivendon's sounding—"Why, then I'd be one of the birds that picks the shreds of flesh from between the teeth of the monster." Then blinding hooting contempt in the tone, and Morgan Aye was in the street and running from it.

But the echoes of that intonation were everywhere in that part of town, soon to be all over the town, all over the world. It was an epidemic of snorting at the Crocodile's Mouth itself. Fools! Did they know that this was but one step from snorting at the very Crocodile?

The ring had closed. The informal league had formed now. The three randoms had met and united. The Mouth was affronted. Worse than that, all the outpour of the Mouth was nullified. The whole world was rejecting the catchwords that came from the Mouth, was laughing at them, was throwing them away with the uttermost gesture, was monkey-facing them, was snorting them down, was casting them out with bottomless contempt.

This was the short reign of the secret society of three, who did not know that they were secret. But in their day they closed the Mouth down completely. It was filled with mud and swamp reeds and rotting flesh.

The Secret Crocodile was lashing its tail with acute displeasure now. The Crocodile's Mouth had become quite nervous. And what of the little birds that fly in and out of that mouth, that preen the teeth and glean scraps of flesh and slogans and catchwords there? The birds were in quite an unhappy flutter.

"There is open conspiracy against us by a

secret society of three persons," Mr. James Dandi was saying, "and all the world abominates a secret society. We have this thing to do this day—to cripple it forever in its strength. Otherwise we will be cast out and broken as ineffectual instruments and the Crocodile will bring in strong persons from the Cocked Eye or the Cryptic Cootie to take our places. Surely we are not without resources. What is the logical follow-up to the Fruitful Misunderstanding?"

"The Purposive Accident," John Candor said immediately. John was sound on tactics.

"Take care of it, John," Mr. James Dandi said. "Remember, though, that he whose teeth we preen is the very bowels of compassion. I believe this is the salient thing in the world in our day, the Compassion of the Crocodile."

"Take care of it, people," John Candor said to his seven talented ones, "remembering always that the Crocodile is the very belly of compassion."

"Take care of it," the seven said to the computer, "always within the context of the jaws of compassion."

The computer programed a Purposive Accident to happen and manufactured such props as were needed. And the Purposive Accident was very well programed.

There was no great amount of blood poured out. No persons were killed except several uninvolved bystanders. The secret three were left alive and ambulant and scathed only at their points of strength.

It happened in the block between the Blind Robbin Bar and Speedsters' Café when all three members of the secret society happened to be walking together. The papers called it a bomb; they call everything a bomb that goes off like that. It was really a highly sophisticated homing device with a tripartite programing and it carried out its tripartite mission.

All three randoms, former members of the short-lived secret society, are well and working again. Mike Zhestovitch is no longer a zipper repair man (it takes two talented hands to fix those zippers), but he still works at the Jiffy Nifty Dry Cleaners. He runs one of those big pressers now which he can easily do with his powerful and undamaged left hand and his prosthetic right hand. But without his old right hand he can no longer make the contagious primordial gesture that once dumbfounded the Mouth and all its words. You just cannot make the big gesture with a false hand.

Mary Smorfia still works at the King-Pin Bowling Alley as hamburger waitress and beer buster. She is still small, dark, unpretty (except for her high-frequency eyes), lively, smart, and Italian. Her mouth is still a gash across her face, but now it is twice as great a gash as it used to be, and it no longer has its curled liveliness. Its mobility is all gone, it will no longer express the inexpressible, will no longer shatter a phrase or an attitude. Mary Smorfia is as she always was, except that now she is incapable of the famous grimace.

Clivendon Surrey is again a motorcycle mechanic at Downhillers' Garage and again he spends most of his time in Speedsters' Café. His vocal cords are gone, of course, but he gets by: he is able to speak with a throat microphone. But the famous intonation, the neigh, the destroying snort are all impossible for him.

The trouble is over with. Now again there is only one organization in the world to create the images and attitudes of the world. This insures that only the standard attitudes of the Disestablishment shall prevail.

In our opening catalog we forgot one group. There is another secret society in the world composed of the good guys and good gals. It has no name that we have ever heard except just the Good Guys and Good Gals. At the moment this society controls nothing at all in the world. It stirs a little, though. It may move. It may collide, someday, even with the Secret Crocodile itself.

As noted in the previous selections by Kas Kalba and Shepherd Mead, the enrichment of our leisure through major new uses of telecommunications is closer to actuality than most futurists would have deemed possible even a decade ago. If Mead wears the hat of a somewhat cynical realist, perhaps it's because he had spent much of his life writing ads on Madison Avenue before he defected from Persuasionville, U.S.A. He's not very optimistic that certain powerful interests who profit from the status quo want the American people to have as much choice in their popular culture as these new systems would provide. Still, there are other powerful groups, such as the computer industry, who stand to gain a lot.

Most Americans living today will partake in this Brave New World of telecommunications, unless a covey of twenty or thirty neutron bombs lofted by cruise missiles wipes out this planet in a few spectacular hours.

Our concluding essay is by Erik Barnouw, a distinguished analyst and historian of American mass media systems. Professor Barnouw is on the side of the optimists concerning the future of telecommunications. Nevertheless, he, too, is worried about the "software" aspects of this revolution, if and when it comes to pass. If someday we won't have to stir from our homes to go to the office or the department store and supermarket or the university classroom, what will we do with all this blessed leisure? Technology may well provide the breakthroughs to give us the gadgetry so excitingly described by Barnouw, but how we use it will, indeed, be the $64-million question.

So You Think TV Is Hot Stuff?
Erik Barnouw

Don't look now, but your television set is about to be replaced by something more up-to-date. As with many giant steps in technology, it will involve ideas that science-fiction people have been picturing for decades—in fact, for a century or so. Now, at last, in diverse laboratories and field tests, their visions are turning into practical hardware. The ingredients seem to be right at our hands.

Your television set, your stereo, your telephone are really quite primitive—"tom-toms" compared to what is now possible and inevitable, according to Peter C. Goldmark, the far-sighted retired chief of CBS Laboratories, responsible for many electronic breakthroughs.

A factor behind the euphoria is a development relating to cable television. This system has long been able to deliver 20 channels or more—a versatility impossible to over-the-air television—so far not at a sensational profit. Now it is about to be expanded further, in a fashion: it may soon offer a choice of hundreds of channels, along with another dramatic option—two-way communication, the chance to talk back.

The key to all this is a mysterious "optical

fiber," now emerging from the laboratory. This glass fiber looks like a thin violin string. Laser beams can travel through it and—incredibly—carry innumerable streams of communication simultaneously in both directions. Combine this virtuosity with various "miracles" already familiar to us—computers, satellites, cassettes, facsimile transmission—and what do you have? A "telecommunications" revolution, it would seem. What its social implications may be, is not clear. To Goldmark, it will be a momentous "democratizing" development, involving an unprecedented government-citizen dialogue. Others see it as opening a new era in education. Still others see it as a breakthrough for minority interests of all sorts, offering them a diversity of special channels.

There are also less optimistic opinions, but problems of use, in the view of most telecommunications technicians, are for later. They themselves are developing the "hardware." "Software" problems can be settled in due time by writers, teachers, performers, producers, graphic artists, musicians and so on—the software people, as they are known in telecommunications language. (Software people don't seem to care for this term. In fact, hardware and software people tend to be kept apart by their vocabularies. But let us set this problem aside and see what the hardware people have in mind.)

It goes like this. In one wall of your room will be a telescreen. It will be able to bring you a wide range of images and sounds and data, via push-button controls. In the first place, you can summon up current events, drama offerings, game shows, athletic contests—not unlike your current television choices. But you may also decide to see a classic film which a computerized switching system can call forth from an archive. Or you may decide to take a university course, prepared and stored in an electronic repository; each lesson, as and when you need it, can be summoned by your push buttons.

When ready, you can order the exam: question after question will appear on your telescreen, to be answered by push button, and the sequence will be climaxed by your grade, which will at once be recorded somewhere in a data bank.

For intensive study you may want some information on paper rather than on the screen. Pushing the right buttons, you can bring it spilling out in the form of a "printout." Your income tax forms may reach you in the same way—unless that primitive business is abolished for an entirely new system, to be mentioned presently. Your daily newspapers may also reach you in this way.

Instead of conversing with a computer you may prefer to talk to a human being—your daughter in St. Louis, for example. There seems no reason why the telephone function, including sight, should not be incorporated in the telecommunications system. Thus you and your daughter will be able to speak to each other while each appears on the other's screen. For conference calls, split-screen arrangements can be used, so that face-to-face business conferences can involve representatives of widely scattered offices, even on several continents. Much business work can be done at home, with instructions, reports and statistics transmitted electronically—via words or visual display or printout, or a combination of them. The insanity of rush-hour travel may gradually pass into history.

One of the most irrational of modern logjams, the postal system, may also yield to tomorrow's telecommunications. The telescreen engineer sees every home or office as a "terminal." The well-equipped terminal of the future will be able to send, as well as receive, official documents and letters.

It is assumed by most telecommunications futurists that some of the choices available via your push-button (digital) controls will be free—sponsored by advertisers or available as a government service—while others will involve payment. Tuning to an

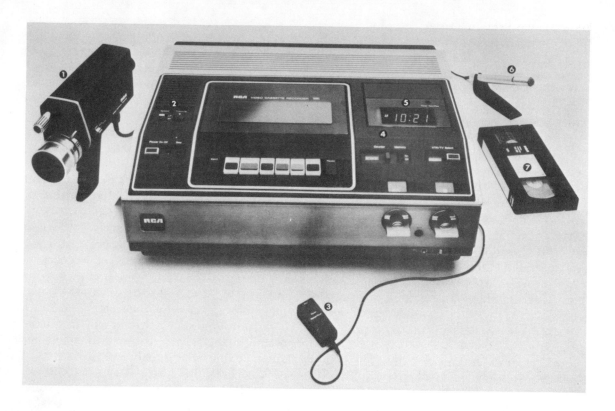

opera performance will probably involve a fee. For a university course you will likewise be charged something, corresponding to current tuition fees. The method of payment will probably be made as painless as possible. The act of tuning may simply deduct the fee electronically from your bank balance. Perhaps, as you tune, an appropriate WARNING will appear on your screen—like the highway phrase, LAST EXIT BEFORE TOLL.

One of the forces propelling telecommunications toward a new era is the computer. Data banks are already, of course, a reality for insurance firms, banks, law enforcement agencies, health agencies; access to such data banks is available over long distances via cable or microwave or satellite. A Milwaukee hospital, about to perform an emergency operation on a patient from Los Angeles, can get the patient's computer-stored medical history in seconds. A New Orleans newspaper, instead of trying to maintain its own massive newsclipping "morgue" on international events, can purchase access to the *New York Times* computerized morgue or information bank. An FBI agent investigating a case in Albuquerque can instantly check fingerprints and other data in Washington computers. One computer can feed its data to another. In telecommunications scenarios, computers are constantly talking to each other.

In all such communication transactions, the term long distance is losing much of its meaning. When television programs or documents or data are transmitted by satellite, 3,000 miles involve no greater difficulty than 300 miles. In phone calls of the future, with two-way video in color, distance may no longer be a cost factor.

Thus the ingredients of the revolution are with us; their wider use seems certain to affect home and office, business and pleasure, information and persuasion, student

Video Cassette Recorder. Much of the hardware for a telecommunications revolution already exists. Features of this video cassette recorder include (1) optional camera that allows production of home shows, (2) speed switch that allows up to four hours recording time, (3) remote pause control, (4) tape counter with memory, (5) electronic digital clock/timer for unattended recording, (6) optional microphone, (7) cassettes with four-hour recording capacity. Courtesy RCA News.

and teacher, citizen and government, in ways that may be startling. Optical glass fiber is based on cheap and plentiful silicon, whereas coaxial cables use scarce, expensive copper. The difference may hasten the wiring of communities throughout the world. What the scientist foresees is that the virtuosity of the fibers, combined with that of satellites and computers and electronic recorders, will tend to integrate various communication systems and purposes into an extraordinary multichannel, interactive communications world: communication of one to one, one to many, many to one, many to many.

Can Future Hardware Needs Be Met?

So confident are scientists of this development that intensive meetings have already been held to work out details, to anticipate what hardware may be needed. Meetings have been held in the United States under the auspices of the National Research Council, sponsored by a consortium of government departments—Commerce; Health, Education and Welfare; Housing and Urban Development; Transportation—with participation by representatives of the Federal Communications Commission, the U.S. Postal Service, and the White House Office of Telecommunications Policy. All feel that the impending communications revolution may radically alter the context of their work. And all look to the revolution for answers to their increasingly pressing problems.

The scientists brought together in such meetings are from diverse fields, representing television, telephone, telegraph, aerospace, computer and other industries. They see their interests converging—but also clashing. Thus the emerging telecommunications visions involve a power struggle, which will be, in fact, a continuation of struggles almost as old as the Republic. . . .

Who will be the gatekeepers of the evolving system? Will authority be dispersed, or concentrated? Will the multiplicity of channels provide a rich diversity of choice, or only seem to? Who will decide what treasures are to be stored in the electronic archives available to your push buttons? Our whole history teaches us that these are crucial questions. More recent history confronts us with still further questions. Will the right of privacy survive the telecommunications revolution and its network of data banks? For the moment such questions remain unanswered, and unanswerable. The current focus is on hardware miracles.

Meanwhile, dreams of things to come lure us on. They offer a heady mixture of possibilities. Ithiel de Sola Pool of the Massachusetts Institute of Technology points out that nowadays an average family, settling down for an evening, generally has three television network programs to choose from. This has been, he feels, "a powerful force toward conformity. Wherever one goes in the United States, the same fads, the same styles, the same scandal of the week, the same ball scores, the same entertainments are on people's lips." He feels that in contrast the emerging technology can then help to "individualize people rather than to homogenize them."

He predicts: "Increasingly, communications devices will be adapted to individualized use by the consumer where and when he wants, on his own, without the cooperation of others; he will use machines as an extension of his own capabilities and personality, talking and listening worldwide, picking up whatever information he wants."

Pool apparently feels that Man himself

will be changed by the emerging technology. "For the computer promises to make it possible to interrogate an inanimate data base with the same ease and success with which we now ask questions of a friend or colleague." He sums up: "A picture begins to emerge of a society ever more individualized in its interests and tastes."

The added factor of two-way "interactive" communication seems invaluable to Pool, as to others. Replacing an era in which "the citizen hears but is not heard," they see an era of citizen feedback. The economist Harold J. Barnett feels this factor will be especially important to local politics, restoring the "community ethos" which mass-audience television has helped to undermine. The factor is also considered important in "telemedicine," a subject of endless futuristic scenarios. These picture the physician examining and interviewing remote patients via telecommunications. A patient need not be brought to the electrocardiograph: the telecommunications system can provide the link.

The two-way factor will also be important in the use of special shoppers' channels. The buyer at home will be able to survey available merchandise, then place orders and authorize payments.

The possible impact of telecommunications on finance is particularly intriguing. The financial world is drowned in waves of paper—currency, checks, stocks, bonds, bills, orders, accounts—that flow endlessly from office to office via messenger or the postal system. That all this is obsolete is being shown by computer networks. "Computers and wire," writes Barnett, "are moving us to a cashless society." Payments will flow over the telecommunications system. In the computerized financial world, taxation may even be simplified by diverting to the government small fractions of all individual transactions.

In the magazine *Science*, Edwin B. Parker and Donald A. Dunn describe the system of the future as a "combined library, newspaper, mail-order catalog, post office, classroom, and theater." It will resemble current television, yet change it radically. "Broadcast television is like the passenger railroad, taking people to scheduled places at scheduled times." Tomorrow's wired system is expected to be "like a highway network, permitting people to use their television sets in the way they use their personal automobiles; they may be able to select information, education, and entertainment at times and places of their own choosing." This will presumably foster "equal social opportunity in the United States."

We should recognize that new technology readily evokes rosy expectations. Possible blessings are more easily glimpsed than problems, and are more gratifying to contemplate. As we have seen, visions of the wired world have been with us ever since the invention of the telephone. As early as 1882, an artist pictured a woman shopping via television, and another taking a course via television. In the early 1900s, the motion picture was expected to have many of the same effects predicted for telecommunications—wide dispersal of knowledge, equalization of opportunity, strengthening of democracy and of international understanding. Broadcasting, at the very hour of its birth, was expected to have similar effects. The first issue of *Radio Broadcast*, launched early in 1922, predicted that broadcasting would

. . . elicit a new national loyalty and produce a more contented citizenry. . . .

. . . the government will be a living thing to its citizens instead of an abstract and unseen force. . . .

. . . at last we may have covenants literally openly arrived at. . . .

. . . elected representatives will not be able to evade their responsibility to those constituents who put them in office. . . .

. . . the people's University of the Air will have a greater student body than all the rest of our universities put together. . . .

That same year a former Secretary of the Navy, Josephus Daniels, joined in the sanguine predictions: "Nobody now fears that a Japanese fleet could deal an unexpected blow on our Pacific possessions. . . . Radio makes surprises impossible." Magazine articles of the day featured such titles as "How Radio Is Remaking the World" and "Radio, the Modern Peace Dove" and "Ether Waves vs. Crime Waves."

Telecommunication May Improve Our Lives

Were they wrong, or are some of these predictions only premature and about to come true in a new "telecommunications" phase of the electronic epoch?

In the already large and growing literature on the wired world of tomorrow, a persistent theme relates to transportation. For it is expected that "message movement" will eventually replace much "people movement"—thus relieving our glutted transportation system, easing problems of the use of energy and improving the quality of our air.

Again and again we are told that the "symbolic interchange" offered by telecommunications can and must replace a large percentage "of the physical encounters now serviced by physical travel." We will become telecommuters, teleshoppers and televoters. In the view of Dr. Gerhard J. Hanneman of the Annenberg School of Communication, University of Southern California, all this can lead to a more rational distribution of the population and ease the current pollution crises.

But what will all those people be doing—those human beings who no longer need to stir from home, who will save endless hours of mass transport and be blessed with leisure? What will they do with their lives? What will their lives mean to them?

At this point, the hardware man invokes the software people. *They* are to enrich the citizen's life with a vast assortment of video services and packages: entertainment, education, art, culture. But the software man tends to be baffled by the assignment.

It seems to software people that the hardware specialist loves smoothly functioning equipment but does not love people, who are messy and disorganized. Why else would he devise these scenarios which always seem to eliminate people—or at least keep them out of the way, at home?

The root of all art is the fantasizing characteristic of human beings, by which they cope with the pressures and perplexities of their lives. Art serves the artist—and the audience, when art succeeds—as interpretation, clarification, redemption. What pressures will haunt the telecommunications viewer of tommorow? What fantasies from the studios of software will fruitfully engage his attention, ease his tensions, keep him content before the telescreen and push buttons? The hardware emerging from our laboratories is truly miraculous. Designing the software may prove to be far more difficult.

THE AUTHORS

SHELLEY ARMITAGE is a professor of English at Tarrant County Junior College in Fort Worth, Texas, and a free-lance writer, contributing to popular magazines and scholarly journals. In 1976 she participated in the Olympic trials for the first women's basketball team to represent the United States.

BEN H. BAGDIKIAN (1920–) is professor of journalism at the University of California, Berkeley. He previously was a reporter and chief Washington correspondent with the *Providence Journal*, a contributing editor to the *Saturday Evening Post*, and assistant managing editor of the *Washington Post* and *Columbia Journalism Review*. He is the author of *In the Midst of Plenty: The Poor in America*, *The Information Machines*, and *The Shame of the Prisons*.

ERIK BARNOUW (1908–) is currently a Woodrow Wilson Scholar at the Smithsonian Institution. Long a member of the faculty at Columbia University, he served as professor of dramatic arts in charge of film, radio, and TV from 1964 to 1969. He was also an editor for Columbia University Press's Center for Mass Communication and an occasional writer and adapter for Theater Guild radio and TV programs. His many books include *Mass Communications*, *The Television Writer*, *Tribe of Plenty: The Evolution of American Television*, and the multivolume, prize-winning *A History of Broadcasting in the United States*.

CARL BELZ (1937–) teaches art history at Brandeis University, where he joined the faculty in 1968. He previously taught at the University of Massachusetts and Mills College. He is the author of *The Story of Rock* and *Robert Rohm, Christopher Sproat*.

DANIEL J. BOORSTIN (1914–) is currently the Librarian of Congress, having served as director of the National Museum of Science and Technology and later as senior historian of the Smithsonian Institution in Washington, D.C. From 1944 to 1969 he was a member of the history department at the University of Chicago. His many books include *The Lost World of Thomas Jefferson*, *The Image*, *The Genius of American Politics*, and the multivolume study, *The Americans*, which won the Bancroft, Francis Parkman, and Pulitzer Prizes.

RAY B. BROWNE is director of the Center for Popular Culture at Bowling Green State University in Ohio. He previously taught at the University of Maryland and Purdue University. The founder and editor of the *Journal of Popular Culture*, he is the author of more than twenty books, including *The Popular Culture Explosion*, *Popular Culture and the Expanding Consciousness*, and *Dimensions of Detective Fiction*.

DAVID BURNER (1937–) has been a member of the history faculty at the State University of New York at Stony Brook since 1966. He is author of the *Politics of Provincialism* and editor of *The Diversity of Modern America* and *The Varieties of American History*.

JOHN G. CAWELTI (1929–) is professor of English and humanities at the University of Chicago, where he joined the faculty in 1957. Among his books are *The Six-Gun Mystique*, *Why Pop?* and *Adventure, Mystery, and Romance: A Theory of Popular Story Formulas*.

R. SERGE DENISOFF is an associate professor of sociology at Bowling Green State University in Ohio. He is also editor of *Popular Music and Society*. He is the author of *Great Day Coming: Folk Music and the American Left* and *Sing a Song of Social Significance*, and coauthor of *Social and Political Movements* and *Solid Gold: The Popular Record Industry*.

REUEL DENNEY (1913–) is professor of American Studies at the University of Hawaii, having previously taught for many years at the University of Chicago. His books include *The Lonely Crowd* (coauthored with David Riesman and Nathan Glazer), *Astonished Muse*, and *Conrad Aiken*.

MARTIN DWORKIN is a photographer, writer, and editor. A teacher at Teachers College, Columbia University, he is general editor of their series, *Studies in Culture and Communication*. He has published more than 700 pieces, including stories, poems, and articles in film criticism and media for such journals as the *New Republic*, *New Leader*, and *The Progressive*. His photos have appeared in magazines all over the world, and he has had several photographic exhibitions.

WILLIAM K. EVERSON (1929–) is film curator of the School of Visual Arts at the New School for Social Research, and an instructor in film history at New York University. He has also served as writer, editor, and researcher for several TV and theatrical releases. His books include *The Films of Laurel and Hardy*, *The Art of W. C. Fields*, and *The Western: From Silents to the Seventies*, which he coauthored with George N. Fenin.

GEORGE N. FENIN (1916–) is a film correspondent for magazines and newspapers in Italy and other countries. A frequent juror at film festivals, he is the author of *Italian Cinema* and coauthor, with W. K. Everson, of *The Western: From Silents to the Seventies*.

MARSHALL FISHWICK (1923–) has been professor of art and history, head of the division of humanities, and director of the American Studies Institute at Lincoln University (Pennsylvania) since 1968. He previously taught at Washington and Lee University and served as president of the Popular Culture Association. His books include *The Hero: American Style*, *Icons of Popular Culture* (edited with Ray B. Browne) and *Heroes of Popular Culture*.

BETTY FRIEDAN (1921–), a feminist lecturer and author, founded the National Organization for Women and served as its first president from 1966 to 1970. Her book *The Feminine Mystique* (1963) is generally credited with having sparked the modern women's movement. She is also the author of *It Changed My Life* and numerous magazine articles.

HERBERT J. GANS (1927–) is the Ford Foundation Urban Chair professor of sociology at Columbia University and senior research associate at the Center for Policy Research. He has also taught at the University of Pennsylvania and the Massachusetts Institute of Technology. A specialist in urban studies and planning and in mass media and popular culture, he is the author of more than one hundred articles and of eight books, including *The Urban Villagers*, *The Levittowners*, *The Uses of Television and Their Educational Implications*, and *Popular Culture and High Culture*.

GEORGE GERBNER (1919–) is professor and dean of the Annenberg School of Communications,

University of Pennsylvania, where he joined the faculty in 1964 after teaching at the University of Illinois. He has held several grants from federal agencies to investigate such subjects as popular conceptions of mental illness and violence in network television drama. He edits the *Journal of Communication* and has written numerous journal articles in the field of communications.

JEFF GREENFIELD (1943–) is a consultant with Garth Associates in New York and an author, having previously served as an assistant to the late Senator Robert Kennedy and to New York Mayor John Lindsay. He is the author of *Where Have You Gone, Joe DiMaggio, Tiny Giant: Nate Archibald*, and *The World's Greatest Team: A Portrait of the Boston Celtics*.

LARRY GROSS is an associate professor at the Annenberg School of Communications. He is coauthor, with George Gerbner and William H. Melody, of *Communications Technology and Social Policy*.

RONALD GROSS (1935–) is adjunct assistant professor of social thought at New York University and vice-president and editor-in-chief of the Academy for Educational Development in New York City. The recipient of the Philip M. Stern Fund grant for magazine writing, he is the author of *Learning by Television*, *Pop Poems*, and *The Arts and the Poor*.

DAVID GRUNWALD is a journalist who worked for the *Washington Post* and the *New York Post* and edited a weekly paper, *Town and Village*, in New York City.

He has also written articles for the *New York Times*, the *Sacramento Bee*, *People Magazine*, and *American Way*, among others.

OSCAR HANDLIN (1915–) is the Carl H. Pforzheimer University Professor at Harvard University, where he first joined the faculty in 1939 as an instructor in history. He has also served as director of the Center for the Study of Liberty in America and the Charles Warren Center for Studies in American History, both at Harvard. The recipient of numerous awards, including the Pulitzer Prize for history, he is the author of *Boston's Immigrants*, *The Uprooted*, *American Principles and Issues*, *The Americans*, and *The American College and American Culture*.

MOLLY HASKELL has worked as a film critic for *The Village Voice* for ten years. She is also the author of *From Reverence to Rape*, which documents the treatment of women in the movies, and of numerous articles that have appeared in *Ms.* magazine and other publications.

NAT(HAN IRVING) HENTOFF (1925–) is a staff writer for *The New Yorker*, columnist for *The Village Voice*, and adjunct associate professor at the Graduate School of Education of New York University. He was also cofounder and coeditor of *The Jazz Review*. He is the author of more than a dozen books, including *The Jazz Life*, *I'm Really Dragged but Nothing Gets Me Down*, *Journey into Jazz*, and *This School Is Driving Me Crazy*.

ROBERT HILBURN (1939–) has been rock music critic of the *Los An-*geles Times* since 1970. He previously served as public information officer for the Los Angeles City Board of Education and as a reporter for the *North Hollywood Valley Times*. He has written for various music publications including *Rolling Stone* and *Melody Maker*.

JERRY IZENBERG has a syndicated sports column appearing in the *Newark Star Ledger*. A contributor to *Sport* magazine and *TV Guide*, he is producer and anchorman for the Channel 5, ten o'clock sports program on Sunday night in New York City. He has also written, directed, and produced eight television programs.

REX L. JONES , an anthropologist, was an assistant professor at the State University of New York, Stony Brook, until 1976. He now resides in California, where he is researching and writing about American culture, particularly gambling in Southern California. His books include *The Himalayan Woman* and *Spirit Possession in the Nepal Himalayas*.

KAS KALBA is president of Kalba Bowen Associates, Inc., a communications consulting company that is involved in telecommunications planning. He previously taught in the Department of City and Regional Planning at Harvard University. He is the author of *City Meets Cable* and several articles, including "Electronic Media Coverage of the U.S. House of Representatives" for the *Congressional Record*.

ELAINE KENDALL (1929–), a writer, is the author of *The Upper Hand*, *The Happy Mediocrity*, and *Peculiar Institutions: An Informal History of the Seven Sister Colleges*. She has also contributed numerous articles on the American scene to such magazines as *Harper's*, *Saturday Review*, and *The New York Times Magazine*.

R(APHAEL) A(LOYSIUS) LAFFERTY (1914–) combined a career as a buyer for an electrical supply company with writing. The recipient of the Hugo Award at the World Science Fiction Convention in 1973 for the year's best short story, he has contributed more than 150 short stories to magazines and other publications. Among his books are *Past Master*, *Space Chantey*, *The Flame Is Green*, and *Strange Doings*.

ROBERT LIPSYTE is currently a columnist for the *New York Post* and sports commentator for the National Public Radio Network. From 1947 to 1971 he was in the sports department of *The New York Times*, as reporter and later as an internationally syndicated columnist. The recipient of numerous awards, including the Meyer Berger Award for Distinguished Reporting, he is the author of eight books, among them *SportsWorld: An American Dreamland*, *The Contender*, and *One Fat Summer*.

JOHN McCARTHY is an associate professor at Catholic University of America and a research associate at their Boys' Town Research Center. He is the author of *Social Movements in Modern America* and of articles in professional sociology journals, including the *American Journal of Sociology*.

ROBERT D. McCLURE is an associate professor of political science at Syracuse University. Formerly a reporter for the *Rocky Mountain News*, he is coauthor, with Thomas Patterson, of *The Unseeing Eye*.

EDWARD MAPP is professor and chairman of library science at New York City Community College in Brooklyn, New York. He is the author of *Blacks in American Films: Today and Yesterday* and *Puerto Rican Perspectives* and editor of *Directory of Blacks in the Performing Arts*.

ROBERT D. MARCUS (1936–) is associate professor of history at the State University of New York at Stony Brook, where he joined the faculty in 1967. His books include *Grand Old Party, A Giant's Strength*, and *America: A Portrait in History*.

GERALD MAST (1940–) teaches English at Richmond College (New York). He is the author of *A Short History of the Movies, The Comic Mind: Comedy and the Movies*, and *Filmguide to Rules of the Game*.

(EDWARD) SHEPHERD MEAD (1914–) is an author who was associated with Benton and Bowles, Inc., in New York for twenty years, serving as vice-president from 1951 to 1956 before working as a consultant to a London firm. Among his many books are *How to Succeed in Business Without Really Trying, How to Succeed with Women Without Really Trying, Free the Male Man!: The Manifesto of the Men's Liberation Movement*, and *How to Get to the Future Before It Gets to You*.

MARION MEADE (1934–), a free-lance writer, is the author of *Bitching, Free Woman: The Life and Times of Victoria Woodhull, Women in Sports: Tennis*, and numerous magazine articles.

TRUMAN E. MOORE is a free-lance writer and photographer in New York City. His photos have appeared in *Life* and other national magazines. His book, *The Slaves We Rent*, is considered a classic study of migrant labor in the U.S. He is also the author of *The Traveling Man* and *Nouveaumania: The American Passion for Novelty*.

JAMES P. MURRAY (1946–) is editor of the *Amsterdam News* in New York City. He has also served as editor-in-chief of *Black Creation* magazine. He is the author of *To Find an Image*.

JACK NACHBAR is assistant professor of popular culture and director of the Film Studies Program at Bowling Green State University in Ohio, where he joined the faculty in 1975. He has written *Focus on the Western* and *Western Movies: An Annotated Bibliography* as well as numerous articles in journals such as *American Film, Journal of Popular Film*, and *Popular Culture Methods*. He is also coeditor of the *Journal of Popular Films*.

MICHAEL NOVAK (1935–) has had a varied career as writer, lecturer, professor, and editor of *Christianity and Crisis* and *Christian Century*. He is currently associate director for humanities at Rockefeller Foundation. Among his many books are *All the Catholic People, The Rise of the Unmeltable Ethnics, Choosing Our King*, and *The Joy of Sports*.

RUSSEL B. NYE (1913–) is distinguished professor of English at Michigan State University, where he has been a member of the faculty since 1940. He has also served as president of the Popular Culture Association and the American Studies Association. The recipient of the Pulitzer Prize in biography for *George Bancroft: Brahmin Rebel*, he is also the author of *Cultural Life of the New Nation, This Almost Chosen People*, and *The Unembarrassed Muse*.

J. K. OBATALA has served as staff writer and editor for the *Los Angeles Times*. He was previously a professor of black studies.

ARNOLD PASSMAN is a free-lance writer who is the author of *The Deejays* and of articles that have appeared in *Playboy* and other magazines.

WILLIAM PAUL , a film critic, teaches a course on film at Haverford College and at Columbia University, where he is a doctoral candidate. He is a reviewer for *The Village Voice* and *Rolling Stone*, and has also contributed to *Film Comment, Film Heritage*, and other magazines.

THOMAS E. PATTERSON is an associate professor of political science at Syracuse University. He is coauthor, with Robert McClure, of *The Unseeing Eye*, a study of TV's impact on the 1972 presidential campaign, funded by the National Science Foundation.

JOHN PENDLETON has taught American history at the University of

California, Santa Barbara, and at Golden West College. A specialist in popular culture, he has contributed to the *Journal of Popular Culture* and *Popular Culture Methods*.

RICHARD A. PETERSON is professor of sociology at Vanderbilt University in Nashville, Tennessee. The author of several articles in sociology journals and in the *Journal of Country Music*, he is also editor of *The Production of Culture* and coeditor, with R. Serge Denisoff, of *The Sounds of Social Change*.

RON POWERS (1941–) is critic at large for WMAQ-TV in Chicago, having previously served as a reporter for the *St. Louis Post-Dispatch* and as TV critic for the *Chicago Sun-Times*. The recipient of the 1973 Pulitzer Prize for criticism, he is the author of *The Newscasters: The News Business as Show Business*.

MICHAEL R. REAL is an assistant professor in the communications program at the University of California, San Diego, where he joined the faculty in 1971. An ordained minister, he previously served as chaplain of the Newman Foundation at the University of Illinois. He is the author of *Mass-Mediated Culture*.

ROGER ROSENBLATT (1940–) has been literary editor of *The New Republic* magazine since 1975. He previously taught English at Harvard University and was director of education at the National Endowment for the Humanities. He is the author of *Black Fiction* and numerous newspaper and journal articles.

PETER SCHILLACI (1929–) is a free-lance media consultant and lecturer on film arts and television. He has taught at Fordham University, Union Theological Seminary, and the New School for Social Research. A frequent contributor to journals on film and television, he wrote a thirty-program television series, "Film and Society." He is also the author of *Movies and Morals* (under the name of Anthony Schillaci) and a film guide to *Life Goes to the Movies*.

HERBERT I(RVING) SCHILLER (1919–) is professor of communications at the University of California, San Diego, where he joined the faculty in 1970 after teaching at Pratt Institute in Brooklyn, New York, and at the University of Illinois. He is the author of *Mass Communications and American Empire* and *The Mind Managers*, in addition to numerous journal articles.

TONY SCHWARTZ is a communications consultant and lecturer, specializing in the design and preparation of radio and television political campaigns, including those of Edward Kennedy, Patrick Moynihan, and Jimmy Carter. He has also served as a media consultant for such large corporations as Mobil Oil, McGraw-Hill, and Coca-Cola. He is the author of *The Responsive Chord* and of a weekly column for *Media Industry Newsletter*.

ROBERT LEWIS SHAYON has had a varied career as a radio-TV critic for *Saturday Review* and as a writer-director-producer for numerous radio and television shows, including "The Big Story," "You Are There," and

"What Shall We Do for Thursday's Child?" The recipient of several critics awards, he is the author of *Open to Criticism*, *The Eighth Art*, *The Crowd-Catchers—Introducing Television*, and *Parties in Interest—A Citizen's Guide to Improving Television and Radio*.

ROBERT SKLAR (1936–) is professor of cinema and chairman of the Department of Cinema Studies at New York University, having previously taught history at the University of Michigan from 1965 to 1976. The author of more than fifty articles and book and film reviews, he received the Theater Library Association Award for *Movie-Made America: A Cultural History of the American Movies*. His other books include *F. Scott Fitzgerald: The Last Laocöon*, and *The Plastic Age: 1917–1930*.

WILLIAM SMALL has been senior vice-president and director of news, CBS News, since 1974. He was formerly president of the Radio and Television News Directors Association, and he served as news director of WLS in Chicago and WHAS-TV in Louisville, Kentucky. He is the author of *To Kill a Messenger* and *Political Power and the Press*, both of which won the Distinguished Service Award for research in journalism from Sigma Delta Chi.

BENJAMIN STEIN is a free-lance writer and a creative consultant for television programs, including "Fernwood Tonight" and "All's Fair." Formerly a speech writer for Richard Nixon and a television and popular arts columnist for the *Wall Street Journal*, he is co-author, with his father, Herbert Stein, of *The Brink*.

CSANAD TOTH is vice-president of Inter-American Foundation, a government agency involved in grants to Latin America. It is the largest foundation of its kind. The director of research for a government publication *They Know How*, he is also the author of several journal articles.

HARRY F. WATERS joined the staff of *Newsweek* in 1968 and is presently general editor of the magazine, responsible for the TV/Media section. One of his arti-cles was selected for publication in *Best Sports Stories of 1972*.

DAVID MANNING WHITE is professor of mass communications at Virginia Commonwealth University. From 1964 to 1972, he was chairman of the Journalism Division at Boston University, where he joined the faculty in 1949. He served as general editor of the *New York Times'* Arno Press series on *Popular Culture in America, 1800–1925* and was coeditor, with Bernard Rosenberg, of *Mass Culture: The Popular Arts in America*, which was influential in creating interest in popular culture research among academicians. Other books include *The Celluloid Weapon: Social Comment in American Film*, *Journalism in the Mass Media*, and *Pop Cult in America*.

WILLIAM L. YANCY is associate professor of sociology at Temple University, where he joined the faculty in 1972. A frequent contributor to sociology journals, he is also coauthor of *Structures of Ethnicity in Urban America* and *The Moynihan Report and the Politics of Controversy*.

FURTHER READINGS

Popular Culture:
What Manner of Mirror
David Manning White

Browne, Ray B., Marshall Fishwick, and Michael Marsden, eds. *Heroes of Popular Culture*. Bowling Green, Ohio: Popular Press, 1972. Valuable collection of essays on men and women who achieved fame and fortune through the media.

Burner, David, Robert D. Marcus, and Jorj Tilson, eds. *America Through the Looking Glass: A Historical Reader in Popular Culture*. Englewood Cliffs, N.J.: Prentice-Hall, 1974. Examines popular culture from colonial days to present.

Cawelti, John G. *The Six Gun Mystique*. Bowling Green, Ohio: Popular Press, 1973. Definitive study of the American West as portrayed in popular culture.

Lewis, George H. *Side Saddle on the Golden Calf: Social Structure and Popular Culture in America*. Pacific Palisades, Calif.: Goodyear, 1972. Thoughtful and comprehensive anthology with excellent commentary throughout by compiler.

Nye, Russell B. *The Unembarrassed Muse: The Popular Arts in America*. New York: Dial Press, 1970. Comprehensive account of popular culture's growth in the United States; indispensable book for all students of popular culture.

Real, Michael. *Mass-Mediated Culture*. Englewood Cliffs, N.J.: Prentice-Hall, 1977. Popular culture as seen by a cultural anthropologist; innovative and well-written case studies of such phenomena as the Super-Bowl, Disneyland, Marcus Welby, et al.

Rosenberg, Bernard, and David Manning White, eds. *Mass Culture: The Popular Arts in America*. New York: Free Press, 1957. Pioneer anthology credited with stimulating much subsequent interest in popular culture.

Rosenberg, Bernard, and David Manning White, eds. *Mass Culture Revisited*. New York: Van Nostrand Reinhold, 1971. Updated version of editors' 1957 anthology.

Story-Tellers and
Story-Sellers: The Makers
of Popular Culture
Herbert J. Gans

Note: This bibliography covers only entertainment and is mainly about the mass media; it leaves out the news. Also, I have left out all individual biographies or autobiographies of popular culture makers. Most actually are about top executives like David Sarnoff, Louis B. Mayer, et al., or about performers such as Clark Gable, Marilyn Monroe, and so forth.

Articles

Baldwin, Thomas F., and Lewis Colby. "Violence in Television: The Industry Looks at Itself." In *Media Content and Control*, Vol 1. of *Television and Social Behavior*, edited by George Comstock and Eli Rubinstein, pp. 290–373. Washington, D.C.: National Institute of Mental Health, 1972. A study of the television producers of violent programs, with lots of quotes, suggesting why they use violence and how they rationalize it.

Cantor, Muriel G. "The Role of the Producer in Choosing Children's Television Content." In *Media Content and Control*, edited by George Comstock and Eli Rubinstein, pp. 259–289. Washington, D.C.: National Institute of Mental Health, 1972. A quicker study, this time of producers of children's television, and not as detailed.

Gans, Herbert J. "The Creator Audience Relationship in the Mass Media: An Analysis of Movie-Making." In *Mass Culture*, edited by Bernard Rosenberg and David M. White, pp. 315–324. New York: Free Press, 1957. A sociological analysis, drawn from Lillian Ross's book,

Picture, of how movie makers take the audience into account when making a film.

Greenfield, Jeff. "The Fight for $60,000 a Half-Minute." *New York Times Magazine*, September 7, 1975. A description of how NBC put together its 1975 program schedule.

Halberstam, David. "CBS: The Power and the Profits." *The Atlantic*, January and February 1976, pp. 33–71 and 52–91. A critical analysis of the executive suite at CBS, though mostly about its news practices and policies.

Hirsch, Paul M. "Processing Fads and Fashion: An Organization-set Analysis of Cultural Industry Systems." *American Journal of Sociology*, January 1972, pp. 639–659. A superb sociological analysis of the mass media as a general type of industrial organization, comparing the media to other industries that sell "fads and fashions." Scholarly; already a classic.

Marcuse, Herbert. "Repressive Tolerance." In *A Critique of Pure Tolerance*, edited by Robert Wolff, Barrington Moore Jr., and Herbert Marcuse. Boston: Beacon, 1969. One statement of the position that popular culture diverts us from political activities.

Books

Bogart, Leo. *The Age of Television*. 3rd ed. New York: Ungar, 1972. A scholarly general book, drawing on and reporting academic studies, mostly about the social impact of television.

Brown, Les. *Television: The Business Behind the Box*. New York: Harcourt Brace Jovanovich, 1971. To my mind, still the best general book about television, especially on the economics. Informally written, it focuses mainly on what I call the sellers of popular culture.

Cantor, Muriel G. *The Hollywood TV Producer: His Work and His Audience*. New York: Basic Books, 1971. A sociological study, based on interviews with eighty producers and producer-writers, depicting graphically although in academic language the situation in which they work, and the pressures they are under.

Comstock, George, and Marilyn Fisher. *Television and Human Behavior: A Guide to the Pertinent Scientific Literature*. Santa Monica, Calif.: Rand Corporation, 1975. The most recent bibliography on the effects of television, containing mostly research reports and scholarly writings.

Duncan, Hugh Dalziel. *Language and Literature*. Chicago: University of Chicago Press, 1953. Chapter 4 is a brilliant analysis of the complex relationship between artists and audiences, as well as critics.

Dunne, John Gregory. *The Studio*. New York: Farrar, Strauss & Giroux, 1969. An acerbic study of one year in the life of Twentieth Century Fox, emphasizing the commercial considerations and the interpersonal jockeying that go into every decision. Not analytic, but well written.

Faulkner, Robert. *Hollywood Studio Musicians*. Chicago: Aldine-Atherton, 1971. A sociological study of the people who perform the background music for the film; interesting particularly because it shows how and why "serious" musicians work in popular culture.

Friedrich, Otto. *Decline and Fall*. New York: Harper & Row, 1970. A dispassionate, well-written analysis of the decline and fall of the *Saturday Evening Post* and the people involved, by one of its last editors.

Gans, Herbert J. *Popular Culture and High Culture*. New York: Basic Books, 1974. An analysis of taste differences in America, a defense of popular culture, questioning whether it really has harmful effects.

Gill, Brendan. *Here at the New Yorker*. New York: Random House, 1975. A breezy history of what it's like to work at the magazine, which unintentionally emphasizes how much the makers of this particular popular magazine are upper-class people.

Himmelweit, Hilde, A. N. Oppenheim, and Pamela Vince. *Television and the Child*. London: Oxford University Press, 1958. Probably the first study of the effects of television on children, and now a classic. It demonstrates, among other things, that "realistic" violence may have harmful effects.

Jacobs, Norman. *Culture for the Millions*. Princeton, N.J.: Van Nostrand, 1961. An anthology of articles that present high culture's case against popular culture.

Lynes, Russell. *The Tastemakers*. New York: Harper's, 1954. A journalistic survey of a variety of popular culture makers, notable mostly for introducing the term "tastemakers" and for the chapter "Highbrow, Middlebrow, Lowbrow."

Rosten, Leo C. *Hollywood: The Movie Colony.* New York: Harcourt, Brace, and World, 1941. Now thirty-five years old, and in many respects outdated because of the decline of the studio system, but still worth reading for the feeling one gets of that era's Hollywood.

Schramm, Wilbur, Jack Lyle, and Edwin B. Parker. *Television in the Lives of Our Children.* Stanford, Calif.: Stanford University Press, 1961. An early American study of the effects of television on children.

Surgeon General's Scientific Advisory Committee on Television and Social Behavior. *Television and Growing Up: The Impact of Televised Violence.* Washington, D.C.: National Institute of Mental Health, 1971. The official report on whether television violence has harmful effects, which suggests that it does, but qualifies its conclusion.

Tuchman, Gaye, ed. *The TV Establishment.* Englewood Cliffs, N.J.: Spectrum Books, 1974. An anthology of various, mostly critical, articles about television; contains an interesting article by the editor on how a national network talk show is produced.

Wakefield, Dan. *All Her Children.* Garden City, N.Y.: Doubleday, 1976. A sympathetic account of the people who write and produce the popular soap opera "All My Children."

White, Theodore. *View From the 40th Floor.* New York: Wm. Sloane, 1960. An account of the decline and fall of *Collier's.*

The Popular Culture Industry: Big Business
George Gerbner

Articles

Gerbner, George. "Communication and Social Environment." *Scientific American*, September 1972, pp. 153–160.

Parker, Edwin B. "Technology Assessment or Institutional Change?" In *Communications Technology and Social Policy*, edited by George Gerbner, Larry Gross, and William Melody. New York: Wiley Interscience, 1973.

Books

Brown, Les. *Television: The Business Behind the Box.* New York: Harcourt Brace Jovanovich, 1971. A breezy but expert description of the economic and business background of programming and management.

Bunce, Richard. *Television in the Corporate Interest.* New York: Praeger, 1976. An economic study by a sociologist of FCC policy and corporate practice.

Gerbner, George, ed. *Mass Media Policies in Changing Cultures.* New York: Wiley Interscience, 1977. National and international systems and theories of mass communications.

Schiller, Herbert I. *The Mind Managers.* Boston: Beacon Press, 1973. A critical account by an economist of manipulated information and "packaged consciousness" from entertainment through polling to advanced communications technology.

White, David Manning, and Lewis Anthony Dexter. *People, Society and Mass Communications.* New York: Free Press, 1964. Some excellent analyses of media culture.

Change or Continuity
Ray B. Browne

Note: For special topics, issues of the Journal of Popular Culture *should be consulted.*

Articles

Cawelti, John G. "Notes Toward an Aesthetic of Popular Culture." *Journal of Popular Culture*, Fall 1971, pp. 255–268. Distinguishes between popular and "elite" cultures and demonstrates what kinds of standards popular culture should and does have.

Clareson, Thomas D. "The Other Side of Realism." In *SF: The Other Side of Realism*, pp. 1–25. Bowling Green, Ohio: Popular Press, 1971. Surveys science fiction and points out its significance in and reflection of literature and life.

Landrum, Larry, Pat Browne, and Ray B. Browne. "Introduction." In *Dimensions of Detective Fiction*, pp. 1–10. Bowling Green, Ohio: Popular Press, 1976. Analyzes detective fiction from its very first manifestations and demonstrates its complexities, especially in recent examples, among most of its authors.

Madden, David. "The Necessity for an Aesthetics

of Popular Culture." *Journal of Popular Culture*, Summer 1973, pp. 1–13. Analyzes the accomplishments and failings of popular culture, insisting that it should try to improve itself.

Books

Cawelti, John G. *Adventure, Mystery and Romance*. Chicago: University of Chicago Press, 1976. A study of the general theory of popular literary formulas and formulaic literature.

Gowans, Alan. *The Unchanging Arts*. Philadelphia: Lippincott, 1970. Surveying art of the world, this book demonstrates that all art begins with utilitarian purpose and must retain one in order to remain alive.

Goulart, Ron. *Cheap Thrills*. New Rochelle, N.Y.: Arlington House, 1972. A detailed study of pulp magazines, by far the best.

Kunzle, David. *The Early Comic Strip*. Berkeley: University of California, 1973. Surveys the "true" comic strip, tracing it back to European broadsheets.

Tebbel, John. *The Media in America*. New York: Mentor, 1974. Surveys the media and their impact.

Toll, Robert C. *Blacking Up: The Minstrel Show in 19th-Century America*. New York: Oxford University Press, 1974. This book is the most comprehensive history and analysis of this medium of entertainment yet to appear. It supersedes all others, and demonstrates how important minstrelsy was to both blacks and whites in the nineteenth and early twentieth centuries.

————. *On with the Show*. New York: Oxford University Press, 1976. A comprehensive and fascinating survey of all forms of entertainment in America, demonstrating how vital the various forms of theater have been in the United States.

Hollywood: The Dream Factory— Movies
Robert Sklar

Drew, Bernard. "Gorilla Power." *American Film*, December–January 1977. An interesting account of the contemporary movie spectacle, referring particularly to the 1976 version of *King Kong*.

French, Philip. *The Movie Moguls*. Chicago: H. Regnery, 1969. See particularly Chapter 3, "Chance and Chutzpah," for a useful, concise account of the origin and character of the moguls.

Kael, Pauline. *Going Steady*. Boston: Little, Brown, 1970. See particularly the essay "Trash, Art and the Movies" for an account of movies as entertainment.

Münsterberg, Hugo. *The Film: A Psychological Study*. New York: Dover, 1969. Originally published in 1916 as *The Photoplay*. Although more than fifty years old, this remains the clearest and most provocative explanation of the psychology of movie-going.

"Production Code of the Motion Picture Producers and Distributors Association." In Garth Jowett. *Film: The Democratic Art*. Boston: Little, Brown, 1976. The prohibitions of this early document on censorship make interesting reading, particularly in light of today's movies.

Rosen, Marjorie. *Popcorn Venus: Women, Movies and the American Dream*. New York: Avon, 1973. A useful account of women in the movies.

Ross, Lillian. *Picture*. New York: Harcourt Brace, 1952. A case study of the people who made *The Red Badge of Courage*. Of particular interest are Arthur Mayer's views on American values and their decline in movies since the time of the Andy Hardy films. This section is contained in Chapter One.

Sklar, Robert. *Movie-Made America: A Cultural History of the American Movies*. New York: Random House, 1975. See particularly pp. 14–19 on early movie audiences.

In addition to the above suggestions, the following books pertain in general to the role of movies in American popular culture.

Jarvie, I. C. *Movies and Society*. New York: Basic Books, 1970.

Powdermaker, Hortense. *Hollywood: The Dream Factory*. Boston: Little, Brown, 1950.

Smith, Julian. *Looking Away: Hollywood and Vietnam*. New York: Scribner, 1975.

White, David Manning, and Richard Averson. *The Celluloid Weapon: Social Comment in the American Film*. Boston: Beacon Press, 1972.

———. *Sight, Sound, and Society: Motion Pictures and Television in America*. Boston: Beacon Press, 1968.

Wolfenstein, Martha, and Nathan Leites. *Movies: A Psychological Study*. New York: Atheneum, 1970.

Wood, Michael. *America in the Movies*. New York: Basic Books, 1975.

Hollywood: The Dream Factory— Television
Robert Sklar

Articles

Rosten, Leo. "A Disenchanted Look at the Audience." In *The Eighth Art*, pp. 31–38. New York: Holt, Rinehart and Winston, 1962. A clear and precise presentation of most of the issues that have occupied thought about television from its beginning.

Sklar, Robert. "The Backlash Factor." *American Film*, December–January 1977, pp. 61–67.

———. "The View from the Television Tower." *American Film*, February 1977, pp. 62–67. Two articles on the recent revival of the TV violence issue, one from the critics' perspective, the other from that of the networks.

———. "Electronic Americana." *American Film*, March 1976, pp. 60–64. A broad look at television content from a cultural perspective.

Books

Adler, Richard, and Douglass Cater, eds. *Television as a Social Force*. New York: Praeger, 1975.

———. *Television as a Cultural Force*. New York: Praeger, 1976. These two volumes of essays were published by the Aspen Institute Program on Communications and Society.

Barnouw, Eric. *Tube of Plenty: The Evolution of American Television*. New York: Oxford University Press, 1975. A one-volume version of his three-volume *A History of Broadcasting in the United States*.

Barrett, Marvin, ed. *Survey of Broadcast Journalism, 1969–1970*. New York: DuPont Foundation/Columbia University School of Journalism, 1970. This volume contains some interesting documents on television and the news. Particularly recommended are "Transcript of the Address by Vice-President Spiro T. Agnew, Des Moines, Iowa, November 13, 1969" (pp. 131–138) and the excerpt from the CBS Evening News with Roger Mudd (pp. 145–146).

Hall, Monty, and Bill Libby. *Emcee Monty Hall*. New York: Grosset & Dunlap, 1973. There are some fascinating descriptive passages on the television game show and its audience in this volume by an insider.

Johnson, William O., Jr. *Super Spectator and the Electric Lilliputians*. Boston: Little, Brown, 1971. A good account of television and sports. Particularly interesting is the description of a day in the life of a television sports spectator (pp. 3–17).

Mayer, Martin. *About Television*. New York: Harper & Row, 1972. This book has some thoughtful insights on the impact of television.

Newcomb, Horace. *TV: The Most Popular Art*. Garden City, N.Y.: Doubleday, 1974. A study of television programs as popular art.

Shanks, Bob. *The Cool Fire: How to Make It in TV*. New York: Norton, 1976. An insider's view on how the television industry works.

Shayon, Robert Lewis. *The Crowd-Catchers: Introducing Television*. New York: Saturday Review Press, 1973. A clear and simple statement of many of the issues surrounding the topic of television and violence is contained in Shayon's discussion of the Surgeon General's Report on Television and Social Behavior.

Wakefield, Dan. *All Her Children*. Garden City, N.Y.: Doubleday, 1976. A discussion of the soap opera.

Popular Culture and Music
Nat Hentoff

General

Mellers, Wilfred. *Music in a New Found Land*. New York: Hillstone, 1975. The most musically knowledgeable and probingly original survey of the history of American music, including popular music.

Folk

Lawless, Ray M. *Folksingers and Folksongs in America*. New York: Duell, Sloan and Pearce,

1960, 1965. A comprehensive account, spanning country and other popular performers and composers.

Lomax, Alan. *Folk Songs of North America.* New York: Doubleday, 1960. The roots of all our popular music, with incisive history and analysis.

Country

Hemphill, Paul. *The Nashville Sound: Bright Lights and Country Music.* New York: Simon and Schuster, 1970. Brilliantly observed, anecdotal, and historical accounts of the rise of country music to national popularity.

Malone, Bill C. *Country Music, U.S.A.: A Fifty-Year History.* Austin: University of Texas Press, 1968. A basic, essential overview.

Malone, Bill C., and Judith McCulloh. *The Stars of Country Music.* New York: Avon Paperback, 1976. Profiles of a wide range of country songsters including their socioeconomic backgrounds.

Black Music

Ellison, Ralph. *Shadow and Act.* New York: Vintage, 1972. Some of the most illuminating writing on jazz and the ways of life and survival that are its roots.

Hentoff, Nat. *Jazz Is.* New York: Ridge Press/Random House, 1976. Profiles of key jazz creators, with emphasis on the customs, history, and economics of the music.

Jones, LeRoi. *Blues People.* New York: William Morrow, 1963. A black perspective on the socio-cultural-political history of black music.

Levine, Lawrence W. *Black Culture and Black Consciousness.* New York: Oxford University Press, 1977. A historian's journey into the richness and diversity of black culture, including music, from slavery on.

Popular Music

Spaeth, Sigmund. *A History of Popular Music.* New York: Random House, 1948; eighth printing, 1962. A bountiful compendium of facts and interpretations, starting at the very beginning.

Rock

Marcus, Greil. *Mystery Train: Images of America in Rock 'n' Roll Music.* New York: Dutton,

1975. The most serious and vivid attempt yet to place rock and its roots within the overall context of American culture.

The Rolling Stone Illustrated History of Rock & Roll. New York: Random House, 1976. By far the most comprehensive and best written cross-section of the key figures in the evolution of rock.

Popular Culture and Sports
Robert Lipsyte

Articles

Commager, Henry Steele. "Give the Games Back to the Students." *The New York Times Magazine,* April 16, 1961.

Ford, Gerald, with John Underwood. "My View of Sport." *Sports Illustrated,* July 8, 1974.

Hart, Marie. "Sports: Women Sit in the Back of the Bus." *Psychology Today,* October 1971.

Ogilvie, Bruce C., and Thomas Tutko. "Sport: If You Want to Build Character Try Something Else." *Psychology Today,* October 1971.

Rosellini, Lynn. "Homosexuals in Sport." *Washington Star,* December 9ff, 1975.

Scott, Jack. "It's Not How You Play the Game, But What Pill You Take." *The New York Times Magazine,* October 17, 1971.

Books

Beisser, Arnold. *The Madness in Sports.* New York: Appleton-Century-Crofts, 1967. A psychiatrist presents fascinating case histories of athletes and fans dealing with the problems of competition, victory, and defeat.

Bouton, Jim. *Ball Four.* Edited by Leonard Shecter. New York: Dell, 1971. The controversial best-seller is actually a love-poem to baseball, and a fine introduction to the game's subculture by an insider.

Bradley, Bill. *Life on the Run.* New York: Quadrangle, 1976. The thinking person's basketball star illuminates the often alienated existence of the celebrity-athlete in America.

Cosell, Howard. *Cosell.* New York: Pocket Books, 1974. *Like It Is.* New York: Pocket Books, 1975. The well-known commentator refracts his life and times in lively fashion.

Hoch, Paul. *Rip Off the Big Games.* New York: Anchor Books, 1972. A Marxist interpretation of sports as a form of exploitation by the power elite.

Holtzman, Jerome, ed. *No Cheering in the Press Box.* New York: Holt, Rinehart and Winston, 1974. Interviews with old-time sportswriters add up to an oral history of twentieth-century sports that rarely got printed.

Lipsyte, Robert. *SportsWorld: An American Dreamland.* New York: Quadrangle, 1975. The best anecdotal overview of sports and its impact on popular culture and the individual as yet written. (If I say so!)

Meggyesy, David. *Out of Their League.* New York: Warner, 1971. One man's microcosmic odyssey from super-Jock to radical ex-All-Pro.

Noll, Roger G., ed. *Government and the Sports Business.* Washington, D.C.: The Brookings Institution, 1974. An economic study of sports ownership, municipal impact, salaries, and so forth, which is critical to understanding the big business aspect of sports.

Scott, Jack. *The Athletic Revolution.* New York: Free Press, 1971. One of *the* basic books by the leader of the progressive sports movement of the 1960s.

Wolf, David. *Foul.* New York: Holt, Rinehart and Winston, 1972. This carefully detailed story of the exploitation of one black ghetto basketball player, Connie Hawkins, is a monumental study of the manipulation of the sports star from grammar school to the pros.

Popular Culture and Politics
Andrew Hacker

Books

Key, Vladimer O. *The Responsible Electorate.* Cambridge: Harvard University Press, 1966. A political scientist argues that despite all the emotional overtones to campaigns, most Americans cast "rational" ballots on election day. An analysis of voting in presidential elections is offered in support of this proposition.

Efron, Edith. *The News Twisters.* Los Angeles: Nash, 1971. An impassioned essay, bolstered by original research, purporting to prove the "liberal" bias of television coverage of politics.

Epstein, Edward J. *News from Nowhere.* New York: Random House, 1973. A study, based on interviews and observation, showing how organizational, technological, and commercial factors shape the presentation of television news.

White, Theodore H. *The Making of the President, 1960.* New York: Atheneum, 1961. A description in depth of the 1960 television debates between John Kennedy and Richard Nixon, which were much more revealing than the Ford-Carter encounters of 1976 (Chapter Eleven).

McGinnis, Joe. *The Selling of the President, 1968.* New York: Pocket Books, 1970. The whole public relations package behind Richard Nimon's ascent to the presidency, including excerpts from television scripts, spots, speeches, and interoffice memos by those conducting the campaign.

Periodicals

Discussions of political themes in the popular media appear from time to time in the following publications:

Rolling Stone (biweekly) publishes occasional articles on the political predispositions of popular musicians and songwriters.

Jump Cut (bimonthly) offers semiacademic analysis of the ideological assumptions inherent in recent films, usually from a left-wing perspective.

TV Guide (weekly) has discussions of how entertainment television treats political issues, often saying more than a quick flip-through might suggest.

Popular Culture: Minorities and the Media
Nathan Irvin Huggins

Articles

Baldwin, James. "Sidney Poitier." *Look,* July 23, 1968, p. 56ff. A critical assessment of the man and the image.

Compton, Neil. "Consensus Television." *Commentary,* January 1966. If the goal is consensus, there is slight chance for the authentic minority voice.

Cripps, Thomas. "The Myth of the Southern Box Office." In *The Black Experience in America*, edited by James Curtis and Lewis Gould. 1970.

Dworkin, Martin. "The New Negro on the Screen." *The Progressive*, November 1960, p. 35ff. An optimistic view of changes that were first being perceived.

Green, Theophilus. "The Black Man as Movie Hero." *Ebony*, August 1972. Popular culture media looks at popular culture media with an appreciative eye, but the doubts are there between the lines of self-congratulation.

Holly, Ellen. "Where Are the Films About Real Black Men and Women?" *New York Times*, June 2, 1974, Part II, p. 11. To ask the question is to raise the point about mass media's capacity or interest in dealing with real people.

Johnson, Albert. "Beige, Brown, or Black." *Film Quarterly*, Fall 1959, p. 40.

Johnson, Albert. "The Negro in American Films: Some Recent Examples." *Film Quarterly*, Summer 1965, p. 22.

Killens, John O. "Hollywood in Black and White." In *White Racism*, edited by Barry Schwartz and Robert Disch, 1970. The theme of racist character of the industry is emphasized.

Kupferman, Theodore, and Philip J. O'Brien. "Motion Picture Censorship—The Memphis Blues." *Cornell Law Quarterly*. Spring 1951. Reflects the heavy hand of racial taboos on industry but focuses on the legal challenge.

Metzger, Charles. "Pressure Groups and the Motion Picture Industry." *Annals of the American Academy of Political Science*, November 1947. Dated, but the analysis raises important and lasting questions.

Moss, Carlton. "The Negro in American Films." In *Harlem, U.S.A.*, edited by John Henrik Clarke. New York: Macmillan, 1971.

Murray, James P. "Do We Really Have Time for a Shaft?" *Black Creations*, Winter 1973. The "We" is black people, and the question comes from one of the many challenges of the blaxploitation film.

Trumbo, Dalton. "Minorities and the Screen." In *Proceedings of the Writers Congress*. Berkeley: University of California Press, 1944. This is quite dated, but it is by a writer sensitive to the problems. There is nothing that I know of that is more up-to-date.

Zanuck, Darryl F. "Controversy Is Box Office." *International Film Annual*, edited by Campbell Dixon, 1957. Reflects the film industry's modest adventures into controversial subjects in the post-McCarthy years. It remains interesting to see what constituted "controversy" and what the limits were.

Zito, Stephen. "The Black Film Experience." In *The American Film Heritage*, edited by Tom Shales, *et al.* Washington, D.C.: Acropolis Books, 1972.

Books

Barnouw, Erik. *Tube of Plenty: The Evolution of American Television*. New York: Oxford, 1975. The definitive work that is a condensation and updating of the history of television in his monumental, three-volume work, *A History of Broadcasting in the United States*.

Barrett, Marvin, ed. *Survey of Broadcast Journalism, 1968–69*. New York: DuPont Foundation/ Columbia University School of Journalism, 1969.

————. *The Politics of Broadcasting: Survey of Broadcast Journalism, 1971–72*. New York: Thomas Y. Crowell, 1973. These surveys are the best single source to get at the scope and character of news reporting on television.

Blumer, Herbert. *Movies and Conduct*. Original edition: 1933; reprinted, New York: Arno Press, 1976. A sociologist's analysis of the relationship between movies and social attitude and behavior.

Bogle, Donald. *Toms, Coons, Mulattoes, Mammies, and Bucks*. New York: Bantam, 1973. The first of three modern books on blacks in film. The emphasis in this one is on the manipulation of stereotypes.

Cripps, Thomas. *Slow Fade to Black: The Negro in American Film, 1900–1942*. New York: Oxford University Press, 1977. The most recent study. It is a social history that provides a solid background for understanding what was being changed in the postwar industry, and how much change there really has been.

Dandridge, Dorothy, and Earl Conrad. *Everything and Nothing*. New York: Tower, 1970. The autobiography of an early "starlet," whose career was tragic.

Ewers, Carolyn. *Sidney Poitier: The Long Journey*. New York: New American Library, 1969.

A biography that is naturally appreciative of Poitier's achievement. It is useful in what it tells of the nature of his struggle and in the corrections we must make with hindsight.

Hunnings, Neville. *Film Censors and the Law*. Atlantic Highlands, N.J.: Humanities, 1967. This British book is about legal controls and civil liberties, but the questions raised do apply to the industry's management of the minority image. Cost is a censor of a kind, but it is not treated adequately here or elsewhere.

Leab, Daniel J. *From Sambo to Superspade: The Black Experience in Motion Pictures*. Boston: Houghton Mifflin, 1975. Sees progress and is more optimistic and more readable than Thomas Cripps, but it is not very deep.

Mapp, Edward. *Blacks in American Film, Today and Yesterday*. Metuchen, N.J.: Scarecrow, 1972. Much of the same.

Mills, Earl. *Dorothy Dandridge*. Los Angeles: Holloway, 1970. The tragedy of being beautiful and black before the media was ready for the black sex object.

Noble, Peter. *The Negro in Film*. Original edition 1947; reprinted, New York: Arno Press, 1972. One of the first full-scale efforts to summarize. It is by an English author, and the book has been superseded by more recent ones.

Racial Justice in Broadcasting. New York: The United Church of Christ, 1970. Part of the pressure that brought change.

Popular Culture and Women
Betty Friedan

Gornick, Vivian, and Barbara K. Moran, eds. *Woman in Sexist Society—Studies in Power and Powerlessness*. New York: Basic Books, 1971. See especially "The Image of Woman in Advertising," pp. 207–217. One of the most salient explanations of the demeaning role given the image of women in American advertising.

Hole, Judith, and Ellen Levine. *Rebirth of Feminism*. New York: Quadrangle, 1973. See especially "Media," pp. 247–277. The authors provide a thoughtful analysis of the overall use of the mass media in the portrayal of women in our contemporary society and offer some ameliorative suggestions.

Mead, Margaret, and Frances Balgley, eds. *American Women. The Report of the President's Commission on the Status of Women*. New York: Charles Scribner's, 1965. See Appendix III, "Portrayal of Women by the Mass Media." The section on women in the mass media in the early 1960s may be contrasted with today's media image to indicate that substantial strides forward have been made in the last decade or so.

Morgan, Robin, ed. *Sisterhood Is Powerful: An Anthology of Writings from the Women's Liberation Movement*. New York: Random House, 1970. See especially "Women in the Professions" (pp. 62–86), "Women in Television" (pp. 70–76), and "Media Images" (pp. 175–197). One of the best anthologies on the women's liberation movement; the section on the media is valuable background material.

Special Publications

"Guidelines for the Treatment of Women in the Media." In *To Form a More Perfect Union—Justice for American Women*. Washington, D.C.: Department of State, 1976. A succinct summary of where the media have been in their depiction of women, where they are going, and how changes can best be implemented.

"Sex Role Stereotyping in Prime Time Television." Study by United Methodist Women, March, 1976. A recent study conducted for a concerned group of women in the Methodist Church reveals that stereotyping of women is decreasing in programming but remains strong in advertisements.

"Survey of Women's Attitudes Toward the Media." In *American Women Today and Tomorrow*. Washington, D.C.: Department of State, March 1977. A concise summary of a study on how *women* feel about the images of themselves in the media.

Popular Culture and American Life Styles
Bennett Berger

The quickest and easiest access to a representative sampling of the literature on popular culture and life-styles is through several an-

thologies which, over the years, have collected some of the more interesting current writings: for example, the following:

Cantor, Norman, and Michael Werthman. *The History of Popular Culture.* New York: Macmillan, 1968. Corrects the general misapprehension that "popular culture" is a child of the age of electronics by tracing its origins back to the early nineteenth century and bringing its history down to the late 1960s. A very broad selection.

Denisoff, R. Serge, and Richard Peterson. *The Sounds of Social Change.* New York: Rand McNally, 1972. A collection of articles on popular music selected by two sociologists, emphasizing the relation of recent developments to changes in the character of the audiences.

Eisen, Jonathan. *The Age of Rock.* New York: Vintage, 1969. Another collection, this time on rock music, selected by a member of the age group which created the music, from mostly journalistic sources.

Feldman, Saul, and Gerald Thielbar. *Life Styles: Diversity in American Society.* 2nd ed. Boston: Little, Brown, 1975. An anthology designed as a textbook for a course on American society which successfully represents the diversity of American subcultures by organizing them under such sociological headings as regionalism, sex roles, ethnicity, family, and social stratification.

Larrabee, Eric, and Rolf Meyersohn. *Mass Leisure.* Chicago: Free Press, 1958. Now unfortunately out-of-print, this collection organizes a wide variety of the uses of mass media and popular culture as ways of disposing of free time and discretionary income. Includes a sampling of both democratic and elitist (or aristocratic) viewpoints.

Lewis, George. *Side Saddle on the Golden Calf.* Pacific Palisades, California: Goodyear, 1972. With good running commentary by its sociologist-editor, this collection attempts consistently to connect expressions of contemporary popular culture with the social groups who originate it and the audiences upon which it impacts.

Rosenberg, Bernard, and David Manning White. *Mass Culture.* New York: Free Press, 1957.

This, the first and probably the most influential collection of writings in the field, did much to set the terms of the major debates about mass (or popular) culture. Rosenberg (anti) and White (pro) select articles from the major media and the major theorists which characterize mass culture as, alternately, a threat to traditional values and civilized sensibilities, or as charming and authentic expressions of the culture we actually live in.

Four books which had a strong impact in shaping the images of the counterculture among the reading public:

Reich, Charles. *The Greening of America.* New York: Random House, 1970. Perhaps the most famous and successful of the books on the counterculture which treated it as the latest revolution in popular consciousness, slated to replace the earlier two which have historically dominated in America.

Roszak, Theodore. *The Making of a Counterculture.* New York: Doubleday, 1969. The book which popularized the term "counterculture," describing it as an attempt to transcend the secular scientific rationality of modern life through the search for spiritual experience in a variety of religious and other contexts.

Slater, Philip. *The Pursuit of Loneliness.* Boston: Beacon Press, 1970. A book which treats the counterculture less thoroughly and explicitly than the previous two, but which is far more thorough and profound in its treatment of the dominant American culture whose pathologies made the counterculture and the greening of America inevitable.

Wolfe, Tom. *The Electric Kool-Aid Acid Test.* New York: Farrar, Strauss & Giroux, 1968. The book which made Tom Wolfe's reputation as a reporter and interpreter of unusual scenes of American life; this one a report of the nationwide bus trip of Ken Kesey and his "merry band of pranksters," one of the first major events that brought the hippies to national attention.

Three influential books on the meaning of popular culture:

Boorstin, Daniel. *The Image.* New York: Harper & Row, 1961. The book which introduced the term "pseudo-event" to the language of popular culture, a *pseudo* event being one that occurs *in order to* be reported, rather than one that is reported *because* it is important—hence reversing the relationship between "news" and publicity. A devastating account of the ways in which images become more real than reality.

Gans, Herbert. *Popular Culture and High Culture*. New York: Basic Books, 1974. A tightly compacted treatise on the relationship between subcultures of taste and the socio-economic characteristics of the "taste-publics" which share such tastes. A "democratic" viewpoint arguing against the inherent superiority of "high" culture to the three or four major lower varieties of it.

Real, Michael. *Mass-Mediated Culture*. Englewood Cliffs, N.J.: Prentice-Hall, 1977. A view of mass culture as mediated through oligopolistic culture *industries*, which purveys distracting images to mass audiences. Interesting case studies of Disneyland, the Superbowl spectacle on TV, and Billy Graham "crusades."

Articles on the youth culture of the 60s:

Berger, Bennett. "Hippie Morality: More Old than New." *Transaction*, December 1967. Connects the subculture of hippies of the 1960s to bohemian traditions which antedate it, and describes what is new in the contribution of the 1960s to this continuous tradition of bohemianism.

————. "Audiences, Art, and Power." *Transaction*, May 1971. Describes changes in the relationships between performers and audiences in the counterculture which transformed teachers (as performers) as well as show business figures into *leaders* and audiences into quasi-political constituencies.

Davis, Fred. *On Youth Subcultures*. A short but thorough treatment of the situation of youth in the 1960s which produced the subcultural explosion it did. An excellent general source with which to begin understanding cultural developments among youth.

Flacks, Richard. "Social and Cultural Meanings of Student Revolt." In *Youth and Sociology*, edited by Peter K. Manning and Marcello Truzzi. Englewood Cliffs, N.J.: Prentice-Hall, 1973. A very influential and widely reprinted article verifying the middle-class origins of most of the student rebels of the 1960s.

Matza, David. "Subterranean Traditions of Youth." *Annals of the American Academy*, November 1961. Sees deviance among youth as divided into three major traditions of rebellion: delinquency, bohemianism, and political radicalism; connects these traditions with mainstream traditions in American culture.

The Future of Popular Culture
David Manning White

Articles
Burgess, Anthony. "Music at the Millennium." *Hi Fi*, May 1976. What will our music sound like in the year 2000? Novelist and composer Burgess offers some intriguing speculations.

Commager, Henry Steele. "Commitment to Posterity—Where Did It Go?" *American Heritage*, August 1976. A leading historian questions some current practices that our popular culture reflects.

Books
Lundberg, Louis B. *Future Without Shock*. New York: Norton, 1975. A quasi-optimistic view of the future. Chapter 4, "Counter-Culture, Youth Culture, and the New Values," is particularly germane to popular culture.

Servan-Schreiber, J. J. *The American Challenge*. New York: Avon, 1969. This distinguished French writer points out both the perils as well as the positive challenges of America's future.

Toffler, Alvin. *The Eco-Spasm Report*. New York: Bantam, 1975. If the dire prognostication of the future articulated by Toffler happens, the structure of popular culture institutions will be affected in most drastic ways.

————. *Future Shock*. New York: Random House, 1970. Definitive book on the challenges of the future. Chapter 10, "The Experience Makers," and Chapter 12, "Origins of Overchoice," are particularly relevant to the future of popular culture.

Vacca, Roberto. *The Coming Dark Age*. New York: Doubleday, 1975. This analysis by Vacca is in the tradition of gloom-and-doom futurists and bears careful scrutiny.